BEN-GURION AGAINST THE KNESSET

CASS SERIES: ISRAELI HISTORY, POLITICS AND SOCIETY
Series Editor: Efraim Karsh
ISSN: 1368-4795

This series provides a multidisciplinary examination of all aspects of Israeli history, politics and society, and serves as a means of communication between the various communities interested in Israel: academics, policy-makers, practitioners, journalists and the informed public.

1. *Peace in the Middle East: The Challenge for Israel*, edited by Efraim Karsh.
2. *The Shaping of Israeli Identity: Myth, Memory and Trauma*, edited by Robert Wistrich and David Ohana.
3. *Between War and Peace: Dilemmas of Israeli Security*, edited by Efraim Karsh.
4. *U.S.-Israeli Relations at the Crossroads*, edited by Gabriel Sheffer.
5. *Revisiting the Yom Kippur War*, edited by P. R. Kumaraswamy.
6. *Israel: The Dynamics of Change and Continuity*, edited by David Levi-Faur, Gabriel Sheffer and David Vogel.
7. *In Search of Identity: Jewish Aspects in Israeli Culture*, edited by Dan Urian and Efraim Karsh.
8. *Israel at the Polls, 1996*, edited by Daniel J. Elazar and Shmuel Sandler.
9. *From Rabin to Netanyahu: Israel's Troubled Agenda*, edited by Efraim Karsh.
10. *Fabricating Israeli History: The 'New Historians'*, second revised edition, by Efraim Karsh.
11. *Divided Against Zion: Anti-Zionist Opposition in Britain to a Jewish State in Palestine*, 1945–1948, by Rory Miller.
12. *Peacemaking in a Divided Society: Israel After Rabin*, edited by Sasson Sofer.
13. *Israeli-Egyptian Relations: 1980–2000*, by Ephraim Dowek.
14. *Global Politics: Essays in Honour of David Vital*, edited by Abraham Ben-Zvi and Aharon Klieman.
15. *Parties, Elections and Cleavages; Israel in Comparative and Theoretical Perspective*, edited by Reuven Y. Hazan and Moshe Maor.
16. *Israel and the Polls 1999*, edited by Daniel J. Elazar and M. Ben Mollov.
17. *Public Policy in Israel*, edited by David Nachmias and Gila Menahem.

Israel: The First Hundred Years *(Mini Series)*, edited by Efraim Karsh.

1. *Israel 's Transition from Community to State*, edited by Efraim Karsh.
2. *From War to Peace?* edited by Efraim Karsh.
3. *Politics and Society Since 1948*, edited by Efraim Karsh.
4. *Israel in the International Arena*, edited by Efraim Karsh.
5. *Israel in the Next Century*, edited by Efraim Karsh.

Ben-Gurion against the Knesset

GIORA GOLDBERG
Bar-Ilan University

Translator
CHAYA NAOR

LONDON AND NEW YORK

First published in 2003 in Great Britain by
FRANK CASS PUBLISHERS

This edition published 2005 by Routledge
2 Park Square, Milton Park, Abingdon, Oxfordshire OX14 4RN
711 Third Avenue, New York, NY 10017

First issued in paperback 2014

Routledge is an imprint of the Taylor and Francis Group, an informa business

British Library Cataloguing in Publication Data

Goldberg, Giora
Ben-Gurion against the Knesset. – (Cass series. Israeli history, politics and society; 32)
1. Ben-Gurion, David, 1886–1973 2. Israel. Knesset 3. Israel – Politics and government – 1948–1967
I. Title
956.9′4052′092

ISBN 13: 978-1-138-87012-3 (pbk)
ISBN 13: 978-0-7146-5556-7 (hbk)

ISSN 1368-4795

Library of Congress Cataloging-in-Publication Data

Goldberg, Giora, 1948–
Ben-Gurion against the Knesset / Giora Goldberg.
p. cm. – (Cass series – Israeli history, politics, and society)
Includes bibliographical references and index.
ISBN 0-7146-5556-2 (cloth)
1. Israel – Politics and government – 1948–1967. 2. Israel. Knesset – History – 20th century. 3. Legislative power – Israel – History – 20th century. 4. Ben-Gurion, David, 1886–1973. 5. Representative government and representation – Israel – History – 20th century. 6. Ministerial responsibility. I. Title. II. Series.

JQ1830.A792O64 2003
328.5694′09′045–dc21 2003051463

Typeset in 10.5/13pt Palatino by Servis Filmsetting Ltd, Manchester

Contents

Foreword: The Theory of the Status of Legislatures

Any attempt to ascertain the status of legislatures with the help of models of regimes suffers from fundamental flaws. One criterion for classifying such models is the independence of the executive arm. In the assembly model, for instance, there is no real separation between the executive and the legislature. The government is merely a parliamentary committee whose task is to implement the resolutions adopted by the legislature. The supremacy of the legislature is reflected in the fact that all government ministers are members of parliament, so that the government derives its authority from the legislature and is not, in itself, an autonomous legal entity. This assembly model, however, is an ideal type which is almost non-existent in practice.

The opposite type of administration is represented by the presidential model, in which there is a distinct separation between the executive and the legislature. Here the president, elected directly by the people, is not subject to the authority of the legislative body. That is, the president is not responsible to the legislature, nor is it empowered to depose him for reasons of policy. At most he can be removed from office for moral failings or ill health. The separation of powers is clearly indicated by separate elections for the presidency and the legislative body. On the other hand, the president is not independent of the legislature, as evidenced by a series of checks and balances, such as the need for the president to obtain the legislature's ratification of budgetary allocations and certain official appointments. The United States is one of the few examples of a presidential model.

To a certain extent, the parliamentary model constitutes a compromise between the conflicting principles inherent in the assembly and the presidential regimes. Whereas the government is elected by the parliament, responsible to it, and subject to its authority, it remains a separate legal entity. Subordination to the legislature is not absolute and is expressed mainly in the legislature's power to dissolve the government. Of the three models, the parliamentary is the most common, with the example usually cited being Britain. Some models are a combination of two types: France, for example, switched in 1958 from a parliamentary to a 'semi-presidential' model, combining elements of the two regimes. In Israel, direct election of the Prime Minister, enacted by the Knesset in 1992 and first implemented in 1996, introduced a typically presidential element into what until then had been a parliamentary system.

The differences between the three models would appear to suggest that legislative bodies are weakest under presidential systems, have much greater power in parliamentary regimes, and are strongest in assembly systems. In practice, however, this is not the case. The strongest legislative body, the US Congress, operates in a presidential system. Although there is a considerable similarity between the regimes in the United States and France (since the establishment of the Fifth Republic in 1958), the large discrepancy between the powers of their legislative institutions illustrates the shortcomings of an attempt to explain the status of parliaments on the basis of models.

The distinction between the three types of regime is long-standing, rooted in a time when most legislatures were stronger than their governments. An additional drawback to this approach is the formalistic/legal nature of the distinction, which takes into account not the true balance of powers, but only the formal constitutional powers. Moreover, the distinction is mainly valid for the period before the emergence of modern political parties, when legislatures and governments were in constant conflict. From the nineteenth century on, the ascendance of political parties, in the modern meaning of the term, shifted the focus of internal political dynamics to inter-party contention. In a world of political parties, the status of the legislature is enhanced by a state of high (though not excessive) competitiveness between them.

Instead of explaining the status of parliaments on the basis of type of regime, two alternative explanations related to the process of party growth might be suggested. First, the deeper the parties' penetration into society, the more detrimental the impact on the status of the parliament. Second, the stronger a certain party and the longer it holds sway, the more negative the impact on the legislature. In other words, a high level of partisanship and low level of competitiveness are harmful to the status of a parliament.

In a situation of high partisanship, the members of the legislature are mainly concerned with party interests. Members of the ruling party are expected, above all, to help maintain the existing balance of power. Thus they find it very hard to criticize the government and oversee it, since this could lead to loss of power. A high level of partisanship is therefore damaging to parliaments because it intensifies three types of discipline: party discipline, whereby party institutions and apparatuses control the parliamentary arm of the party; factional discipline, whereby the faction leaders (the party's parliamentary arm) control the activities and voting patterns of other members of the faction; and coalitionary discipline, which subjects the parliamentary conduct of the members of small coalition partners to the will of the largest party in the coalition, and sometimes even to the will of the government.

In a situation of high competitiveness with a reasonable prospect of change of government, the ruling party will not undermine the status of the legislature, nor will the opposition automatically support the consolidation of its powers. Given the feasibility that the ruling party will find itself in the opposition, and the opposition will assume power, both sides are dissuaded from adopting inflexible positions. Under conditions of low competitiveness, on the other hand, the ruling party may be tempted to undermine the status of the legislature by the fact that the opposition automatically rallies to its support. In the United States, although parties emerged at an earlier stage than in Europe, the low level of partisanship and high level of inter-party competition contributed to establishing the strong standing of Congress. Parliaments with a high level of partisanship and high competitiveness, like the House of Commons, will be weaker, but will still enjoy greater status than parliaments with low competitiveness and high partisanship, such as those in communist countries, for example. In some multi-party systems with a dominant party, the legislatures also display this pattern of high partisanship and low competitiveness. Israel was an apt example until 1973, when party dominance ended, bringing about a marked increase in inter-party competitiveness.[1] As the legislatures of some developing countries are characterized by low partisanship and low competitiveness, their status is higher than that of legislatures in communist states, but considerably lower than that of institutions such as the British parliament, which are characterized by high partisanship and high competitiveness.

The decline in the level of partisanship seen in almost all democratic countries since the 1970s might have been expected to enhance the status of their legislatures. However, the influence of other factors, referred to below, seems to have neutralized the anticipated effect of this decline. Israel, for example, is undergoing a process of decreasing partisanship, while at the same time there has been an increase in the level of inter-party competitiveness, particularly since 1973. The 1981 transition to a two-bloc structure is a clear manifestation of this trend, which was also reflected in the first change of government in 1977, the partial changeover in 1984 and 1988, and the changes in 1992, 1996 and 1999. These two processes, the decline in partisanship and rise in competitiveness, should have enhanced the status of the Knesset.

Mezey's theoretical analysis may assist us in identifying additional factors impacting on the standing of parliaments. His distinction between three types of parliament is based primarily on the perception of its functions. According to the first, the policy-making model, a legislature is meant to be the source of national policy and laws. The second, the representational model, places emphasis on giving expression to the particularist interests of the voters and organized groups. The representatives are charged with the task of safeguarding the interests of the voters on the national level. The third option, the system maintenance model, assumes that the government, not the legislature, is the source of policy. The main function of the legislature, therefore, is to provide backing for the government and to recruit support for its policies, making it an instrument for explaining government policy. Generally speaking, extra-parliamentary elite groups prefer the system maintenance model, the general public tends to prefer the representational model, and members of the legislature support the policy-making model.[2]

Mezey created a typology of legislatures based on two criteria: its power to determine policy, and the support it receives from elite groups and from the public. A strong legislature can alter and even veto policy proposals originating in the executive body; a legislature with limited power to determine policy can amend elements of the proposed policy, but cannot veto it; a weak legislature can neither change nor quash the proposed policy or any of its components. Furthermore, a legislature can enjoy considerable or scant support. Mezey cites five types of legislature:

- An active legislature enjoys a high degree of support and wields considerable power in determining policy. The US Congress and state legislatures, as well as the Congress of Costa Rica are examples of this type.
- A vulnerable legislature has considerable power in policy-making, but enjoys little support. To this model belong the legislatures of Italy, the Third and Fourth Republics of France, Weimar Germany, Chile, Uruguay and the Philippines.
- A reactive legislature wields limited policy-making power and enjoys a high degree of support. Mezey classifies the Knesset as this type, together with the legislatures of Austria, Australia, the Fifth Republic of France, Japan, Turkey, Ireland, Switzerland, Norway, Sweden, Britain, Canada, Finland, Mexico, Denmark, Belgium, Holland, West Germany, India and New Zealand.
- Marginal legislatures receive little support and have limited policy-making power. To this type belong developing countries such as Thailand, Pakistan, North Vietnam (till 1975), South Korea, Kenya, Uganda, Malaysia, Colombia, Peru, Brazil, Afghanistan, Iran, Ethiopia, Syria, Jordan, Zambia, Nigeria, Argentina, Bangladesh, Guatemala and Lebanon.
- Finally, minimal legislatures enjoy a high degree of support, but have little power to determine policy, such as the legislatures of communist countries like the former Soviet Union, Poland and Yugoslavia, as well as Tanzania, Singapore, Tunisia, Taiwan, the Ivory Coast and Ghana under Nkrumah.[3]

The problematic element in Mezey's typology is his view of support. Instead of being treated as a single factor, it should perhaps be divided into three separate components – the support of elite groups, the support of the general public and the support of the chief executive. If elite groups and the public offered the same level of support in all countries, one could make appropriate use of the typology. However, in many cases there are differences between the two types of support. According to Mezey's classification, both the legislatures of Britain and the former Soviet Union enjoy a high degree of support, yet in Britain the main source of support is the public while in the former Soviet Union it was the elite. Moreover, Mezey's typology fails to distinguish between the support of elite groups and that of the chief executive. Although it is true that the chief executive is a member of the elite, his weight is such that he deserves separate attention.

Rather than employing only two criteria, policy-making power and degree of support, four could be used: policy-making power, support of the elite, support of the head of the executive branch, and the legitimacy of the legislature in the eyes of the public. In this classification, there are more than five types of legislature, and legislatures can shift from one type to another. To cite one example, the steep decline in the public legitimacy of the Knesset in the 1970s would have been expected to transform it from a reactive to a marginal type. However, the increase in its policy-making power and the degree of support it has received from the elite have largely counter-balanced the negative impact of its reduced legitimacy. Thus, the six factors which determine the status of a legislature are: the degree of partisanship, the degree of inter-party competitiveness, policy-making power, support of the elite, support of the chief executive and public legitimacy. Moreover, there may well be a certain interdependence among these factors. It may be assumed, for example, that the greater the support of elite groups for the legislature, the greater its policy-making power.

A distinction should also be made between the four factors which directly shape the status of a legislature – its policy-making power, the support of the chief executive and of the elite, and public legitimacy – and the two indirect factors – partisanship and competitiveness. The indirect factors exert influence on one or more of the direct factors, so that their impact is mediated by the direct factors. Furthermore, the two indirect factors are interrelated, as are the four direct factors.

The best possible situation for the status of a legislature is one of low partisanship, high competitiveness, considerable power to determine policy, strong support from elite groups and the head of the executive, and high public legitimacy. In the case of the Knesset, the only one of these components which has declined over time is its legitimacy in the eyes of the public. On the other hand, the decline in partisanship and increase in the support of the chief executive, competitiveness, policy-making power and degree of support of the elite have aided in enhancing its status. Mezey's assertion regarding the difference in the perception of the functions of different legislatures can help to explain the fact that legitimacy has declined while the other five factors have improved. Whereas this improvement has shifted the Knesset from the system maintenance model to the policy-making model, the positive change did not satisfy the public's expectations from the Knesset, which should have led it toward the representational model. Public frustration at the fact that the representational model was not being implemented was among the causes of the decline in legitimacy.

One might also take issue with Mezey's focus on policy-making, and his disregard for the classic parliamentary functions – investigation of the activity of the executive arm, monitoring, criticizing and controlling the executive, and maintenance of a supreme national forum for public debate on major issues. According to the perception inherent in Mezey's analysis, the government and legislature are engaged in a battle over responsibility for the same functions. It might be better, however, to regard them as bodies charged with fulfilling different functions. The further we advance along the continuum from the assembly to the presidential model, the greater the separation of powers and the distinction between the functions of the two authorities. In the intermediary parliamentary model, there is a certain lack of clarity with regard to the functions of the legislature.

There may also be some connection between the expectations of the public, which find expression in the representational model, and the power of a legislature to determine policy. In other words, certain sectors of the public seek parliamentary expression of their interests and desires in a situation in which the general interest and 'general will' are expressed by the government. These expectations are largely on the level of policy-making rather than in the realm of proper administration, that is, where the legislature investigates and criticizes the government, monitors it and conducts discussions of public issues of major importance. It is possible, therefore, for a legislature to win scant public acknowledgement of its legitimacy even though it is carrying out the classic parliamentary functions in reasonable fashion. The level of legitimacy depends above all on fulfillment of the representational function through intervention in the policy-making process on behalf of groups and individuals.

A distinction should also be made between the institutional status of the legislature and the individual standing of its members. These two elements are related and exert mutual influence on each other. Generally speaking, an improvement in institutional status contributes to enhancement of individual standing and vice versa. The individual dimension is of particular significance with regard to the question of public legitimacy. Indeed, while the decline of the legitimacy of the Knesset in the eyes of the public may be more closely allied with the personal, rather than the institutional factor, since the two are interrelated, there are implications for the institutional issue as well.

The importance of the distinction between the institutional and individual factors for analysis of the status of legislatures lies in the fact that there may be a discrepancy between the institutional power of a parliament and the personal power of its members. Individual power may even increase without an accompanying rise in institutional status. For example, a very high level of inter-party competitiveness, such as when the legislature is divided between two parties or two party blocs of equal size, will not necessarily increase the institutional authority of the legislature, but is likely to reinforce the power of its members. The decision of several of them, or in extreme cases only one, to transfer allegiance from one party to another can seal the fate of the government, but will have no direct bearing on the institutional power of the legislature.

OBJECTIVES

This book deals with one of the six factors which determine the status of the legislature – namely, the degree to which it enjoys the support of the chief executive. The study focuses on David Ben-Gurion's role in shaping Israeli parliamentarism, with reference to the other five factors. To date, the numerous historical studies devoted to Ben-Gurion have not addressed the parliamentary issue, while political science investigations of the Knesset have not touched on Ben-Gurion's contribution. The present study is an initial attempt to understand the roots of Israeli parliamentarism through analysis of Ben-Gurion's role. This link between Israeli parliamentarism and Ben-Gurion is achieved by combining political science theories with historical methodology.

While serving as Prime Minister and Minister of Defence, Ben-Gurion held most of the power of the political elite, which was concentrated in the executive body. As is true of all legislatures, the early years of statehood were of great significance in determining the status of the Knesset. Indeed, Ben-Gurion himself was well aware of the importance of this period, stating: 'These are the years of foundation-laying, and the foundations we lay now will determine the future for generations to come.'[4] One of the fathers of Israeli parliamentarism, Yochanan Bader, had this to say about Ben-Gurion's influence:

> In the formative years of the state, Ben-Gurion had the power to determine its image, to mold the patterns, regulations and

> procedures which, for better or worse, became the status quo – and not only on religious matters; they became deeply rooted in the life of the state . . . Of these matters, people will say in years to come: this was decided at the time of the Provisional Government, that was determined by the First Knesset and cannot be changed. That is the way it is. And some will take a favourable view and praise it, while others will condemn it.[5]

It is the contention of this study that the fact that Ben-Gurion gave the Knesset little support explains, at least to a certain degree, its present fundamental weaknesses. Ben-Gurion denied the Knesset the right to take part in the policy-making process, caused a decline in the support of the elite and the general public, encouraged partisanship and endeavoured to reduce competitiveness. His own perception of the Knesset was in line with the model of system maintenance, whereas the Knesset members advocated the policy-making model, and the public favoured the representational model. This assertion tallies with Mezey's theory regarding the different perceptions of the function of a legislature.

Ben-Gurion's approach to the Knesset is typical of premiers and of nation-building leaders in particular. He was able to exert such tremendous influence on the status of the Knesset due, *inter alia*, to four factors: his extensive power within the government; his considerable authority within his own party; the fact that he headed a dominant party whose strength far exceeded its electoral gains; and the unique formative period, when massive public sympathy and support was extended to a leader of his magnitude who was identified with the establishment of the state and even with the state itself.

It is reasonable to assume that leaders who emerge from a legislature will have greater sympathy for it than extra-parliamentary leaders. Ben-Gurion rose to power without a parliamentary past. Such leaders, who before assuming supreme office engaged largely in administrative activities, tend to perceive the legislature as an impeding factor. They believe the lack of experience of members of the legislature renders them incapable of comprehending practical political work and its constraints. On the other hand, leaders who emerge from a legislature, such as the British premiers, tend to be more sympathetic toward it. Their lengthy parliamentary service typically inspires deep understanding of the roles of parliament, and in some cases even identification with it. This phenomenon is particularly striking among leaders of a parliamentary opposition. One such example is Menachem Begin, who attained the premiership after 29 years as leader of the opposition. Members of the opposition find it easy to attack the government in the name of parliamentary interests.

Although Ben-Gurion exerted considerable influence on the status, powers, strength and image of the Knesset, as we will see below, he was not the sole formative force. The present study is not concerned with the additional factors which helped shape Israel's legislature. It is necessary to stress this important reservation: Ben-Gurion's influence was decisive, but not exclusive. An additional reservation relates to Ben-Gurion's political strength. Despite the extraordinary power he wielded – unparalleled among Israel's leaders – Ben-Gurion was not omnipotent. His authority should not be overestimated. On several occasions he found himself in the minority in the government or the party. The government rejected some of his proposals regarding the waging of the War of Independence, and did not adopt his scheme to change the electoral system into a combined regional–personal-majority system; his party chose Sharett rather than Eshkol as Prime Minister when Ben-Gurion retired to Sede Boker in 1953, and in the same year, rejected his plan to declare the Israel Communist Party illegal.[6] It also turned down his proposal to establish the 'People's Front', an extra-party organization which was to stand for election to the Knesset in order to win support for the reform of the electoral system.[7] Nor did the party adopt his position during the final stages of the 'Lavon affair', and even decided, against his wishes, to form an alignment with Achdut Ha'avoda (the *Ma'arach*). In the course of this book, we will see how Ben-Gurion's plans were foiled even on a variety of issues relating to the standing of the Knesset. On some parliamentary matters he prevailed, and on others his ideas were rejected. Yeshayahu Leibowitz's assertion that 'for many years, Ben-Gurion was seen to be adept at party and parliamentary stratagems',[8] is essentially correct. However, his further claim that Ben-Gurion 'exerted total control over his party and over political life in Israel, and even those of his colleagues who had second thoughts about his direction and methods subjected their will to his'[9] is correct only in part, and was valid mainly in times of war. Whenever Ben-Gurion tried to impose his views in a way which was liable to undermine the power of certain politicians or organizations, he encountered resistance. He succeeded in overcoming some, but not all, of this opposition.

Mezey lists several types of pressure that can be applied to the legislature by the extra-parliamentary political elite, including dissolving the legislature by force or constitutional amendment, and verbal attacks on the institution and its members.[10] In the case of Israel, the legislature has never been dissolved by force; however, two legislative bodies – the Provisional State Council and the Constituent Assembly – disappeared prematurely at Ben-Gurion's initiative, and verbal attacks on the Knesset and its members were his daily bread. Moreover, Ben-Gurion battled the Knesset on a number of issues, his main aim being to restrict its powers and undermine its status in the eyes of the public.

He was involved in such questions as the number, immunity and salary of Knesset members, and their right to leave the country; the location of the Knesset; its agenda; the organization and powers of its committees; coalitionary discipline in the plenum and committees, and more. This list reveals two related aspects: the power of the Knesset as a governing institution (as reflected, for example, in the organization and powers of the committees) and the status of the individual members of the Knesset (as reflected in their immunity and salary).

The low level of competitiveness and high level of partisanship which prevailed in Ben-Gurion's time had a negative effect on the status of the Knesset. In addition, Ben-Gurion employed several means of his own to weaken the Knesset both institutionally and on the personal level. His strong influence over the composition of his party's Knesset slate assisted him here. This is an interesting example of the discrepancy between the formal/legal level and the political/party level. In theory, the Knesset elects the government, since the government is responsible to it. In practice, however, under Ben-Gurion the situation was almost completely reversed. The Party Nominations Committee, which selected the party's Knesset candidates, was composed of the senior ministers, headed by Ben-Gurion. As we will see below, Ben-Gurion made skillful use of this instrument in order to further his aims.

Although this study does not deal with the post-Ben-Gurion period, it may be assumed that the end of his term of office as Prime Minister marked the beginning of a process that strengthened the Knesset and improved its status. Such a process is identified by Blondel in his discussion of Third World countries. He argues that in the Third World, after the departure of charismatic leaders who have been identified with the gaining of national independence, it becomes possible to bolster the status of the legislature.[11] While the comparison between Israel and the Third World may be problematic, the principle is not invalid. Among the Western democracies, France is the most apt example for comparison with Israel here. The rise to power of de Gaulle in 1958 and the transition from a parliamentary system to the semi-presidential system brought with them a decline in the authority of the French legislative institutions. The transition also heralded a certain reduction in the level of partisanship and competitiveness, but the important factor in the weakening of the parliament was associated with de Gaulle's character and the actions he took. Goguel believes that de Gaulle's influence was one of the most important causes of the enfeebling of legislative institutions under the Fifth Republic.[12] The process has also been analyzed by Williams,[13] Derfler[14] and Wright,[15] whose description of De Gaulle's negative attitude toward the legislative institutions appears very similar to that of Ben-Gurion toward the Knesset.

Blondel classifies the legislative institutions of de Gaulle's period as the type of 'inhibited' parliament characteristic of Latin American countries such as Venezuela and Uruguay, and developing countries such as India and Lebanon.[16] The parliaments of Western Europe and the US Congress, on the other hand, belong to another category, that of strong parliaments. Blondel believed that after de Gaulle, France was likely to join this category of strong legislatures. According to his typology, which differs from that of Mezey, the weakest parliaments, or nascent legislatures, are characterized by a low level of activity and deal only with issues on the micro-level. The East German parliament and the Supreme Soviet under Stalin are examples. The second category, the truncated legislature, consists mainly of African states, whose legislatures conduct significant debate, but only on certain subjects. These legislatures have no impact on foreign affairs and socio-economic policy. An inhibited parliament, like the legislative institutions of de Gaulle's France, deals with all issues, but lacks the power to influence the executive arm in regard to important and decisive matters. Finally, the strong parliaments in Western Europe and the United States are characterized by wielding considerable influence over such important issues as foreign policy and social and economic policy.

Blondel does not discuss the Knesset; however, the Knesset of Ben-Gurion's era can be classified in his typology as an inhibited parliament. After this period, it began moving toward the model of a strong legislature, thus diverging from the patterns of Third World countries and drawing closer to the model of Western democracy. De

Gaulle's resignation and Ben-Gurion's retirement had similar effects on the power and status of the legislatures in their countries.

STRUCTURE OF THE BOOK

The first part of the book deals with the establishment of Israel's parliamentary institutions, primarily in the first years of statehood. Chapter 1 discusses Ben-Gurion's crucial influence on shaping parliamentary life in the early period from the foundation of the People's Council on the eve of the establishment of the State until the convening of the First Knesset in 1949. Chapter 2 highlights Ben-Gurion's role in determining the organization and powers of the Knesset committees. Other subjects are divided into those relating to the institutional power of the Knesset and those concerned with Ben-Gurion's struggles with Knesset members. As each issue obviously has both institutional and personal aspects, the division is based on their relative weight, rather than on any clear-cut distinction. The second section relates to Ben-Gurion's conflict with the institutional power of the Knesset. Chapter 3 deals with the dissolving of the Knesset, Chapter 4 analyzes Ben-Gurion's attitude toward the Knesset's investigative function and Chapter 5 discusses the symbolic aspects of his relationship with the Knesset. The third section of the book concerns his clashes with members of the Knesset. Chapter 6 analyzes his critical attitude toward the members' privileges, particularly immunity; Chapter 7 is devoted to Ben-Gurion's attempts to subject the parliamentary conduct of coalition Knesset members to the will of the government through legislation aimed at establishing collective responsibility and specifying sanctions against its violation and Chapter 8 addresses internal party appointments and politics, including the relations between the Mapai faction in the Knesset and the government and its leader. Part 4 deals with Ben-Gurion's verbal attacks on the Knesset, its members, the parliamentary opposition and the political parties, and his caustic parliamentary style, which had a negative impact on the character of Knesset debates. Chapter 9 presents Ben-Gurion's contribution to creating a crude, acrimonious style of parliamentary life in Israel, and Chapter 10 relates to his attacks (most of them extra-parliamentary) on two vital components of the parliamentary system – the opposition and the political parties. The concluding chapter deals with Ben-Gurion's overall influence in shaping Israeli parliamentarism.

METHODOLOGICAL REMARKS

The study is based on a systematic survey of the material in several central archives. The deliberations of the Knesset committees were examined in the State Archive; documents relating to the preparations for statehood were found in the Central Zionist Archives; study of partisan aspects drew on the abundant data in the archives of the Israel Labour Party at Beit Berl; and the Ben-Gurion Research Center Archives at Sede Boker served as the main source of data for the book as a whole. Further sources of information were provided by *Divrei Haknesset* (*Knesset Record*) and the contemporary press. Ben-Gurion's historical awareness and remarkable habit of keeping a written record of his actions, decisions, statements and thoughts greatly facilitated the research. At the same time, however, after delving into the plethora of archival material for several years, students of Ben-Gurion might gain the impression that this unique personality was cognizant of the possibility that the material might some day be perused by scholars who were not necessarily uncritical of him. One can only hope that this is a mistaken impression, or at least that it does not cast doubt on the validity of the data. Ben-Gurion's attitude toward historical research can be ascertained from a letter to Amitai Etzioni in 1952:

> I do not attribute great value to 'historians' whose writing is based on documents and research – most of which are but wishful thinking. True history is that in which a man writes his own experiences (if he is a man of truth), for he may know only this: what he himself has experienced, what he himself thought and felt.[17]

Uri Avneri, one of Ben-Gurion's avowed opponents and a member of the Knesset from 1965–73, sounds a cautionary note: 'I would not be exaggerating greatly if I said that relying on Ben-Gurion's papers to write history is like recording the history of the Jewish people according to the "Protocols of the Elders of Zion".'[18] Avneri may be right with regard to Ben-Gurion's books, in which he aspired to write the history of Zionism, but his statement is groundless with respect to the comprehensive archival material.

Although a large amount of material was collected for this study, additional data undoubtedly still exist and can cast further light on the subject. It is to be regretted that it was no longer possible, for obvious reasons, to interview the actual participants in the events of the period. Particular effort was made to avoid analyzing the data from a modern perspective, and thereby distorting the picture. In other words, it would be a grave error to refer to the period of a mobilized democracy of the 1950s in terms of modern Western democracy.

NOTES

1. For the term 'dominance', the character of a multi-party system with a dominant party, and application of these terms to the case of Israel, see Giora Goldberg, *Political Parties in Israel – from Mass Parties to Electoral Parties* (Hebrew), Tel Aviv: Ramot, 1992, pp. 23–51.
2. Michael L. Mezey, *Comparative Legislatures*, Durham, NC: Duke University Press, 1979, p. 20.
3. Ibid., p. 36.
4. Archives of Israel Labour Party, conferences, women's meeting, 11 July 1951.
5. Yochanan Bader, *The Knesset and I* (Hebrew), Jerusalem: Idanim, 1979, p. 146.
6. For this fascinating affair see: Giora Goldberg, 'The Jewish Factor in the Israeli Reaction to the Doctors' Plot in Moscow', in Eliezer Don-Yehiya (ed.) *Israel and Diaspora Jewry*, Ramat-Gan: Bar-Ilan University Press, 1991, pp. 183–203.
7. Giora Goldberg, 'Ben-Gurion and the "People's Front"' (Hebrew), *Medina, Mimshal Veyahasim Beinleumiim* (State, Government and International Relations) No. 35, (Autumn–Winter 1991), pp. 51–66.
8. Yeshayahu Leibowitz, *Encyclopedia Hebraica* (Hebrew), addendum vol., p. 674.
9. Ibid.
10. Mezey, *Comparative Legislatures*, p. 28.
11. J. Blondel, *Comparative Legislatures*, Englewood Cliffs, NJ: Prentice-Hall, 1973, p. 141.
12. François Goguel, 'Parliament under the Fifth French Republic: Difficulties of Adapting to a New Role,' in Gerhard Loewenberg (ed.) *Modern Parliaments: Change or Decline?*, Chicago and New York, Aldine-Atherton, 1971, pp. 81–95.
13. Philip Williams, 'Parliament under the Fifth French Republic: Patterns of Executive Domination', in Gerhard Loewenberg, Ibid., pp. 97–109.
14. Leslie Derfler, *President and Parliament: A Short History of the French Presidency*, Boca Raton FL: University of Florida, 1983.
15. Vincent Wright, *The Government and Politics of France*, New York: Holmes and Meier, 1978, p. 116.
16. Blondel, *Comparative Legislatures*, p. 138.
17. Ben-Gurion Research Center Archives, correspondence, Ben-Gurion to Amitai Etzioni, 19 November 1952.
18. Uri Avneri, 'Liars should have good memories' (Hebrew), *Ma'ariv*, 9 February 1994, p. 2.

PART ONE

The Establishment of Parliamentary Institutions

1 From the People's Council to the First Knesset

The Israeli parliamentary system was not born in a vacuum. In the pre-state period, the institutions of the Zionist movement as well as those of Knesset Israel (the Jewish community in Palestine) were quasi-parliamentary bodies. The Zionist Congress, the representative institution of the Zionist movement, established when the movement was founded in 1897, was essentially a forum for debate and discussion. *Asefat Hanivharim* (the Elected Assembly), the representative arm of Knesset Israel's institutions, was established in 1920 and functioned under the auspices of the *Vaad Le'umi* (National Council) and its executive.

The institutions of Knesset Israel dealt mainly with internal affairs. The Zionist movement's institutions, on the other hand, were broader and were active mainly in the spheres of foreign affairs and immigration. The Zionist Congress and the Elected Assembly were not legislatures, since they did not deal with legislation, nor did they convene regularly. Their importance lay in the very fact that Zionists from Palestine and the Diaspora as well as Palestinian Jews were given a share in the democratic electoral process even before the state came into being. In general, the Congress and the Assembly were representative bodies that did not fulfil vital parliamentary functions such as supervision, investigation and control. The relations between the two bodies and the executive authorities which grew out of them were largely similar to those prevailing within political parties between broad bodies like the convention or the central committee and executive bodies like the directorate or the secretariat. In other words, most, if not all of the power was concentrated in the executive bodies, while the quasi-parliamentary bodies were essentially representative and charged mainly with electing the executive institutions.

The important point in our context is that, until the establishment of the state, Ben-Gurion, who was at the head of the executive pyramid of the Zionist movement's institutions in the 1930s, was never confronted by a strong legislature capable of investigating, supervising or criticizing the activities of the executive level. The weakness of the quasi-parliamentary institutions in the pre-state period is understandable since they had neither sovereign power nor legislative power, which is the basic authority of a parliament. Once the state was established, the formal status of the legislature underwent a transformation. This change was not sudden, but was part of the process that led to the establishment of the First Knesset in 1949. Three new bodies were involved in this process – the People's Council, the Provisional State Council and the Constituent Assembly.

The present chapter deals with Ben-Gurion's role in this process, while the next will focus on the parliamentary committees in the same period. The two subjects have been separated in view of the great importance of the committees.

THE PEOPLE'S COUNCIL

The establishment of the provisional institutions of government at the beginning of 1948 was overshadowed by the fierce conflict over who would be the supreme national authority on security matters. Ben-Gurion succeeded in abolishing the position of Haganah commander – held by Israel Galili – which could have been a barrier between the Minister of Defence and the Chief of Staff. The establishment of the People's Council, on the other hand, was not accompanied by any political furor. A provisional state government was to be established by the end of 1948 under the UN Assembly resolution. The UN and the leaders of the Yishuv did not intend to create a structure composed of a government and a legislature, but rather to establish a single institution which would constitute an executive authority. How, therefore, did the distinction between the People's Council and the People's Administration come about?

Ben-Gurion wanted the powers of all the political bodies dealing with security, as well as those dealing with other areas, such as the Jewish Agency Executive and the *Vaad Le'umi*, to be transferred to the provisional state government. At the beginning of April 1948, he declared that it was essential to treat each and every issue as if it were of significance to the country's security.

> It is necessary that all these matters be dealt with in the Yishuv by a single authority. Two authorities would be anarchy, three would be twofold anarchy . . . At this time of crisis – we need one supreme authority, with decisive authority on all matters pertaining to the life of the Yishuv, not only security in the limited sense of the term, but all aspects of economic, public and cultural life, and this institution must be granted authority by the Yishuv and the Zionist movement. Until we prevail, it alone must control all our affairs in this country.[1]

He demanded that 'the ruling institution which will come into existence, the sole and supreme body, be granted all the authority of the Yishuv and of the Zionist movement'.[2]

Zeev Sherf, Secretary of the People's Administration, explained that it was necessary to separate the People's Administration and the People's Council because the Council had grown to an unwieldy size:

> It was impossible to believe that a council with 37 members could constitute a practical national administration. From the outset, we did not intend to set up so large a body; when the various parties were approached to give power of attorney to the implementation committee, it became evident that none of the parties or bodies would grant it unless one or more of their representatives were included in the council.[3]

The solution was to establish an additional, smaller body, to be called the People's Administration (or the Thirteen), which could adopt resolutions with relative ease, and would constitute the basis for the provisional government. The People's Council was composed of members of the Jewish Agency Executive in Jerusalem, members of the *Vaad Le'umi* Executive and representatives of parties which had not participated in the Jewish Agency Executive and the *Vaad Le'umi* Executive.

Although Ben-Gurion agreed that the Administration would be responsible to the Council,[4] it was not clear initially whether the reference was to an extended government and cabinet or to a parliament and a government. Sherf asserts that the name 'People's Council' was selected mainly 'in order to avoid a superfluous and useless dispute with the mandatory government',[5] since a provisional government council was planned. Mapam's proposal that the People's Administration be elected 'in parliamentary fashion',[6] namely by the People's Council, was rejected. The Council did not elect the Administration nor could it dissolve it. The Administration drew its authority not from the Council, but from the Zionist Executive.

Several days before the first meeting of the People's Council, David Remez, a Mapai leader, protested to Ben-Gurion that it was being ignored:

> If the 'Thirty-Seven' is the legislative institution, it is inconceivable for it to be unaware, before a meeting of the Thirteen is held, that such an event is going to take place. If the thirteen-member institution is established, they will feel they are being ignored. There is a feeling that the Thirty-Seven was established so as not to exist.[7]

Ben-Gurion's reply was: 'We must discuss this matter on its merits, and not because of any fear that the Thirty-Seven may be dissolved; this will not happen if the parties participating in the Thirteen do not run away from the Thirty-Seven.'[8] Remez continued to demand that the People's Council be convened in order to inform it of the existence of the Administration, but Ben-Gurion objected to the idea that the Administration could only be convened if a prior meeting of the People's Council were held, and the proposal was rejected.

In fact, the Administration began operating before the Council convened for its first session. On 18 April 1948, the Administration held its first session, during which it clarified the nature of its relations with the Council. Sherf reported that the meeting 'noted that the People's Administration has the authority to deal with matters of security, transportation, supplies, commerce and industry, labour, manpower, agriculture, immigration, police etc.'.[9] In practice, the People's Council was left without any power or specific tasks. The sole function assigned it was to serve as a forum for the proclamation of the establishment of the state.

The day after the first meeting of the Administration, in response to pressures to convene the Council, Ben-Gurion dispatched a letter to its members, warning that 'postponement of the activity of the

Administration until after the Council meets will, in my opinion, constitute a grave threat to the security and strength of the Yishuv in the trying days which lie ahead . . . and there can be no fundamental arrangement now except for the Thirteen'.[10] A practical obstacle was now added to Ben-Gurion's reluctance to convene the Council. The Jerusalemite members were unable to attend the Tel Aviv meetings because of the security situation.

The first meeting of the People's Council finally took place on 4 May 1948, ten days before the proclamation of statehood was scheduled to take place. Ben-Gurion, who was chairman of the Council without having been elected to this position, conducted the meeting and was the sole speaker. He confined himself to delivering a general report on the situation. The meeting was conducted without an agenda. Ben-Gurion announced that the Administration was not a government and the Council was not a legislature. What existed was an 'emergency command . . . and as such, we may perhaps be unable to observe all the precepts of democracy'.[11] This ceremonial pattern was reiterated the next day. The Council members listened to Ben-Gurion's speech and dispersed without having uttered a word. Ben-Gurion exploited the inability of the Jerusalem members to attend as a pretext for gagging the Council: 'There is a justified demand by the Jerusalem members not to commence the Council's work as yet, since they have been unable to reach us . . . the honour of the Council and of our Jerusalem members requires that we do not start without them'.[12]

The Council was not made privy to the preparations for the establishment of the state and the formulation of the Declaration of Independence. Sherf reports on the criticism evoked by the relegation of the Council to the sidelines:

> The Council members from outside Jerusalem were angered by the fact that it was not convened. Particularly incensed were those parties which were not participating in the People's Administration and hence were not made privy to the deliberations in the final days.[13]

The communists protested vehemently against the non-convening of the Council,

> and in other parties as well there was anxiety as to the active existence of the Council as a legislative body, and as a body

> supervising the activities of the Administration, and in the future – the government. The fact that no meetings had been held in the month between the establishment of the Council and that day, aroused certain anxieties.[14]

The very fact that someone close to Ben-Gurion like Sherf noted this, however indirectly, attests to the gravity of the issue, particularly since he did not refer to the festive gatherings held on 4 and 5 May as meetings.

The first session of the People's Council at which important issues were discussed was held on 14 May 1948, the day that statehood was proclaimed. This was also the last day of the People's Council, before it was transformed into the Provisional State Council. Ben-Gurion asked the Council for its unanimous approval of the text of the Declaration of Independence, in whose formulation it had played no part, as noted above. The Council acceded, but not before Meir Vilner of the Communist Party protested that: 'I received information on the agenda of this meeting only two hours ago.'[15] Herzl Rosenbloom of the Revisionist Party asked: 'Will the Council members be permitted to sign at the festive meeting, and incidentally to submit their reservations to any of the clauses?'[16] Ben-Gurion hastened to reply: 'Not today . . . today we can't do it',[17] then announced the agenda of the festive meeting and added 'there will be a proclamation and there will be no debate, because the debate has been held here'.[18]

The Council went on to discuss the manifesto (an additional legal document) and dealt Ben-Gurion his first defeat. His version of the first clause in the manifesto dealt with the powers of the Provisional State Council, successor to the People's Council: 'The Provisional State Council is the legislative authority. The Council is empowered to and hereby bestows this authority on the government for purposes of urgent legislation.' Nachum Nir (of Achdut Haavoda Poalei Zion which was then part of Mapam) questioned the term 'urgent legislation'. Ben-Gurion hastened to promise that the provisional government would not exploit its right to adopt urgent legislation until the Provisional State Council was convened two days later. Nir expressed his objections to the proposal:

> If so, I do not see why it is necessary . . . there is a danger that the Council will become a fiction. I have the impression, on the basis of my experience in the past month in the People's

> Council and the Administration, that someone would like to turn it into a fiction.[19]

It was evident that Nir was referring to Ben-Gurion's involvement. Vilner seconded Nir's objections: 'This is an anti-democratic practice . . . Simple logic says that thereby we, the Council, are taking the decision to abolish the Council.'[20] Golda Meir, one of the pillars of Mapai, proposed erasing the words 'and it hereby bestows', thereby, in effect, ranging herself against Ben-Gurion. The latter defended his stand, saying that

> any ordinary parliament, particularly during an emergency, invests such powers in the executive body. We are at war, and none of us knows what will happen tomorrow . . . I believe that the members of the Administration merit the confidence of the Council.[21]

Some Mapai members of the Council did not support Ben-Gurion's proposal, which was rejected after the omission of the four words. This attempt to divest the Provisional State Council of some of its legislative powers, even before it had come into being, did not succeed. Immediately after the ratification of the manifesto, the People's Council convened for a festive session at which Ben-Gurion proclaimed the establishment of the state. From now on, the Provisional State Council was to replace the People's Council without any change in the composition of its membership.

Ben-Gurion succeeded in reducing the Council's role to a marginal one. It was he who decided whether and when the Council would convene. It had no rules of procedure and he controlled its agenda. He did not inform the Council of the preparations for the establishment of the state. The decision to proclaim statehood was dealt with by the Mapai institutions, ratified by the People's Administration, but never appeared on the agenda of the People's Council. The members of the Council did not take part in formulating the Declaration of Independence. Ben-Gurion refused even to listen to their reservations regarding the proposed text. Only on 16 May 1948, two days after the proclamation, did he permit the People's Council members, who meanwhile had become members of the Provisional State Council, to voice their comments on the clauses of the Declaration.[22]

THE PROVISIONAL STATE COUNCIL

At the first session of the Provisional State Council, two days after the proclamation of statehood, it turned out that the establishment of the state had not brought far-reaching changes. Ben-Gurion continued to conduct the Council meetings. The first proposal submitted to the Provisional State Council concerned the election of Haim Weizmann as its president. Ben-Gurion admitted that the Council was not empowered to co-opt members and change its composition 'but sometimes there is a sense of justice which is above the law'.[23] Nir insisted that the question of Weizmann's election should not be placed on the agenda, since the Council had not decided whether there should be a presidency at all and, if so, what its powers and functions should be. Rosenbloom questioned the election of a person who was not a member of the Council as president. Weizmann's election was ratified by the Council, but not before Ben-Gurion had ruled that 'according to our constitution, the president of the Council possesses neither political power nor constitutional rule',[24] and that Weizmann's election did not imply that he would be a member of the government.

At the same meeting, the government tabled the Law and Administration Ordinance before the Council. Nir protested that the Council had not been given sufficient time to peruse the proposed text before the discussion:

> For five or six weeks the members of the People's Council have been idle, despite their position. The document could have been prepared earlier, and we could have examined it properly. Now they come and propose that we approve the entire law this evening.[25]

The government proposal stated that the government would operate in accordance with the policy decided on by the Council, would implement its resolutions and report to it on its activities. Nir protested at the discrepancy between the formal powers proposed for the Council and its weak status in practice:

> We have not determined any policy, have taken no decisions; you have not permitted us to take any decisions. We should have decided who our chairman is. I see that Mr Ben-Gurion is fulfilling this function honourably, but I did not elect him. If we have already elected a president today, we should also have

> elected a chairman, in order to know who is going to conduct the meetings here.[26]

Nir objected to the arrangement proposed in the Law and Administration Ordinance regarding emergency regulations, which would empower ministers 'to amend any law, change it, suspend it or introduce conditions'. In his opinion, 'the power to legislate is ostensibly assigned to us, but the provisional government can empower the prime minister or any minister to pass an ordinance which will revoke the law we have passed. This is an anti-democratic law'.[27] Moreover, he criticized the handing over of all the powers formerly wielded by the British monarch (or one of his ministers, the High Commissioner or the Palestine government) to the provisional government and 'not to the Council, which is the source of government'. If the emergency regulations were adopted and all these powers were granted to the provisional government, 'the Council members can go home and not be summoned for another month or two or three . . . this is a total abolition of democracy . . . on the basis of these laws, we can abolish the Council'.[28]

Nir's most vigorous protest was reserved for the proposal that the Council could approve or reject the expenditure budget, 'but is not empowered to increase it'. 'What is the source of power in our country – the government or the Council?' he asked.

> As far as I am concerned, it is the Council. The government derives its power from the Council. This being so, why is the government granted the right to decide on any budget while the Council only has the right to say yes or no. Why are we being deprived of the right to make allocations? Why do you think the Council should limit its sovereignty? Moreover, there is a certain insult implied here – why do the government ministers think that we are less responsible than they are? Why do they regard us with mistrust?[29]

Mordechai Shatner of Mapai and David Zvi Pinkas of the Mizrachi Party echoed Nir's criticism on the budget and the emergency regulations. Shmuel Mikunis of the Communist Party argued that 'they want to turn the Provisional State Council into a fiction'[30] and added that the government's proposal contained 'several clauses which reveal a desire to destroy the powers of the Council'.[31] Oblique criticism was also voiced by Meir Argov of Mapai:

> What will the authority of the Council consist of, in effect, if it is convened only formally . . . if it is not treated as a parliament – because then it will be empty of real content, will become a forum for speeches and proclamations, or will be regarded as a council for times of crisis, as noted by the chairman at the first meeting of the Council. This can be done by submitting reports on every government meeting, if not orally, then in writing. This would allay the suspicion held by many that the Council would be only an incidental body, not something serious.[32]

In light of the criticism from representatives of the parties in the government and from Mapai, Ben-Gurion was forced to postpone the vote on the Law and Administration Ordinance. A five-member committee was set up to reformulate the clauses of the ordinance. It was also decided that the committee would draft a proposal to regulate the working procedures of the Council.

At the second meeting of the Provisional State Council on 19 May 1948, the Law and Administration Ordinance was adopted. At the beginning of the meeting, Ben-Gurion announced that he would survey the security situation 'on the assumption that I can trust all those present here – not only Council members, but also journalists and guests; these remarks are not for publication, although I will reveal no secrets'.[33] The statement 'not for publication' is indicative of Ben-Gurion's attitude towards the Council. At the same meeting, in a discussion of the 'Shipping Vessels Ordinance (Nationality and Flags)' he again noted that several matters were 'not for publication'.[34]

At the conclusion of the meeting, the issue was raised in a question which Nir directed at Ben-Gurion:

> I have been shown a letter in the press relating to the agenda of the Council, containing the text of an order prohibiting the publication of any informative material on the meetings apart from the official communiqué. I would like to know: when did we decide that? And if we did not decide it – then this means that it is permissible to publish the material, with certain censorship, of course.[35]

In his reply, Ben-Gurion admitted that no debate had taken place on this question, and added:

> Of course there is censorship. Each of us knows that there is a need for censorship, and it is to be regretted that things have been published which are useful to the enemy. On the other hand, censorship should be strict only when publication could prove harmful, but not on controversial internal matters. Thus, there is no ban on publication of matters discussed by the Council, apart from cases where it is stated specifically that such a ban exists.[36]

In making this statement, Ben-Gurion was deciding procedure without being empowered to do so. He did not even take the trouble to specify who was authorized to ban publication. On the basis of his comments in the earlier part of the meeting, one can, perhaps, deduce that he was referring to himself.

In the debate on the Law and Administration Ordinance, the Council members succeeded in amending some of the original proposals. One important amendment, adopted at Nir's initiative, stated the responsibility of the provisional government towards the Provisional State Council. The government waived the proposed clause limiting the authority of the Council to increase the budget. The government also withdrew the clause which stated that the Council was authorized to transfer its legislative powers to the provisional government for purposes of urgent legislation. The authority to promulgate emergency regulations was not revoked, but was rendered conditional on the Council's proclamation of a state of emergency. On the same day, the Council approved Ben-Gurion's proposal and proclaimed a state of emergency. Appended to the Law and Administration Ordinance was a list of members of the Council and a list of government ministers. The ratification by the Council of the entire ordinance, including the appendices, was for the purpose of reaffirming that the government was subject to the Council. Rachel Cohen of Wizo asked that the vote on the list of Council members be separated from the vote on the list of ministers. Ben-Gurion decided otherwise: 'This list is not to be voted on – we must accept it, but not vote against it.'[37] He was implying that the existence of the government was not conditional on the approval of the Council.

In the two weeks following the ratification of the ordinance on 19 May, the Council was not convened. At its third meeting, on 3 June, criticism was again voiced about its limited powers and its mode of operation. Shatner of Mapai complained that the Council was convening too infrequently. Pinkas (HaMizrachi) asked the ministers 'to come to the Council and explain the main points of their functions and of the ministries', and demanded 'that the Council participate in the discussions and in the decision-making on important and weighty matters relating to the administration of our state'.[38] Argov (Mapai) said that the government should 'bring matters before us in a broader manner and in greater detail'.[39]

After the general discussion and before the Council went on to discuss a series of draft laws, Ben-Gurion expressed the hope 'that the Council will demonstrate its efficiency so that we can cover the entire agenda'.[40] When the meeting opened, Nir proposed to begin by discussing the Council's rules of procedure, but he was outvoted. Ben-Gurion, skilled in fixing agendas and conducting meetings, did not even raise the subject for discussion although it appeared on the agenda. The lack of rules of procedure was very convenient from his point of view. Towards the end of the meeting, when it was clear that Ben-Gurion was evading the subject, Nir demanded that the debate on the rules of procedure be the first item on the agenda of the next meeting. Ben-Gurion was unwilling to commit himself: 'No commitment made by this meeting will be valid, since there is no way of knowing what will happen next week.'[41] And, indeed, the following week the Council was not convened.

In the first month after the proclamation of statehood, Ben-Gurion convened the Council for only three sessions. He conducted the meetings and the agenda with an iron hand. The absence of rules of procedure helped him in his skilful manoeuvring. He prevailed on the question of the emergency regulations, despite his failure at the People's Council when the manifesto was approved, and notwithstanding the fact that the Provisional State Council approved a more moderate approach to urgent legislation than he would have wished. At this early stage one can discern a pattern, based on the wide gap between constitutional arrangements and political practice. The most striking example is the clause in the Law and Administration Ordinance which stipulates that the government will operate according to the policy laid down by the Council, implement the resolutions of the Council and report to it on its activities. The significance of this clause was that it would be a government based on the assembly model. The reality was totally different.

The following are some of the reservations voiced by the members of the Council with regard to its powers and its operation. Vilner of the Communist Party demanded 'that the Council be convened before the government takes decisions and not afterwards'.[42]

Aryeh Altman of the Revisionist Party asked: 'What is the actual role of the Council? Is it only to be faced with facts, to hear post factum about resolutions which have already been implemented?'[43] He also complained about the dearth of information which the government was supplying to the Council. Argov of Mapai blamed the weakness of the Council and the fact that it was not being convened on 'all members of the government and not on the Prime Minister alone . . . The government can prevent this by coming to the Council and presenting the issues seriously, not only as statements for outward show.'[44] Pinkas of HaMizrachi asserted that 'as regards discussions and decisions on political matters there is at present no difference between ordinary citizens of this country and the representatives of the people who are members of this Council'.[45]

Ben-Gurion continued to conduct the Council meetings in an authoritarian fashion. Before one of the votes, the Minister of Justice, Pinchas Rosen, pointed out to him that Council member Eliyahu Dobkin (Mapai), who had not been present at the beginning of the meeting, had arrived. The Prime Minister commented: 'He will not vote at this meeting' and Beba Idelson of Mapai was outraged: 'Is there a law that states that if a Council member arrives late, he is denied the vote?'[46] Ben-Gurion did not even reply.

On 17 June 1948, the Council began to debate the rules of procedure. A fierce debate raged on the question of the procedure for conducting meetings. Nir demanded that the rules of procedure stipulate that ministers could no longer conduct the meetings. By a majority of 11 to 9 it was decided that a minister could not serve as Chairman of the Council, and by 12 to 8 that deputy chairmen could not be members of the government. Ben-Gurion had lost the battle, but still refused to submit. Towards the end of the meeting he called on Argov, who claimed

> that there was a misunderstanding on the previous vote on the composition of the presidium, and we want to request a revote on this question, either now or at the next meeting. I propose that the presidium be composed of the President of the Council, the Prime Minister and three elected deputies who are not members of the government.[47]

This proposal, which makes no mention of the position of Chairman of the Council, was submitted by Mapai, the Yemenite Party and the four religious parties. It was based on the fact that in the absence from the country of Weizmann, President of the Council, Ben-Gurion, as Prime Minister, could continue conducting the meetings.[48] By a majority of 13 to 10 the Council decided to hold an additional vote on this question, and by 12 to 11 it cancelled the resolution passed earlier at the same meeting. The lack of clarity enabled Ben-Gurion to continue to chair meetings for the coming month. Only after it transpired that the Mapai–Yemenite–religious coalition on this matter no longer existed, did Mapai agree to elect a chairman (speaker) for the Council who was not a minister. On 15 July 1948, some two months after the state came into being, Yosef Sprinzak was elected to this position.[49] Immediately after the vote, Ben-Gurion yielded his seat, and handed the gavel to Sprinzak. Three years later, in his speech on the occasion of the completion of the First Knesset's term of office, Nir referred to the 'battle' over the separation of the positions of Prime Minister and Chairman of the Council. 'I recall our first steps at the Provisional State Council. We fought for two months for something which now seems self-evident, that the Prime Minister cannot serve as Chairman of the Council.'[50]

From the moment Ben-Gurion was forced to give up chairmanship of the Council meetings, his involvement in parliamentary affairs decreased. The election of a Council speaker heralded its enhanced status. This was reflected, *inter alia,* in the separation of the Council secretariat from the government secretariat, which enabled the formation of a separate administrative staff for the parliament. Nir reported that 'six months lapsed before we understood that the government secretariat could not be identical with the Provisional State Council secretariat'.[51] And, in fact, several months after Ben-Gurion ceased chairing the Council meetings, an independent secretariat was established for the Council. The presidium of the Council decided to appoint 'a special secretary under the presidium's authority', and in August 1948 the Council Chairman reported on this to the Minister of Finance, Eliezer Kaplan, and requested funding for the new position.[52] The secretary was appointed only at the end of October 1948. The Council's administrative separation from the government was an important step in the development of Israeli parliamentary life. This separation was given formal expression later, in January 1949, with the enactment of the Transition to the Constituent Assembly Ordinance. The change abolished the linkage between the government secretariat and the Council secretariat. In the debate on this clause, Baruch Weinstein of the Revisionist Party said: 'It is unthinkable for the apparatus at the disposal of the executive authority to serve as the apparatus of the legislature as well.'[53] However, despite the separation, the salaries and employment conditions of the administrative staff of the parliament remained inferior to those of the administrative staff of the government.[54] Once an independent apparatus was established for the parliamentary institution, its status vis-à-vis the government was improved.

The Council's independence is further reflected in Sprinzak's letter to Sherf, the Government Secretary, in which he asked for 'copies of the questions and the responses *before* the meeting of the Council'.[55] On the other hand, the Council remained largely financially dependent on the government. When Sprinzak wanted to train stenographers, he submitted a request to the Ministry of Finance for an allocation of 750 Israeli liras.[56] This financial dependence continued after the 1949 elections. More than three months after the elections, a request was submitted by the Knesset secretariat to the Prime Minister's office for the funding of stencil machines, and 'I also request approval for a machine with a double cart, as well as an order for two steel filing cabinets for our archive, in accordance with our discussion when the archive was established'.[57]

The extent to which the Council was under the government's control can be ascertained from three resolutions which the government adopted at its session of 30 May 1948. It decided to approve the resignation of three members of the Provisional State Council and the co-opting of three replacements. It also decided that the Council should pass a law granting participation rights to proxies at Council meetings. The third resolution stated that the government, not the Council, would issue a response to the UN Security Council resolution on the armistice. The fact that this last resolution was passed by a majority of six to four indicates the extent to which differences of opinion existed inside the government on the status of the Council.[58]

The Council's rules of procedure were ratified on 17 June 1948, at the meeting at which it failed to decide on a speaker. The rules of procedure stipulated that the Council would convene once a week. This was an improvement over the frequency of meetings till then, but a legislature which convenes only once a week cannot fulfil its functions adequately. In such a situation, parliamentary activity is not perceived as a full-time occupation, but rather as a secondary occupation. According to the proposed rules of procedure, the agenda was to be decided by the government, but the Council could add items to it. When several Council members protested at the privilege granted to the government, Ben-Gurion intervened and said:

> Those who believe that through amendments [to the agenda] they will enhance the Council's democracy, are doing the exact opposite. If the Council devotes one session a week to discussing the agenda – what to add and what to omit – the public will cease to take an interest. In several weeks' time, the war may be resumed, and the public will not be interested in such idle debates. The situation is that the government is not dependent on the Council, nor is the Council dependent on the government. The Council will be of some value if it has value in the eyes of the public; and this will happen if it discusses issues, not agendas.[59]

This statement also indicates that Ben-Gurion understood only too well the importance of public support for the legislature.

The draft rules of procedure included a clause empowering the chairman to distinguish between a debate on a fundamental issue and other kinds of debate. The intention was that debates on fundamental issues be held on a party (factional) basis, and that other issues be discussed on an individual basis, free of party constraints. Nir questioned the chairman's authority to make this distinction. His stand was backed by a majority of 11 to 9. The shadow of Ben-Gurion, who still headed the Provisional State Council at that time, apparently loomed over the vote.

The rules of procedure included several clauses which indicated the inferior status of the Council in comparison to the government. For example, they stipulated that the government secretariat should also serve as the secretariat of the Council. As noted above, the two were separated at a later stage. The rules of procedure authorized the government (and the presidium of the Council) to decide on closed sessions of the Council. This meant that even if most members of the Council supported open deliberations, the government's viewpoint would prevail. This constituted clear interference on the part of the executive authority in the internal affairs of the legislative authority. The rules of procedure stated that the Treasury would pay the Council members for travel costs and for the 'loss of a day's work'. Council members did not, in effect, receive salaries, but only expenses, the level of which was determined by government officials. The spirit of these remarks clearly suggest that this body was not regarded as a true parliament, the workplace of its members, but rather as a supplementary occupation.

The ministers were granted unlimited right to speak. The rules of procedure permitted the government to refrain from responding to questions, although it obliged them to state the reason for the refusal. On the demand of the government (or ten members of the Council) a personal ballot or secret written vote would be held. The Council members were not authorized to receive copies of the minutes of closed debates. All these clauses, which became part of the rules of procedure of the Council, undermined its status and gave the advantage to the government.

Meanwhile, the infant state was reeling under the impact of the *Altalena* affair (an armed ship brought to Israel by the Revisionists and shelled by the army). The Council discussed the subject at the initiative of several members, who cited the rules of procedure, and not at Ben-Gurion's behest. Weinstein of the Revisionist Party and Zerach Vahrhaftig (Hapoel Hamizrachi) demanded the establishment of a parliamentary committee of investigation on the *Altalena.* The proposal was rejected when Ben-Gurion opposed it: 'I will not undergo interrogation by Begin, even if someone else on the Council carries out the task for him.'[60] Ben-Gurion preferred a ministerial committee for this purpose. The Provisional State Council decided to co-opt four more members of the Council to the three-member ministerial committee. The initiative for this move came from Vahrhaftig. Beforehand, Ben-Gurion, asked what the committee's authority would be, replied that: 'there is no authority, just a task . . . to create a certain type of rule in a state which has a united army . . . if this task is fulfilled, it will ensure that all the crimes committed in this area concerning the army, concerning the revolt against authority – will be obliterated'.[61] Later in the debate, he announced: 'This committee will take no decisions by majority vote. It will merely clarify, summarize and propose.'[62] These comments indicate the role Ben-Gurion had adopted as the supreme national authority, establishing norms and making arrangements without any legal basis. He succeeded, therefore, in preventing the setting up of a parliamentary committee of investigation and in depriving the Council of its natural task as an institution investigating the activity of the government, although he was forced to accept the participation of Council members in the committee. His original intention was to prevent the subject from being dealt with by the parliamentary institution. When he was unable to do so, he demanded that the government, through the ministerial committee, deal with the matter. In other words, instead of the Council investigating the government's functioning in this affair, the government would do the investigating itself. He did not achieve his aim in full, but to a large extent did check the Council's attempt to gain the authority to investigate the government. The same meeting of the Council approved an amendment to the Law Courts Ordinance proposed by Vahrhaftig, concerning the appointment of Supreme Court justices. Whereas the government had proposed that the Minister of Justice appoint the justices and the government approve the appointment, Vahrhaftig demanded that they be appointed by the government, with the approval of the Council.[63] This was a defeat for the government and the Prime Minister, and an achievement for the Provisional State Council.

Ben-Gurion's concern regarding the flow of information to the legislative branch was clearly evident from the early stages of the development of Israeli parliamentary life. For example, when he was asked at a meeting of the Council by the Minister of the Police and Minority Affairs, Bechor Shitrit, about the proportion of Oriental Jews among the immigrants from Cyprus, Ben-Gurion replied: 'I cannot give information on that matter in this forum.'[64] He sometimes justified the refusal to provide information to the Council by claiming that the government had not yet discussed the matter. At the beginning of July 1948, for example, in response to a demand by Altman of the Revisionist Party that the government supply the Council with information on the proposals of the UN mediator, Count Bernadotte, Ben-Gurion said that the government could not bring this matter before the Council for discussion since 'the Government has not yet had time to discuss it'.[65] Berl Repetor (Mapam) tried to raise the question again and Ben-Gurion responded emphatically: 'The question was whether there is information, and the answer was : there is no information.'[66]

Generally speaking, Ben-Gurion tended to justify the dearth of information provided to the Council on security grounds. Vahrhaftig submitted the following question to Ben-Gurion (in his capacity as Minister of Defence): 'Can we, at this meeting of the Council, be given a survey by the Minister of Defence on our security situation, and on the means we are adopting to prepare for the imminent war?' Ben-Gurion replied briefly and emphatically: 'No. This is not advisable.'[67] Security considerations were also cited with regard to publication of details about the Council's meetings. At the end of the debate on the government's response to Bernadotte's proposals, Ben-Gurion informed the Council members that 'this was a closed session. You can publish only the resolution which was adopted, and not the other proposals . . . an announcement will be issued to the press in accordance with the spirit of that resolution.'[68]

Ben-Gurion intervened in the conduct of the meeting which discussed the report of the UN mediator and the instructions which the government had conveyed to the Israeli UN delegation. After the lengthy debate, the Mapam representative, Zvi Luria, insisted on putting his own proposals to the vote. The Speaker, Sprinzak, objected. Ben-Gurion explained the matter as follows:

> The government is not requesting ratification of the instructions, since in the event that the Council is not opposed to the instructions, the government regards the fact that no resolution is adopted as approval. Only in the event that the Council does not agree to this line, is it necessary to adopt a resolution – there is no need for a resolution, if the Council accepts the government line.[69]

This attitude is strange, since there was no way of knowing without taking a vote whether the Council did in fact support the line proposed by the government. However, Sprinzak did not call for a vote when the debate ended and he closed the session.

A fascinating incident, which indicates Ben-Gurion's unwillingness to provide the Council with much information, occurred in November 1948 in the wake of the demand for a Council debate on foreign policy. The Foreign Minister, Moshe Sharett, was then in France and Ben-Gurion was Acting Foreign Minister. On 11 November, the Council was due to hold a wide-ranging political debate. Ben-Gurion cancelled the debate on the grounds that, in Sharett's absence 'there is no point in holding this debate today'.[70] On 21 November, three Revisionist members of the Council dispatched a letter of protest to the Council presidium after the rejection of their demand for a debate: 'We protest vigorously at this method of conducting affairs which confronts the State Council with established facts.'[71] Two days later, Sprinzak approached the government on behalf of the Council presidium, requesting a political debate 'in light of various requests on the part of Council members who wish to hold a political debate in the Council'.[72] Ben-Gurion continued to refuse until a political debate was scheduled in the plenum at the initiative of Council members.

The debate was held in a closed session on 25 November 1948. Ben-Gurion confined himself to a few brief remarks and explained that the initiative for the debate stemmed from the Council and not from the government. It may well be that Ben-Gurion provided only a limited amount of information in order to signal to the Council that a parliamentary debate held against his own wishes would not achieve its aim. In response to the dearth of information and to the brevity of Ben-Gurion's statement, several members of the Council expressed their dissatisfaction. Weinstein of the Revisionists was particularly incensed:

> I fear that there is no point to such a meeting, in any event not to this closed session. After the official announcement that this session is solely for members of the Council, the impression will undoubtedly be created in the public that fateful political decisions are being taken here . . . you should have had consideration for the Council members and not banished the public. At least we would have had an audience . . . parliaments in other countries do not discuss foreign affairs in this way . . . if we demanded a debate on foreign policy problems, it was because we wanted to hear from the Prime Minister, from the authoritative source, and not just isolated, fragmented information.[73]

Vahrhaftig believed that 'at a closed session we were entitled to hear somewhat more',[74] while Altman expressed his regret that 'the Prime Minister did not find it necessary to give us information even at this closed session'.[75] Two Mapai representatives, Avraham Katznelson and Argov, also demanded more information from Ben-Gurion. Argov stated this explicitly:

> I join in the complaint of the members of the State Council that this is not the first time that political questions have not been submitted for debate on time. As for the debate itself, it did not reflect the necessary serious approach as befits the Council and the government. I protest at the fact that the Prime Minister did not give us a comprehensive survey of all that has occurred in these past three weeks.[76]

Ben-Gurion responded to these complaints, by feigning ignorance: 'I cannot give you information which I do not possess, and I am incapable of pretending I have secrets which I cannot divulge to you.'[77]

The issue of coalitional discipline had already come up in the early stage of the Provisional State Council. The government had decided on several occasions to forbid ministers to vote at the Council against government resolutions.[78] One example was the Election Law, regarding which Nir dispatched a sarcastic question to Ben-Gurion:

> Doesn't the government think that the resolution of 19 November 1948 is illegal, since it forbids members of the Council (who are ministers) to vote according to their conscience, and therefore changes the balance of power in the Council itself? And if the government considers this resolution to be legal, what are the arguments in favour of this legality?

Ben-Gurion defended himself by saying that the government was not aware of 'any law banning the government from adopting such a resolution'.[79] In later periods, Ben-Gurion endeavoured to impose coalitional discipline not only on ministers, but also on members of the Knesset. At this preliminary stage of the Provisional State Council, the lack of any legal basis for government resolutions regarding the votes of ministers in the Council was of cardinal importance.

The government's control of the Council's agenda often evoked the criticism of its members. Sprinzak protested at the fact that the government did not show enough consideration for the Council:

> I do not know who to approach on this matter, perhaps the Minister of Justice, to consult with him about how we can get the government to foresee, to know in advance when certain laws lapse. We have to be able to know things several weeks ahead, because we are becoming an institution which simply swallows and issues ordinances. But there are other matters too, and ordinances should not be passed under the threat that today is already the 9th of the month, and the ordinance will lapse if the Council does not extend it immediately.[80]

This sense of insult was not linked directly to Ben-Gurion, but clearly reflected the attitude towards the parliamentary branch of the government he headed.

Ben-Gurion persisted in his systematic disregard for the clause in the Law and Administration Ordinance that determined the principle of the government's subordination to the Council. He now also cited the argument that there was no clause in the law which restricted the government. Nir submitted a question to Ben-Gurion after the Prime Minister's declaration to the foreign press that Israel would not align herself 'with one world bloc against another'. He wanted to know 'on the basis of what authority this declaration was made, without it having been discussed by the State Council; and was it made after a government resolution or at the initiative of the Prime Minister alone'.[81] Ben-Gurion replied that the Law and Administration Ordinance contained no instruction precluding the Prime Minister 'from telling a foreign journalist what should be said, in his opinion – for the good of the country'.[82]

Nir pursued the point, and raised the question of the government's attitude towards the Council on various occasions. For example, during the political debate held on 11 January 1949, he asked,

> why, on many issues, and particularly foreign affairs, the government does not deem it necessary to take the Council into its confidence, and at best, gives us a report – good or bad, that is another matter – and even if they give us the opportunity after having heard the report, to express our satisfaction or dissatisfaction, this can have no effect, because we hear of things only after they have been done . . . I do not think that the government is acting wisely by accustoming us to think only post-factum. We are a young parliamentary state and it is the government's duty to teach us and to guide us into parliamentary life.[83]

Nir went on to attack Ben-Gurion directly: 'When he answers me that the Prime Minister can say whatever he likes, if he thinks it is for the good of the country – then I have the impression that he has still not entered into the role of Prime Minister.'[84] Ben-Gurion interrupted him by heckling him, but Nir did not shrink from clearly stating his views:

> The law says that policy is determined by the State Council. And when you, as Prime Minister, say that you will join a regional bloc – you are determining policy. This policy should have been determined by me and not by you. That is what the law says. When the Prime Minister speaks, he makes me responsible for what he said. The result is that I am responsible . . . I do not wish to be responsible except for my own actions. If the State Council decides something against my views – I am still responsible, because I am a member of the State Council,

> but to determine policy which could prove harmful, without consulting the State Council – I think the Prime Minister should know that that is unacceptable.[85]

Some two weeks before the elections to the Constituent Assembly, the Provisional State Council held a debate on the Ordinance of Transition to the Constituent Assembly. This ordinance revoked the Assembly's dual structure as a conventional legislature and a body charged with the task of framing a constitution. The majority of the members of the Constitution Committee of the Council favoured including a clause which would charge the Assembly with the task of framing a constitution within two years. Ben-Gurion, on the other hand, represented the stand of the government in favour of omitting both that clause and the one that would restrict the term of office of the Constituent Assembly to two years. His main argument was that the Provisional State Council was not an elected body, and hence was not empowered to determine such binding procedures:

> This Council lacks the authority to constrain the voters and to impose its views on them. Even if the Council tries to do so – this will be of no value. Who empowered this Council to impose its will on the people? . . . This Council has no binding authority on the Constituent Assembly. The Assembly will determine how many years it will serve . . . the authority to define the powers of the Constituent Assembly rests solely with the Assembly and not with this Council. This Council can make decisions only until a new institution has been elected . . . The Council cannot approve the proposals of the committee, and if they are passed – they have no legal validity, since the Constituent Assembly can revoke any ordinance passed by the Provisional Council.[86]

Ben-Gurion proposed that initially a vote be held on the government's proposal, and only if it was ratified, would the law committee's proposal be put to the vote. Vahrhaftig, chairman of the committee, objected to the proposed procedure on the grounds that 'the government has the prior right to submit the proposal itself to the State Council, but not its formulation'.[87] Ben-Gurion demanded that Vahrhaftig specify the legal basis for his demand, and the reply was that it was to be found 'in our rules of procedure. There is a majority and a minority. Therefore, we must put to the vote first the majority proposal and then the minority proposal.' Sprinzak ruled in favour of Ben-Gurion, and held a vote on the government resolution which was adopted by a majority of 16 to 7. Ben-Gurion's struggle in this regard reflects his basic approach, which was to achieve a political majority free of any binding restrictions or procedures.

At the same debate, the Prime Minister made some interesting comments on the nature of Israeli democracy:

> Most of the members of the committee have apparently forgotten the essence of the Provisional Council and the essence of democratic elections and the sovereignty of the people. The State of Israel was established in revolutionary fashion, without elections and without democracy. Otherwise it could not have come into being, and establishing the state was more important than scrupulously observing democratic procedures.[88]

The Council was only a 'temporary arrangement', particularly since

> the Council members have forgotten that it is the electorate which is sovereign and not this Council, and the Constituent Assembly can also change the name 'Constituent Assembly' if it so chooses, and it will determine its own working procedures and tasks. There is now one thing which is above all others – the sovereign voter.[89]

Ben-Gurion also intervened in the procedures of the Provisional State Council at its session on 13 January 1949, which was scheduled to vote on the recommendations of the Foreign Affairs Committee. The Committee's proposals were submitted to the Council, as were the proposals of Yaakov Riftin of Mapam. According to Clause 3 of Riftin's proposal,

> the State Council regards the lifting of the siege of Rafiah as a grave military and political error. The State Council expresses its regret at the fact that the withdrawal from the Egyptian border, which is the outcome of Anglo–American intervention and is a threat to our security and political position in the Negev, was carried out without prior discussion at the State Council.[90]

According to Clause 4: 'The State Council declares that the Prime Minister's statement on the regional treaty was made without the knowledge of the Council and is at odds with its political line.'

Ben-Gurion argued that the Council could not vote on Clause 3 because 'this is not a matter of foreign policy, but of conducting a war'.[91] Nir objected to Ben-Gurion's comment and received the reply that 'the State Council is not conducting the war'.[92] Sprinzak sided with Ben-Gurion and proposed that no vote be taken on Clause 3 of Riftin's proposal 'because it was not within the authority of the Foreign Affairs Committee to deal with this'. Argov, despite his Mapai affiliation, thought otherwise:

> In my opinion, the Prime Minister has misinterpreted the proposal of Council Member Riftin. Riftin did not raise a military question. According to the interpretation of the Prime Minister, this clause should be transferred to the Security Committee, and from the Security Committee it will be returned here. We have no interest in this . . . We propose a vote on Riftin's proposal – for and against, without confining ourselves to a formal announcement.

Sprinzak held a vote on the procedural question of whether to hold a vote on Clause 3 of the Riftin proposal. Argov's stand won greater support than Ben-Gurion's and the Council voted on Clause 3. Before the vote on Clause 4, Ben-Gurion again intervened and claimed 'that this clause states an incorrect fact. The Prime Minister did not make any announcement on a regional treaty, but rather on a Jewish–Arab alliance.'[93] As a result, Sprinzak proposed that no vote be taken on this clause. Most of the Council members supported the Speaker's stand.

In several cases, Ben-Gurion disregarded resolutions adopted by his party's institutions in regard to the Mapai faction's stand in the Provisional State Council. A striking example was the issue of granting voting rights in the forthcoming elections to the Constituent Assembly to immigrants who had been banished to Cyprus by the British. On 10 November 1948, the Mapai Bureau adopted a resolution in support of this proposal. The Bureau also decided that 'a government minister or faction member that opposes this stand – is entitled to abstain from voting'.[94] Ben-Gurion, who believed that the Cyprus exiles should not be granted voting rights, refused to withdraw his objection. He appeared before the members of his faction and persuaded them to vote with him on this matter. Zalman Aranne protested, at the Mapai Bureau meeting on 16 November, that

> Ben-Gurion appeared at the faction meeting and said that all these arguments endanger the very existence of the state and its legality . . . When one of us cites this argument – it is not considered important. When Ben-Gurion says it – it is important and all our comrades voted against the Bureau resolution. We had cabled the Cyprus exiles that the party decided to give them the right to vote.[95]

Ben-Gurion succeeded, in this case, in prevailing over his party's institutions.

Another subject placed on the agenda before the elections to the Constituent Assembly was that of election propaganda in the armed forces. Ben-Gurion objected to the proposal that the Minister of Defence's appeal against a resolution of the Central Elections Committee should be brought before the Council.[96] Consequently, this authority was granted to the government instead of to the Council. While he prevailed on this matter, Ben-Gurion failed on the issue of supervision of written propaganda. The government demanded that the Central Elections Committee be required to approve all party publications, but the Council denied the government any involvement in this issue.[97] Ben-Gurion was furious. In his letter to the Chief of Staff, specifying the voting procedures in the army, he noted that 'the Government's instruction regarding material dispatched to the armed forces – which should not include incitement, slander and provocation – was revoked by the State Council'.[98] Ben-Gurion suffered a further parliamentary defeat on the proposal to restrict the size of the daily newspapers. The Council rejected the government's draft legislation.[99]

On several occasions, the question of the rights of the State Council members vis-à-vis the censor was raised. Moshe Kol, Chairman of the Foreign Affairs Committee, complained to Ben-Gurion that the correspondence of Council members was being opened. In his reply, Ben-Gurion confirmed that there was censorship on all letters sent abroad, and explained that this was due to the state of war. He assured Kol that he would instruct the censor to inform the sender if there were delays in transmitting cables.[100] There were also cases in which Ben-Gurion himself censored news items in the press. Thus, for example, he was dissatisfied with the press release issued by the Minister of Labour and Construction, Mordechai Bentov of Mapam, and decided to bar its publication. He wrote to Bentov: 'I have been informed of the text of your press release – and I have banned its publication.'[101] He justified the ban on the grounds that a minister must not express open disagreement with other ministers in the press. Another minister, Peretz Bernstein of the General Zionists, then Minister of Trade, Commerce and Supplies had serious complaints which he submitted to the Prime Minister:

> All my correspondence, that which comes by post (inside the country!) and even most of the letters which reach my office by messenger service in the administration campus, have been clandestinely opened and sealed. I do not know who is conducting this internal espionage . . . Whoever is acting in this matter has a free hand within the state and government service . . . I am endeavouring to convey this letter to you without it falling into spying hands.[102]

Kol and Bernstein's appeals to Ben-Gurion are also discussed in Chapter 6, which deals with immunity, since the lack of immunity was one of the factors which enabled such involvement on the part of the security services.

Council Member Mikunis of the Israel Communist Party complained that he had been barred from entering 'the Arab ghetto in the town of Acre' where he had been scheduled to deliver an election address. Mikunis claimed that the military governor had informed him on arrival that the meeting had been cancelled and that he could not enter the area. 'Such an attitude towards a member of the State Council violates the most fundamental rights of Council members', Mikunis wrote in a question he submitted to Ben-Gurion. Ben-Gurion's reply was unequivocal: 'The state's regulations apply equally to all its citizens, and State Council members have no special privileges in areas under military rule.'[103]

In conclusion, the Provisional State Council benefited from the fact that in its time there was no coalition and in practice, no parliamentary opposition. In place of debate between the coalitional majority and the oppositional minority, the main debate was conducted between the government, headed by Ben-Gurion, and the Council. The fact that the existence of the government was not dependent on Council approval was advantageous to the Council in fulfilling its duties, since criticism of ministers and of the government as a whole on the part of members of factions represented in the government could not bring down the government. On the other hand, the Council suffered by not being an elected body, and hence its members were deprived of the right to initiate private legislation. The main obstacle to the development of the Provisional State Council was Ben-Gurion.

THE CONSTITUENT ASSEMBLY

At the last session of the Provisional State Council, several days before the convening of the Constituent Assembly, Ben-Gurion summed up as follows:

> I am convinced that the Council will willingly hand over its authority to the Constituent Assembly. Just as no man should envy his son or his disciple, so this Council, which was a provisional body, should not envy the Constituent Assembly which is elected and which will be permanent.[104]

Ben-Gurion's wish as to the duration of the Constituent Assembly's tenure was not fulfilled in full. The Assembly convened for two whole days and on the third day decided, at Ben-Gurion's behest, to dissolve itself and to be replaced by the First Knesset.

The question of the election of the Deputy Speakers of the Constituent Assembly arose at its first session on 14 February 1949. The Ordinance of Transition to the Constituent Assembly, adopted by the Provisional State Council, stipulated that until the Assembly adopted new rules of procedure, it would operate on the basis of the rules of procedure of the Provisional State Council. These stated that there should be three deputy speakers. Mapai wanted only two deputies, in order to prevent Herut from being allotted one of the positions. After the election of Sprinzak (Mapai) as Speaker, it was clear that the positions of deputies would be allotted to the other factions in accordance with their size. Mapam and the United Religious Front were the two largest factions after Mapai. The next was Herut which had 14 representatives in the Knesset. Ben-Gurion had no problem in explaining his viewpoint:

> There is no legal question involved here which requires an expert opinion. The Constituent Assembly is a sovereign body,

> and is no longer bound by the resolutions of the Provisional State Council, if it decides otherwise. Even if the clause regarding the presidium were part of the rules of procedure of the Provisional State Council, the Constituent Assembly is empowered to revoke it. If the Assembly decides on four, six, two or one deputy it thereby revokes that clause and its full authority to cancel or amend does not require the opinion of any legal expert. It is a sovereign body, and the proposal to elect two deputies or any other number is completely legal, and depends only on whether the Constituent Assembly decides thus or otherwise.[105]

The Herut representatives demanded a legal opinion. The Minister of Justice, Rosen, took issue with Ben-Gurion: 'If the intention today is to decide on the final composition of the presidium, then those who propose it should first propose cancelling this clause in the rules of procedure of the Provisional State Council, and then putting to the vote the proposal regarding two deputies.'[106] Ben-Gurion was not ready to accept the opinion of his Minister of Justice. The festive session of the Constituent Assembly was in an uproar. Yosef Sapir (General Zionists) protested that the election of deputies had not been on the agenda of the meeting.[107] The meeting eventually decided on the election of two deputies without changing the rules of procedure. On the following day, Nir and Burg were elected Deputy Speakers of the Constituent Assembly. Herut was excluded from the presidium.

On the same day, 15 February 1949, the government placed the Transition Law on the table of the Assembly and it was ratified on the following day. The central clause in the law dealt with the transition from the Constituent Assembly to the First Knesset. Having enacted the law, the Assembly ceased to exist, and was replaced by the First Knesset. As regards the relations between the executive and legislative bodies, the law marked the transition from an assembly system to a parliamentary system. The Law and Administration Ordinance stated that the government would act in accordance with the policy established by the Provisional State Council, implement the resolutions of the Council and report to it on its activities. The Transition Law omitted the first two components – policy-making by the Council and government implementation of Council resolutions. Nir's proposal that the status quo continue was put to the vote and rejected.[108] The Transition Law did not determine the term of office of the First Knesset. One change for the better as far as the parliamentary body was concerned was the fact that the Law specified that the government served as long as it enjoyed the confidence of the Knesset, which was empowered to pass a vote of no-confidence.

THE FIRST KNESSET

Immediately after enacting the Transition Law, the First Knesset elected Haim Weizmann, who had served as President of the Provisional State Council, as President of the State of Israel. The government resigned, and in accordance with the Transition Law, the President charged Ben-Gurion with the task of forming a new government. On 10 March 1949, the new government, headed by Ben-Gurion, won a vote of confidence in the Knesset.

At a meeting with leaders of the General Zionists in February 1949, Ben-Gurion revealed his contemptuous attitude towards the Knesset. He did not even want to grant it full legislative powers:

> The legislature will discuss the laws. Members will make their comments. There will be a debate on principles and details and a just government takes note of what is said in parliament . . . The ministers must listen to the amendments proposed by the members of parliament, and only then take their final decisions.[109]

The conclusion is that even in the legislative realm, the most natural function of a parliament, its task was not to take decisions but to confine itself to serving the government in an advisory capacity. In order to carry out this limited task, the legislature was dependent on the government's sense of fair play. Ben-Gurion perceived Government–Knesset relations in a one-sided manner: 'The Government is the leader, its duty is to lead the legislature. It appears before the legislature with initiatives . . . there will be a debate, clarification and the government must listen.'[110]

One of the changes for the worse in the Knesset at this stage was the abolition of the institution of the presidium and its replacement by a forum which included the Speaker of the Knesset and his deputies. This change was not only of semantic significance. It concealed a tendency to belittle the Knesset and to increase the powers of the Speaker vis-à-vis his deputies. In the era of the Provisional State Council – after Ben-Gurion had been deposed as chairman of the meetings and Mapai failed to include him in the presidium – the presidium had consisted of the President of the Council, the Chairman of the Council and his three deputies. When a controversy broke out in March 1949 in the Standing Committee over the question of the presidium versus the forum of the Speaker and his deputies, Israel Guri did not hesitate to reveal Mapai's standpoint. He said that his party would not agree to remain in the minority, since two representatives of the other big parties (Mapam and the United Religious Front) were liable to collaborate and to leave the Speaker in the minority. Since Mapai was much larger than the other two parties together 'this is not feasible. Mapai would never agree to such a thing.'[111] Eliezer Peri of Mapam claimed that Mapai had misled his party on this matter: 'I do not know if we would have voted for Mr Sprinzak if the Mapai members had revealed to us that they had decided to abolish the presidium. I think that this is a betrayal of trust in our faction.'[112] Hillel Kook of Herut considered this change to be a yardstick for the status and sovereignty of the Knesset. The abolition of the presidium turned the Knesset into 'a kind of appendix, more in the sense of a department of the Government'.[113] The protests of the opposition did not succeed in preventing the abolition of the presidium.

Although at the stage of electing the deputies, Ben-Gurion ignored the rules of procedure of the Provisional State Council, he chose to exploit them in fixing the agenda of plenum sessions. Since the rules of procedure stated that the government would decide the agenda, it was advantageous to Ben-Gurion to refer to them. After expressing confidence in the government, Sprinzak reported to the Knesset that 'we can provide information on our working procedures and our future meetings only after clarifying the matter with the Government'.[114] At the first session after the government had won a vote of confidence, Ben-Gurion tried to impose the government's will on the agenda of the Knesset. At the beginning of the session, Sprinzak announced that Eliyahu Eliashar (Sephardim) and Haim Landau (Herut) wanted to place on the Knesset's agenda the question of the plight of Iraqi Jewry, while Landau wanted to raise the question of Jerusalem. The Speaker was unable to inform the Knesset if and when these subjects would be discussed and noted that the matter was being dealt with by the government.[115] The session was devoted entirely to discussion of the US Credit Law. When the law had been ratified towards the end of the meeting, the Prime Minister mounted the rostrum and began to read out the agenda of the next meeting: 'In accordance with Clause 13,3 of the Law and Administration Ordinance, 1948, I hereby announce the agenda of the next meeting of the Knesset: a. the election of committees; b. The State Comptroller Law; c. the Soldiers Employment Law.'[116] This evoked protests in the plenum and heckling by members, who demanded that a debate be held on the Prime Minister's announcement. Sprinzak ruled that the matter would be discussed at the next meeting, and hastened to adjourn the meeting.[117]

And, indeed, at the next meeting a debate was held on this matter. Israel Bar-Yehuda (Mapam) declared: 'All of us, including those who did not vote for him, owe respect to the Prime Minister on condition that he respects the Knesset . . . I must express my amazement and regret at conduct which violates procedure.'[118] Begin asked:

> How will the sovereignty of the Knesset find expression, if the head of the executive body determines the agenda of its meetings? The Prime Minister is of course entitled, in the name of the executive body, to propose subjects for the agenda. But he is not entitled to lay down the law: this and that are what you are going to discuss.[119]

Peri was no less emphatic:

> It is inconceivable that the Knesset, which is sovereign, should take orders from the government, discuss issues and determine its working arrangements on the basis of government instructions . . . if the Prime Minister is permitted to impose his will on us, as occurred at the previous meeting, we will demand that a special committee be elected at once, to determine the rules of procedure of the Knesset.[120]

Mikunis joined in the criticism: 'For the first time the Prime Minister appeared and announced in a dogmatic tone that the following was the agenda of the next meeting. The Knesset members rightly regarded this as a slight to the sovereignty of this house.'[121] Landau claimed that Ben-Gurion's action reflected the government's tendency 'to impose the will and the actions of the executive branch on the legislative branch'.[122] One of the important consequences of this criticism was the declaration of the chairperson of the Standing Committee, Beba Idelson of Mapai, that although the government had the right to fix the agenda of the Knesset, it did not have the right to inform the Knesset of this.[123] It was highly significant that a Mapai rerpesentative, who held an official position in the Knesset, issued a statement which constituted criticism of the Prime Minister's actions. Henceforth Ben-Gurion refrained from informing the Knesset of the agenda. Later at the same session, Sprinzak was unable to announce if and when the debates proposed by Eliashar and Landau would take place: 'I announced that we had held discussions with the government and had not yet received their reply.'[124]

The day after the parliamentary discussion on Ben-Gurion's intervention in the Knesset agenda, the Prime Minister made reference to the term 'the sovereignty of the Knesset' which had been cited several times in the discussion:

> The sovereignty of the Knesset is not the sovereignty of this or that faction, whether in the opposition or the coalition, but the sovereignty of the Knesset as a whole and its democratic decisions, whether unanimous or majority decisions. The Knesset's sovereignty requires that the will of the Knesset, expressed and embodied in decisions on the government's programme of action and on the election of the government, will be carried out with great efficiency and speed . . . after the law has been ratified, there is no discussion and no appeal against it, unless it is revoked.[125]

On the following day, 23 March 1949, Landau continued to protest at the fact that the items he had asked to place on the agenda were not being discussed by the Knesset. He also demanded a discussion of the armistice agreements and insisted that Sprinzak put to the vote the question of whether to discuss this matter in the plenum.[126] The Speaker, torn between the devil and the deep blue sea, refused to initiate such a vote. He gave a confused reply, arguing that it was the duty of the Speaker to inform the government of the wish of Knesset members to discuss certain matters and 'whether I received an answer or not – it is within the authority of the Speaker' and promised 'at the end of the meeting this evening, I will make an announcement on the questions raised by Knesset Member Landau'.[127] Towards the end of the meeting, the Speaker summoned up the courage to refer to the demand of Knesset members that urgent issues be placed on the agenda. He turned to the Prime Minister and asked him for his views on the subject. Ben-Gurion did not agree to an immediate discussion of the two issues. On the question of the

Iraqi Jewish community, he said that 'the Government has placed the matter on its agenda and will discuss it next week', and as regards Jerusalem and the armistice agreements, he did not hesitate to state that 'we are not placing this subject on the agenda now'.[128] The Herut members continued to insist on a debate on the armistice agreements, but the Prime Minister was adamant:

> The Government is opposed to discussion of the armistice agreements at the present time . . . In our opinion the time has not yet come to discuss them, and we cannot take part in such a debate. I do not think there is any benefit to discussion before you hear a survey of the situation, and hence this is premature. I propose that we wait on this clause until the government submits a proposal.[129]

Herut persisted, arguing that the negotiations might end before the Knesset was given the opportunity to discuss the agreements. The Mapam representative, Bar-Yehuda, proposed a compromise, whereby the issue would be referred to a committee, but the plenum voted in favour of the government's stand and the subject was not discussed by the plenum.[130]

A week later, the Prime Minister kept his promise to the Knesset and brought the Iraqi Jewish question before the plenum. His speech was very brief and did not include new information. His argument ran as follows: 'The grave concern for the plight of more than a quarter of a million Jews in the Arab states precludes me now from giving a detailed statement on this matter.'[131] In light of the brevity of Ben-Gurion's speech, Sprinzak raised the possibility of postponing the debate, but most of the Members of the Knesset (MKs) present voted for continuation.[132] Shmuel Merlin (Herut) expressed his disappointment that so important a subject had been allotted only 90 minutes: 'For only ninety minutes, in great haste, and in order to fulfil an obligation – but nonetheless the question is on the agenda. I say this with bitterness, and not only because the problem is not being discussed in the appropriate manner.'[133] Yehiel Duvdevani of Mapai also had reservations as to the form of the debate: 'Until now our parliament has not been miserly about clarifying questions of secondary importance. I can only regret that such miserliness is being displayed with regard to this particular problem of the Jewish people.'[134]

The parliamentary discussion of the armistice agreements took place the day after the signing of the treaty between Israel and Jordan at Rhodes. After the Prime Minister's statement, members voiced their disappointment at the fact that the Knesset had not been informed of the moves leading up to the treaty. Dov Bar-Nir of Mapam protested against 'being faced with a fait accompli'.[135] Riftin complained that 'the Government was not accredited to take so fateful a decision without a democratic debate, without the decision of the Knesset'.[136] Yitzhak Ben-Aharon of Mapam levelled serious charges at the government:

> We cannot accept the government's ruling with regard to this Knesset. It might be that the majority in the Knesset may not deserve better treatment than the government has accorded the Knesset as a whole. At the time when they were discussing the treaty, the Knesset was in session, we were assembled here, doing our duty and fulfilling our tasks. Therefore, I direct this question at the government and the Prime Minister . . . Did not the Knesset and the Foreign Affairs and Security Committee, which has recently been appointed, deserve to express their views before this treaty was signed?[137]

Sapir of the General Zionists had similar complaints, and even Yizhar Harari of the Progressive Party, a member of the coalition, was critical.[138] Ben-Gurion, however, went even further. Towards the end of the term of office of the First Knesset, he expressed the hope that the government's influence over parliamentary procedure would increase in the Second Knesset: 'We will have to introduce an ordinance so that Vilner or anyone else will not be able to stand up every day and submit motions for the agenda and change the working procedures proposed by the government.'[139]

An incident which occurred in February 1950 illustrates Ben-Gurion's utter contempt for the Knesset. Due to the crisis generated by the controversy over the type of education to be given to new immigrants, three religious ministers boycotted government meetings. Ben-Gurion refused to permit them to serve in office and wanted to fire them without himself being forced to resign. He convened his government, which approved his proposal that the ministers be dismissed: 'A minister who refused to take part in government meetings or to implement government resolutions, cannot remain a member of the government and continue to head his ministry. The government will regard him as having resigned.'[140] The intention was that the government decision should not be the basis for legislation, but rather the end of the affair. The fact that the government adopted a resolution on so fundamental a constitutional matter was a slap in the face for the legislature. At most, the Prime Minister permitted the Knesset to discuss the matter: 'The government has charged me with the task of bringing its decision to the knowledge of the Knesset. The government is not proposing to the Knesset that it hold a debate on this question, but the Knesset is entitled to discuss it if it sees fit.'[141] Shortly afterwards, a compromise was reached between Mapai and the religious parties which averted the need to implement the government decision. Chapter 2 discusses various aspects of this affair as they related to the Knesset committees.

In August 1950, the Mapai faction in the Knesset discussed the new rationing regulations with the party secretariat and the Mapai members of the Histadrut Executive. The Prime Minister threatened that the government would resign if it did not receive the backing of the Knesset on this matter: 'The Knesset alone can debate and decide this matter. The Knesset can also annul it, but if it does so – it will have to establish a new government.'[142] According to this outlook, the Knesset was a mere rubber stamp. However, it was not only the Knesset that received harsh treatment from Ben-Gurion. The judges also suffered at his hand. In October 1950, he wrote to the Attorney General, denying the right of judges to convene for discussion of their working conditions:

> I read this morning that there has been a meeting of judges to discuss their working conditions. I do not believe this is acceptable . . . They are not entitled to establish a trade union and to organize a kind of strike. Each of them should resign individually. Such a meeting cannot be allowed.[143]

The intervention of the Prime Minister on so delicate a matter and his tendency to make assertions of constitutional significance were also a form of attack on the Knesset.

That same month, Ben-Gurion submitted to the Mapai central committee his plan for the establishment of an economic council, to constitute a framework for consultations between the government and representatives of large economic organizations from the private and Histadrut sectors. His explanation for this corporatist initiative was that the Knesset 'not only does not exhaustively relate to the economic affairs of the country, but it does not directly represent them

. . . There should be a place where complaints can be submitted directly to the government.'[144] This proposal meant that the Knesset's authority would be weakened to some extent. However, in December 1951, during a discussion by Mapai's political committee of ways of increasing output, Ben-Gurion expressed his doubts as to the value of agreements with industrialists and workers organizations:

> I do not believe in any agreements or in persuasion, neither of the Industrialists Association nor of the workers . . . we will determine the minimal standard of output in each occupation and the factory owner who does not achieve this output will not receive raw materials, the factory will be closed and the workers will be unemployed, and we will say to the factory owner: if you do not reach the minimum, you will engage in buying plots of land, but we will ban the purchase of plots . . . if vital factories strike – we will reopen them . . . I have the feeling that what the public wants is government, not wild government, but real government.[145]

Nonetheless, after the elections to the Second Knesset, the government announced in the Knesset, within the framework of its guidelines, the establishment of an economic council with advisory authority, which would operate through the Prime Minister's office, and the first meeting of this body, which was not long-lived, was scheduled for 2 March 1952. Ben-Gurion himself dispatched the letters of appointment to its members and invited them to the meeting.[146]

Ben-Gurion's influence on the first steps of Israeli parliamentary life was destructive. In those formative years, his sense of identification with the state was at its height. As a result, the Knesset was assigned a marginal position. Ben-Gurion acted as if the Zionist revolution was still in full swing, while the Knesset in fact represented the end of the revolutionary situation and the transition to routine life and normalcy.

NOTES

1. Central Zionist Archives (CZA), Zionist Executive meeting, 6 April 1948.
2. Ibid.
3. Zeev Sherf, *Three Days* (Hebrew), Tel Aviv: Am Oved, 1965, p. 101.
4. Ibid., p. 39.
5. Ibid., p. 100.

6. CZA, Zionist Executive meeting, 11 April 1948.
7. Ibid., Jewish Agency Executive meeting, 14 April 1948.
8. Ibid.
9. Sherf, *Three Days*, p. 39.
10. Ibid., p. 42.
11. People's Council (minutes), 4 May 1948, p. 6.
12. Ibid., 5 May 1948, p. 10.
13. Sherf, *Three Days*, p. 220.
14. Ibid., p. 221.
15. People's Council (minutes), 14 May 1948, p. 13.
16. Ibid., p. 20.
17. Ibid.
18. Ibid., p. 21.
19. Ibid., p. 22.
20. Ibid.
21. Ibid.
22. Provisional State Council (minutes), 16 May 1948, pp. 18–20.
23. Ibid., p. 5.
24. Ibid.
25. Ibid., p. 9
26. Ibid., p. 10.
27. Ibid.
28. Ibid.
29. Ibid., p. 11.
30. Ibid., p. 15.
31. Ibid., p. 16.
32. Ibid.
33. Ibid., 19 May 1948, p. 4.
34. Ibid., p. 12.
35. Ibid., p. 13.
36. Ibid.
37. Ibid., p. 7.
38. Ibid., 3 June 1948, p. 23.
39. Ibid., pp. 24–5.
40. Ibid., p. 26.
41. Ibid., p. 32.
42. Ibid., 17 June 1948, p. 15.
43. Ibid., p. 18.
44. Ibid., p. 22.
45. Ibid., p. 24.
46. Ibid., 24 June 1948, p. 5.
47. Ibid., 17 June 1948, p. 41.
48. Weizmann arrived in Israel only in late September, 1948. The Provisional State Council welcomed him on 30 September.
49. Provisional State Council (minutes), 15 July 1948, p. 7.
50. *Knesset Record*, 20 August 1951, p. 2,204.
51. Ibid.
52. Yosef Sprinzak, *Letters* (Hebrew), Vol. 3, Tel Aviv: Ayanot, 1969, pp. 21–2.
53. Provisional State Council (minutes), 17 June 1948, p. 40.
54. State Archives, 20/25, minutes of House Committee meeting,15 November 1949.
55. Ibid., 20/4, Sprinzak to Sherf, 15 September 1948.
56. Ibid., Sprinzak to Head of Budget Section, 19 December 1948.
57. Ibid., K. Aharonovitch to S. Even-Tov, 29 April 1949.
58. CZA, 8181–S25, 30 May 1948.
59. Provisional State Council (minutes), 17 June 1948, p. 37.
60. Ibid., 23 June 1948, p. 42.

61. Ibid., 24 June 1948, p. 5.
62. Ibid., p. 8.
63. Ibid., pp. 22–3.
64. Ibid., 1 July 1948, p. 15.
65. Ibid., p. 4.
66. Ibid.
67. Ibid., 8 July 1948, p. 10.
68. Ibid., 5 July 1948, p. 18.
69. Ibid., 27 September 1948, p. 43.
70. Ibid., 11 November 1948, p. 4.
71. State Archives 20/4, Altman, Weinstein and Tzui Segal to the presidium of the Provisional State Council, 21 November 1948.
72. Ibid., Sprinzak to the Government Secretariat, 23 November 1948.
73. Provisional State Council (minutes), 25 November 1948, pp. 13–14.
74. Ibid., p. 10.
75. Ibid., p. 8.
76. Ibid., p. 15.
77. Ibid., p. 18.
78. See Ben-Gurion's remarks, Ibid., 2 December 1948, p. 4.
79. Ibid.
80. Ibid., 9 December 1948, p. 20.
81. Ibid., 6 January 1949, p. 6.
82. Ibid.
83. Ibid., 11 January 1949, p. 22.
84. Ibid., p. 23.
85. Ibid., p. 24.
86. Ibid., 13 January 1949, p. 11.
87. Ibid., p. 12.
88. Ibid., p. 10.
89. Ibid.
90. Ibid., p. 5.
91. Ibid., p. 8.
92. Ibid.
93. Ibid., p. 9.
94. Israel Labour Party Archives, 48/25, Mapai Bureau meeting, 10 November 1948.
95. Ibid., Mapai Bureau meeting, 16 November 1948.
96. Ben-Gurion Research Center Archives. Correspondence, Ben-Gurion to Pinkas (chairman of Security Committee of the Provisional State Council), 16 December 1948.
97. Provisional State Council (minutes), 16 December 1948, pp. 39–43.
98. Ben-Gurion Research Center Archives, correspondence Ben-Gurion to Chief of Staff Yaakov Dori, 23 December 1948.
99. Provisional State Council, 25 November 1948.
100. Ben-Gurion Research Center Archives, correspondence, Ben-Gurion to Kol, 7 January 1949.
101. Ibid., Ben-Gurion to Bentov, 16 December 1948.
102. Ibid., Bernstein to Ben-Gurion, 16 October 1948.
103. Provisional State Council (minutes), 6 January 1949, pp. 4–5.
104. Ibid., 10 February 1949, p. 14.
105. *Knesset Record*, 14 February 1949, p. 9.
106. Ibid.
107. Ibid., p. 11.
108. Ibid., 16 February 1949, pp. 42–3.
109. Ben-Gurion Research Center Archives, minutes of meetings, coalition files, meeting with General Zionist leaders, 24 February 1949.
110. Ibid.

111. State Archives, Standing Committee meeting minutes, 3 March 1949.
112. Ibid.
113. Ibid.
114. *Knesset Record*, 10 March 1949, p. 145.
115. Ibid., 17 March 1949, p. 147.
116. Ibid., p. 169.
117. Ibid.
118. Ibid., 21 March 1949, p. 171.
119. Ibid., p. 172.
120. Ibid., p. 175.
121. Ibid., p. 176.
122. Ibid.
123. Ibid.
124. Ibid., p. 178.
125. Ibid., 22 March 1949, p. 192.
126. Ibid., 23 March 1949, pp. 195–6.
127. Ibid., p. 196.
128. Ibid., p. 220.
129. Ibid., pp. 220–1.
130. Ibid., p. 221.
131. Ibid., 30 March 1949, p. 266.
132. Ibid., pp. 266–7.
133. Ibid., p. 270.
134. Ibid., p. 274.
135. Ibid., 4 April 1949, p. 289.
136. Ibid., p. 291.
137. Ibid., p. 292.
138. Ibid., pp. 295–6.
139. Ben-Gurion Research Center Archives, minutes of meetings, meeting of candidates for ministerial posts, 10 July 1951.
140. *Knesset Record*, 21 February 1950, p. 831.
141. Ibid.
142. Israel Labour Party Archives, meeting of Mapai faction with Mapai Secretariat and Mapai members of Histadrut Executive, 6 August 1950.
143. Ben-Gurion Research Center Archives, correspondence between Ben-Gurion and Attorney General, 1 October 1950.
144. Israel Labour Party Archives, Mapai Central Committee meeting, 22 October 1950.
145. Ibid., meeting of Mapai Political Committee, 20 December 1951.
146. Ben-Gurion Research Center Archives, correspondence, letter of appointment and invitation to first meeting of the Economic Council, 25 February 1952. On the establishment of the Economic Council see also: Israel Labour Party Archives, meeting of Mapai Secretariat, 10 January 1952.

2 Parliamentary Committees

COMMITTEES DURING THE TENURE OF THE PEOPLE'S COUNCIL AND THE PROVISIONAL COUNCIL OF STATE

The People's Council functioned without any committees. Even after the establishment of the state, when the Provisional Council of State came into operation, Ben-Gurion was not at all eager to establish parliamentary committees. On 24 May 1948, he wrote in his diary about his meeting with Mikunis of Maki (the Israeli Communist Party): 'He asked about including them in committees. I told him no committees had been set up, and that I don't believe we will set up any, there is only the defence commission. If it continues to exist, there is no point in changing its composition.'[1] At the meeting of the Council of State on 3 June, it was in fact Mordechai Shatner of Mapai who first proposed the establishment of a Finance Committee.[2] Ben-Gurion, who was chairing the meeting, did not react to the proposal. He did not table it for discussion, nor did he hold a vote on it. The Council continued to operate without any committees, with the exception of ad hoc committees established for the discussion of particular laws.

Ben-Gurion was particularly concerned about the possible establishment of a defence committee that might curb his powers. As far as he was concerned, the ideal situation would be to avert the establishment of a parliamentary defence committee and the renewed activity of the defence commission, which had been established outside of the parliamentary framework prior to the establishment of the state. Of the two, his highest priority was to oppose the establishment of a parliamentary defence committee. When he reached the conclusion that he would be unable to achieve both of these goals, he hastened to renew the activity of the pre-state defence commission. This was on 16 June 1948, one day before the Council's scheduled discussion on the draft Rules of Procedure, which included the establishment of permanent committees. The creation of permanent parliamentary committees might establish a precedent liable to serve as a basis for a demand to establish a parliamentary defence committee. Ben-Gurion informed the members of the pre-state defence commission – a body that was not linked to the Council – that the commission was in operation and that he was its chairman. Moreover, he laid down the working procedures of the commission. For example, he stated that the establishment of sub-committees for special duties required the approval of the Minister of Defence. The chairman of the commission, or his representative, would present proposed resolutions to the committee. Other decisions taken by the commission would 'require the approval of the Minister of Defence or the provisional government. The chairman of the commission has the right of veto.'[3] In this way, Ben-Gurion ensured his control over the defence commission, whose activity, composition and working procedures did not need to be approved by the Council. Moreover, some of its members were not members of the Council and others were ministers in the government.

On the following day, 17 June, the Council was engaged in establishing committees as part of its deliberation on the Rules of Procedure. The draft referred to the establishment of four permanent committees: constitution, preparations for elections to the Constituent Assembly, finance and legislation. Nir proposed the establishment of a foreign affairs committee and a defence committee. Ben-Gurion immediately notified the Council that if a defence committee were set up, 'Not all secrets would be divulged to the members of such a committee', adding that

> It will not be helpful or advantageous, nor is there anything democratic about it, if apart from this committee, which is known as the government, there were another committee. What is the function of such a committee? Decisions? That would rule out the government. Advice? It will not be able to provide any advice either, for it will not know what the government can know. Parliamentary committees do not know all the secrets – they convene from time to time and receive information . . . A defence committee will have no more authority than

> the defence commission has. It is impossible to take away any of the government's authority in these matters, and the same is true for foreign affairs.[4]

Ben-Gurion took a particularly resolute stand on this issue. It was his wish to sidetrack the slightest possibility of parliamentary interference in or supervision of security matters. The Provisional Council of State did not immediately resolve the issue, but decided in principle that permanent committees would be established, without noting what they would be. In keeping with Ben-Gurion's suggestion, a finance committee and a committee to propose the composition of the committees were established.

The establishment of the constitution, legislation and elections committees dragged on until 8 July. Weinstein of the Revisionist party suggested the establishment of two other committees – foreign affairs and security. Ben-Gurion took advantage of his authority as chairman of the meeting to avoid raising the subject for discussion or putting it to a vote, arguing that it was not on the agenda. His interpretation of the item 'composition of the presidium and the committees', which was on the agenda, was puzzling: 'A suggestion of this sort was brought up at one of the previous Council meetings, but it is not related to the committees about which decisions have now been taken.' He was referring to the three committees whose establishment had been approved at that meeting – legislation, constitution and elections. Ben-Gurion tried to placate Weinstein by saying: 'You can do that at the next meeting and it will be put on the agenda.'[5]

At the next meeting, when Ben-Gurion was replaced by Sprinzak, the new chairman did in fact give Weinstein the floor. Ben-Gurion intervened: 'The government has not dealt with this matter. I ask that we allow the government to address the proposal, and then we can express a position.' Weinstein was insistent, saying 'I had been promised that the matter would be raised for discussion today; it is on the agenda',[6] but the members voted to discuss the matter at the next meeting in order to give the government an opportunity to formulate a position.

At the Council meeting on 22 July, Ben-Gurion presented the government's position, which was opposed to the establishment of committees on foreign affairs and security: 'The government is itself the largest and most authoritative committee on matters of security.'[7] Moreover, he added, there is a committee of five ministers dealing with matters of security. The defence commission established by the

Jewish Agency and the Vaad Le'umi discusses security matters once a week. 'It is the government's opinion that there is no point in the Council adding a fourth institution', but rather that the existing defence commission should be expanded 'so that those circles who are not represented in it can also join it, and representatives of certain other circles that are in it will no longer remain'.[8] In so far as the foreign affairs committee was concerned, Ben-Gurion's position was unequivocal:

> The only effective foreign affairs committee of the Council of State is the committee known as the 'Provisional Government', all of whose members are members of the Council, who twice a week, that is, at each and every meeting, discuss questions of foreign policy. There is, therefore, no point in adding another institution to the one called the 'Provisional Government'.[9]

The Council accepted Ben-Gurion's position on the defence committee and charged the committee on committees with the task of preparing an amended proposal on the changed composition of the defence commission. However, on the issue of the foreign affairs committee, Ben-Gurion did not get his way. In the discussion, Argov of Mapai supported the establishment of a foreign affairs committee. The Minister of Foreign Affairs, Sharett, surprised Ben-Gurion by announcing that he did not object to the establishment of such a committee and had expressed a similar position in the government meeting that had discussed the issue. After Sharett's announcement, there was no longer any point in Ben-Gurion's persisting in trying to prevent the establishment of a foreign affairs committee. The Council unanimously approved the committee's establishment,[10] and on 29 July 1948, it approved its composition.[11]

The security committee was established on 12 August 1948 against Ben-Gurion's wishes. The new committee did not include the four ministers – one of whom was Ben-Gurion – who had served as members of the pre-state defence commission. However, since the new committee was based on the defence commission, it did include members who were not members of the Provisional Council of State. Varhaftig (HaPoel HaMizrachi) objected vigorously:

> Now that we have a Council of State, it is in fact a parliament, which sets up parliamentary committees on all important issues, and security is the foremost issue . . . I am opposed, now

> that we already have a Council of State, to have people added from the outside to deal with such an important issue as security, as if we do not trust the Council of State to deal with this particular matter. I want this committee to be a parliamentary committee like all the parliamentary committees . . . I ask that we reject this proposal and decide on a normal parliamentary committee.[12]

Varhaftig's position did not receive a majority. Although Ben-Gurion did not succeed in blocking any parliamentary involvement in questions of security, he did manage to set a precedent according to which the parliamentary body would handle this issue differently from other questions of policy.

The establishment of a security committee entailed the loss of some of Ben-Gurion's power. As long as the defence commission had existed, he had been its chairman, but when the security committee was established, Pinkas of the Mizrachi Party was chosen to chair it. After Ben-Gurion was forced, in July, to relinquish the chairmanship of the Council of State, in August he lost another important function, as chairman of the defence commission.

Early in October 1948, the security committee held an intriguing discussion on its powers. Some of its members demanded that Ben-Gurion provide the committee with information about the arrest of Lehi members following the murder of Count Bernadotte. Ben-Gurion refused, claiming that the matter was outside of the committee's authority. He argued that 'It is a question of security, but it is internal security, not external . . . it is an internal political issue . . . not a matter for the security committee . . . that committee exists for the defence of the state'.[13] Arrests, Ben-Gurion claimed, are carried out by the police, while the army 'provides assistance, but not everything the army helps with concerns the security committee, since the control of and war against terror is not an army matter'.[14] He continued to explain his opposition by stating that he was not dealing with the subject as the Minister of Defence, but as the Prime Minister. The pressures brought to bear by the committee chairman, Pinkas, Sapir (General Zionists) and Argov were futile. Ben-Gurion remained entrenched in his position and declined to provide the committee with any information on this subject.

Just as Ben-Gurion dragged his feet concerning the Council's discussion of foreign policy in November 1948 – a subject covered in the previous chapter – he resorted to similar behaviour regarding the involvement of the Council's foreign affairs committee. The chairman of this committee, Moshe Kol of the Progressive Party, accused Ben-Gurion of refusing to appear before the committee:

> I had planned to convene the foreign affairs committee during this fortnight, but only on condition that the acting Foreign Minister, who is now Prime Minister, would attend the meetings. Since I never received a positive reply – I did not convene the committee.[15]

Ben-Gurion's great concern about any interference by the security and foreign affairs committees in his affairs is also revealed in the letter sent by the Council secretary, Asher Tzidon, to the chairmen of the Council's committees towards the end of the Council's term of office. In it, he notified them that at the last meeting of the Council, they would be able to review the activities of the committees. To the letters addressed to the chairman of the defence committee (Pinkas) and the chairman of the foreign affairs committee (Kol), he added 'You need to consult the Minister of Defence regarding the material and its contents.'[16]

At the time the security committee was established in August 1948, other changes took place in the work of the committees of the Provisional Council of State. These important changes were not grounded in the Rules of Procedure, which, as mentioned previously, referred to the establishment of four committees (legislation, constitution, finance and elections) without instituting the principle of attaching the parliamentary committees to government ministries. Now the finance committee became the finance and economics committee and was attached to the five ministries dealing with economic subjects. The legislation committee was attached to the Justice Ministry, in addition to its normal duties. In addition, three new committees were established and attached to government ministries: the internal affairs committee (the Ministries of Interior Affairs, Police, Minorities and Religion), the immigration committee (Ministry of Immigration), and the public services committee (Ministries of Welfare, Health and War Victims). The proposal to establish a system of parliamentary committees attached to government ministries was adopted in the committee on committees. The State Council decided that 'each committee will determine and define its content and powers in conjunction with the appropriate ministry to which it is connected'.[17] The ministers attended nearly all the meetings of the committees, usually held in their own offices. The reason for the establishment of the additional committees and their attachment to government ministries is linked to the establishment of the foreign affairs and security committees, in particular the latter. Once these two important committees were established, it was no longer possible to continue objecting to parliamentary involvement in the other ministries. The expansion of the number of committees and their attachment to the government ministries heralded some improvement in parliamentary control of the executive branch.

THE ESTABLISHMENT OF COMMITTEES IN THE FIRST KNESSET

The decisive stage in the development of a system of parliamentary committees occurred early in 1949, when the committees of the First Knesset were organized. On 14 February 1949, the Constituent Assembly elected a standing committee charged, among other tasks, with preparing the organization of committees. The chairman of this committee came from the ranks of Mapai. At first, it was Zalman Shazar, and later Beba Idelson acted in this capacity. Representation was given to all the factions on this committee, and hence, it had 33 members. To make its work more efficient, a smaller sub-committee of seven members, was set up. Known as the 'Committee of Seven', it was chaired by Guri of Mapai, and its other members were: Pinkas of the Religious Front, Harari of the Progressives, Moshe Ben-Ami of the Sepharadim, Hanan Rubin of Mapam, Sapir of the General Zionists and Landau of Herut. This committee agreed on the organization, composition and powers of the committees. Although there were a few minor points not finally agreed upon in the committee, there was agreement on most of the important topics, in particular on the principle of attaching Knesset committees to government ministries:

> The basic assumption underlying the committee's proposals is that every matter that one of the ministers is responsible for will be included in a parliamentary committee's area of competence. In general, the committee adopted the principle of attaching every committee to a specific ministry.[18]

The committee of seven decided to establish 15 permanent committees, most of which were attached to government ministries. For example, the transportation committee was attached to the Ministry of Transportation and the foreign affairs committee to the Ministry of Foreign Affairs. Some committees were to handle several ministries, for example, the social services committee was attached to the Ministries of Welfare and Health, while others were to handle subjects not directly related to any government ministries, for example, the state apparatus committee, the law and justice committee, the Knesset committee and the constitution committee. The proposed structure was similar in several respects to the one existing during the tenure of the Provisional Council of State. A final decision on the establishment of a security committee was postponed until the committee could hear Ben-Gurion's view on the matter.

The most important outcome was the agreement of all the members of the coalition, Mapai in particular, to formulate, with the opposition, a joint document expressing the interests of the Knesset and its ability to oversee the activities of the government and its ministries. In the initial stage, the government respected the principle of the non-intervention of the executive branch in the internal affairs of the legislative branch, and refrained from interfering in the work of the Committee of Seven.

Ben-Gurion, displeased with the Committee of Seven's decisions, began to 'steamroll' the committee in order to obstruct their implementation. Sapir (General Zionists) described the course of events as follows:

> The Committee of Seven completed its work and submitted its conclusions to the standing committee. Under the pressure of the Speaker of the Knesset, the standing committee decided to convene a special session, on a Friday, if I'm not mistaken. The Speaker demanded that the committee step up its work, in order to present the question of the committees to the Knesset, but the meeting that we decided to convene never took place. It turned out that in the meantime, the government had called a meeting of the coalition factions, at which it cancelled the decisions taken by the Committee of Seven, in most cases with a majority of all the members from all the factions – in relation to the number of committees, their composition and duties. The Mapai representative notified us afterwards: 'We are hereby notifying you that we are withdrawing our agreement' . . . And in bringing proposals of its own, the government displayed no small measure of brutality, after all the factions in the

> standing committee and in the Committee of Seven had agreed . . . it is obvious that the government wants to deprive the Knesset and its committees of the practical possibility to scrutinize the matters that it is dealing with.[19]

Rubin (Mapam) also protested against the government's intervention in this issue and the 'government's attempt to impose its will on the House'.[20] Kook (Herut) recounted how the Committee of Seven had arrived at 'certain conclusions, and here out of a clear blue sky – on Monday morning – when all the members came to the committee meeting, they found the government's own version of proposals, and we all knew in advance what the results would be when these proposals were brought to the Knesset for a vote'.[21] Vilner (Communists) inveighed against 'the Government's sudden intervention in a matter that, as a government, it was precluded from interfering with'.[22] Moshe Aram (Mapam) stated his protest at a meeting of the standing committee:

> An attempt was made in the Committee of Seven to achieve agreement among all the factions. The government factions could have come and told us that they were withdrawing their agreement. Why didn't they do that very simple thing? . . . We are all sitting here with the same view. What point is there after everything is finished, after we've agreed, for the government to come and say it's all cancelled?[23]

Based on the government's proposal, it was decided that the parliamentary committees would be organized according to subjects and would not be attached to government ministries. This method significantly curtailed the Knesset's ability to oversee the work of the government. It represented a regression in comparison to the situation that had existed during the tenure of the Provisional Council of State. According to the government's proposal, the committee on the state apparatus was annulled; the constitution committee and law and justice committee were combined into one, and the same was done in regard to the security and foreign affairs committees. This time, Ben-Gurion succeeded in achieving what he had failed to do in the Provisional Council of State. The most important government ministry, the Ministry of Defence, was left without a committee to oversee its work. Ben-Gurion's explanation for this decision was:

> that matters of security and foreign affairs are 'organically' connected. Security is a function of the external political situation . . . and since these committees are not attached to the ministers, but are auxiliary committees of the Knesset, to more effectively deal with these matters, we believe these two subjects – security and foreign affairs – are interrelated and constitute one complex. The security situation is linked to an external political situation, worldwide or regional, or both.[24]

The left-wing factions, Mapam and the Communists, demanded that each of these subjects – security and foreign affairs – should be treated separately by a parliamentary committee. Vilner quoted a member of the standing committee who had sarcastically remarked about the joint committee for these two areas, that 'you will have the security of knowing that we will be "foreign" [external] to these matters'.[25] Ben-Aharon (Mapam) asked: 'Are we to see in this move a step taken for the sake of economizing or one taken for the sake of secrecy? What benefit will be derived from having one committee and why is it better than two committees?'[26] Herut supported the government's proposal to combine these two subjects, 'in the hope that a new leaf may be opened in which our military strength will not be squandered by our political blunders'.[27] Ben-Gurion derided Herut's position:

> I am grateful to MK Kook, who has given us a lesson in the importance of power. One ought not to withhold reward for a kindly phrase, but we knew the secret of the importance of power long before we were graced by MK Kook's teaching . . . you also discovered the 'secret' of an army, after we established the Israel Defence Forces.[28]

On the same occasion, Ben-Gurion informed the Knesset that,

> this government will not bring before this committee those things which it believes are not ready for publication or discussion . . . there is no need to fear that we will divulge matters prematurely – we really will not do so, if we believe that would damage vital interests of the state, whether matters of security or of foreign policy.[29]

In a meeting of the Mapai directorate and the faction secretariat, Beba Idelson explained why Ben-Gurion was so adamant on the issue of the Knesset committees: 'Ben-Gurion says that since there are parties now represented in the Knesset that did not participate in the Provisional Council, we cannot allow ourselves to be as liberal as we were in the committees of the Provisional Council.'[30] He was obviously referring to Herut and the communists. Naturally, Ben-Gurion did not dare state these views publicly. Instead, he attributed his objection to the attachment of committees to government ministries to the fact that in a parliamentary system, there is collective responsibility, which precludes 'making committees an adjunct to ministers'.[31] He argued that the opposition wanted 'a rule of committees which is contrary to a parliamentary form of government'.[32] In the United States, the committees serve as a line of communication between the President and the Congress because of the separation that exists in a presidential system between the two branches. In contrast,

> in a parliamentary system, there is no separation between the government and the parliament. Only in a non-parliamentary system is government alone and the legislature alone . . . in our case . . . we have a parliamentary form of government. The government and the parliament are directly linked, the Knesset elects the government, and the government is at the head of the Knesset.[33]

The government is the

> executive and guidance committee that the parliament selects for itself . . . in our system, the ministers have no individual authority drawn from a supreme source outside of the government. Each minister receives instructions from the entire government, and the entire government is responsible for each minister. The minister does only what the government tells him to. In a form of government like ours, it is impossible to dissolve the government. You can only replace it. For this reason, we have opposed and continue to oppose the establishment of committees alongside the ministers whose function is to advize and guide each and every minister. The minister does not take guidance from any committee, but only from the government, and the entire government is at the disposal of the Knesset and only at its disposal. The opposition wants an arrangement in which the committees are attached to the ministers, to continue

> the system that existed in the time of the Provisional Council of State, when each minister was a kind of federation unto himself, and had a committee to guide and direct him. This will not do now that we have established the collective responsibility of the government by law. The committees will no longer be attached to ministers. Instead they will be auxiliary tools for the Knesset; they will specialize in various matters, and clarify them in order to make the work of the Knesset more efficient. The committee is not for a minister – but for a particular matter or matters. It gives no guidance to the minister. The Knesset as a whole provides guidance to the government . . . for this reason we insist that there be committees for particular matters and not for ministers.[34]

The same restrictive approach was adopted in relation to the committees' powers. The Rules of Procedure of the Provisional Council of State, formulated before the expansion of the committees and their attachment to government ministries, did not specify what their powers were. Later, the Council did authorize each committee and the ministry or ministries to which it was attached to determine the committee's authority. In the Council's Rules of Procedure, there was a particularly severe clause stating that 'No proposal on any matter shall be discussed, or put to a vote, unless it has first been proposed in a committee one of whose functions is to discuss proposals relating to that matter.'[35] The original proposal, which was rejected by the Council, was even more stringent, since it stated that proposals to the committees must come only from government ministers. With the establishment of the committees in the First Knesset, in March 1949, a majority in the standing committee suggested that the committees be authorized to discuss bills, regulations that have been enacted and requests submitted by citizens to the Knesset or to the government and passed on by them to one of the committees. In fact, in this proposal the committees were authorized to deal with subjects referred to them by the Knesset or the government, but they were not authorized to initiate discussions on any subject. Based on this proposal, their status would have been limited to that of a body that responds but does not take any initiative. However, owing to Pinkas' amendment, the committees' powers were expanded and it was decided that a committee could also discuss 'any other matter that falls within the sphere of its interests'.[36] In addition, the committee was to receive from the ministers (or their representatives) an explanation and information on any matter referred to them for discussion and was also entitled to receive information from ministers on other subjects that belong to the area of its duties and to hold discussions on them. The opposition was strongly opposed to any attempt to stifle the Knesset committees. Sapir proposed that the committees be authorized to propose legislation, as well as to 'present to the Knesset proposals on any matter it sees fit'.[37] In fact, he demanded that the committees be granted an authority they had had during the tenure of the Provisional Council of State – to submit bills to the plenum. In addition, his suggestion was to expand the committees' right to receive information from the ministers:

> The committee will receive from the relevant minister or his representatives, at its request or at set times, information on the actions taken in the said ministry that fall within the committee's sphere of activity . . . whenever possible, the committee is entitled to receive from the minister or his relevant representatives, information on the planned actions of the said minister.[38]

Landau proposed a similar formulation: 'the continual receipt of information from the ministries included within the committee's area of duties, on their activities, to ensure the effective and faithful implementation of the Knesset's decisions'.[39] Bar-Yehuda suggested, among other things, that a minister called to appear before a parliamentary committee be obliged to do so within ten days. All the proposals made by representatives of factions in the opposition were rejected in the plenum.

BEN-GURION'S ATTITUDE TO THE COMMITTEES OF THE FIRST KNESSET

Ben-Gurion did not keep the foreign affairs and security committee informed about the developments and decisions connected with the armistice agreements. In April 1949, Sapir protested, without directly attacking Ben-Gurion, about the fact that the armistice agreement with Jordan was not brought in advance to the foreign affairs and security committee and the Knesset:

> I should like to register my protest about the fact that the proposed agreement was not brought before the foreign affairs and

> security committee and the Knesset before it was signed . . . we ought to warn against the recurrence of such cases, in my view, not only as far as the oppositionary factions are concerned, but also in relation to the procedures of this house . . . we should make sure that such matters are not presented to us incidentally to the presentation of questions or their placement on the agenda.[40]

Ben-Aharon and Harari also expressed their objections to the fact that the security and foreign affairs committee was not privy to the details of this agreement.[41]

Ben-Gurion was outspokenly scornful of the constitution, law and justice committee, when it was discussing the establishment of a constitution. In May 1949, Minister of Justice Rosen suggested that the committee invite Ben-Gurion to a discussion on the necessity for a constitution in light of the controversy on this issue among the government ministers.[42] At the beginning of June, the committee decided to summon the Prime Minister to a meeting, but he put off his appearance time after time. Committee meetings were cancelled twice because of Ben-Gurion's failure to attend. On this point, he had the backing of the Mapai faction, a fact noted in Chapter 8, which deals in intra-party politics. Early in July, the committee chairman, Nir, told the other members that 'after the last meeting, I spoke to the Prime Minister officially and told him we had waited for him three times. He replied that the government actually has not formed an opinion yet . . . he explained that he is very preoccupied.'[43] On 13 July, Ben-Gurion finally condescended to appear before the committee.[44]

In June 1949, the government secretary, Sherf, wrote to the ministers – apparently at the suggestion of the Prime Minister – clarifying the powers of the Knesset committees. These guidelines to the ministers, with the clear aim of limiting the committees' authority, were given following the questions addressed to the Commissioner of Police in the Internal Affairs Committee about the establishment of a gendarmerie. In his letter Sherf stated:

> The committees do not serve as institutions that provide general guidelines to the government ministries, but only do so on matters referred to them for discussion. The committee is also entitled, of course, to receive information on other matters that enter into the sphere of its interests. However, the practice that has now been introduced in the internal affairs committee

> of summoning ministers to hear general talks from them about the entire area of their work exceeds the framework of these decisions by the Knesset and is contrary to the desire of the government[45]

A committee, with the exception of the finance committee when discussing the budget, was precluded from summoning a minister and asking him to deliver an overall talk about his ministry. 'If such a demand is made, in my view, the members of government ought to oppose it and bring it to the entire government for discussion.'[46] An issue that had not yet been discussed by the government, or the deliberation on which had not been completed in the government, could not be raised in a committee by a minister or his representative, nor could it be discussed in a parliamentary committee. As an example, Sherf cited the question of the gendarmerie which had been raised in the internal affairs committee and the readiness of the Police Commissioner to discuss it. Only in a discussion on the budget, was it permissible to 'discuss a government ministry as such',[47] however this was a prerogative solely of the finance committee. Ministers were not permitted to pass on budgetary material to the Knesset committees. In accordance with the government decision, only the Minister of Finance was authorized to do so. 'The budgetary proposals of ministries that have been submitted to the Minister of Finance or brought before the government, are internal material of the government and hence may not be published or provided to anyone.'[48]

Two days after Sherf wrote this letter to the ministers, Ben-Gurion sent two letters referring to the discussion held in the internal affairs committee on the issue of a gendarmerie. To the chairman of the committee, Benjamin Minz (*Poalei Agudat Israel*), he wrote that the question of a gendarmerie had not yet been brought up in the government, adding that 'This is not yet a matter for discussion in a committee.'[49] To the police commissioner Ben-Gurion wrote instructing him to refrain from giving information to the committee:

> Since the parliamentary frameworks have not yet been clearly formulated, a committee may at times discuss a matter prematurely and address questions to the wrong party. However, for the sake of good order, I must inform you that an answer on an issue such as this is a matter for the government, and if in future you are asked questions of this sort, ask [the questioners] to apply to the government.[50]

Minister Dov Joseph's statement to members of the Mapai faction, in November 1949, is indicative of the government's attitude to the Knesset committees:

> There are no grounds for the allegation that I refuse to appear before the Knesset committees. However, the government forbids its ministers from reporting to a committee. The members of the government report only to the Knesset. But I always willingly respond to the request of every committee that calls upon me to give it information.[51]

The prohibition imposed by the government, at the behest of the man who was at its head, against the provision of reports to the Knesset committees, as well as the very distinction it made between the plenum and the committees, definitely had an adverse effect on the standing of these committees.

In December 1949, Ben-Gurion decided to transfer the Knesset from Tel Aviv to Jerusalem. The symbolic implications of this move are analyzed in Chapter 5. The Speaker of the Knesset, Sprinzak, and other members of Knesset were not in favour of this decision. Sprinzak made his views known in a meeting of the Mapai faction's directorate: 'If I had been asked, I would have said: for a year or two the Knesset has to take shape in a suitable climate, and that's in Tel Aviv.'[52] He believed that the Knesset plenum should convene two days a week in Jerusalem and that the third day should be devoted to work in the committees, which would meet in Tel Aviv. Aranne was also in favour of alloting two days to the capital and one day a week to Tel Aviv.[53] However, Ben-Gurion sent a letter to Harari, the chairman of the House committee, informing him that the ministers would not appear before the Knesset committees if their meetings were held in Tel Aviv.[54] Sprinzak, at a meeting of the Mapai faction's directorate, remarked: 'It's strange that he sent the letter to Harari, without informing me about it', adding, 'I don't see that it would in any way impair the transfer [of the Knesset] if some of the committee meetings were held in Tel Aviv.'[55]

Early in 1950, as noted in Chapter 1, the religious parties imposed sanctions in the wake of the ongoing quarrel between them and Mapai about education in the immigrant camps. Their ministers stopped attending government meetings. The government reacted by deciding that a minister who failed to participate in government meetings would be regarded as having resigned. As soon as Ben-

Gurion had announced this decision in the plenum, Nir, the chairman of the constitution, law and justice committee, approached him and invited him to a discussion on the matter at the committee meeting the following morning. According to Nir, the Prime Minister agreed to appear before the committee on condition that the meeting be held that evening. Nir replied that he was not prepared to deviate from the normal practice of holding committee meetings in the morning.[56] Ben-Gurion did not appear at the committee meeting the next day, and the Mapai representatives on the committee boycotted the meeting. The representatives of the religious parties, as well as those of the opposition and the Progressives, argued in the discussion that the government's decision had no legal validity.[57]

In the discussion on this subject by the constitution, law and justice committee several days later, representatives of the opposition once again expressed their support for the religious parties' claim. Ben-Gurion, who this time did consent to attend the meeting, argued that since the law does not address a case of ministers boycotting meetings, then

> as long as the Knesset does not amend the law according to the internal logic of the matter, any government can . . . inform a member that he can no longer serve as a member of it. The government is obliged to inform the Knesset of such an instance, since it is a political event . . . the government's decision is not a law . . . the government has interpreted for itself in what way the law of collective responsibility applies to the specific case.[58]

Harari responded that the government ought to have at least consulted the committee on this matter, 'since the legislator in this country is the Knesset, not the government'.[59] Ben-Gurion, however, did not accept Harari's criticism.

> The constitution committee has no authority and the government need not consult it, but only the Knesset. The government's committee is the Knesset . . . There is only one committee that the government goes to, and that is the finance committee, which replaces the Knesset, according to a Knesset decision, in relation to certain matters . . .[60]

Despite Ben-Gurion's position that the government was competent to act as it saw fit and had no obligation to consult with the constitution, law and justice committee, the committee adopted Harari's proposal and took the decision that the government's announcement regarding the religious ministers had raised legal issues that called for a legislative solution. A more radical proposal made by Yochanan Bader stating that the government's decision 'has no grounds in the existing law', was supported by nine members, but it was not adopted, since nine others opposed it.[61] This incident demonstrates Ben-Gurion's hostile attitude to the Knesset committees, and reveals his profound contempt for the Knesset too. When he appeared before the constitution, law and justice committee, he complimented the Knesset committees, while at the same time he levelled criticism at the plenum, expressing his wish that the Knesset would do more to educate the public:

> Every time I am in some committee, I ask myself why matters are not dealt with in the same way by the Knesset. If they would do so, I think the Knesset would become the highest institution for educating the people. In any event, whenever I am in committees, everyone really speaks to the point.[62]

Thus, while praising the committees, Ben-Gurion added a remark that implied he would have liked to see the Knesset's status lowered and its functions lessened: 'The Knesset does not choose the government . . . the Knesset's function is to express confidence or non-confidence in the government.'[63]

In July 1950, the Minister of Justice, Rosen, sent an angry letter to the Prime Minister about judges' salaries. Rosen protested that the government was preventing the Knesset, and in particular the finance committee, from dealing with the question: 'It seems to me that it is fitting and proper for the government to leave the decision about the salaries of judges, who belong to a separate branch, to the Knesset.'[64] He was turning to Ben-Gurion in the wake of the government's refusal to approve the decisions taken by the finance committee on this matter, although at an earlier stage, the government had decided to authorize the finance committee to resolve it.

The economics committee also incurred Ben-Gurion's ire. In September 1950, he summoned the Police Commissioner and his deputy; the Minister of Supply and Rationing, Dov Joseph; and two Mapai members of Knesset, Abba Chushi and Arye Bahir. Ben-Gurion expressed his interest in the work of the inquiry commission on the black market, headed by Chushi. As a matter of fact, the economics committee had been authorized to inquire into the matter. Later in the meeting, the Prime Minister said he had heard there were many thefts in the Haifa port, some of them perpetrated by the workers. The Haifaite, Chushi, replied that this was occurring on a minor scale. Then Ben-Gurion made a telling remark that reflected his attitude towards the Knesset committees: 'A committee on behalf of the Knesset should not be the one investigating this matter. It is a labour matter.'[65] This affair is mentioned here briefly against the background of the economic committee's involvement. The investigative aspects of the affair are covered at length in Chapter 4.

Another affair, in April 1951, concerned the fixing of the date for elections to the Second Knesset. Mapai was then interested in holding early elections, while the other parties were opposed. Mapai was disgruntled by the fact that this issue was dragging on due to the small parties' opposition to holding earlier elections. The subject was held up in the constitution, law and justice committee chaired by Nir. In order to expedite the legislation, Sprinzak announced in the plenum on 27 March 1951, that the plenum would discuss the matter on 2 April.[66] On the date the discussion on early elections was to be held, Nir came to the plenum and requested a two-day delay. The request was made in the name of the constitution, law and justice committee, which had taken the decision that morning. Nir undertook, on behalf of the committee, to bring the subject to the plenum within two days.[67] Sprinzak put this request to a vote, and stated that even if the committee did not meet its commitment, the matter would be placed on the agenda of the plenum in two days' time. The plenum voted to grant the committee's request.[68]

Later that day, the members of the Mapai faction met to discuss the matter. The Prime Minister, very angry, appeared and demanded that he be allowed to speak to the plenum to change the decision it had taken:

> No committee other than the finance committee has any authority. According to the law, the government determines the agenda. Nir had no right to take the floor and say what he did . . . I want to make a revision in the Knesset, and I see no reason not to do so . . . They want a transition law in order to postpone the election date. I consider it my duty to come to the Knesset and explain what damage they are causing the state.[69]

Sprinzak, who did not want Ben-Gurion to reopen the issue in the plenum, stated:

> It was not a change in the agenda but a postponement. I set the date, not the government. What the constitution committee had to inform me before, Nir told me. There is no law in the world that rejects such a proposal . . . on that basis, I suggest that we don't raise the issue again. If Ben-Gurion appears, a thousand will sign up to take the floor . . . Kaplan and Lavon, two members of the government, were at the Knesset meeting and didn't intervene. Changes can be made in the agenda at any time. Someone has to notify all those who need to know.[70]

David Bar-Rav-Hai said that Nir had announced in the constitution, law and justice committee that the matter was up for discussion and that the Mapai representatives had objected, but remained in the minority. Like Sprinzak, he also suggested that the matter not be raised again in the plenum. Joseph Lam was the only one who supported Ben-Gurion's proposal, when it was put to a vote in the Mapai faction.[71]

In July 1951, Nir rejected Ben-Gurion's demand that the constitution, law and justice committee move more quickly in its discussion of the equality for women bill. During the committee meeting, Nir received a letter from the Prime Minister, in which he wrote: 'Since the government plans to ask the presidium to convene the Knesset next week for the last reading of the women's equality bill, I am asking you to conclude the discussions in the committee this week.'[72] Nir asked the committee members if they agreed that he should notify the Prime Minister that they could not possibly complete preparation of the law by the coming Monday. Bar-Yehuda suggested that they tell the Prime Minister that when the committee has completed its deliberations on the law, it will so inform the government.[73] Nir accepted Bar-Yehuda's suggestion and the committee finished preparing the law after several more meetings. In this instance, Ben-Gurion did not succeed in imposing his will.

The decisions taken during the tenure of the First Knesset were supposed to be temporary, since the committees' powers were to be anchored in future legislation and in the Knesset Rules of Procedure, which had not yet been finally formulated. It later turned out that the decisions taken in that initial stage had become the basics of Israeli parliamentarism.

BEN-GURION'S ATTITUDE TO THE KNESSET COMMITTEES

After the elections to the Second Knesset, the General Zionists renewed their demand that the Knesset committees be attached to government ministries, but Mapai representatives removed the subject from the agenda.[74] In a few of the meetings of the Mapai faction in the Knesset, some criticism of the work of the committees was also expressed. In November 1952, two Mapai MKs gave vent to their frustration. Meir Argov (Grabovsky), chairman of the foreign affairs and security committee, related to the limitations placed on the committee by the Prime Minister:

> I cannot invite any minister without Ben-Gurion's or Sharett's consent . . . after the committee has heard a report, it takes no steps, it makes no visits. I cannot take a single step or answer a single letter without approval . . . all the other committees have a great deal more work than the foreign affairs and security committee.[75]

Genia Tversky, a member of the public services committee, admitted that the committee had overstepped the instructions in the Rules of Procedure: 'We discussed all the issues of the ministry. In these Rules of Procedure it is written that we are not allowed to hold discussions, we did all that. Our committee did everything that we were forbidden to do under the Rules of Procedure.'[76] The difficulty of working within the rigid procedures created in the committees at Ben-Gurion's behest, led to illegal behaviour in the legislature itself.

In a meeting of the faction in 1955, in Ben-Gurion's absence, David Hacohen proposed that separate parliamentary committees be established for foreign affairs and security. He even went so far as to complain about the weakness of the foreign affairs and security committee: 'The work in this committee on defence matters is superficial . . . I am a member and I don't know what is going on in this area. Every year, they take us on tours, but we don't actually know what is being done there. And these are very serious problems.'[77] In January 1956, during a meeting between leaders of the three labour parties, Galili protested to Ben-Gurion about what was happening in the foreign affairs and security committee: 'I have a very bitter feeling of dissatisfaction as a member of the foreign affairs and security committee . . . we never have any really thorough discussions on security matters.'[78] In June 1956, Ben-Gurion rebuffed

Argov's suggestion that a 'liaison officer' be appointed between the chairman of the committee and the General Staff and Ministry of Defence: 'The Minister of Defence is the "liaison officer", and any other officer for this purpose is out of the question.'[79]

Ben-Gurion did not keep the foreign affairs and security committee informed about plans and preparations for the Sinai campaign. In his speech before the Mapai central committee, about two months after the war, he expressed his lack of confidence in the committee, as well as in the Knesset as a whole:

> Constitutionally, although we don't have a written constitution – but it should be self-evident – the government cannot go to war without the consent of the Knesset. However, the circumstances in this case did not permit us to bring the matter to the Knesset, nor even to the Foreign Affairs and Security Committee.[80]

In November 1956, he wrote to Argov, telling him how astonished he was at the 'grevious error' Argov had made in the foreign affairs and security committee meeting, by inviting Galili to eulogize General Asaf Simchoni, since Galili 'had never served in the IDF'.[81]

Ben-Gurion's attitude towards the foreign affairs and security committee is also evident from the letter he sent to Argov in February 1957, in reply to Argov's complaints that the committee holds far fewer meetings than the government does and that Ben-Gurion rarely appears before it. Ben-Gurion responded by saying he failed to understand the committee members' complaint about his failure to appear before the committee, since he is entitled to send someone else to provide information to the committee. He added that

> The Knesset decides how many meetings should be held with the foreign affairs and security committee, and whether the Prime Minister has to come in person to give it information . . . The government, if it sees fit, will meet twice every day, and I don't see that that would oblige me to go to the foreign affairs and security committee twice a day or even every day.[82]

Ben-Gurion was also critical about the composition of the foreign affairs and security committee. He wanted former army officers to serve on it rather than members of Knesset who had no military experience. He referred to that preference in a meeting of the Mapai central committee, in which he presented the party list for the Third Knesset, by saying:

> Mapai did something for the army, and to this very day there has not been a single member on the foreign affairs and security committee who knows anything about military matters. There are some good, loyal members – Herzl Berger, Argov, Ben-Asher – but not a single one of them served in the army . . . I want us to have members in the Knesset who are closely acquainted with military and security matters.[83]

This is a rather puzzling complaint, since Ben-Gurion strongly influenced the choice of candidates for the Mapai lists for the first two Knessets, as we shall see in Chapter 8. Later in his speech, Ben-Gurion criticized the leaders of the *Ihud*, the kibbutz wing of Mapai, for having recommended five candidates for the list, none of whom was a 'soldier' – 'and they do have such men. If I were the one to decide on my own, I would do that.'[84]

In October 1956, Ben-Gurion complained to the Director-General of the Ministry of Finance, Jacob Arnon, that information was being leaked to the press about payments made to ministers for per diem expenses and official apartments. In his letter, the Prime Minister referred to the finance committee as one of the possible sources of the leak:

> In the government, there is justified indignation at items published in the press about payments made to ministers for their per diem expenses and official apartments. This information emanates from the finance committee or the Treasury. The material – according to the members of the government – was given to the finance committee without the ministers' knowledge, and they were not given the opportunity to check whether the figures were correct. If you can, I should like you to: 1) stop supplying these figures; 2) find out why this information was given to the press; 3) explain why the government members were not given the opportunity to examine the figures first.[85]

In fact, Ben-Gurion was demanding that the Director-General of the Finance Ministry refrain from giving information on this matter to the finance committee.

In June 1957, during a parliamentary discussion on the role of the security service, the Prime Minister lavished compliments on the foreign affairs and security committee for conducting discussions without resorting to demagogy, unlike the irresponsible plenum, but added, 'however, there too, details that are not vital will not be provided'.[86] In other words, although the foreign affairs and security committee is better behaved than the contumacious plenum, still it does not deserve to receive full information. A further analysis of Ben-Gurion's attitude to the Knesset committees will be made by partially reviewing three affairs – the Lavon affair, the Laskov affair and the Soblen affair.

THE LAVON AFFAIR

The debate about the powers of the committees, particularly the foreign affairs and security committee, was renewed in relation to the investigation of what came to be known as the 'security mishap' involving an abortive Israeli military-intelligence plot in Egypt in 1954, when Lavon was serving as Minister of Defence and Sharett as Prime Minister following Ben-Gurion's resignation in 1953. After the committee had begun to investigate the matter at the end of 1960, Ben-Gurion refused to accede to its demands for the documents relating to the affair, including the report of the Cohen committee.[87] 'They did not want to submit a single document to the foreign affairs and security committee',[88] Bader said, adding that Peres, who had appeared before the committee, refused to answer some of its questions, claiming that the Minister of Defence had forbidden him to do so.[89] As soon as Ben-Gurion realized that the committee's investigation would not yield the result he wanted, at the end of 1960, he voiced his objection to the committee's handling of the affair:

> I objected and I continue to strenuously object to the foreign affairs and security committee meddling in this matter, because there are several members on that committee who are preparing another 'Dreyfuss affair'. Someone who has taken a position in advance cannot be an objective investigator, and that's Bader. I can live without this matter being re-investigated . . . I would not suggest conducting a new investigation, and I did not do so for five years . . . I do not suggest a re-investigation. I am only saying: not the foreign affairs and security committee.[90]

After the committee had been engaged in investigating the affair for several months, and after Lavon, Peres and Sharett, among others, had appeared before it, Ben-Gurion succeeded in halting its inquiry into this subject.[91] Bader asserted that, owing to his support for Lavon, 'my telephone has been tapped and my house has been under constant surveillance, so they could know who has been visiting me'.[92]

In January 1961, Ben-Gurion told the Mapai central committee his version of the foreign affairs and security committee's involvement in the 'affair'. Lavon demanded that Ben-Gurion clear his name, to which Ben-Gurion replied, 'I did not dismiss you, and I am not the one to clear you.'[93] Lavon then told him of his desire to involve the foreign affairs and security committee. 'I replied that I doubt whether this committee is the most appropriate place for this investigation, but he was adamant.'[94] Ben-Gurion said the following things in the committee:

> an investigation of the guilt or innocence of people in acts committed in 1954 – I think that is not a matter for the foreign affairs and security committee – it is not a legal committee, in my view it's a matter for a legal instance in the state – but less than anything else, in my view, is it a matter for the foreign affairs and security committee.[95]

In January 1961, Ben-Gurion wrote to the Justice Minister, Pinchas Rosen, that Lavon had 'desecrated the sanctity of security',[96] by involving the committee in the investigation of the 'mishap'. Until then, Ben-Gurion claimed, there had been no leaks from the committee's deliberations. But as soon as the investigation was opened, the leaks began. In that same meeting of the party's central committee, Lavon argued that once Ben-Gurion had informed him that he did not want to investigate the matter, his only option had been to apply to legal instances. 'I notified the Prime Minister', he stated, 'that he had left me no choice but to go to the foreign affairs and security committee.'[97] According to Lavon's version, Ben-Gurion had acknowledged his right to apply to the committee. Lavon asserted that he had appeared before the committee with the consent of both the party and Ben-Gurion.[98] In early February, the Mapai central committee convened for the purpose of ousting Lavon from his position as Secretary-General of the Histadrut. Sharett, who was opposed to the move, argued that Lavon had appeared before the foreign affairs and security committee with the knowledge and consent of the party. But Sharett's opposition was of no avail; at that meeting Lavon was removed from his high office.[99] When the plenum discussed the affair in 1961, the Prime Minister referred to the involvement of the foreign affairs and security committee by saying: 'I also know what took place in that institution then called the foreign affairs and security committee, which did not have the authority to discuss this dispute.'[100]

In regard to Ben-Gurion's complaints about the many leaks from the foreign affairs and security committee, the following remarks by Bader, one of Lavon's staunchest supporters, should be treated with some circumspection. He stated:

> during the committee's deliberations on the affair, its doors were thrown wide open. It began with the publication of details, taken directly from the recorded minutes, and these were aimed against Lavon. The military censor gave his tacit approval to these leaks, by not preventing their publication in full in the press.[101]

Bader blamed Ben-Gurion for the leaks: 'The leaks originated mainly from Ben-Gurion's close associates or from Ben-Gurion himself.'[102]

The Knesset's involvement in the Lavon Affair did not end with the brief inquiry conducted by the foreign affairs and security committee. In December 1960, the government decided to approve the conclusions of the 'Committee of Seven' which were not at all to Ben-Gurion's liking, because the committee had absolved Lavon of responsibility for the 'security mishap'.[103] In January 1961, Ben-Gurion informed the Knesset of his resignation, which automatically led to the resignation of the government. In his announcement to the Knesset in July 1961, he made clear that his resignation, and consequently that of the government, meant the cancellation of the government's decision to approve the December 1960 conclusions of the Committee of Seven.[104] The Knesset was immediately summoned to a special meeting to revoke the Prime Minister's announcement. Even the Justice Minister, Rosen, spoke out against words uttered by Ben-Gurion in the plenum, such as 'I have dismissed the government', or 'I have removed the government', and said the Prime Minister's announcement about the cancellation of the government's December 1960 decision should not be accepted.[105] In that Knesset session, the December 1960 decision was approved, with

Mapai abstaining. The alliance that was formed in order to defeat the Prime Minister crossed both coalition and ideological lines. The eight factions that were opposed to Ben-Gurion were Herut, the Liberals (which then already included the General Zionists and the Progressives), Mapam, Achdut Avodah, the National Religious party, Agudat Israel, Poalei Agudat Israel and the Communists.

Ben-Gurion did not give up, however. When he presented his new government in November 1961, the issue re-emerged. He stated

> the Knesset is sovereign, but we need to know what it is sovereign for. It is not sovereign to rule on the question of whether Job was created or not. Even if the Knesset should decide unanimously that Job never existed, any Jew can say: I am telling you that Job existed, or vice-versa . . . Nor is the Knesset competent to decide on the exodus from Egypt.[106]

At this point, he came to the subject of the 'Affair', and said:

> Nor about something that happened eight years ago. Whether something happened or did not happen eight years ago – neither the Knesset nor the government has the legal authority to decide. Its determination is valueless . . . There are some things that the Knesset's sovereignty does not apply to . . . It is not authorized to write history . . . and no decision taken by the Knesset can have the effect of upholding anything that is detrimental to the foundations of the law, and the Knesset is definitely not competent to determine what the facts were in 1954, which it did not even attempt to investigate.[107]

On another occasion, Ben-Gurion criticized the Knesset's decision to approve the government's decision of December 1960. This was in his speech to Young Mapai in December 1964:

> But the Knesset members did not read anything and did not know anything. They got together, all the factions, and decided: these conclusions are firm and abiding, and we shouldn't touch them. Such a thing has never happened in any parliament in the world. You know that the parliament is sovereign. It can do everything – but not everything. It cannot say that two times two are five, and if it does say that, then I won't give two hoots about it and neither will anyone else.[108]

He told his audience that in his speech to the Knesset when he presented his government in November 1961,

> I told them: 'What you decided at the end of the Fourth Knesset has no substance, the Knesset has no authority, the government has no authority [to do so]', and I was astonished that no one reacted. I was sure that first of all the opposition would rise and say: 'What!? The Knesset is not sovereign to decide?' . . . No one uttered a word . . . Until this very day, I am amazed that they were all silent. Usually, when I'm not in the Knesset, they don't keep quiet. And never before, had I said anything so heretical . . . It's possible that in another week or two, the Knesset will convene again and decide: the government's decisions of 25 December 1960 are firm and abiding. That won't be the end of the matter, because the Knesset does not have the final say! There is something else, above the Knesset – that is the Jewish people.[109]

THE LASKOV AFFAIR

Another affair that reveals Ben-Gurion's attitude to the Knesset committees is one that involved the end of Haim Laskov's term of service as Chief of Staff in 1960. The circumstances in which he left this position are not clear. He resigned following a lengthy, ongoing dispute with Shimon Peres, the Deputy Minister of Defence, about Peres' right to meet with senior officers without first co-ordinating these meetings with Laskov.[110] According to Bader, Laskov was the one who asked the foreign affairs and security committee to inquire into this matter. Ben-Gurion refused to approve Laskov's appearance before the committee, 'based on the claim that he is authorized to represent the IDF in the committee'.[111] Tzidon explained that Ben-Gurion had refused to permit Laskov's appearance because he feared Laskov would reveal the reasons for his resignation to the foreign affairs and security committee.[112] According to Mordechai Naor, the committee discussed the subject in Laskov's absence.[113]

Following Ben-Gurion's refusal to permit the outgoing Chief of Staff to appear before the committee, the Knesset for the first time in its history convened in a closed session, on 26 December 1960, five days before Laskov was replaced by Tzvi Tzur. In this session, the

Herut representative was given the opportunity to argue why it was proper to summon Laskov to the foreign affairs and security committee. Then another member of Knesset spoke and suggested that the subject be referred to the committee.[114] Ben-Gurion objected both to the demand made by Herut and to the suggestion to refer the matter to the committee, and the plenum accepted his position.[115] In January 1961, the Prime Minister, in a meeting of the Mapai central committee, expressed his criticism of the fact that the Knesset had been called to a closed session.[116]

THE SOBLEN AFFAIR

The Soblen affair, in the summer of 1962, provides yet another example of Ben-Gurion's attitude to the Knesset committees. Dr Soblen was an American Jew sentenced to life imprisonment in the United States for espionage. After he was released on bail, he escaped to Israel and requested the status of a new immigrant. He was arrested, and before the court had an opportunity to rule on the matter, a deportation order against him was issued, and speedily executed, under US pressure. The opposition criticized the government, whose representatives had provided the Knesset with very sparse information on the deportation proceedings. Bader tried to obtain information in the framework of the finance committee's discussion on the budget for the Transportation Ministry. The finance committee was discussing approval of allocations to El-Al, the national airline, which had flown Soblen outside the state boundaries. Bader exploited the opportunity, as part of the opposition's routine activity, to pose a series of questions to the Minister of Transportation, Bar-Yehuda, such as:

> Was it permissible to put certain persons into a charter plane? . . . There was an unscheduled stop of one plane in Athens. For that we have to pay money to Greece. Why was this done, and how much did it cost? . . . Three airplanes left on the same day in the same direction, nearly empty. What were the expenses of these flights, what were the incomes from these flights, how much is the deficit, the loss?[117]

The Minister of Transportation declined to answer these questions. Herut regarded this refusal as one more in a series of incidents demonstrating 'contempt for the Knesset and its rights',[118] and on this basis, proposed a vote of no-confidence in the government.

Bader explained the no-confidence motion by saying:

> What is the main right of the opposition, a modest, limited right, and yet one we cannot do without? It is the right to receive information. And if it is our right to criticize and our duty not to criticize without good reason, then it is impossible to do so unless we receive information . . . it is written in the regulations that 'a permanent committee is entitled to demand that the relevant minister provide it with explanations and information on a matter referred to it for discussion or one that falls within the area of its functions, and the minister is obliged, himself or through his representative, to provide the requested explanations or information'. There are no conditions here, it is the right of a parliamentary committee. In the finance committee, we posed a series of questions to the honourable Minister of Transportation who is responsible for El-Al, responsible for it before the Knesset and the finance committee for the governmental allocations to El-Al, responsible for the financial management of the El-Al company, for the moral and social level of the services rendered by El-Al and for its good reputation. Of course, he is responsible together with the government as a whole. But from the standpoint of the Rules of Procedure (clause 13(b)), he is the one who is responsible, and he must give answers to the competent committee, to the finance committee which is dealing with allocations to El-Al and is entitled to consider giving or withholding these allocations for whatever reason . . . If no answers to these questions are forthcoming, if there is no possibility of parliamentary supervision, if everything is hidden, stage after stage, behind excuses . . . then that is a serious infringement on the authority of the parliament and of the opposition.[119]

In his reply, Ben-Gurion defended the Transportation Minister's decision to decline to reply to the questions posed to him in the finance committee:

> Mr Bader's claim that it is the opposition's right to ask questions in the finance committee does not have a leg to stand on. It is the right of every member of a Knesset committee to ask

> questions – but this right is defined and limited in the Knesset Rules of Procedure, and if he asks questions that are not within the committee's competence – the minister is not obliged to reply . . . the Minister of Transportation did not reply to unauthorized questions . . . I, at any rate, concur completely with the minister's decision to refuse to reply to questions that are a matter for an inquiry committee and not for the finance committee . . . The investigation into Soblen's deportation was not referred to the committee by the Knesset and it is not the finance committee's affair.[120]

The Rules of Procedure state, as mentioned earlier, that a committee is entitled to demand information from a minister, not only if the matter has been referred to it for discussion, but also if it 'is within the area of its functions', and the areas of the committee's work are, as determined in the Rules of Procedure: 'the state budget; taxes of all types; customs and excise; loans; currency and foreign currency; banking and bills; state incomes and expenditures; liaison with the State Comptroller'. According to the Prime Minister's argument, the subject about which the Transportation Minister had been questioned in the finance committee did not fall within the area of the committee's duties: 'If I were at a meeting of the Foreign Affairs and Security Committee and someone began to ask me questions about banking, I would tell them: I won't answer that, because it is not a matter for the Foreign Affairs and Security Committee but for the finance committee.'[121] Unquestionably, Bader, one of the finest parliamentarians Israel had ever known, knew in advance what arguments the Prime Minister would put forth. His questions to the Transportation Minister did not touch directly on the Soblen Affair, but were directed at areas considered in the Rules of Procedure to fall within the purview of the finance committee, such as the state budget and its expenditures.

Ben-Gurion continued his attack on Bader and the finance committee:

> When the finance committee begins to take an interest in this question, it stops being a finance committee. It becomes a group of people who are curious, perhaps legitimately curious, but the minister is not obliged to satisfy the curiosity of every private person . . . If what I have been told is true, that the finance committee decided to invite an attorney, who is

> Soblen's counsel – it has gone completely mad and has made the Knesset and its committees an object of ridicule . . . It had no right to decide to invite Soblen's attorney and to question him. It is none of its affair, unless the Knesset takes an extraordinary decision to that effect. It was contempt of the Knesset Rules of Procedure and of the rights of the Knesset committees. A Knesset committee is, after all, a very respectable institution, although it is not a sovereign institution like the Knesset . . . The Transportation Minister was perfectly correct in teaching Mr Bader and the committee to respect the Rules of Procedure and the laws . . . And I commend him for having preserved the honour of the Knesset Rules of Procedure before those members who have no respect, other than their respect for themselves.[122]

In the course of his speech, Ben-Gurion did not even shrink from denouncing the finance committee for its 'slackness': 'Here it is 1 August, and the budget has not yet been approved, because the committee was preoccupied with matters that were not referred to it and did not get around to completing its discussion on the budget.'[123] Moshe Sneh (Communists) referred to the Prime Minister's denunciation as an 'insult to the Knesset', and added some strongly worded comments:

> You have attacked the finance committee for not having completed the budget on time. We, the Communists, are not represented on the finance committee, and we have a complaint in this regard; but the finance committee is the Knesset in miniature. Is it really the Knesset that did not complete the budget? It was the government! When did you submit the budget? Four months after the set date. At least you should remain silent. Why are you complaining about the Knesset? Why are you criticizing the finance committee for not having completed its work on the budget? It is not a contractor who is obliged to supply you with budgets. It can discuss as long as it wants, it can also not end [its deliberations]; it can also end them by taking a negative decision.[124]

Sneh accused the government of adopting 'an attitude towards the Knesset that is characterized by evasion, neglect, concealment and deception, disregard and the spinning of webs of lies'.[125]

The spokesmen for the other oppositionary factions were no less outspoken in their criticism of the government. Shlomo Lorenz (Agudat Israel) protested about 'the refusal of the Transportation Minister to provide the information requested in the finance committee', and asserted that 'this is not an isolated case of the government's contempt for the Knesset'.[126] Rubin (Mapam) rejected the Prime Minister's argument that the questions posed by Bader to the Transportation Minister exceeded the bounds of the committee's area of work. He added that 'the government did not want to give the Knesset the full picture. It is clear that incorrect and incomplete pieces of information came one after the other, while the government never told the Knesset the truth, nor does it want to.'[127] Harari (Liberals) explained why the opposition was forced to make use of the finance committee in order to obtain information about Soblen: 'Once again the coalition, in the House Committee, in its wisdom decided there would be no discussion. When the decision is taken not to hold a discussion in the Knesset, the opposition has the legal means to ensure that there will be a discussion.'[128] In his reply, the Prime Minister expressed his displeasure with the co-operation of all the parties in the opposition on this matter, and took a very firm stand in relation to the committee:

> The finance committee, and any other committee, must do what the law charges it to do. It is precluded from doing what the law does not permit it to do. It cannot do what it wants; there is no arbitrariness in this country . . . the Minister of Transportation was right in preventing the finance committee from exceeding the limits of the law in this matter. And no committee, neither until now nor in the future, will do whatever it wants to.[129]

Although Ben-Gurion did succeed in defeating the no-confidence motion, the fact that all the opposition factions aligned themselves with Herut on this issue shows that they regarded it as a question of principle. The position taken by Ben-Gurion is indicative of his basic view that favoured the existence of parliamentary committees which have very few powers and duties, and do not deserve to receive from the government the information they need to carry out their work. The three affairs – the Lavon Affair, the Laskov Affair and the Soblen Affair – all occurred during Ben-Gurion's last years as Prime Minister. It is evident from his fierce struggle against the committees that his attitude to the Knesset did not improve over the years. In the early 1960s too, when Israel had overcome its birth pangs, Ben-Gurion persisted in his vigorous opposition to the Knesset.

NOTES

1. Ben-Gurion Research Center Archives, Ben-Gurion's diary, 24 May 1948.
2. Provisional State Council, 3 June 1948, p. 6.
3. Archives, Ben-Gurion Research Center, correspondence, Ben-Gurion to Remez, 16 June 1948.
4. Provisional State Council, 7 June 1948, p. 39.
5. Ibid., 8 July 1948, p. 13.
6. Ibid., 15 July 1948, p. 9.
7. Ibid., 22 July 1948, p. 15.
8. Ibid., p. 16.
9. Ibid.
10. Ibid., p. 21.
11. Ibid., 29 July 1948, p. 33.
12. Ibid., 12.8.48, p. 16
13. Ben-Gurion Research Center Archives, minutes of meetings, meeting of security committee, 1 October 1948.
14. Ibid.
15. Provisional State Council, 25 January 1948, p. 9.
16. State Archives, 20/4, Tzidon to chairmen of committees of the Provisional Council of State, 4 January 1949.
17. Provisional State Council, 12 August 1948, p. 23.
18. State Archives, 20/4, Committee of Seven proposals.
19. *Knesset Record*, 23 March 1949, p. 198.
20. Ibid., p. 199.
21. Ibid.
22. Ibid., p. 200.
23. State Archives, 20/3, minutes of meeting of the standing committee, 21 March 1949.
24. *Knesset Record*, Ibid., pp. 219–20.
25. Ibid., p. 218.
26. Ibid., p. 217.
27. Ibid.
28. Ibid., p. 219.
29. Ibid., p. 220.
30. Israel Labour Party Archives, meeting of the faction directorate and the Mapai secretariat, 28 February 1949.
31. *Knesset Record*, Ibid., p. 219.
32. Ibid., p. 218.
33. Ibid., p. 219.
34. Ibid.
35. Provisional State Council, 4th meeting, 17 June 1948, p. 46
36. *Knesset Record*, 23 March 1949, p. 210.
37. Ibid., p. 204.
38. Ibid.
39. Ibid., p. 206
40. Ibid., 4 April 1949, p. 296.
41. Ibid., pp. 292, 295.
42. Giora Goldberg, 'You Don't Need a Constitution to plant Trees On State-Building

and Constitution Framing', (Hebrew), *Medina, Mimshal Vihasim Benleumiyim* (State, Government and International Relations), 38, Spring–Summer 1993, p. 36.
43. State Archives, 20/21, minutes of meeting of the constitution, law and justice committee, 6 July 1949.
44. Goldberg, 'You Don't Need a Constitution'.
45. Ben-Gurion Research Center Archives, correspondence, Sherf to government ministers, 26 June 1949.
46. Ibid.
47. Ibid.
48. Ibid.
49. Ibid., correspondence, Ben-Gurion to Mintz, 28 June 1949.
50. Ibid., correspondence, Ben-Gurion to the Police Commissioner, 28 June 1949.
51. Israel Labour Party Archives, meeting of the Mapai faction in the Knesset, 13 November 1949.
52. Ibid., meeting of the Mapai faction directorate in the Knesset, 18 December 1949.
53. Ibid.
54. See Sprinzak's statement, Ibid., meeting of the Mapai faction directorate in the Knesset, 2 January 1950.
55. Ibid.
56. State Archives, 20/21, minutes of a meeting of the constitution, law and justice committee, 22 February 1950.
57. Ibid.
58. Ibid., minutes of a meeting of the constitution, law and justice committee, 27 February 1950.
59. Ibid.
60. Ibid.
61. Ibid., minutes of a meeting of the constitution, law and justice committee, 14 March 1950.
62. Ibid., minutes of a meeting of the constitution, law and justice committee, 27 February 1950.
63. Ibid.
64. Ben-Gurion Research Center Archives, correspondence, Rosen to Ben-Gurion, 27 July 1950.
65. Ben-Gurion Research Center Archives, minutes of meetings, consultation on ways to combat the black market, 27 September 1950.
66. *Knesset Record*, 27 March 1951, pp. 1,446–7.
67. Ibid., 2 April 1951, p. 1,544.
68. Ibid., p. 1,547.
69. Israel Labour Party Archives, meeting of Mapai faction in the Knesset, 2 April 1951.
70. Ibid.
71. Ibid.
72. State Archives, 20/21, minutes of meeting of constitution, law and justice committee, 3 July 1951.
73. Ibid.
74. See statement by M. Argov, Israel Labour Party Archives, minutes of a meeting of the Mapai faction in the Knesset, 3 September 1951.
75. Ibid., meeting of Mapai faction in the Knesset, 18 November 1952.
76. Ibid.
77. Ibid., meeting of Mapai faction in the Knesset, 15 August 1955.
78. Ben-Gurion Research Center Archives, minutes of meetings, meeting of leaders of the three labour parties, 30 January 1956.
79. Ibid., correspondence, Ben-Gurion to Argov, 17 June 1956.
80. Israel Labour Party Archives, meeting of Mapai central committee, 3 January 1957.
81. Ben-Gurion Research Center Archives, correspondence, Ben-Gurion to Argov, 11 November 1956.
82. Ibid., Ben-Gurion to Argov, 19 February 1957.

83. Israel Labour Party Archives, meeting of Mapai central committee, 9 June 1955.
84. Ibid.
85. Ben-Gurion Research Center Archives, correspondence, Ben-Gurion to Director General of the Ministry of Finance (Jacob Arnon), 3 October 1956.
86. *Knesset Record*, 19 June 1957, p. 2,194.
87. Yochanan Bader, *The Knesset and I*, p. 133.
88. Ibid., p. 174.
89. Ibid., p. 133.
90. See statement by Ben-Gurion, Israel Labour Party Archives, meeting of Mapai central committee, 19 October 1960.
91. Bader, *The Knesset and I.*
92. Ibid., p. 134.
93. Israel Labour Party Archives, meeting of Mapai central committee, 12 January 1961.
94. Ibid.
95. Ibid.
96. Ibid.
97. Ibid.
98. Ibid.
99. Ibid., meeting of Mapai central committee, 4 February 1961.
100. *Knesset Record*, 3 July 1961, p. 2,131.
101. Bader, *The Knesset and I*, p. 132.
102. Ibid., p. 133.
103. Ibid., p. 144.
104. *Knesset Record*, 3 July 1961, p. 2,132.
105. Ibid., 24 July 1961, p. 2,147.
106. Ibid., 2 November 1961, p. 247.
107. Ibid.
108. Israel Labour Party Archives, conference, conference of secretariats of youth clubs, 3 December 1964.
109. Ibid.
110. Mordechai Naor, *Laskov* (Hebrew), Tel Aviv: Ministry of Defence and Keter, 1988, pp. 291–2.
111. Gevirtz, 'The Good Soldier', (Hebrew), *Chadashot*, 9 January 1987, p. 45.
112. Asher Tzidon, *Beit HaNivcharim* (The Parliament), Jerusalem: Achiasaf, 1969, p. 267.
113. Naor, *Laskov*, p. 297.
114. Tzidon, *Beit HaNivcharim*, p. 150.
115. Ibid.
116. Israel Labour Party Archives, meeting of Mapai central committee, 12 January 1961.
117. *Knesset Record*, 1 August 1962, pp. 2,989–90.
118. Ibid., p. 2,988.
119. Ibid., pp. 2,988–90.
120. Ibid., p. 2,990.
121. Ibid., p. 2,991.
122. Ibid.
123. Ibid.
124. Ibid., p. 2,994.
125. Ibid.
126. Ibid., p. 2,995.
127. Ibid., p. 2,994.
128. Ibid., p. 2,992.
129. Ibid., p. 2,998.

PART TWO

The Struggle Against the Knesset's Institutional Power

3 Dissolving the Knesset

In the opening chapter, Mezey's distinction between the types of pressure applied to a parliament by the extra-parliamentary political elite was mentioned. These are: the forcible dissolution of the parliament; its dissolution through constitutional change; and verbal attacks on the parliament and its members. This chapter deals with the issue of dissolution, whereas Chapter 9 discusses Ben-Gurion's verbal attacks on the Knesset and its members. Chapter 1 described Ben-Gurion's major role in dissolving the Provisional Council and the Constituent Assembly.

ATTEMPTS TO DISSOLVE THE KNESSET THROUGH CONSTITUTIONAL MEANS

When the Constituent Assembly was elected in 1949, it was not clear how long it would serve. Even after passage of the Transition Law, which provided for the replacement of the Constituent Assembly by the First Knesset, it was still not known when the First Knesset would be dissolved and elections held for the Second Knesset. In November 1949, Nir, chairman of the constitution, law and justice committee criticized this anomalous situation and, referring to the belief that the Knesset would serve a four-year term, remarked: 'We have this legend about four years. It originates in the government's four-year plan. In any event, the legal situation is that the First Knesset can serve interminably.'[1] As the representatives of the opposition continued to deplore this irregular situation, Ben-Gurion promised that elections would be held after the First Knesset completed a four-year term. In November 1949, he assured the Knesset that 'no later than four years after the establishment of the Knesset, new elections will be held, whether there is a constitution or not'.[2] The next day, Begin expressed his criticism of Ben-Gurion's statement: 'Who decided that this body would sit for four years? When was this decision taken? Does the Prime Minister believe that as the head of the executive body he is entitled to decide the length of the legislative body's service?'[3]

In July 1950, Ben-Gurion reiterated his promise. Since the government's plan, which was approved by the Knesset when the government was established, was a four-year plan, then obviously 'no later than four years from the establishment of the Knesset, new elections will be held'.[4] However, he did not see fit to accede to the demands of the opposition and to fix by law the length of the Knesset's terms or the timing of elections. Bar-Yehuda of Mapam stressed the need for legislation that would determine who was competent to dissolve the Knesset, when it was possible to do so, and the length of time between its dissolution and the election of a new Knesset. He added that a state could not be run on the basis of promises, and that laws were necessary for that purpose.[5] In the same discussion, Ben-Gurion said he supported the idea of giving the government a legal right to dissolve the Knesset: 'It is possible to have a constitution that enables the government to dissolve the Knesset before its term is out – such a system is not bad at all.[6] I am in favour of the British system, in which the government can dissolve the parliament', Ben-Gurion said, but he limited this right to a situation in which 'there is a serious issue, and the government feels that the Knesset is not expressing the will of the people on that matter'.[7] However, in relation to a comparison with the British system, one point must be clarified. A distinctly coalition-type government is not the same as a two-party system of government. Since the ruling party in Britain nearly always enjoys an absolute majority in the parliament, whereas in Israel no party has ever achieved an absolute majority in the Knesset, any comparison between the two is basically flawed. If Mapai had achieved an absolute majority in the Knesset and was interested in holding early elections, it would not have needed a constitutional clause permitting the government to dissolve the Knesset, but could have done so through legislation. However, during Ben-Gurion's term as Prime Minister, with the exception of the nine months of the provisional government's tenure, Mapai had a majority in the government, but not in the Knesset.

At the end of October 1950, Ben-Gurion promised the Knesset that the government would propose a law fixing the Knesset's term of service – and once again mentioned a four-year period.[8] Indeed, a week later, he submitted to the Knesset a bill determining the Knesset 's term of office. It stated that the Knesset is elected for four years and that the President has the authority to dissolve the Knesset before the end of its term. However, this Presidential act is not independent; it requires the signature of the Prime Minister or of another minister.[9] The opposition objected to the suggested wording. However, the bill was sent to the constitution, law and justice committee,[10] where it was 'buried' and never returned to the plenum. Ben-Gurion continued to advocate a system in which the government had the right to dissolve the Knesset. A few days after the government resigned in February 1951 – following its defeat in the Knesset vote on education – the Prime Minister wrote to Justice Minister Rosen: 'If a government decides upon something that it regards as fundamental to its policy, and is prepared to resign, dissolve the parliament and hold early elections because of it – in parliamentary language that is known as presenting the question of confidence.'[11]

When the Transition Law to the Second Knesset was being enacted, in mid-1951, there were echoes of the concerns felt by various factors vis-à-vis the dissolution of the Knesset. The government demanded that it be authorized to determine the date on which the Second Knesset would be convened; however in the vote taken in the constitution, law and justice committee only nine members supported this demand, against 11 who were in favour of authorizing the Speaker of the First Knesset and his deputies to do so. Mapai's demand that the First Knesset be dissolved a month prior to elections was also rejected.[12] During the second reading of the bill, Mapai proposed that the First Knesset be dissolved one day before elections to preclude the possibility that the elections would be cancelled by the First Knesset – but this proposal was defeated by a majority of 51 members against 41. Nir's reaction to the proposal was that it is easier for the government to carry out a coup than it is for the Knesset.[13] In this discussion, Ben-Gurion announced that 'this government does not want to continue in its capacity, and has decided to turn to the people in order to challenge the Knesset majority'.[14] He was also opposed to the addendum suggested by Joseph Burg, which would make it impossible to dissolve the Knesset during the first year of its term, and it was not accepted.[15] In

April 1951, the Knesset approved a law fixing the date of elections to the Second Knesset.[16]

After the elections, Ben-Gurion tried to introduce a constitutional change that would enable the government to dissolve the Knesset. In light of his bitter experience during the First Knesset, when his party was prevented from holding early elections after the government fell, Ben-Gurion was anxious to change the law to enable the government and the Prime Minister to dissolve the Knesset and to bring about early elections. While coalition negotiations were being conducted after the elections to the Second Knesset, Ben-Gurion made this a key demand by Mapai of its potential partners.

At first, the matter was discussed in Mapai's political committee. Ben-Gurion reported that during the coalition negotiations he had notified the General Zionists that the Knesset would be dissolved 'according to a proposal by the Prime Minister to the President',[17] and that they had not reacted. His demand of the HaPoel HaMizrachi was even harsher:

> I told the HaPoel HaMizrachi that my condition for serving as Prime Minister in the coalition was that the Prime Minister could dissolve the Knesset . . . for six months I have been heading a government which has no Knesset behind it. In other countries that would also be a bad thing, but in our case it is a thousand times more serious, it is catastrophic, I won't do that any more. The only guarantee to keep this situation from recurring is the possibility, should it happen again, to dissolve the Knesset, so it will be impossible for a minister to vote against the government and for the government to continue to exist, because there is not a majority in the Knesset to support its dissolution.[18]

Like the representatives of the General Zionists, the representatives of the HaPoel HaMizrachi did not react to Ben-Gurion's demand either. He told the members of his party's political committee:

> I do not think we necessarily have to have a government for four years. The question facing us is whether there is a possibility that we will control the dissolution of the Knesset . . . if it depends on us, there won't be the kind of carrying on that we saw in the previous Knesset. If they know it is in our hands, they will restrain themselves . . . if they accept this condition

> that we can dissolve the Knesset – that is the best guarantee that they won't become unruly.[19]

Aranne and Joseph were skeptical about the readiness of the coalition partners to accept this condition. Shazar said: 'This demand, that the Prime Minister be entitled to disssolve the Knesset, will be very unpopular in the country.'[20] Ben-Gurion stuck to his position:

> You cannot resign. If it were possible to resign, I wouldn't have been sitting in the government for the past four months. I tried to do it and saw that I couldn't. I could only abandon the Ministry of Defence and tell the army: there is no one dealing with the matter . . . As a matter of fact, I don't care what the wording is. I just want them to know that we can dissolve the Knesset. During the negotiations, the General Zionists said neither yes nor no.[21]

Aranne asked what Ben-Gurion would do if the religious parties did not accept his proposal. Ben-Gurion replied that in that case he would leave the religious parties in the opposition and set up a coalition with the General Zionists, on condition that they agree to his demand. Aranne persisted, asking Ben-Gurion what he would do if the General Zionists also refused to accede to his demand. 'I will inform Weizmann that I do not accept the task of forming the government'[22] Ben-Gurion replied. Aranne asserted that Ben-Gurion's demand that 'a coalition will not be formed unless the government's right to dissolve the Knesset is assured'[23] amounted to an undesirable ultimatum, and added: 'You are not conducting the negotiations personally, but rather on behalf of the party.'[24] Lavon came to Aranne's aid by stating: 'It will be hard to prove that this is not an attempt by Mapai to impose its dictatorship.'[25] The Mapai leaders were not inclined to agree to Ben-Gurion's demands and did not give him the backing he needed in the coalition negotiations.

Three days later, the political committee convened again to discuss the matter. Argov reported that the leaders of HaPoel HaMizrachi had not agreed to accept Ben-Gurion's demand in full. Instead they had proposed that the law be brought to the Knesset only after the government had been in office for six months, and that it stipulate that every Knesset would exist at least 18 months, and if afterwards a motion of no confidence in the government were passed and the President failed twice within two months to bring about the formation of a government, then he was entitled, based on the government's proposal, to announce new elections.[26] Mapai was opposed to delaying the legislation and to leaving the final decision in the President's hands; it also refused to accept the limitation of 18 months. Kaplan reported to the committee members that the General Zionists wanted a separation between the dissolution of the Knesset and the fixing of a new date for elections, and agreed that the President would have the authority to set the date for elections, but not to dissolve the Knesset.

A few days later, Argov informed Mapai's political committee of progress in the negotiations. The HaPoel HaMizrachi had moderated its demand about the 18-month period during which the Knesset could not be dissolved, and was now asking for 12 months. It had also shortened the length of time required before the President could call new elections from two months to six weeks. Its leaders were demanding that a Knesset remain in office until the next Knesset is seated, to avoid a situation in which there would be no Knesset.[27] Ben-Gurion was enraged by the refusal of his potential coalition partners to accept his conditions, and announced that he would form a minority government, all of whose ministers were members of Mapai. He assumed that Mapam would abstain in a vote to approve a minority government.[28] At this stage, the coalition negotiations with the HaPoel HaMizrachi and the General Zionists broke down, but a compromise was finally reached between Mapai and the religious parties, which in fact amounted to a defeat for Ben-Gurion. The compromise reached was not included in the basic principles of the new government and remained an 'oral agreement'.[29] Its essence was that the new legislation would be enacted after one year and would state that if the government resigned and the President was unable, within six weeks, to form a government, the government would be entitled to compel him to act to dissolve the Knesset and to announce new elections. The resignation of the Prime Minister would be regarded as the resignation of the entire government.[30] The last clause was intended to give Ben-Gurion the indirect authority to dissolve the Knesset. If he wanted to, he could resign and then the entire government would have resigned. And if there were difficulties in forming a new government – and he was likely to see to that – the government would act through the President, who had no discretion in the matter, to dissolve the Knesset and call early elections. The agreement between Mapai and the religious parties did not come to fruition, and the legislation Ben-

Gurion was so eager to achieve was not passed. After the ultra-orthodox parties left the coalition, Ben-Gurion brought up the agreement that had been reached a year earlier. He was very aggressive in his attitude towards parties that were not prepared to join the coalition and threatened 'that there will be no government at all'.[31]

The issue of dissolving the Knesset came up again at the end of 1952 following the death of President Weizmann and the need to elect a new President. Rozen regarded himself as a candidate for the office of president and demanded that Ben-Gurion expand his powers. In November 1952 Ben-Gurion argued with Rozen about the President's powers and expressed his opposition to some of the powers Rozen wanted the President to have, in particular the authority to declare new elections. Ben-Gurion was convinced that if the government resigned or was defeated, and for a fortnight or a month it was impossible to form a new government, 'the Prime Minister would advise the president to dissolve the Knesset and announce new elections, and then the President would have to do so . . . it is unthinkable, in my view, to have two executive powers in the state'.[32]

ATTEMPTS TO DISSOLVE THE KNESSET BY NON-CONSTITUTIONAL MEANS

At times, Ben-Gurion went even further than entertaining the idea of dissolving the Knesset. Occasionally he would threaten to abandon his office as Prime Minister and Minister of Defence, even if no replacement could be found for him. One of the serious implications of this threat was contempt of the Knesset and the readiness to violate the laws it had enacted. For example, in May 1953, after the four General Zionist ministers resigned,[33] a furious Ben-Gurion appeared before Mapai's political committee and declared that he would inform the Knesset of his readiness to serve in the government 'until the end of June and not one day longer, not as Prime Minister nor as Minister of Defence'.[34] Minister Joseph rebuked him: 'There's a law, why would you violate the law?'[35] But Ben-Gurion replied: 'There is an Attorney General, let them put me on trial. It is not a matter for discussion here.'[36] Argov cautioned against creating 'one crisis on top of another',[37] and Aranne said that if Ben-Gurion refused to accept the task of forming a government, the result would be chaos in the state and in the party.[38] The political committee decided, against Ben-Gurion's wishes, that he would not announce his resignation. A few months later, Ben-Gurion did in fact resign.

While he was at Sede Boker, Ben-Gurion's hostility to the Knesset increased. He systematically boycotted meetings of the plenum and its committees. He did not regard his membership in the Knesset as a job or office, not even as filling a public function. In January 1954, he wrote in a letter: 'As for my duties in the Knesset, I will fulfill them *based on my understanding* [emphasis in the original] within the bounds of the existing laws.'[39] In February 1954, he wrote to Mordechai Nesiyahu: 'I no longer am active in public affairs, and other than the work I do on the kibbutz – I only watch and observe.'[40] The same day he wrote to someone else that he no longer was engaged in 'public life' and was only 'one of the workers on the Sede Boker kibbutz'.[41]

During that period, Ben-Gurion refused to attend events, even those that were not political. In September 1954, when he was invited by the President of the state, Yitzhak Ben-Zvi, to a party given for Knesset members, he refused to go. He thanked the President and his wife in a letter, adding a few words that testified to his attitude towards the Knesset: 'To my great regret, I am unable to come, and hence am conveying my sincere wishes that the reception given by the President and his wife will inspire all of the guests with a spirit of unity and responsibility.'[42] When the Israeli management of the World Jewish Congress invited him to the ceremony at which Speaker of the Knesset, Sprinzak, would be awarded the Wise prize, he refused to attend. In his reply to the invitation, he heaped praises on Sprinzak – 'Sprinzak's role in shaping the parliamentary image of the State of Israel is indeed unique'[43] – but he declined to take part in the ceremony, 'since in the next few months, I am unable to move from here'.[44]

Several citizens wrote to the former Prime Minister, expressing their disapproval of his failure to resign from the Knesset although he did not participate in the work of that body. One of them was particularly critical of Ben-Gurion and posed the question:

> If your common sense and clear conscience have led you to choose the path you are taking, why do you continue to serve as a member of Knesset when, according to your own plan, you won't be able to come to Jerusalem and take part in the deliberations of the Knesset?[45]

Another asked 'Is it proper from a social and moral standpoint, to be a member of Knesset . . . and at the same time not to take part in even one of its sessions for such a long time, not to play an active role, not even to vote?'[46] The writer also wanted to know whether the salary Ben-Gurion received from the Knesset was sent to his kibbutz or directly to him. Ben-Gurion replied that when he resigned from the government, he thought about whether he should continue his membership in the Knesset, and

> I decided not to leave the Knesset. To my regret, the law does not compel Knesset members to attend meetings. If it were up to me, I would pass a law stating that a Knesset member who fails to attend the Knesset for a long time, without a good reason, will lose his membership.

He added that even if there is a 'good reason' for his absence, he should not be paid a salary.[47] To the question about his own salary, Ben-Gurion declined to give a straightforward answer: 'As to the question about what I do with my salary as a Knesset member – there would be some point in my replying in a public statement (if people believe there is a need to do so) . . . there is some point only in a public reply.'[48] Ben-Gurion did not give up his salary. In February 1954, Mordechai Namir wrote to Ben-Gurion's wife regarding the account in the Knesset and stated that the matter had been arranged 'so that yours and Renana's checks will be regarded as payments on account of the salary'.[49]

Ben-Gurion's correspondence with Moshe Baharav in January and February of 1954 further reveals his negative attitude towards the Knesset. Baharav had introduced himself as a member of the Shahal organization (The Israeli Pioneering Service), whose activists were former IDF and Haganah officers. In his first letter to Ben-Gurion, he wrote that 'the situation in the country is intolerable', and referred to a social gathering of IDF officers and ex-officers, at which he had witnessed 'among those present, the readiness to *take up their guns, and to purge the Knesset of all the underhanded dealings . . . and to clean up some of the dirt* [emphasis in the original] of the government ministries'. He reported that one of the attendees had said (adding that he himself was of the same opinion, and nearly all had agreed)

> that only after the 'clean-up' in the government ministries and the Knesset, would they go to Sede Boker and ask you to come

> back and take the reins of power into your hands . . . it is possible, and I am confident, that the entire nation will agree to that – to forego the need for any representatives in the Knesset – because all those representatives in any case represent no one, and all of the wheeling and dealing in seats should be done on Lilienblum Street, in real seats. The people will not object to giving up the democratic foolishness known as a parliament for a period of at least five years, and you are the only man suitable for the task.[50]

Ben-Gurion did not relate to this strange letter as just one more attempt by cranks to submit all manner of suggestions and requests to politicians. A few days later, he took the trouble to reply to it, expressing his serious reservations about the revolutionary ideas put forward by Baharav: 'I do not agree with the soldier who suggested "taking the gun in hand to oust the Knesset and the like"; I believe in democracy, despite all the difficulties it entails.'[51] However, after expressing his disagreement with the idea of eliminating the democratic system of government, Ben-Gurion did convey good wishes to Baharav and his comrades: 'I wish you success . . . do all the positive things that you wish to do . . . carry out acts of pioneering, show an example of the pure life.'[52]

A few days later, Baharav wrote to Ben-Gurion again, expressing his regret that Ben-Gurion could not join him and his people. This time, he refrained from bringing up the idea of using weapons, but he did not abandon his hope of dissolving the Knesset: 'Just very, very simply, to go in and dissolve the Knesset for several years . . . and to install for several years, say five years, a great man who stands above the nation as head of the state.'[53] Ben-Gurion replied to this letter by referring Baharav to a verse in the Book of Kings, which says 'Let not he who girds on his harness boast', and emphasized, 'I do not mean by that to discourage you, on the contrary.'[54] In his third letter to Ben-Gurion, Baharav did not refer to the Knesset.[55] Ben-Gurion carried on the correspondence and this time ordered his admirers: 'And as for the organization – first of all actions, actions, actions.'[56] Ben-Gurion's intent was not to see the Knesset dissolved by force; he was referring rather to pioneering deeds, but the very fact that he was corresponding with a man who was opposed to the very foundations of democratic rule is no small matter. Ben-Gurion began to grow suspicious of Baharav. On the day he sent him his third letter, he also wrote to Levi Sarid, one of Shahal's leaders, asking him for information about Baharav: 'I received a letter from someone called M. Baharav. Who is this M. Baharav? His letters to me have aroused my doubts about him. He also seems to be an organizer of Shahal.'[57] Not only did Ben-Gurion fail to defend the Knesset in his letters to Baharav, but his letter to Sarid shows that he was carrying on this lengthy correspondence with a person unknown to him.

The preparations made by Mapai for the passage of the first basic law also reveal how important the issue of dissolving the Knesset was to Ben-Gurion. The heads of the faction left it up to Ben-Gurion to decide on the wording of those sections of the law dealing with the dissolution of the Knesset.[58] Mapai had a hard time arriving at a unified position on this issue. An internal document, written by the legal advisor of the Mapai faction in the Knesset in June 1957, notes that there are three possibilities for dissolving the Knesset – by the Knesset itself by means of a special dissolution law, by the President on the advice of the Prime Minister, and by the Prime Minister himself. The document states that the faction will continue to discuss the matter after it hears Ben-Gurion's views.[59] Since Mapai was unable to impose its view in this matter on its coalition partners, it was forced to agree to authorize the Knesset as the sole body that could dissolve itself.

Frustrated by this situation Ben-Gurion, in November 1958, delivered a speech to the Mapai central committee, in which he mentioned the dissolution of the Knesset several times:

> Several years ago, some people came to me and said that we ought to remove the Knesset and set up a dictatorship. I was stunned, because these people were not fascists, but men who saw how this system was being abused. I cannot name names. But I cannot guarantee that what happened in Sudan, in Iraq, in Egypt, in Lebanon, will not happen here. If it hasn't happened until now, perhaps I know the reason why. I will not speak about it. But I cannot give any assurances. This government is not adding any honour to democracy . . . I am not sure how many years this form of government will prevail . . . a democracy that does not inspire respect – will not endure for long . . . I can tell you who could be the force that would destroy the democracy. It takes an army to destroy a democracy. In all countries, it was done by the army . . . I can't swear that it isn't likely to happen here – I won't say what happened in Iraq,

> where they hung people, but what happened in Sudan. They didn't hang people, they didn't do anything, just annulled. I am sure that if the present form of government continues, it will happen in one way or another . . . Is this people really so idiotic that it can be so abused? . . . There is opposition to political parties . . . This has got to lead to the downfall of the democracy and to a coup.[60]

Despite his pessimistic forecasts, Ben-Gurion did express some words of support for the existence of the Knesset, along with some serious reservations: 'I deny the sovereignty of the Knesset. I am one of those who calls into question the Knesset's sovereignty, but since there is no other institution, even this Knesset is better than anarchy.'[61] This speech to the Mapai central committee led to an adjournment motion by the opposition.[62]

On the eve of the 1959 elections, Ben-Gurion proudly declared to the members of the Mapai central committee that despite the danger existing in Israel of a military coup, nothing of the kind had happened. Because 'we have succeeded in establishing an army which serves only as an executive arm of the state'.[63] The danger of a military coup, according to Ben-Gurion, stemmed from the poorly functioning government. He continued his speech with words of encouragement for the activists of his party: 'we can get a majority in the Knesset, and that is what the state needs. And that is required for only one thing, in order to pass one law – a law of regional elections, and then we will dissolve the Knesset and hold regional elections.'[64]

In June 1964, after his resignation from the government, Ben-Gurion put forth an idea which, had it been implemented, would have caused a profound parliamentary crisis. It was during a party symposium that he proposed that Mapai go to the forthcoming elections on a platform that had only one item – a change in the electoral system. All those public figures who were not Mapai members, but supported a change in the system – even those from other parties – could join the list. All the candidates would commit themselves in advance to engage in only one activity, if elected – to promote legislation changing the election system. After the new law was enacted, elections would be held according to the new system. The candidates would undertake in advance to resign immediately after the elections to the Knesset if Mapai did not win an absolute majority, enabling it to change the electoral system. Since this meant the resignation of all those on the list of candidates, not only those who had been elected to the Knesset, the Knesset would remain with a very small number of members, 65 according to Ben-Gurion's calculations. Mapai, the largest party, would boycott the Knesset. In effect, he was suggesting a partial dissolution of the Knesset which would paralyze it, based on his estimation that the government that would be formed would not last long. Moshe Dayan was opposed to Ben-Gurion's proposal.[65] Ben-Gurion's proposal testifies to the fact that he believed it was necessary to create a severe crisis to pave the way for political reform. He did not even shrink from a partial dissolution of the Knesset and the complete disruption of its work and public status. This proposal was one more in a series of threats to resign. Another instance occurred when a coalitional crisis broke out in December 1957, and he notified the leaders of the Progressives that the following day he would resign, and 'the country would remain without a government'.[66]

While Chapters 1 and 2 depicted Ben-Gurion's enormous influence in shaping parliamentary life in Israel, this chapter describes a series of failures on his part. All of his attempts, of various kinds, to dissolve the Knesset ended in failure. Although he did succeed in dissolving the Provisional Council of State and the Constituent Assembly, he never achieved more than that. The forces that allied themselves against him at times included some from the coalition parties, even from Mapai. One cannot conclude from this chapter that Ben-Gurion wanted to see the Knesset dissolved. On the contrary, he wanted it to exist, but on condition that it serve the interests of the state. It is worth noting that none of the prime ministers who served after Ben-Gurion was involved, in any way, in so sensitive an issue as the dissolution of the Knesset.

NOTES

1. State Archives, minutes of meeting of constitution, law and justice committee, 16 November 1949.
2. *Knesset Record*, 21 November 1949, p. 128.
3. Ibid., 22 November 1949, p. 133.
4. Ibid., 12 July 1950, p. 2,180.
5. Ibid., p. 2,181.
6. Ibid., p. 2,180.
7. Ibid., p. 2,181.
8. Ibid., 30 October 1950, p. 102.
9. Ibid., 8 November 1950, p. 202.
10. Ibid., 16 November 1950, pp. 236–48.

11. Ben-Gurion Research Center Archives, correspondence, Ben-Gurion to Rosen, 19 February 1951.
12. State Archives, minutes of meeting of constitution, law and justice committee, 3 April 1951.
13. *Knesset Record*, 4 April 1951, p. 1,577.
14. Ibid., p. 1,581.
15. Ibid., pp. 1,580–2.
16. Ibid., 12 April 1951, p. 1,697.
17. Israel Labour Party Archives, meeting of Mapai political committee, 10 September 1951.
18. Ibid.
19. Ibid.
20. Ibid.
21. Ibid.
22. Ibid.
23. Ibid.
24. Ibid.
25. Ibid.
26. Ibid., 13 September 1951.
27. Ibid., 16 September 1951.
28. Ibid.
29. Ben-Gurion Research Center Archives, minutes of meetings, meeting of ministers-designate, 7 October 1951; Ben-Gurion Research Center Archives, correspondence, Ben-Gurion to Pinkus, 2 December 1951.
30. Ibid.
31. Israel Labour Party Archives, meeting of Mapai's political committee, 24 September 1952.
32. Ben-Gurion Research Center Archives, correspondence, Ben-Gurion to Rosen, 14 November 1952.
33. The General Zionist ministers resigned from the government after red flags were waved and the Internationale was sung in the schools on 1 May.
34. Israel Labour Party Archives, meeting of Mapai's political committee, 25 May 1953.
35. Ibid.
36. Ibid.
37. Ibid.
38. Ibid.
39. Ben-Gurion Research Center Archives, Ben-Gurion to Gershon Namir, 11 January 1954.
40. Ibid., Ben-Gurion to Mordechai Nesiyahu, 1 February 1954.
41. Ibid., Ben-Gurion to Gabriel Rakach, 1 February 1954.
42. Ibid., Ben-Gurion to Ben-Zvi and his wife, 3 September 1954.
43. Ibid., Ben-Gurion to Dr L. Bernstein, 23 December 1953.
44. Ibid.
45. Ibid., C. Levinsohn to Ben-Gurion, 25 February 1954.
46. Ibid., Gideon Idelman to Ben-Gurion, 8 February 1954.
47. Ibid., Ben-Gurion to Gideon Idelman, 11 February 1954.
48. Ibid.
49. Ibid., Mordechai Namir to Paula Ben-Gurion, 17 February 1954. Paula was Ben-Gurion's wife and Renana, his daughter.
50. Ibid., Moshe Baharav to Ben-Gurion, 25 January 1954.
51. Ibid., Ben-Gurion to Moshe Baharav, 1 February 1954.
52. Ibid.
53. Ibid., Moshe Baharav to Ben-Gurion, 5 February 1954.
54. Ibid., Ben-Gurion to Moshe Baharav, 10 February 1954.
55. Ibid., Moshe Baharav to Ben-Gurion, 11 February 1954.
56. Ibid., Ben-Gurion to Moshe Baharav, 20 February 1954.

57. Ibid., Ben-Gurion to Levi Sarid, 20 February 1954.
58. Israel Labour Party Archives, meeting of Mapai faction in the Knesset, 20 May 1957.
59. Ibid., 11 June 1957. The document was attached to Akiva Govrin's letter to Ben-Gurion dated 12 June 1957.
60. Ibid., meeting of Mapai central committee, 27 November 1958.
61. Ibid.
62. *Knesset Record,* 7 January 1959, pp. 797–805.
63. Israel Labour Party Archives, meeting of Mapai central committee, 6 September 1959.
64. Ibid.
65. Ibid., conferences, a one-day symposium at Beit Berl, 13 June 1964.
66. Ben-Gurion Research Center Archives, minutes of meetings, Ben-Gurion's meeting with leaders of the Progressive party, 29 December 1957.

4 Investigation of the Government by the Knesset

One of the traditional roles of a parliament is to investigate the activity of the government and the administration. A parliamentary investigation, unlike a criminal investigation conducted by the police and the legal authorities, is a public inquiry into the government's activity and its policies. Several basic assumptions suggest that a parliament is an almost ideal body to conduct an investigation, and it is not by chance that investigation is one of the major activities of one of the most powerful legislatures in the world, the US Congress in both its houses.

The first basic assumption is that there is a vital need to investigate certain public matters. The second is that a body cannot investigate itself. The third is that the investigating body should not be dependent on the investigated body, and it is desirable for the former to have a higher status than the latter. A fourth basic assumption is that in order for the conclusions of the investigation to carry greater weight in the public eye, the investigating body should be distinctly political in its nature. While an investigative body that is not political may very well arrive at the facts, due to its character, it is likely to avoid raising the conclusions that stem from its investigation. When these four assumptions are taken into account, the parliamentary arena is the most appropriate one for an investigation.

A parliament is likely to avail itself of the assistance of various authorities, for example the State Comptroller, in regard to the technical aspects of the investigation. The administration can be investigated by the State Comptroller, but a governmental policy investigation must be carried out by a political body capable of considering its implications and arriving at conclusions. Overly strict party discipline may impair the parliament's ability to investigate, and particularly to arrive at conclusions, since supporters of the government are liable to try and protect it, while its opponents will tend to be excessively critical. The US Congress can properly fulfill its investigative function because of the low level of party discipline in that body. When the parliament is perceived as a body lacking in autonomy, whose major function is to give the government backing, there is very little chance that it will fulfill its investigative role properly.

Ben-Gurion did not conceive of the Knesset as a body empowered to investigate the activity of the government, the administration and the government's policies. He prevented the Knesset from becoming an investigative body and did his best to hamper this aspect of its work. He tried to curtail investigation in general and parliamentary investigation in particular. In the few cases in which an investigation was unavoidable, the initiative for it was to come from him or from the government, but not from the Knesset. Members of the Knesset were sometimes included in an investigation, but Ben-Gurion endeavoured to prevent the Knesset from engaging in investigation as an independent institution. There was a turnabout when Ben-Gurion, as Prime Minister, appointed members of Knesset to governmental inquiry committees.

The discussion in this chapter is in two parts. It first discusses the subject of investigation by means of parliamentary questions, and then analyzes the issue of investigative committees.

PARLIAMENTARY QUESTIONS

A parliamentary question is one of the tools Knesset members have at their disposal in order to obtain information from ministers. The question may also have other purposes, but the receipt of information is the major one. Traditionally, this important parliamentary tool is regarded with disdain by the ministers. They tend to delay providing answers in the plenum and often the scope of the information given in these answers does not satisfy the questioners.[1] To a great extent, Ben-Gurion is responsible for the lowly status of the question in Israeli parliamentary life.

Until 1950, the ministers were not obliged to give answers in the plenum. A staff member of the Knesset secretariat would read out the question and the answer. Hence, it was impossible to ask the minister an additional question. The possibility of asking the minister, or his representative, an additional question was created only in 1950. In the first two years of the state, the ministers were entitled to decline to provide an answer. They were required to state the reason for their refusal, but it was not limited by the Rules of Procedure. Only later were certain limitations set on the ministers' right to refuse to reply to questions. The time period within which the ministers had to reply to questions gradually increased from 48 hours in 1948 to 49 days in 1961.

In September 1948, Sprinzak, chairman of the Provisional State Council, asked Sherf, the government secretary, to 'provide me with copies of the questions and the answers to them, *before* the Council meets'[2] (emphasis in the original). In November 1948, the Prime Minister responded to a question put by Weinstein regarding the military censor's deletion of part of a statement by Weizmann, the President of the Council, that Arab refugees ought to be returned to Israel: 'The Prime Minister does not feel there is any room for a question of this sort. It is not the government's affair to confirm or deny rumors.'[3] Not only did the person posing the question receive no information; he was also rebuked for having raised it in the first place. This reply is representative of Ben-Gurion's tendency to reject questions, in whole or in part. In December 1948, the Deputy Secretary of the Knesset wrote to the Prime Minister's Office, asking it to speed up the answers to the questions submitted by Mikunis of the Communists. This request was made following the receipt of a letter by Mikunis to the Knesset secretariat.[4]

In January 1949, Nir asked Ben-Gurion about the widespread use the government was making of the emergency regulations. He referred in particular to a regulation introduced by the Minister of the Interior levying a one-time tax on residents of Tel Aviv, which 'renders null and void the State Council's right to legislate, since in another three months, when the regulation comes to the Council for its approval, it will already be *ex post facto,* since the tax will have been collected in the meantime'.[5] The Prime Minister's reply was both evasive and general ('a one-time action is sometimes required for the sake of the wartime effort'),[6] and in no way did it really respond to the specific problem raised by Nir, nor to the principle involved.

On the very first occasion on which Ben-Gurion replied to questions as Prime Minister, during the term of the First Knesset, he gave brief and unsatisfactory answers. Pinkas asked him about keeping his promise to finance religious services, and Ben-Gurion replied that the issue was being discussed in the government and would soon be submitted to the Knesset.[7] To all the other questions, he also gave very brief replies. In April 1949, Ben-Gurion displayed his disdain for the Knesset and its members when responding to his very first question as Minister of Defence. To Haim Megurei-Cohen's (Herut) question as to whether the government knew about the military conscription of fathers of large families, Ben-Gurion response was terse and vague.[8]

That same day, Bar-Yehuda (Mapam) was critical, in the plenum, of the ministers' delay in replying to questions.[9] Nir, Deputy Speaker of the Knesset, responded in his report that the Speaker and his deputies had written to the Prime Minister and his ministers asking them to reply promptly to questions.[10] In May 1949, all 19 Knesset members from Mapam submitted a question to Ben-Gurion in which they complained that many questions were never answered. They added that the request made by the Knesset Speaker in the plenum to the ministers to reply within 48 hours was not complied with and asked what the Prime Minister planned to do to ensure that the ministers would act according to the law.[11] Ben-Gurion replied that he had conveyed their 'justified' request to his ministers and had asked them to expedite their replies to questions. He added, however, that there was a need to formulate a regulation in regard to questions, 'because in some cases, Knesset members submit questions about matters that should not be brought to the Knesset for reasons of security, or which do not constitute a question in the parliamentary sense of the word'.[12] That same month, Ben-Gurion persisted in his criticism of the manner in which questions were submitted. Writing to Riftin (Mapam) in response to a question, he stated that in posing the question, he had revealed details about the dismantlement of certain military brigades, remarking that 'it is regrettable that an attempt was made to circumvent the prohibition and to publish such information in an open Knesset meeting'.[13] Ben-Gurion's reply to Riftin's question was given in writing and contained no details that in any way could have been considered a reasonable answer to the query. He adopted this brusque approach not only towards Knesset members from the opposition. He also replied in writing to Yehiel Duvdevani, a Mapai MK by stating: 'For security reasons, I am not giving this question and the answer in the Knesset.'[14]

In June 1949, Ben-Gurion tried to teach Vilner of the Communist Party how to formulate a question: 'If the intent is not to slander but to clarify facts, MK Vilner would do well in future not to ask the government "why", but rather "whether" it is true that the government . . .'.[15] The same day he replied laconically to Rubin (Mapam), without taking the trouble to properly respond to his question: 'From time to time the Knesset and the committees will be given a review of the situation regarding employment and construction – and the Knesset can at any time discuss the matter.'[16]

Ben-Gurion's remarks in September 1949 at a forum of leaders of Mapai and senior army officers also reveal his disrespect for the institution of parliamentary questions. The forum was discussing the Prime Minister's proposal for a daily newspaper to be published by the army. Ben-Gurion attacked the existing newspapers, adding that he anticipated criticism of the new newspaper: 'No apology is necessary. I can already see what will happen: first there will be a question in the Knesset. I've already prepared my reply.'[17]

In December 1949, MK Yaacov Meridor (Herut) raised once again the subject of the delay in providing replies to questions by the Prime Minister himself. Meridor submitted a question to Ben-Gurion, in which he asked, 'What is the maximum amount of time you need to answer a question?'[18] Ben-Gurion replied in January 1950 with marked scorn: 'The government sees no benefit stemming from a discussion of the questions raised by the questioner.'[19] The same day, obviously reluctant to supply any information, he replied briefly to another MK from Herut, Shmuel Katz, about development in the Negev: 'Experts are examining several areas in the Negev. There would be no point in giving out any details at this time.'[20] Two days later, he gave a polemical reply to Meridor's question about the President's failure to visit the graves of fallen soldiers: 'These so-called questions do not reflect any respect, on the part of the questioner, for our soldiers who fell in wartime', and advised him to show more respect for the President and not to make the victims of war 'a target for his barbs'.[21] In several cases he wrote to those posing questions, that it was not at all desirable to present their questions to the Knesset. He often used the wording: 'It is best that your question not be brought to the Knesset',[22] or 'It is not desirable to raise these questions in the Knesset.'[23]

It was Ben-Gurion who instituted the inefficient system existing in the Knesset, according to which ministers do not provide relevant answers to the questions, but instead refer the questioners to other sources. In May 1950, he replied to a question by Sneh of the Communist Party (about the prohibition against the performance of a play by the Soviet author Simonov) after nearly six months, by referring him to another source. 'There is nothing to add to the reply by the Minister of Interior on this matter, given on 28 October 1949', was the complete wording of the reply.[24] The Prime Minister referred Sneh to the statement in this regard made by the Minister of the Interior more than a month before Sneh had submitted his question. Why could not Ben-Gurion have given this worthless reply, containing no more than 14 words, within a reasonable time period?

In June 1950, Ben-Aharon submitted a question to Ben-Gurion regarding the government's attitude towards the publishing house of the HaKibbutz HaMeuchad, which was controlled by the Achdut Havoda faction in Mapam, of which he was a member. Ben-Gurion did not reply in the Knesset, preferring to do so in a personal letter he sent Ben-Aharon in August 1950: 'I choose to answer you personally, because your letter contains "questions" that are polemical in nature and have nothing to do with the Knesset . . . and if you wish to adopt this means of argumentation, that is your affair.'[25] Ben-Aharon was concerned about the restrictions placed on Haim Guri's book, but Ben-Gurion's pretext for this was:

> Haim Guri revealed high-level military secrets, and this is a very serious matter since he came into possession of the information not as an author, but as a major in the IDF . . . to our great regret, a number of copies of this book have been circulating, and if the question is discussed in public, unquestionably spies of the Arab countries (who abound in this country) will do their utmost to obtain a copy of the book, and if your question is publicized, it will undoubtedly harm state security.[26]

In June 1950, Aharon Tsizling, who had served as a Mapam minister in the provisional government, made the claim, in a meeting of the House Committee, that four ministers, including Ben-Gurion, had given incorrect answers to questions. For example, the Prime Minister had undertaken, in replying to a question, to implement a certain action related to educational policy. However, despite his assurance, 'to this day, it has not been carried out. Are these proper parliamentary relations?'[27] Tsizling demanded that the House Committee rule on this matter. In addition, he complained about Ben-Gurion's reply to his question about the curfew in Jaffa. Ben-Gurion had denied that the incident Tsizling was asking about had taken place, and the former demanded that the House Committee 'decide here and now by a majority which of the sides is speaking the truth'.[28] In November 1951, Ben-Gurion interjected some harshly critical remarks about Knesset members into his reply to a question. In response to a routine question about the difficulties encountered by the police in helping farmers in cases of property theft, the irate Prime Minister argued that 'it's not easy to recruit the right kind of people because of the low wages and particularly because of the unfair attitude towards policemen held by some important segments of the population, journalists, and some Knesset members as well'.[29]

In May 1952, Ben-Gurion complained to the Speaker of the Knesset about a question posed by Ben-Aharon, commenting that

> Many Knesset members abuse the right of parliamentary questions, and add whole articles to a question that should be asked and given a reply in public, but at least they stick to the formalities, and end the article with a question. The Knesset regulations state: 'The parliamentary question must be brief and to the point and take the form of a question only, and be signed by the questioner.' I am not complaining in this case about the absence of brevity; many of those posing questions are guilty of that. But Mr Ben-Aharon's composition contained no question at all, and in no way resembled a parliamentary question. Does this not show disrespect to the Knesset and to a parliamentary institution which is so necessary in a democratic country – the institution of parliamentary questions? I don't know if there is an authorized institution in the Knesset to which one can apply in such a case, but first of all, I saw it as my duty to call the attention of the Speaker and his deputies to this strange behaviour, which, in my view, is an insult to the Knesset and its regulations.[30]

Again, in May 1953, the Prime Minister complained to the Deputy Speaker, Yaacov Klebanov, about the fact that when chairing the Knesset session, he had permitted Tsizling to ask the Minister of Interior a second additional question, after the minister had replied to the first additional question.[31] But Ben-Gurion did not let it go at that. The following day, he sent another letter to Klebanov, with copies to the Speaker and to the Chairman of the House Committee, stating how taken aback he was when after Tsizling had been permitted to ask two additional questions, Klebanov had allowed him to exploit a clause in the Rules of Procedure in order to make a personal statement.[32]

INQUIRY COMMITTEES 1948–50

In February 1949, Ben-Gurion had already set up the pattern of inquiry – not investigation – committees, meaning those established by him and made up of Knesset members. It was the Prime Minister who determined the composition of the committees, but he did not undertake in advance to adopt their conclusions. He did not even involve the government in this matter. Following a quarrel between the Minister of Justice, Rosen, and Judge Gad Frumkin, who Rosen did not want as a Chief Justice, Ben-Gurion sent a letter of appointment to three Knesset members (from parties in the coalition) informing them: 'You have the right to summon anyone, as you see fit, in order to clarify the matter. Your conclusions will be submitted to the Prime Minister.'[33] The three Knesset members were in effect appointed as the Prime Minister's assistants to help him arrive at a decision regarding Frumkin's appointment as a Chief Justice. Ben-Gurion did not even intend to involve the government in a discussion of the committee's conclusions. At a later stage, MK Ben-Zion Dinur of Mapai was also added to the committee as its chairman. Knesset members from the opposition were not included in the committee. According to Bondi, after the committee found that Frumkin was not suited for the position of Chief Justice, Ben-Gurion decided to dissolve the committee. Rosen wanted it to continue its inquiry, but

> Ben-Gurion saw no point in prying into Frumkin's past if he were no longer a candidate for the position of Chief Justice, and wanted to close the matter. To sweeten the bitter pill, Ben-Gurion promised Frumkin an honourary appointment to an appropriate government committee.[34]

The most important fact here is that the committee was not a parliamentary investigation committee, but an inquiry committee of the Prime Minister, who for this purpose was assisted by Knesset members.

The first parliamentary conflict over the investigative powers of the Knesset took place in 1949. Two Knesset members from Mapam,

Ben-Aharon and Riftin, sent a letter to Ben-Gurion in July, raising suspicions of embezzlement and mismanagement in the army and the Ministry of Defence. They advocated the establishment of a parliamentary investigation committee to look into the matter, but Ben-Gurion did not agree. Instead, he preferred to set up a special committee headed by a Chief Justice and three Knesset members. This committee was established in co-operation with the foreign affairs and security committee of the Knesset. Ben-Aharon and Riftin stated that they would take a position on the move initiated by Ben-Gurion after they knew what powers the committee had and who was serving on it.[35] Ben-Gurion chose Justice Yitzhak Olshan to chair the committee and Knesset members Haim Ben-Asher (Mapai), Harari (Progressives) and Klebanov (General Zionists) to serve on it.[36] He wrote to them:

> Your committee will determine the procedures for its inquiry. An order will be issued to all the army institutions and to all military personnel to provide the committee with all the information it requires. Your conclusions will be submitted to the Minister of Defence.[37]

The role of the opposition in the committee was minimal; Klebanov was the only member from an opposition party. Since the largest party in the opposition, Mapam, was not given any representation on the committee, despite the fact that its members had raised the issue in the first place, its representatives again entered a demand in the Knesset – after Ben-Gurion had published the composition of the committee – that a parliamentary investigation committee be appointed.[38] They made a point of stressing the difference between a parliamentary investigation committee established by the Knesset and an inquiry committee established by the government, whose members, even if some of them were Knesset members, are appointed by the Prime Minister. As a result, a parliamentary investigation committee would be ensured 'greater freedom, greater latitude and autonomy in its work'.[39] Ben-Gurion reproached the two Knesset members who had raised the matter for not having revealed the source of their information. Mapam's demand did not win a majority in the Knesset and the committee acted in the format determined by the Prime Minister.

Even before this debate in the Knesset, during which it was clear Mapam would demand the appointment of a parliamentary investigation committee, the Prime Minister took several steps to establish hard facts. About a week before the scheduled debate, he wrote urgently to the committee chairman, Olshan, instructing him to convene the committee immediately. He added that it would be best if the committee convened in Tel Aviv.[40] Two days before the Knesset debate he again wrote to Olshan, this time urging him to speed up the investigation, adding that even if one of the committee members were absent, there was no need to discontinue the committee's deliberations.[41]

The committee investigated the matter for nine months and heard scores of witnesses. Its report and work were secret. Ben-Gurion refused to reply in the Knesset to questions about the committee's progress in its work. One instance in which the matter was raised in the Knesset was in March 1950, when Bar-Yehuda of Mapam complained that Ben-Gurion was not reporting to the Knesset on the progress of the committee's investigation. He told the Knesset that in November 1949, MK Eliezer Preminger had asked Ben-Gurion when there would be results and had received no reply.

> Since the Minister of Defence did not answer his question, on 27 December, he turned to the Prime Minister and reminded him of his promise that the ministers would reply promptly. He asked the Prime Minister to press the Minister of Defence to give him a prompt reply. To this very day, the reply has not been received, after four and a half months, neither from the Minister of Defence nor the Prime Minister.[42]

The committee found that there were indeed cases of car theft. Nonetheless, when Olshan gave Ben-Gurion the committee's final report, the Prime Minister asked him whether the complaints of the two MKs who had raised the issue were intended to goad and attack Mapai.[43] Since it was not a parliamentary investigation committee, the committee's report was not discussed either in the plenum or in the foreign affairs and security committee.

Early in January 1950, Begin rose in the Knesset to demand that a parliamentary investigation committee be established regarding the fall of the Old City of Jerusalem during the War of Independence.[44] The Prime Minister's reply in the Knesset was evasive: 'There is not the shadow of a doubt that the Knesset is entitled to demand a report . . . and I will willingly tell these investigators things I have never revealed and would not hasten to state publicly.'[45] He was opposed to the establishment of a parliamentary investigation committee, and stated that Begin had no right to demand an inquiry, since he

> did not take part in the battle. At the moment, I have no complaints to make to him. Before the elections to the Knesset, an amnesty law was passed, and that law applies to Mr Begin, but I do not recognize his right to investigate and ask questions, and owing to the amnesty law, I will not ask him any personal questions.[46]

At the same time, Ben-Gurion appointed an inquiry committee to look into the conduct of the attorney, Gorali, in the Be'eri-Tubiansky affair. In the letter of appointment, he instructed the members of the committee to submit their recommendations to the Minister of Defence and the Minister of Justice.[47] Nir was appointed to head the committee and appointed as its members were Bar-Rav-Hai (Mapai) and an officer with the rank of lieutenant colonel. This mix of Knesset members and an IDF officer was quite unusual. In the appointment letter, the Prime Minister addressed the two Knesset members as 'Mister' rather than by their parliamentary titles. In fact, Nir refused to chair the committee, because 'the law recognizes only investigation committees and not inquiry committees',[48] and because as long as the affair was being tried in the court, there was no room for a public inquiry. Nir, an experienced and sophisticated parliamentarian, was well aware of the Knesset's interests, and consequently was not prepared to serve on an *engagé* committee set up by the Prime Minister.

AN INVESTIGATION OF EDUCATION IN THE IMMIGRANT CAMPS

The crisis relating to education in the immigrant camps gave rise to harsh accusations of anti-religious coercion. When the need to investigate the matter came up at the beginning of 1950, Ben-Gurion decided to establish an inquiry committee in the usual format of a judge and several Knesset members. But now for the first time, he used the term 'investigation committee' instead of 'inquiry committee'. Education Minister Shazar accused the Prime Minister – at a meeting of the Mapai directorate in the Knesset – of not having made the government a party to his decision regarding the committee:

> This committee came out of the clear blue sky. Ben-Gurion said that any five people picked randomly off the street could sit on this committee to investigate the matter. He suggested the committee on his own, without consulting the government.[49]

In Aranne's view the committee was 'absurd', because it was 'composed of bourgeois–religious elements',[50] and Guri called the committee's composition a 'pogrom'.[51] The four Knesset members that Ben-Gurion appointed to the committee were Ben-Zvi (Mapai), Abraham Almaliach (Sephardim) and two representatives of the United Religious Front, Kalman Kahave and Haim Avraham Shag. No seats on the committee were assigned to members of the opposition. Its chairman was Justice Gad Frumkin.

Two days later, a leading forum of Mapai discussed the matter. Aranne, Lavon, Guri and Deborah Netzer criticized the committee's composition. Netzer was of the opinion that the two religious members would behave according to the dictates of their party and added: 'I don't know if the Sephardic committee member has to be Almaliach, or could be one of ours.'[52] The Prime Minister rejected this criticism: 'This is not a political committee; it is an investigation committee. All five people on the committee, as far as I know them, are committed to finding out the truth . . . the committee was charged with clarifying facts, not with setting policy.'[53] In February 1950, Ben-Zvi announced in the Knesset that the committee was preparing to conclude its investigation within a week, and would submit its report in two week's time.[54] In March 1950, a stormy debate ensued in the Knesset centring on the investigation committee. Representatives of Mapam, who, as noted, did not participate on the committee, called it 'your family investigation committee', adding, 'This is an appeasement committee, not an investigation committee!'[55]

The directorate of the Mapai faction discussed the investigation committee's report in June 1950. Shazar stated: 'The blame seems to fall upon the government, that is about the gist of the conclusions, and we cannot let that go by without reacting.'[56] Guri insisted that the fact that Dinur had been prevented from serving on the committee, due to Ben-Gurion's objection, should not be publicized.[57] Ben-Gurion was cutting in his criticism of the committee's report. Upon reading it, he said,

> I was greatly surprised by many things. There is hearsay testimony. There is a prejudicial attitude towards witnesses of one

> type, and the opposite attitude towards witnesses of another type, and there is a huge gap between the report and the conclusions. For this reason, the government has not accepted the report, but only the conclusions, and even those – only in general – because the committee exceeded the bounds of its authority.[58]

The report's bitter fate attests to the danger existing in any government committee, since when all is said and done, it is the government that decides whether or not to accept all or part of the report and the conclusions. From the standpoint of the Knesset's status, participation of its members on a committee is likely to have positive consequences if the report and the conclusions are adopted by the government. However, if the government comes to a different conclusion, that can be damaging to the prestige of the Knesset. The most important point is that in this format, the Knesset has no standing as an institution. In January 1951, MK Ari Jabotinsky (Herut) was critical of the format of the committees: 'In my view, a government committee on which Knesset members serve also blurs the lines between the different domains.'[59] In February 1951, one of the committee members, Ben-Zvi, announced in a meeting of the Mapai faction that the committee did not act 'on behalf of the Knesset, but on behalf of the government, and the committee no longer exists, so no one can speak in its name'.[60]

THE INVESTIGATION OF THE BLACK MARKET

In Chapter 2, dealing with committees, brief mention was made of the investigation of the black market by the economics committee. In the summer of 1950, the opposition called for the establishment of a parliamentary investigation committee on the black market. Mapai voted against this motion and it was defeated in the vote.[61] Bahir's remark in this regard at a meeting of the Mapai faction was that an investigation was needed, but that 'we need to know where to investigate. That calls for consultation with the government. We ought to call in a number of members from the economic institutions of the Histadrut and clarify the matter with them'.[62] Sprinzak and Akiva Govrin, on the other hand, were in favour of a parliamentary investigation.[63] The directorate of the faction decided that the matter would be discussed with the ministers, and that afterwards an investigation committee would be established with Aranne's help.[64]

A majority in the Knesset decided on a compromise between the opposition's desire to establish an independent parliamentary investigation committee and the government's desire not to investigate the matter at all. It would conduct an investigation, not in the form of a parliamentary investigation committee, but by empowering one of the permanent committees – the economics committee – to investigate the matter. It then turned out that this committee could not carry out this task because it lacked the authority to do so. The government, which was not enthusiastic about the conduct of an investigation, was supposed to have vested the necessary powers in the committee, as was the case on previous occasions. MK Landau of Herut reacted by proposing a private bill dealing with the powers of a parliamentary investigation committee. It was intended to do away with the situation that existed then, according to which such a committee was 'at the mercy of the government, which is entitled to grant or not to grant it the powers it needs to fulfill its function'.[65] According to his proposal, the Knesset, not the government, would grant these powers. Witnesses would be compelled to appear before the committee, which would be authorized to question them, to take their testimony, to swear them in, and demand that they produce documents. The government was opposed to the bill, which indeed was defeated in the vote. However, Minister of Justice Rosen promised that the government would grant this committee all the powers it required.[66] Although the Knesset did not adopt Landau's bill, in 1958, 'Basic Law: The Knesset' stated that the powers of a parliamentary investigation committee would be determined by the Knesset whenever it decided to establish such a committee. This constituted a certain improvement over the situation that existed in the first decade of the state's existence.

After the committee investigated the black market, it held several meetings. Ben-Gurion received the minutes of these meetings, and at the end of September he met with the Minister of Rationing and Supply, Dov Joseph, with the chairman of the committee, Chushi of Mapai, and the Police Commissioner and his deputy. The Prime Minister questioned Chushi about what had taken place in the committee's meetings, and Chushi gave him information about the committee members who were 'troublemakers'. Ben-Gurion wanted to know whether the committee had the authority to take testimony under oath. Chushi doubted that it did. The Prime Minister summed up the discussion by expressing his virulent objection to the very fact that the Knesset was investigating the matter.[67] A few days later, he summoned the heads of the Histadrut for a consultation on the matter.[68] He was alarmed by the anticipated conclusions of the parliamentary committee, and reacted by establishing a special ministerial committee to combat the black market.

THE JALAMI INVESTIGATION

The only instance, during Ben-Gurion's premiership, in which a parliamentary investigation committee acted in complete separation from the permanent committees of the Knesset was in 1951, regarding the conduct of the police towards the detainees of the 'Brit Kanna'im' ('Covenant of Zealots') underground. This religious underground group, whose centre was in Jerusalem, resorted to violence, and was also reported to be plotting to attack the Knesset.[69] Members of the underground were caught and placed in detention in the Jalami camp. A short time later, some accusations were made asserting that several of the detainees had been humiliated and mistreated.

During that same period, in the spring of 1951, Mapai did not have a coalitional majority and hence was unable to prevent the Knesset's intervention in this matter. At first, the government refused to accept the Knesset's decision to release the detainees from administrative arrest, arguing that it had no authority to take such a decision.[70] However, Mapai did not have enough leverage in the Knesset to rebuff the demands of the religious parties to establish a parliamentary committee to investigate the affair. The entire opposition was united in supporting the religious parties' claim, and it was clear that if Mapai stuck to its adamant position, it would be defeated in a vote in the plenum. At that time, Ben-Gurion was abroad and was being replaced by the Minister of Foreign Affairs, Sharett. Immediately before Mapai's anticipated defeat, the Minister of Police announced that the government supported the establishment of a parliamentary investigation committee.[71] That was unquestionably a wise move, since the government, as a result, averted public defeat.

After the Knesset's decision to establish the parliamentary committee, an inter-party struggle ensued over the allocation of seats on the committee among the various parties.[72] The balance of power between the coalition and the opposition was reflected in the committee's composition. The four opposition parties – Mapam, Herut, General Zionists and the United Religious Front – were each given a seat on the committee, and only three places were alloted to the coalition – two to Mapai and one to the Progressives. No less important was the appointment of a representative of one of the opposition parties – Chanah Lamdan of Mapam – as chairman of the committee.

In the initial stage of the committee's work, it encountered difficulties in conducting the investigation. It complained to the House Committee that after it had decided to issue a writ of habeas corpus in order to hear the testimony of the detainees, the Attorney General – who expressed the government's position – showed a biased and unfair attitude towards the committee by pressing the judge hearing the committee's motion to reject it. Bar-Yehuda (Mapam) argued that the government's conduct in relation to the investigation committee was 'unjust'.[73] Most of the committee's meetings were held in the Tel Aviv District Court. Bader, a representative of Herut on the committee, remarked that 'We sat there on the dais like judges hearing one witness after another. Police officers testified under oath, and the detainees (who had been released in the meantime) by a sworn statement.'[74] Bader added in relation to the questioning of the Police Commissioner that 'Smiling, and with great courtesy, I got him to admit that the purpose of holding the detainees in Jalami was to interrogate them about their offenses.'[75] Bader was convinced that the committee had succeeded in fulfilling its task and added drolly: 'They say that after the Jamali investigation, the leaders of Mapai went to the cemetery to swear on Berl Katznelson's grave that there would never, ever be another parliamentary investigation committee!'[76]

A week before the elections to the Second Knesset, Mapai's political committee discussed the investigation committee and their fear that the matter would be brought up in the plenum prior to the elections. David Hacohen, one of Mapai's representatives on the committee, took the position that it would be better to postpone publishing the committee's report and conclusions until after the elections: 'We have the feeling it would be best to postpone it until after the elections . . . Should we try to sabotage it, and by no means allow the Knesset to convene before the elections? We need to get Sprinzak's help.'[77] Sprinzak reassured the members of the political committee by telling them that the Knesset would not convene in the week remaining until the elections. Aranne suggested that the publication of the investigation committee's report be postponed, and Ben-Gurion, who had a very low opinion of the Knesset, actually took a different view: 'There is no danger if the Knesset should convene. No one will pay attention. They'll know it's just some election slander.'[78] In the end, the committee did not complete its work prior to the elections.

The committee published its report three days after the elections; however, the government only reacted four months later. The delay in its reaction was further evidence of its contempt for the Knesset and the investigation committee. Since it was the government that had vested the committee with investigative powers, the committee's report was dependent on the government's position. In November 1951, Mapam and the General Zionists, speaking in the plenum, deplored the fact that the government, six months after the committee's appointment and more than three months since the publication of its report, had not yet seen fit to react to it.[79] Ben-Gurion was in favour of giving the government a two-week extension. In this discussion, the Prime Minister let the cat out of the bag. He now argued that although the committee members had unanimously adopted the report, it was impossible to argue that its conclusions had been unanimously accepted.

> The report was not unanimously accepted by the committee members, and they know it. One of the members whose name was added to the report without his knowledge, did not agree to the conclusions nor did he sign the report, and that was David Hacohen.[80]

Further on in his speech, he hinted that the government might not adopt the report at all: 'There is no law, neither in the State of Israel nor in any other country, as far as I know, that the report of a committee, even of a parliamentary committee, is binding on the government.'[81]

Prior to the parliamentary debate, in which the government was supposed to reveal its position on the report, Ben-Gurion telegraphed to Sharett who was in Paris with Hacohen: 'Next week, a debate about Jalami will be held in the Knesset. In my view, it is imperative that Hacohen be in the Knesset then.'[82] That was what the Prime Minister wanted, because he knew that Hacohen could help strengthen his claim that the report was not unanimously accepted. Early in December 1951, the debate on the report was finally held in the plenum. Hacohen, who had been called back urgently from

Paris, claimed that on the day the report was submitted to the Speaker of the Knesset he was ill and was unable to sign it. A day earlier, he had asked his colleague in the faction, Herzl Berger, to represent him at the meeting. Berger, according to Hacohen, signed the report without his authorization. Hacohen stated that he had written to the Speaker of the Knesset and to the chairman of the committee, that he could not approve his signature on the report. He claimed that his comments were not taken into account when the report was written, and expressed 'his total disagreement with the committee's report'.[83] He stated his satisfaction with the announcement made by the government, that there had not been complete agreement with the committee's report, and went even further by asserting that it would have been fitting to include on the investigation committee people who were not members of Knesset.[84] Berger raised counter-arguments, stating that when he signed the report in Hacohen's name, he, like all the other committee members, had been under 'the distinct impression that I was doing so not arbitrarily but because I was entitled to',[85] especially since on the same day, before signing the report, he had spoken on the phone with Hacohen and so had the committee chairman. It is possible that the whole affair in connection with Hacohen was a trick planned in advance, probably by Ben-Gurion, to avoid the impression that the committee had unanimously adopted the report. Suspicion falls on Ben-Gurion because he was the one who had insisted in the Knesset that the report had not been unanimous, and had taken the trouble to bring Hacohen back from Paris to attend the parliamentary debate.

Bader, the moving spirit behind the committee, was deeply disappointed by the Hacohen affair:

> Since the two committee members who spoke with Hacohen – one was even a member of his party – told us we could sign the minutes in his name, I had no doubts whatsoever about this procedure . . . If I had known that the report I was signing was not unanimously adopted, I would have demanded more far-reaching conclusions.[86]

Since the opposition had a majority on the committee, Bader would probably have had no difficulty achieving his aim. His willingness to reach a compromise with representatives of the coalition stemmed from his understanding that the report would carry greater weight if it were adopted unanimously. If the whole Hacohen affair was really a trick thought up by the leaders of Mapai – perhaps even by Ben-Gurion – it succeeded all too well, and the representatives of the opposition on the committee were taken in by it.

More important than the Hacohen affair was the position taken by the government in regard to the committee's report. While the committee placed the responsibility for the ill-treatment of the detainees not only on the local officers, but on the police headquarters as well, the government decided not to assign any responsibility to the latter. This amounted to a slap in the face to the committee by the government, although it did not reject the report in its entirety. The committee recommended that the government draw appropriate conclusions regarding reforms in the police and inform the Knesset of them. The government, on the other hand, merely decided that the Minister of Police would submit a report to the interior affairs committee of the Knesset after the police looked into the matter and took the required steps. It is strange, indeed, that the police headquarters, which was found responsible for what occurred in the detention camp, was authorized by the government to examine and take steps.

The opposition protested against the government's conclusions regarding the report. Sapir (General Zionists) argued that 'The government's conclusions are completely inconsistent with the conclusions of the investigation committee.'[87] Peri's reaction (Mapam) was even more trenchant. He asserted that the committee had charged the government with the task of drawing conclusions, not simply discussing the matter, and added: 'The government's announcement is tantamount to an attempt to place the government, the executive branch, above the Knesset.'[88] The chairman of the committee, Lamdan, was also extremely critical of the government's response.[89] The Minister of Police, on the other hand, did not hesitate to openly find fault with the work of the committee: 'We therefore should investigate to see whether everything was done properly, and whether the committee adhered to the most elementary principles in taking testimony and questioning witnesses, and adopted an approach free of any partisan bias.'[90] In the end, the Knesset accepted the government's announcement in relation to the report with a majority of 52 against 37.[91]

Even though the final outcome amounted to a parliamentary defeat, the parliamentary investigation committee in the matter of the Jalami detainees marked the height of the Knesset's success, one that was never repeated, neither in Ben-Gurion's time nor in later periods. The affair attests to the Knesset's ability and the desire of its members to investigate and supervise the administration. Most important of all is the fact that representatives of the opposition and of the coalition on the committee were able to reach common conclusions – on nearly all the topics. This proves that a parliamentary institution can effectively carry out the task of investigation, despite the fact that its members belong to rival parties.

FURTHER INSTANCES OF DISDAIN FOR THE KNESSET'S INVESTIGATIVE FUNCTION

After the Jalami investigation drew to a close and its echoes died down, Ben-Gurion continued to deride the investigative function of the Knesset. His opposition to a public investigation spilled over from the parliamentary level and applied to his disdain for investigation on other levels as well. After the comptroller of the Jewish Agency published an extremely critical report, in 1952, about the working practices and management of the Agency, Ben-Gurion reacted with unrestrained anger in the Knesset: 'I didn't read this report by the person who was the comptroller of the Agency, nor will I read it.'[92] He defended his new Minister of the Treasury, Levi Eshkol, who had been the Agency's treasurer during the period which was the object of harsh criticism in the Comptroller's report: 'I have no need to read his report to know who Eshkol is.'[93]

In June 1952, he reverted to the practice of appointing committees on behalf of the government on which Knesset members served along with representatives of other bodies. He appointed an inquiry committee on youth communities and instructed it to complete its work within a month and submit its conclusions to the government. Four members – all from Mapai – out of a total of 12, were Knesset members. The others represented various government ministries, the IDF and the teachers' union.[94]

In July 1952, Mapam called for the establishment of a parliamentary investigation committee on the closure of the Israeli Communist Party's newspaper for a week.[95] This time, the Prime Minister did not even see fit to react to the demand in the Knesset and simply ignored it. After two Israeli Arabs were killed in a military incident in 1952, Ben-Gurion preferred to appoint an investigation committee on his own. It was composed of representatives of the IDF, the Ministry of Defence and the Ministry of Justice. Even Rosen criticized him for this procedure.[96] In a conversation held in September

1952 between Ben-Gurion and Peretz Bernstein, a leader of the General Zionists, about his party joining the coalition, Bernstein complained that when he had been chairman of a committee that was supposed to investigate a matter connected with imports, the witnesses were afraid to appear before it, and the government ministries refused to provide the committee with the documents it needed. The Prime Minister evaded the issue and, without replying to Bernstein, changed the subject.[97]

In August 1960, Herut and the General Zionists called for an investigation into the fall of the Old City of Jerusalem during the War of Independence. Their demand was for the establishment of a parliamentary investigation committee following the publication of a book by Dov Joseph, who had been the military governor of the city during the war. Ben-Gurion totally rejected their demand. He argued that any parliamentary committee, even the foreign affairs and security committee, was in essence a partisan committee that cannot write 'objective history'. He related to an investigation as the writing of history and added that

> This committee which is proposed here would be good for partisan backbiting. It will be a place for everyone who wants to prove that he is a greater patriot than all the others . . . The Knesset was created in order to pass legislation, to set policy, and not to write history. This is something that it was definitely not called upon to do, nor was it elected for that purpose. With all due respect to the Knesset – and precisely because I have a great deal of respect for the Knesset as a sovereign institution in the country – I tell you it is not capable of doing this, and this task should be left to future historians who will write the history of past times.[98]

The argument that parliamentary investigation amounts to historical research is truly amazing. The contention that representatives of political parties cannot conduct a fair investigation became a fundamental notion in Israel's political history, and since then has been used by various governments in order to rebuff attempts to assign the Knesset investigative roles.

Ben-Gurion gave similar reasons for his opposition to the acceptance of the conclusions of the Committee of Seven – the ministerial committee that investigated the 'mishap' or Lavon Affair. He then expressed the view that 'You can never get to the truth when people who are prejudiced discuss a problem on the basis of narrow political interests.'[99] Not only did he refuse to accept the conclusions of the ministerial committee; but as already noted in the chapter on Knesset committees, he also was unwilling to make the Knesset a party to the investigation and was in favour of a 'judicial investigation'. Such an investigation, however, is more appropriate in cases of criminal suspicions, while a parliamentary investigation is not intended mainly for such cases, but primarily for cases that fall within the grey area between policy mismanagement and criminal activities. A 'judicial investigation' is not meant to deal with this type of issue.

Regarding a subsidiary issue of the Lavon Affair, Ben-Gurion, after he had resigned from the government, demanded that the Minister of Justice establish a non-parliamentary investigation committee to look into the functioning of the government in 1960 in the matter of the Committee of Seven. Begin regarded this demand as contempt of the Knesset and termed it 'amazing . . . strange, anti-parliamentary, anti-legal'.[100] He believed the body that should supervise the government, check its decisions and decide on their nature, was the Knesset, and not a non-parliamentary investigation committee.[101] It is interesting that Ben-Gurion, even after he had left the government, continued to forcefully demand an investigation on this subject, but even then, when he no longer headed the executive branch, he was unwilling to have the Knesset play a role in the investigation. The Speaker of the Knesset, Kadish Luz, referred to this point in his speech before the Mapai convention in February 1965. 'There is another type of investigation committee – the parliamentary investigation committee – but that is appointed by the Knesset. I am, however, certain that Comrade Ben-Gurion was not referring to that type.'[102]

In February 1963, an acrimonious argument took place in the plenum between Ben-Gurion and Yaacov Meridor (Herut) on the establishment of parliamentary investigation committees.[103] Meridor accused Ben-Gurion of having blocked the Knesset's every move since the establishment of the state:

> Mr Prime Minister, from the establishment of the state, there has been a clear trend on your part – and it continues to this very day – of clipping the Knesset's wings. If you can recall one instance in which you agreed – after scandals that broke out in the country, after catastrophes that occurred – to the establishment of a parliamentary investigation committee, then you really

> deserve a medal. For some reason, you are always wary of parliamentary investigation committees, for some reason, in every instance, minor as well as major, an investigation committee is appointed, a ministerial committee, an inter-ministerial committee – but in any case, a committee composed of people belonging to the executive branch, never one set up by the Knesset, by the parliament. And you always say: Take an example from England, take an example from America. In England after every catastrophe, after every case that arouses waves of negative public criticism, the government initiates the establishment of a parliamentary investigation committee. But not so in this country . . . You are not inclined to give the Knesset, the parliament, what it deserves and let it be what it ought to be. And if there is, to any extent, a diminution of the Knesset's power, I believe you and your ministry are the source. From this standpoint, I would suggest that you rethink this subject.[104]

Ben-Gurion replied derisively, stating that the responsibility for the failure to establish parliamentary investigation committees did not lie with him, since the law empowers the plenum of the Knesset to do so:

> Member of Knesset Meridor complained to me about why I don't establish parliamentary investigation committees. In England, in fact, that is a function of the government. The government appoints parliamentary committees. There they call them royal committees, not parliamentary committees. In our country, the Knesset establishes parliamentary committees. If the Knesset does not want to, MK Meridor, it does not appoint any. It does not want to follow your advice. Why is it obliged to follow your advice? It is true that you belong to a party that was elected to power by God, but the Knesset has the right to decide as it wishes. If it does not choose to do so, it does not. Should I impose my will on the Knesset? Do you want to invest me with such a power? With such authority?[105]

In his reply, the Prime Minister totally ignored the fact that he had been opposed in principle to granting the Knesset an investigative function, and placed all the responsibility upon the majority in the Knesset, which he had created and led, and which he had tried so hard to compel to vote in a uniform and united manner.

NOTES

1. Giora Goldberg, 'The Parliamentary Opposition in Israel (1965–1977)', Jerusalem: The Hebrew University, Ph.D. dissertation, 1980 (Hebrew), pp. 93–122.
2. State Archives, 20/4, Sprinzak to Sherf, 15 September 1948.
3. Provisional State Council, 25 November 1948, p. 5.
4. State Archives, Ibid., Tzidon to Prime Minister's Office, 1 December 1948.
5. Provisional State Council, 6 January 1949, p. 5.
6. Ibid.
7. *Knesset Record,* 28 March 1949, p. 238.
8. Ibid., 11 April 1949, p. 333.
9. Ibid., p. 334.
10. Ibid.
11. Ibid., 16 May 1949, p. 503.
12. Ben-Gurion Research Center Archives, correspondence, Ben-Gurion to members of the Mapam faction, 12 May 1949.
13. Ibid., Ben-Gurion to Riftin, 23 May 1949.
14. Ibid., Ben-Gurion to Duvdevani, 5 June 1949.
15. Ibid., Ben-Gurion to Vilner, 29 June 1949.
16. Ibid., Ben-Gurion to Rubin, 29 June 1949.
17. Ibid., minutes of meetings, meeting between Ben-Gurion and Mapai leaders and army officers about the publication of a daily newspaper for the IDF, 19 September 1949.
18. Ibid., correspondence, Ben-Gurion to Meridor, 26 December 1949.
19. Ibid., Ben-Gurion to Meridor, 9 January 1950.
20. Ibid., Ben-Gurion to Katz, 9 January 1950.
21. Ibid., Ben-Gurion to Meridor, 11 January 1950.
22. Ibid., Ben-Gurion to Meridor, 23 May 1950.
23. Ibid., Ben-Gurion to Moshe Una, 17 May 1950.
24. *Knesset Record,* 23 May 1950, p. 1,444.
25. Ibid., Ben-Gurion Research Center Archives, correspondence, Ben-Gurion to Ben-Aharon, 8 August 1950.
26. Ibid.
27. State Archives, minutes of meeting of the House Committee, 13 June 1950.
28. Ibid.
29. *Knesset Record,* 20 November 1951, p. 419.
30. Ben-Gurion Research Center Archives, correspondence, Ben-Gurion to the Speaker of the Knesset and his deputies, 21 May 1952.
31. Ibid., Ben-Gurion to Klebanov, 10 May 1953.
32. Ibid., Ben-Gurion to Klebanov, 11 May 1953.
33. Ibid., Ben-Gurion to Berlin, Ben-Zvi and Abraham Granowsky, 8 February 1949.
34. Ruth Bondi, *Felix* (Hebrew), Tel Aviv: Zmora-Bitan, 1990, p. 422.
35. *Davar,* 2 September 1949.
36. Ben-Gurion Research Center Archives, correspondence, Ben-Gurion to Aranne, 27 July 1949.
37. Ibid., Ben-Gurion to members of the inquiry committee, 18 August 1949.
38. *Knesset Record,* 1 September 1949, pp. 1,510–12.
39. Ibid., p. 1,510.
40. Ben-Gurion Research Center Archives, correspondence, Ben-Gurion to Olshan, 24 August 1949.
41. Ibid., Ben-Gurion to Olshan, 30 August 1949.
42. *Knesset Record,* 21 March 1950, p. 1,092.
43. Yizhak Olshan, *Controversy and Contention* (Hebrew), Jerusalem and Tel-Aviv: Schoken, 1978, p. 226.
44. *Knesset Record,* 2 January 1950, p. 385.

45. Ibid., p. 436.
46. Ibid.
47. Ben-Gurion Research Center Archives, correspondence, Ben-Gurion to members of the inquiry committee, 2 January 1950. On the affair centring on Captain Meir Tubiansky's execution, see Zeev Segal, *Israeli Democracy* (Hebrew), Tel Aviv: The Ministry of Defence, 1988, pp. 167–8.
48. Ben-Gurion Research Center Archives, correspondence, Nir to Ben-Gurion, 10 January 1950.
49. Israel Labour Party archives, minutes of meeting of Mapai faction directorate in the Knesset, 24 January 1950.
50. Ibid.
51. Ibid.
52. Ibid., minutes of meeting of Mapai directorate and Mapai faction in the Knesset, 26 January 1950.
53. Ibid.
54. *Knesset Record*, 28 February 1950, p. 894.
55. Ibid., 14 March 1950, pp. 1,011–12.
56. Israel Labour Party archives, minutes of meeting of Mapai faction directorate in the Knesset, 6 June 1950.
57. Ibid.
58. Ben-Gurion Research Center Archives, correspondence, Ben-Gurion to Yaacov Shapira, 7 July 1950.
59. State Archives, minutes of meeting of constitution, law and justice committee, 24 January 1951.
60. Israel Labour Party Archives, minutes of meeting of Mapai faction in the Knesset, 7 February 1951.
61. Ibid., minutes of meeting of Mapai faction directorate in the Knesset, 23 July 1950.
62. Ibid.
63. Ibid.
64. Ibid.
65. *Knesset Record*, 31 July 1950, p. 2,361.
66. Ibid., p. 2,362.
67. Ben-Gurion Research Center Archives, minutes of meetings, 27 September 1950, consultation about ways to combat the black market.
68. Ibid., 1 October 1950, consultation with heads of the Histadrut sector about the black market.
69. Bader, *The Knesset and I*, p. 45; Avram Daskal, 'The Activities of the Extra-Parliamentary Opposition during the First Years of the State: Brit Kanna'im and Malkhut Yisrael', MA thesis (Hebrew), Ramat Gan: Bar-Ilan University, Department of Political Studies, 1990.
70. State Archives, minutes of meeting of the House Committee, 23 May 1951.
71. *Knesset Record*, 28 May 1951, p. 1,841.
72. State Archives, Ibid., 4 June 1951.
73. Ibid., 26 June 1951.
74. Bader, *The Knesset and I*, p. 46.
75. Ibid., p. 47.
76. Ibid.
77. Israel Labour Party archives, meeting of the political committee of Mapai, 22 July 1951.
78. Ibid.
79. *Knesset Record*, 14 November 1951, p. 389–91.
80. Ibid., p. 390.
81. Ibid.
82. Ben-Gurion Research Center Archives, correspondence, Ben-Gurion to Sharett, 18 November 1951.
83. *Knesset Record*, 4 December 1951, p. 546.

84. Ibid., p. 547.
85. Ibid., p. 552.
86. Ibid., 10 December 1951, p. 581.
87. Ibid., 4 December 1951, p. 542.
88. Ibid., p. 544.
89. Ibid., 10 December 1951, pp. 571–3.
90. Ibid., p. 577.
91. Ibid.
92. Ibid., 25 June 1952, p. 2,450.
93. Ibid.
94. Ben-Gurion Research Center Archives, correspondence, Ben-Gurion to members of the inquiry committee, June 1952.
95. *Knesset Record*, 8 July 1952, pp. 2,564–7.
96. *Davar*, 29 August 1952.
97. Ben-Gurion Research Center Archives, minutes of meetings, meeting between Ben-Gurion and Bernstein, 30 September 1952.
98. *Knesset Record*, 10 August 1960, p. 2,165.
99. Ibid., 16 November 1960, p. 240.
100. Ibid., 4 November 1964, p. 263.
101. Ibid.
102. Israel Labour Party archives, Mapai convention, 18 February 1964.
103. *Knesset Record*, 25 February 1963, pp. 1,237–8; 26 February 1963, p. 1,270.
104. Ibid., 25 February 1963, pp. 1,237–8.
105. Ibid., 26 February 1963, p. 1,270.

5 Symbolic Competition

In a parliamentary system, the parliament's supremacy over the government also has a symbolic dimension. Since the source of sovereignty resides in the parliament, symbolically it stands above the government. One of the ways that Ben-Gurion impinged upon the status of the Knesset was in the symbolic realm. He relegated it to the sidelines and attempted to pare down its symbolic superiority. Probably one of the reasons, although certainly not the most important, for his objection to the framing of a constitution was his reluctance to allow the Knesset, or the Constituent Assembly, to perform this task rather than him. Since a constitution carries great symbolic importance, he wanted to prevent the Knesset from doing anything that would leave a strong imprint on Israeli society and might outweigh another symbolic act – the declaration of independence, which, in his view, was identified with him and attributed to him.[1]

One indication of how aware Ben-Gurion was of the importance of symbols and how much he took them into account in his political practice is his behaviour in relation to the election of a president after the death of President Weizmann in 1952. Ben-Gurion was adamantly opposed to the candidacy of Knesset Speaker Sprinzak. In a private conversation with Yehudah Erez, he spoke scornfully of Sprinzak's ambitions:

> And he wants to be the President of Israel. He's not content with being Speaker of the Knesset and Chairman of the Zionist Executive, he has a strong desire to become President. He's the very same man who at the time was opposed to the struggle against the British and to the declaration of the state.[2]

In a meeting of the Mapai central committee convened to select the party's candidate for the presidency, Ben-Gurion expressed his regret that Albert Einstein had not responded positively to his request that he accept the office. The Prime Minister proposed Yitzhak Ben-Zvi, although he claimed that he himself would have preferred a President of Yemenite origin. In the vote, 64 members supported Ben-Zvi's candidacy as opposed to 50 in favour of Sprinzak. It is possible that Ben-Gurion's opposition to Sprinzak stemmed from his hostility towards the Knesset, since Sprinzak at the time symbolized that institution more than anyone else. However, he may have been opposed to Sprinzak's candidacy because he regarded him as a weak Speaker, whose pliancy enabled Ben-Gurion to control the Knesset; perhaps he feared that if Sprinzak were elected as President, his successor might be more independent and aggressive and stand in Ben-Gurion's way. The key sentence Ben-Gurion uttered at that meeting was: 'I know that a president is only a symbol, but nonetheless a very important symbol.'[3]

CONTENTION IN THE KNESSET ON A SYMBOLIC BASIS

Before analyzing the symbolic dimension of the Knesset's location, the timing of its sessions, its size, its appellations, holidays and ceremonies, we will briefly review several symbolically significant events on which Ben-Gurion had some influence.

Five days after the establishment of the state, the government appointed a symbols committee, made up of four ministers. This committee 'was given the authority to discuss and decide upon all matters, which involve some external expression of the state (flags, emblems, insignia of the armed forces, stamps, and so on)'.[4] Unquestionably, the Prime Minister played a major role in the decision to assign the executive branch control over the symbolic realm and to divest the Knesset of any part in it.

In August 1949, Ben-Gurion instructed his secretary to apply to the Knesset secretary on the matter of the Speaker's signature on some of the laws passed by the Knesset. Ben-Gurion had noticed that when the Speaker signed in place of the President, as his replacement, he was not content with the title of Acting President, but also usually added his title as Speaker of the Knesset. Ben-Gurion's secretary did, in fact, address a request to the Secretary of the Knesset, on behalf of the Prime Minister, asking that he omit the title of Speaker of the Knesset.[5]

In November 1949, while delivering an important speech in the plenum about the government's activities, Ben-Gurion suddenly said: 'For the sake of our friendly relations with the Soviet Union, I should like the Speaker's permission to stop at this point.'[6] That evening he was invited to a party by the Soviet consul on the occasion of the 32nd anniversary of the October revolution. According to a report in the press, when Ben-Gurion was about to discontinue his speech, someone from the Mapai benches told him that he still had enough time to complete it, to which the Prime Minister responded by adding, in his particular brand of humour: 'After all I have to get dressed in honour of the revolution.'[7] Sprinzak, amazed, did in fact adjourn the meeting. The following day, Ben-Gurion explained the reason for his action: 'Ladies and gentlemen, I regret that due to an important and pleasurable international duty, I was forced yesterday to cut my speech short.'[8] According to the press report, 'A smile lingered on the speaker's lips, when he prefaced this comment to his speech.'[9] The discontinuation of his speech and the adjournment of the meeting did result from the fact that the Prime Minister had to attend an important diplomatic event, but his abrupt announcement, without first preparing the Knesset or at least the Speaker of the Knesset, as well as his amused demeanour at both of these meetings, are typical of his tendency to symbolically denigrate the Knesset.

On two occasions, in November 1949, the House Committee discussed the question of broadcasting Knesset debates on the radio. At that time, the sole radio network was completely controlled by the Prime Minister's office. The radio directors, who appeared before the Committee, were opposed to the need to obtain the approval of the Speaker of the Knesset and his deputies (the presidium of the Knesset) to record parliamentary debates. Bar-Yehuda registered his protest, demanding that the permission to record debates be given only by the Speaker and his deputies: 'The Knesset is not only the government; it is the government and the opposition.'[10] Katz (Herut) inveighed against the freedom of action that the Broadcasting Authority had appropriated to itself: 'The Knesset ought to rule the Knesset.'[11] Sprinzak, however, gave in to Ben-Gurion's functionaries and decided that the situation would remain unchanged. Ben-Gurion emerged as the victor from that struggle, which had a distinctly symbolic dimension.

In October 1950, Israel's ambassador to Britain conveyed Israel's congratulations to Prime Minister Churchill, adding the Knesset to the list of institutions extending their greetings. Ben-Gurion protested vehemently against the mention of the Knesset in this context:

> That is a mistake. He can, on certain occasions, convey greetings on behalf of the government and the people (since the government represents the people), but not the 'Knesset' – the Knesset is an institution, and he does not speak on behalf of that institution; only its Speaker can do so.[12]

Ostensibly, the Prime Minister would seem to have been defending the Knesset. However he was really being facetious, and was actually insulting the Knesset, detracting from its status, and suggesting that it ought to look after its own affairs, without any help from the executive branch.

In June 1951, an idea was broached that had consummately symbolic significance – to grant Israeli citizenship to victims of the Holocaust. Ben-Gurion was invited to the House Committee that was discussing the subject. He proposed that the matter be handled by a public committee composed of three ministers, three representatives of the Zionist Executive, three members of the public and Leo Cohen. To the Knesset, the Prime Minister assigned no role whatsoever on this committee and when someone criticized this omission, he retorted sarcastically: 'If the intent is that this is a matter only for the Knesset – I think that in this country, I'm being turned into an anti-Zionist . . . there is one organization that is more representative of the Jews than any other and that is the Zionist Executive.'[13] There was no room for the Knesset on this committee, because 'no partisan matters are involved . . . we will submit this committee's views to the House Committee. If the House Committee should wish to discuss this matter separately – I am opposed to that.'[14] Bar-Yehuda contradicted Ben-Gurion and demanded that the Knesset be given a role in the process. The Prime Minister's reply was adamant: 'The answer is no, because this is being done on a non-partisan basis.'[15] Tsizling went even further in his criticism; he asserted that Ben-Gurion had made this a partisan issue by denying the Knesset and the House Committee the right to discuss the subject.[16] Ben-Gurion's proposal that the House Committee refrain from discussing the subject was outvoted. Another Mapai member proposed that the Knesset Speaker and his two deputies deal with the matter, but that proposal was defeated as well, and it was finally decided to establish a subcommittee of the House Committee for the purpose. A week later, the co-ordinator of the sub-committee, Mordechai Nurok (United Religious Front), reported that the sub-committee had decided to co-operate with the government's committee, and added: 'I was charged with the task of speaking to the Prime Minister. I did so, and submitted our proposal to him, and he agreed to it.'[17] The idea itself, that of granting citizenship to the Holocaust victims, was never implemented.

Nor did Ben-Gurion hesitate to intervene in financial matters connected with the Knesset. In May 1952, speaking to members of Mapai's political committee, he mocked the Knesset:

> We have the Knesset, its members have read many books and have decided that there should be a separation between the legislative branch and the executive branch. They have decided that the civil service commission can not interfere in matters relating to the salaries of Knesset employees . . . because they are an institution that has 'to keep to itself'.[18]

This was his way of stating his demand that the salaries of Knesset members be determined by the executive branch. In February 1954, after resigning and moving to Sede Boker, he wrote to his secretary Yitzhak Navon, asking him to make some inquiries for him relating to the Knesset's budget: 'What is the meaning of these grants, to whom? And what is a grant?'[19] Even after leaving his post as Prime Minister, his hostility towards the Knesset did not lessen, and in this instance, it was reflected in his scrutinizing the Knesset's budget, in the hope of finding some scandalous element in it.

In February 1953, Mapai's political committee discussed Israel's participation in a worldwide Jewish conference called 'Let My People Go'. The previous week, Foreign Minister Sharett had announced in the foreign affairs and security committee that the Knesset would send a delegation in which all the Jewish organizations would participate. However, the Prime Minister suggested in the political committee that only those factions wishing to take part in the conference should participate. Argov interpreted this proposal as meaning that 'there would not be one delegation on behalf of the Knesset, but delegations of the various factions . . . the advantage of this is that the Knesset does not officially participate'.[20] The political committee approved the Prime Minister's proposal and decided it would not support the suggestion to send an official Knesset delegation to the conference.

In February 1958, Ben-Gurion recommended to the Mapai faction that it abstain in the vote in the plenum on the first basic law passed, called Basic Law: The Knesset.[21] The faction, however, decided to vote in favour of the law. As a result, the humiliation that would have been caused to the Knesset, had the ruling party openly opposed the major legislation dealing with that body, was averted. Ben-Gurion's motive in opposing the law was his desire to bring about a change in the electoral system to the Knesset.

THE KNESSET'S SECURITY

Ben-Gurion also saw fit to intervene in matters relating to the Knesset's security. After the incident in October 1957, when a patient from a psychiatric hospital threw a hand grenade into the hall of the Knesset, wounding several of those present, the Knesset Speaker, Sprinzak, notified the Minister of Interior, Bar-Yehuda, that he had appointed a three-member security committee to investigate the circumstances of the attack, and that he intended to apply to the Security Services to obtain proposals for the appointment of a security officer for the Knesset. The Speaker and his deputies (the presidium of the Knesset) accepted the proposals of the three-man committee, but Ben-Gurion objected to the arrangements contained in these proposals. In a letter to the Minister of the Interior, he claimed that these arrangements were neither practical nor effective.[22] He did not conceal his intentions. Although it is generally accepted that the unit responsible for the security of the parliament is not subordinate to the army or other security branches – a symbol of the autonomy of the legislative branch – Ben-Gurion argued that if the Speaker of the Knesset appointed an independent security officer, 'without constant and organic co-operation with the national security service . . . there is hardly anything to be gained by appointing a special official for this job'.[23] The Prime Minister announced that due to his objection to the proposed procedure, he would not recommend any candidates to the position of officer of the Knesset. The Speaker's proposal, he asserted, was intended to prevent any intervention by the security services and is based on 'miracles', while the Knesset is obliged to see to it that 'no one is murdered inside the Knesset'.[24] In effect, Ben-Gurion was expressing his lack of confidence in the Knesset's professional ability to protect itself.

The following day, the worried Minister of the Interior spoke to the Prime Minister on the subject and a day later also sent him a letter about it.[25] He wrote that in their conversation, they agreed that the Prime Minister would direct the security services to comply with the decisions of the Knesset Speaker and his deputies, but that the Prime Minister could express his dissatisfaction with the new security arrangement. Underlying the arrangement was not only the appointment of the Knesset officer, but also the establishment of a separate unit to be called the Knesset Guard. The Minister of the Interior in his letter reiterated his request that the Prime Minister give no instructions to the security services and the army that would contravene the decisions of the Knesset Speaker and his deputies.[26] Ben-Gurion was very concerned about the establishment of an armed force that would be under the auspices of the Speaker of the Knesset, an attitude which reflected a symbolic humiliation of the Knesset.

In January 1959, the new Knesset Guard, which MK Sneh called 'Sprinzak's private army' held its inaugural parade.[27] The press reports stated that the new unit was subordinate only to the Knesset. In this instance, then, Ben-Gurion had failed to place the security of the Knesset under the responsibility of the security arm that he himself controlled.

Sprinzak died several days after the establishment of the Knesset Guard and the celebrations of the Knesset's tenth anniversary. The day after his death, four huge memorial notices were placed on the front page of the *Davar* newspaper[28] by the Knesset, the Zionist Executive, the Histadrut and Mapai. Oddly enough, the government did not see fit to publish a memorial notice on the death of the Speaker of the Knesset. The Prime Minister delivered a eulogy for the Speaker and, standing at the open grave, said some things that were inappropriate to the occasion: 'We often had disagreements'[29] and spoke about the deceased as the 'second after the President of the State'.[30]

THE SIZE OF THE KNESSET

Ben-Gurion was in favour of a Knesset with a small number of members. Since anything large in size was regarded as important and significant, he would have preferred a smaller Knesset, which would have been less threatening to him, from the standpoint of its legislative capability and its supervision of the government. After the elections committee for the Constituent Assembly had decided on 171 members, the provisional government intervened in favour of reducing the number to 101.[31] The compromise that was reached was for 120 members. When the Knesset was discussing the number of its members in April 1951, Ben-Gurion did not intervene directly, but he was obviously in favour of the minimalist proposal made by one of his associates, Shlomo Lavie, for 71 members. The majority on the constitution, law and justice committee decided to increase the size of the Knesset from 120 members to 150. The chairman of the committee, Nir, explained in the plenum why the government wanted a small Knesset and hinted that he was referring to Ben-Gurion:

> The Knesset knows, and it is obvious, that if there are not 151 members, but only 120, the government will have an easier time . . . I think this strong opposition is strange. In my view, it stems from a desire to minimize the importance of the Knesset, and that is the basis for all this talk about the Knesset and its members not working . . . we all work, but there is this desire to degrade the value of the Knesset's work and to create the impression that it is not working, not doing anything, in order to say that someone else is doing more.[32]

The Knesset dismissed the decision of the constitution, law and justice committee to have 151 members, and also rejected Lavie's suggestion of 71 members, which had the support of the Prime Minister. The compromise reached was 120 members, the number already decided upon, as noted above, prior to the 1949 elections. Ben-Gurion did not always hesitate to express his opinion about the desirable number of Knesset members. For example, at a meeting of the Mapai central committee, in September 1954, he declared his support for a reduction of the number to 71.[33] In a letter he wrote that same month from Sede Boker to a citizen, Ben-Gurion advocated a reduction in the number of Knesset members: 'We are a small state and there is no need for such a large representative body.'[34]

In a meeting with leaders of the Achdut Haavoda party in August 1955, Ben-Gurion once again spoke out in favour of reducing the number of Knesset members.[35] In October 1956, he made his position clear in the plenum of the Knesset. It was during a debate on the first reading of Basic Law: The Knesset. He stated:

> And I believe – although I am not prepared to go to battle on this issue – that the number of 120 in our case is exaggerated

> and out of proportion. We could easily make do with 71. I know of bigger countries that have fewer elected representatives. But I don't want to devote my limited time to this issue.[36]

THE LOCATION OF THE KNESSET

A great deal of symbolic importance is attached to the location of the Knesset. Just as the members of a parliament are sovereign in determining their working arrangements, its autonomy is also expressed in the fact that its members are the ones who decide on its location. The parliament's constitutional superiority to the government means that the government does not interfere in deciding where it will be located; moreover its very location ought to express this superiority. The buildings of the US Congress, for example, are located on a hill and are far more impressive than the White House, which is in a much lower and less central location. The parliament building in London is far more impressive than the Prime Minister's office, which properly demonstrates the supremacy of the legislative branch over the executive branch. When the British Prime Minister leaves his office in order to attend a meeting of parliament, it is symbolically an ascent to a more important, loftier place. In Jerusalem too, the edifice that houses the Knesset (as well as the Supreme Court building) is located above the building of the Prime Minister's office, and is by far the more impressive of the two buildings. However, the Knesset moved to its new home only in 1966. For nearly two decades – during most of which time Ben-Gurion was Prime Minister – the Knesset was in an inferior location, one that did not manifest its autonomy and symbolic pre-eminence.

Before it was installed in its present edifice, the Knesset moved several times. During the tenure of the People's Council and the Provisional State Council, it convened in various places in Tel Aviv, one of which was the Prime Minister's office. When the Constituent Assembly was elected, it convened for the first time in Jerusalem – in the Jewish Agency building – but two weeks later, after having become in the meantime the First Knesset, it returned to Tel Aviv. The Knesset was housed in Tel Aviv in the buildings of the Kessem cinema and the San Remo Hotel. In December 1949, it moved to Jerusalem, where at first it met in the Jewish Agency building, and in March 1950 moved to Beit Froumine, where it remained for 16 years, until it moved to its present building.

The government and the Prime Minister had a great deal of influence on the location of the Knesset during various periods. For example, Ben-Gurion wrote in his diary in December 1948, that Minister Yitzhak Greenbaum had telephoned to inform him that a committee of ministers had decided that the Constituent Assembly would meet in the Kessem cinema and the San Remo Hotel in Tel Aviv. Greenbaum told him that the army had to be evacuated from the San Remo, and the Prime Minister wrote: 'I promised to do that.'[37] In November 1949, Shatner, chairman of the committee for the development of the area of government buildings in Jerusalem, wrote to the government secretary about the search being conducted to find a suitable building for the Knesset. For this purpose, a tour was arranged for the committee members and the Speaker of the Knesset stated that plans would be drawn up for a building adjacent to the conference building on the northern hill of the designated area.[38]

In December 1949, the Prime Minister informed the Knesset of his decision to move the Knesset's sessions from Tel Aviv to Jerusalem:

> When the First Knesset opened on 14 February 1949, the necessary arrangements for its operations in the capital were not yet in place, and it was necessary to temporarily hold its sessions in Tel Aviv. The required arrangements in Jerusalem are nearly complete now, and there is nothing to prevent the Knesset from returning to Jerusalem. And we suggest that you decide to do so.[39]

Sapir, of the General Zionists, insisted that a debate be held on the subject, but Ben-Gurion was opposed. Sixty Knesset members supported his position versus 39 who were in favour of holding a parliamentary debate on the matter.[40] Sprinzak summed up the matter: 'The Knesset has heard the Prime Minister's statement and the statements of the factions . . . and I hereby announce that the meetings of the Knesset after the festival of Hanukkah will take place again in Jerusalem.'[41] The Knesset did not vote on the Prime Minister's proposal that it move to Jerusalem, and this was another expression of his control over the Knesset and the symbolic supremacy of the executive branch over the legislative.

According to Bader, Sprinzak was not really in favour of the move to Jerusalem and said: 'It's enough if my gavel is in Jerusalem, and we'll find a way to hold our sessions in Tel Aviv.'[42] In a meeting of the Mapai faction in the Knesset, Aranne reported that at a meeting of the faction's directorate, the members had expressed surprise that they had not been consulted about the decision. Ben-Gurion replied that the government had made its recommendation to the Knesset about the move to Jerusalem and the Knesset would decide.[43] In actual fact, as we have already noted, the Knesset was not a party to this important decision. This is how Yehiel Flexer, a veteran employee of the Knesset, described Ben-Gurion's sway on the decision about moving to Jerusalem:

> Ben-Gurion presented the Knesset with a fait accompli . . . everyone then understood that this was not a proposal for the Knesset to debate or decide on, but a decision that had to be accepted without any question. And that's how it was. Ben-Gurion had already decided in the name of the Knesset.[44]

There was another reference to the Knesset's move to Jerusalem at a joint meeting of the foreign affairs and security committee and the constitution, law and justice committee, in January 1950, to discuss the 'Law of Jerusalem, the Capital', proposed by Herut. Ben-Gurion was opposed to any legislation in this regard, which would have symbolic significance par excellence, since it would determine the state's capital city. He argued that the Knesset's decision approving the government's statement on this issue was sufficient. The Prime Minister was opposed not only to legislation, but to any special declaration by the Knesset on this matter as well. In the vote, only eight Knesset members supported his proposal that would prevent the Knesset from passing a law or making a declaration about Jerusalem being the capital of Israel. Eleven members voted for the Knesset's involvement in the form of a law or a declaration. In an additional vote, 12 members favoured a declaration by the Knesset and only three favoured legislation. Ben-Gurion did lose in this case, but his attempt to bypass the Knesset on a subject so imbued with symbolic significance attests to his clear tendency to dwarf the Knesset and not to yield it even symbolic supremacy.[45] When the wording of the declaration was submitted to the Knesset for its approval, Herut suggested that Jerusalem be called Greater Jerusalem. Ben-Gurion was opposed to that on the grounds that aspirations or historical objectives are not the Knesset's concern. The Prime Minister's position was accepted by the plenum.[46]

Several days after the Knesset moved to Jerusalem, the Speaker, at a meeting of the Mapai faction's directorate, expressed his rage at the fact that he had not been a party to the decision, nor had he even been asked his opinion on the matter. He asserted that the decision was political in nature. There was not yet a suitable hall in Jerusalem where the Knesset could convene and there were difficulties involved in the transfer. He said he had visited Jerusalem (evidently a few days after the decision about the transfer), and had been dissatisfied:

> My impression was a very unsettling one. It was as if an enemy was invading Jerusalem. I didn't see any of the joy or dancing that were reported in the press, I saw panic . . . I would like to see the Knesset residing in Jerusalem in a befitting manner . . . If anyone had asked my opinion, I would have said – the Knesset needs a year or two to take final shape in a suitable climate, and that's in Tel Aviv.[47]

The Knesset Speaker suggested that the plenum should meet twice a week in Jerusalem and that an additional day be devoted to committee meetings that would convene in Tel Aviv. Moreover, he insisted that the Knesset administration, with the exception of the required minimum for the plenum's sessions, should remain in Tel Aviv.[48] Aranne and Beba Idelson were also in favour of a gradual move to Jerusalem.[49]

The opposition to the Prime Minister's unilateral move did not end there. Now the struggle focused on the location of the committee meetings, a subject partially covered in Chapter 2, which deals with the Knesset committees. The House Committee held a debate on the transfer to Jerusalem following Ben-Gurion's statement that the ministers would not attend the Knesset's committee meetings if they were held in Tel Aviv. It was Minister Joseph who announced: 'I have heard the words of the Prime Minister and the other ministers – that if the committees sit in Tel Aviv, the ministers will not attend. They will only come if the committees hold their meetings in Jerusalem.'[50] Bar-Yehuda interrupted the minister: 'The ministers will attend wherever they are invited to do so.'[51] The conflict between the Knesset and the government reached its peak when the Speaker of the Knesset ruled: 'The ministers attend at the location decided upon by the Knesset.'[52] Minister Joseph informed the committee that the government had decided that the best temporary place for the Knesset was the teachers' seminary in the Beit Hakerem quarter of Jerusalem. Joseph tried to placate the Speaker in so far as the lack of office space for the Knesset was concerned:

> I have some good news for the Speaker of the Knesset. We have decided for the moment to reduce the amount of space taken up by the Prime Minister's office in the wing of the Keren Kayemeth . . . that will enable you to get another 2–3 rooms, or perhaps even more, if you speak to them about that.[53]

Bar-Yehuda tried to defend the Knesset by comparing its transfer to Jerusalem with that of the Prime Minister's office. He alluded to the fact that while Ben-Gurion had transferred the Prime Minister's office to Jerusalem, he still continued to manage the Ministry of Defence from Tel Aviv. Nir was of the view that it was more important to transfer the Foreign Ministry to Jerusalem. Israel Rokach (the Tel Aviv mayor from the General Zionist party) was in favour of the committees meeting in Tel Aviv. He and Bar-Yehuda argued that the transfer was adversely affecting the work of the Knesset. The Speaker of the Knesset, who was furious, expressed his frustration in harsh words that reflected the Knesset's dependence on the government: 'No one ought to assume that there are two authorities – the government and the Knesset. There are not two authorities.'[54]

The House Committee decided to preserve the building in which the Knesset had met in Tel Aviv. Ben-Gurion responded with rage, and wrote to the chairman of the committee, Harari:

> I have heard that the House Committee has decided not to touch the building that previously housed the Knesset in Tel Aviv . . . The House Committee has no authority to decide about a private house and what will be in that private house, even if it was once the Knesset. Once the Knesset has decided to move to Jerusalem – there is no place in Tel Aviv that is under the Knesset's authority, and the House Committee cannot interfere in regard to a house which in no sense belongs to the Knesset. Only in Jerusalem is there a Knesset.[55]

He stated that this was an attempt to breach the decisions taken by the government and the Knesset about the transfer of the Knesset to Jerusalem, and he adamantly stated that: 'The government will not be able to attend any meeting of the Knesset committees, if they are not held in Jerusalem, because the government is obliged to respect the wishes of the Knesset.'[56]

The Speaker of the Knesset was affronted by the fact that this letter was addressed to the chairman of the House Committee and not brought to his attention: 'It's very strange that he wrote the letter to Harari, without informing me of it',[57] Sprinzak remarked at a meeting of the directorate of the Mapai faction in the Knesset. Although

> Ben-Gurion believes that the transfer ought to be in full, the truth of the matter is that the Knesset was the only institution that moved in full to Jerusalem, and I do not see how the transfer itself will be adversely affected if some of the committees hold meetings in Tel Aviv.

Sprinzak's colleagues on the faction directorate were discomfited by the complicated turn of events caused by the Prime Minister's obstinacy. Yonah Kesse stated that the decision to hold committee meetings in Tel Aviv ought to be clarified with Ben-Gurion. Aranne suggested that all the plenum and committee meetings be concentrated in two days each week, so that there would be no need to hold meetings in Tel Aviv. He also promised to discuss the matter with Ben-Gurion. Sprinzak understood that the faction directorate was not the appropriate forum to adopt a clear-cut decision on this matter.[58] The custom they adopted was in keeping with Aranne's suggestion – two days a week of parliamentary work.

A week later, the faction directorate met, along with several members of the Knesset administration, to discuss the matter again. The Speaker of the Knesset made some harsh comments:

> The connection with Tel-Aviv is 'killing' the Knesset. The decision to devote two days to the work of the Knesset is 'murdering' the Knesset. In addition to the fact that most of the Knesset members do not live in Jerusalem, it prevents the Knesset from conducting its work in an orderly and effective manner. The Knesset is made up of people, who need time to think in the framework of the Knesset . . . I do not think it is fair to devote only two days, out of an entire week, to the work of the Knesset. The Knesset should be the major occupation of its members.[59]

The Speaker announced that he was in favour of the Knesset meeting three days during the week, but his position was supported by only one other member, while five others were opposed to it. Kesse suggested a compromise, according to which one week out of a month the Knesset would sit for three days, and during the rest of the month, only two days a week. At the conclusion of the meeting, Sprinzak was in the minority. The directorate did decide to permit him to suggest to the House Committee that the Knesset would sit, as it formerly had, three days a week, but it was also decided that Kesse would propose, in the name of Mapai, that the plenum would sit two days a week and the committees would meet on the third day. Moreover, it was agreed that the plenum would meet once a month three times a week.[60]

In the end, Ben-Gurion did not succeed in imposing his will on the Knesset in this matter. Immediately after the move to Jerusalem, the Knesset began to meet less frequently – twice a week instead of three times – although later this practice was changed and the Knesset continued to meet three times a week. Moreover, on those days when the plenum was not in session, some committees met either in Jerusalem or in Tel Aviv. The move to Jerusalem actually did impair the work of the Knesset. Tzidon reported that the sessions had become shorter after the move to Jerusalem: 'For safety's sake, it was decided to begin later and to adjourn the meetings earlier.'[61] He also added that the Jewish Agency building in Jerusalem, to which the Knesset had moved 'was not at all suitable to its needs'.[62] The move also resulted in the cancellation of several Knesset sessions. The winter of 1949–50 was a very harsh one in Jerusalem, so much so that 'it was necessary to cancel all the meetings of the Knesset (Sprinzak, apparently under Ben-Gurion's pressure, did not want to hold the meetings in Tel Aviv) until the snow melted and the road to Jerusalem was cleared'.[63] Ben-Gurion's abrupt decision to transfer the Knesset to Jerusalem was not accompanied by any advance preparations, which would have made it easier for the Knesset to carry on its regular work in an orderly manner.

The building in which the Knesset was housed from 1950 to 1966, Beit Froumine, was far from meeting the needs of a parliament. The Speaker of the Knesset tried to find some financing for the construction of a new building. The promise given by Minister Joseph in 1949, that within 12–14 months a new building would be erected for the Knesset, was never kept, no preparations were made, nor was a budget for the purpose ever found. Early in June 1952, the Speaker wrote to the Prime Minister, with a copy to the Minister of Finance, about the need to build a building for the Knesset in the *Kiryah,* the complex of government buildings in Jerusalem.[64] In his reply, Ben-Gurion agreed with Sprinzak that there was no point in investing in the construction of an additional wing to the building that housed the Knesset, but he was not prepared to make any commitment about a budgetary allocation for this purpose, and in fact he referred the Speaker to the Minister of Finance: 'The development budget is discussed in a special ministerial committee, and I see that a copy of your letter went to the Minister of Finance, who is the chairman of that committee.'[65]

The Knesset remained in the dilapidated building to which it had moved in March 1950, without Ben-Gurion doing anything about allocating a budget for a new building. The Knesset's deliverance finally came from a completely different direction. In July 1957, it turned out that Baron James de Rothschild had left a legacy of 6 million Israeli pounds for a specific purpose – the construction of a new building for the Knesset. Ben-Gurion rushed to notify the Knesset of this windfall.[66] Now he could no longer prevent the Knesset from establishing its symbolic supremacy. The Knesset's new residence was finally inaugurated in August 1966. Ben-Gurion, who by that stage had not been Prime Minister for more than three years, although he was still a member of Knesset, had not yet shaken off his hostility towards the Knesset. He boycotted the ceremony inaugurating the edifice, and the press expressed its surprise at this behaviour.[67]

THE TIMING OF MEETINGS

In a well-run parliamentary system, the government does not convene on the days when the parliament is sitting; it schedules its meetings according to the dates of the parliament's sessions. In this regard, priority should be assigned to the parliament as an expression of its symbolic supremacy. This, however, was not the case in the first years of Israel's existence as a state. The government met on Tuesdays, thereby preventing the Knesset committees from holding any meetings that day. In May 1948, Bader had already registered a protest about this matter at a meeting of the constitution, law and justice committee: 'I fail to understand this method, whereby if the government meets on Tuesday – no committee is able to meet on a Tuesday.'[68] He demanded that if the Knesset convened on Monday, Tuesday and Wednesday, the government ought to hold its meetings on Thursday. Bader's protest arose from the statement made by the Justice Minister to the chairman of the committee, that although he was interested in attending its meetings, he would be unable to do so because it met on Tuesday, which was the government's regular meeting day.[69]

In February 1950, the House Committee decided to address a request to the government once again, asking it not to hold meetings on the day the Knesset was in session. In the meantime, the government had changed its meeting day to Wednesday, when the Knesset was also in session.[70] Harari complained that committees meeting on Wednesday were unable to invite ministers to their meetings.[71] Two weeks later, Sprinzak informed the House Committee of the forthcoming change: 'I have learned that the government may decide to hold its meetings on Sunday . . . I am opposed in principle to holding any meetings on a day when the government is meeting.'[72] Bar-Yehuda corrected the Speaker's statement: 'On the contrary! The government ought not to hold its meetings at a time when the Knesset is holding its meetings.'[73] In June 1950, Harari, the chairman of the House Committee, reported to the committee members on the government's inconsiderate attitude in regard to the timing of meetings. He told them he had written to the government in the committee's name – after the committee had taken several decisions to do so – and that the Speaker of the Knesset and his deputies (the presidium of the Knesset) had also applied to the government in an attempt to settle the matter. However, he stated, 'In reply to my letter, I received a notice that the government had acceded to our request and moved its meetings from Tuesday to Wednesday . . . this is definitely an impossible situation.'[74] Obviously, the government's reply did not evince any readiness to accede to the Knesset's request; rather it clearly showed contempt for it, since the Knesset also held meetings on Wednesdays.

In December 1950, at a meeting of the House Committee, Harari insisted that if it was the wish of the Knesset, the government was obliged to change the hours of its meetings on Wednesdays.[75] Although in February 1950, the Speaker of the Knesset had already announced that the government would move its meetings to Sunday, the actual change in scheduling government meetings only went into effect at the beginning of 1951. In other words, for two and a half years, the government was flouting the principle of the Knesset's symbolic supremacy, and refraining from scheduling its meetings in accordance with the timing of the Knesset's sessions. At the end of January 1951, the Minister of Justice informed the constitution, law and justice committee that 'the government has finally given in to the pressure of the Knesset to move its regular meetings to Thursday'.[76] Although there is no written evidence of Ben-Gurion's intervention in this matter, this supercilious attitude towards the Knesset unquestionably originated in the Prime Minister's office, which is responsible for the government's connection with the Knesset.[77]

NAMES

The intentional distortion of names is a sign of contempt. Ben-Gurion was in the habit of deliberately mispronouncing the name of his greatest political adversary, Menachim Begin, calling him 'Beygin'. He also employed the tactic of not mentioning the names of his rivals. One example is the appellation he gave Begin: 'The man now sitting to the right of Mr Bader.' From time to time, Ben-Gurion would get the names of various parliamentary institutions wrong. On 15 July 1948, the day he was removed from his position as the chairman of its meetings, instead of writing 'Provisional State Council', in his diary, Ben-Gurion wrote 'the Government Council'.[78] A month after the establishment of the Provisional State Council, he called it in his diary 'the Founding Assembly'.[79] After September 1948, when the security commission was abolished and replaced by the security committee of the Provisional State Council, Ben-Gurion continued to refer to it as the security commission, which he, as mentioned previously, had chaired.[80] In August 1953, in his greeting to the jubilee convention of the Teachers' Union, he referred to 'the legislative institution of Israel', refraining from using the name 'Knesset'.[81]

Ben-Gurion even took it upon himself to decide what names to give the streets in the *Kiryah* in Jerusalem. The usual custom is that the local council or municipality, which is in a sense, a parliament, decides the names of streets, without mayoral interference. This practice is based on the idea that the designation of names has symbolic significance, and hence the parliamentary institution bears the responsibility. In May 1952, the Prime Minister wrote to the President of the Supreme Court, informing him that all the streets in the *Kiryah* would be given biblical names.[82] In October 1952, he also wrote to the government secretary, Sherf, informing him that 'the city of the kingdom of Israel will not be denoted by botany, but by history'.[83] By that he meant that he would not permit streets to be named after biblical plants, but only after biblical figures. In his direct intervention in regard to the naming of streets, the Prime Minister disregarded the fact that the Knesset building was also going to be in the *Kiryah*, and that therefore the Knesset ought to have been consulted on this symbolic matter.

FESTIVALS AND CEREMONIES

Festivals and ceremonies have a special symbolic meaning. It was no accident that Ben-Gurion also waged a battle with the Knesset over this issue. His main focus was on Independence Day, but there were other festivals and ceremonies in regard to which he tried to meddle in the life of the parliament. The Knesset's own holiday is celebrated on the 15th of Shvat – Arbor Day – which is the anniversary of its first meeting. In February 1956, the Prime Minister expressed his disapprobation of the fact that the Knesset celebrated its establishment every year. In an address to the plenum, he expressed his hope that 'we will do away with this multiplicity of years, and have only one New Year. Because today we have a new year that begins on April 1, another that begins on October 1, the first day of the month of Tishri, and the 15th of Shvat.'[84] In addition to the religious New Year, he was referring to the Knesset's anniversary celebration, to the start of the financial year and to the dates when the Knesset annually opens its sessions. In 1957, prior to the forthcoming anniversary of the Knesset, he sent the Speaker a letter protesting the Knesset's decision to move the date of its anniversary celebration a few days.[85] From these two instances it is obvious that Ben-Gurion did not show respect for the Knesset's anniversary, as a Prime Minister should.

In July 1950, Ben-Gurion announced that the government had decided that the 20th of Tammuz (Herzl Day) would not be Army Day, as it had been for the previous two years. His reason for the change was that 'it was not decided by the sovereign authority in the state (the Knesset) but through an act of the army'.[86] However, as Ben-Gurion himself wrote in a letter, it was the government, not the Knesset, that had decided to cancel the celebration of Army Day on the anniversary of Herzl's death.

Ben-Gurion was also very much involved in the debate, in August 1949, on the law about the reinterment of Herzl's remains in Jerusalem. Sprinzak informed the House Committee, apparently after prior consultation with the Prime Minister, that the special law would be passed on condition that no debate on it would be held in the Knesset and no objections would be entered. He also announced that the coffin would be brought to the airport and taken from there to the Knesset hall, where an extraordinary, festive session of the Knesset would be held, at which the Speaker of the Knesset and the Prime Minister would read a proclamation to the nation. Bar-Yehuda suggested that only the Speaker should make a speech, and that if the Prime Minister was allowed to speak, it would be correct to allow every faction with four or more Knesset members to deliver an address. Sprinzak was opposed and defended the Prime Minister's right to speak, since making a proclamation was not the same as making a speech, but rather was the reading aloud of a document.[87] Herut objected to the Prime Minister's participation in the festive session. Katz of Herut stated that he failed to understand why the President had not been invited to take an active part in the ceremony.[88] Ben-Gurion won this battle. The extraordinary session that the Knesset held on the day of Herzl's reinterment was opened by the Speaker of the Knesset and the only one to deliver a speech was, in fact, Ben-Gurion.[89]

In 1958, Israel celebrated its tenth anniversary. Ben-Gurion appointed Meir Weisgal as chairman of the team that planned and co-ordinated the festivities connected with the tenth anniversary. The Knesset had not authorized the Prime Minister to make this appointment. In Weisgal's letter of appointment, Ben-Gurion made no mention of the Knesset or of the possibility that it would play an active role in the festivities.[90] However, the Prime Minister finally decided to include the Knesset partially in the anniversary celebrations. Three days before Independence Day, the Knesset held a festive session to mark the tenth anniversary. This session was addressed by the Speaker, the Prime Minister and spokesmen of the factions. In his long, programmatic speech, the Prime Minister never mentioned the Knesset, not even with a single word.[91]

INDEPENDENCE DAY CELEBRATIONS

Ben-Gurion was particularly aggressive in his behaviour towards the Knesset in relation to Independence Day celebrations. This attitude stemmed from his feeling that as the founder of the state, the state's holiday was actually his own. He was not inclined to include the Knesset in the celebrations and reserved for himself the exclusive right to decide what form they would take. Eliezer Don-Yehiya, who made a study of the Independence Day celebration in the early years of the state's existence, did not actually examine Ben-Gurion's role in deciding on the nature of the festivities, but he did find that 'there was a pronounced tendency to direct the Independence Day ceremonies from "above" and to shape the patterns of the holiday so they would advance political and national goals'.[92] The very fact that

Don-Yehiya devoted hardly any space to the Knesset's role in the festivities, in contrast to that of the IDF, for example, shows how marginal this role actually was.

Prior to the first Independence Day, Ben-Gurion deliberately delayed the legislation determining the form of the festivities. His aim in doing so was to avoid giving the Knesset sufficient time to get organized and intervene in the plans for the holiday. A mere 23 days before Independence Day, the government submitted to the Knesset the draft law on the first Independence Day – an extremely short time for dealing with legislation. Not only that, but two days after the draft law was submitted, the Passover recess of the Knesset began, so that the Knesset did not even have 23 days. Oddly enough, neither Ben-Gurion nor any of his ministers were prepared to present the government's draft law to the plenum. In parliamentary life, it is a rare occurrence indeed when a government does not bother to present to the parliament its reasons for drafting a law. Nir, who was chairing the session, expressed his amazement: 'Which member of the government is proposing this law? I am asking that one of the ministers take the trouble to propose the law.'[93] Since none of the ministers responded to his request, Nir read out the draft law himself. It is not unlikely that the ministers refrained from doing so either because they feared the Prime Minister's disapproval, or resented the fact that he had commandeered nearly all the authority, leaving nothing in the hands of the government.

In the debate that ensued in the plenum after Nir finished reading out the draft bill, the proposed version came under harsh criticism from the benches of the coalition, including even Mapai. Lavie, a close associate of Ben-Gurion's, was opposed to the clause in the draft bill that authorized the Prime Minister to issue orders regarding cessation of work that day, flag-raising ceremonies and the holding of public festivities.[94] Yaacov Gil of the General Zionists concurred with Lavie and stressed the role the Knesset should play in determining the content of the holiday.[95] Implicit in the words spoken by Dinur of Mapai, was also trenchant criticism of Ben-Gurion: 'This is the Knesset's first step in shaping the cultural image of the State of Israel . . . I suggest that the Knesset select an ad hoc committee to thoroughly deliberate this matter. It is a basic right of the Knesset to determine the form of the holidays.'[96] Pinkas supported Dinur's proposal and added his criticism of Ben-Gurion: 'I understand that this holiday has to entail more than simply "orders" issued by the Prime Minister regarding cessation of work, flag-raising ceremonies and the holding of public festivities.'[97] Esther Raziel-Naor of Herut suggested that the draft bill be referred to the constitution, law and justice committee, adding that 'The holiday should be determined over generations by the people and the builders of the nation, and should not take the form of official orders.'[98] Rokach of the General Zionists, who was also the Mayor of Tel Aviv, suggested that the content of the festivities should be determined jointly by the Knesset and the local authorities.[99] Lavie, opposing the referral of the draft bill to a committee, stated:

> It is not a matter for a committee, because it is not a matter for the government either. It is a matter that appertains to the House. What does this have to do with the committees? The committees were not intended to deal only with the wording, but are also supposed to negotiate with the executive powers, as well as to negotiate between the legislative and the executive branch. If we want this holiday to be a holiday of the people, it is not a matter for the government only, but mainly for the Knesset. It is the Knesset of Israel that decides about the holiday . . . The fundamental decision is a matter for the Knesset only, and the government ought not to decide about it . . . It is not the government that decides and imposes its will on the entire Jewish people . . . the Knesset is far more competent; it has the ability and the authority to take the decision and to carry it out.[100]

At the end of the debate, the draft bill was referred to the House Committee. It convened the following morning, the last working day before the Knesset's Passover recess, and decided that, due to the time constraint, it would prepare the draft bill itself, rather than assign it to another committee.[101] Preparation in the House Committee took very little time, and at 10:20 a.m. the draft bill was brought to the plenum for its approval. In the debate in the House Committee, Bar-Yehuda complained about the brief time allowed the Knesset: 'The government . . . has not given us time to prepare ourselves in our committee, so that we can be responsible for the content.'[102] He suggested that the law be restricted to one year and was mocking in his reference to the powers the law bestowed upon the Prime Minister: 'If he wishes to select an advisory committee, he will select an advisory committee, if he wants to consult rabbis, he will consult them. But whatever he does, it will be only for this year.'[103] This proposal, intended to curtail Ben-Gurion's authority, was rejected. Eliahu Mazor of the United Religious Front suggested that the Prime Minister be divested of all the powers granted him in the draft bill and that these be transferred to the Minister of the Interior or to the government, but this proposal was also rejected by a majority of the committee members.

When the proposal was referred to the plenum, Lavie protested that the House Committee had not discussed his suggestions and continued to argue that the Knesset, rather than the Prime Minister, should decide on the content of the holiday:

> First of all, I am opposed to handing the matter over to the government. In my view, it belongs to the Knesset. The government is an executive power, and among Jews a holiday needs no executive power; it needs the authority of the Knesset of Israel. It is a far greater and much stronger authority than that of the government. In this way, the consecration of the holiday and its cultural content are given expression.[104]

The Knesset made a few slight changes in the wording proposed by the government. The only important one amounted to a revolt against Ben-Gurion. While the government's proposal had not stated that in principle Independence Day would be a non-working day, the Knesset passed a law making it a legal holiday. Those making the proposal were, in fact, from the coalition. Moshe Ben-Ami (Sephardim) said:

> This should be determined in a binding law and not left to the Prime Minister's discretion . . . Today we are proclaiming Independence Day in Israel, and it is impossible to make such a proclamation without such a basic thing as the declaration of a non-working day by the Knesset. This is not a matter of discretion and cannot depend on the agreement or non-agreement of the Prime Minister.[105]

Kesse of Mapai concurred with Ben-Ami's view and added: 'The Knesset must declare this day a non-working day for perpetuity, whereas the Prime Minister should be given the authority to decide on the content and arrangements of the holiday.'[106] Although the House Committee had agreed that the decision about making Independence Day a non-working day would be left to the Prime Minister, the plenum changed that and added a clause to the law to that effect. On all other points, the task of determining the content and arrangements of the holiday was left in the hands of Ben-Gurion.

However, this was not the final blow in the series of humiliations the Knesset had to suffer before Israel's first Independence Day. At the end of April, after the law had been passed, Nurok, at a meeting of the House Committee, suggested that the Knesset take an active part in the Independence Day celebrations. His idea was to hold a festive session on Independence Day at which the Knesset Speaker would deliver an address, the national anthem would be sung, in the presence of invited representatives of foreign countries, 'so that the place of the Knesset – the supreme institution of the state – is recognized'.[107] Bar-Yehuda's suggestion was to arrange a ceremony at which the victims of the War of Independence would be mentioned and the Speaker would deliver an address. Kook (Herut) supported Nurok's proposal. The committee accepted it and decided to hold a festive session, although the Speaker was opposed. He argued that it was not clear whether all the Knesset members would attend and added that the foreign diplomats had already been invited by the government to a special ceremony. He suggested another option – that at the end of the Knesset's session on the day before the holiday, he would 'say a few words on the occasion of Independence Day'.[108] Apparently, Sprinzak realized that Ben-Gurion would be opposed to the proposed ceremony and that without the Prime Minister, it would be impossible to hold it.

One day before Independence Day, the House Committee convened again. Sprinzak, who apparently had already learned that Ben-Gurion was opposed to the holding of any ceremony in the Knesset, hardened his position against the decision taken by the committee the previous week:

> I should like to ask you to go back on a vow. At our previous meeting, I told you we would decide about the festive session on Independence Day. Now I have come to the conclusion that we do not need it. First of all, at 11 a.m., there is a prayer service in the synagogue. I myself am engaged elsewhere at 12 . . . everyone is celebrating, there will be a parade, there will be prayer, there will be a children's procession and the Prime Minister will deliver a message for everyone.[109]

Enraged, Nurok reacted aggressively:

> I am opposed to the honourable Speaker's annulment of vows . . . this is . . . a question of principle. It is incumbent upon us to stress the sovereignty of the Knesset on the state's birthday. The parliaments in all countries hold a special festive session on their state holiday.[110]

Bar-Yehuda was direct in his accusation of Ben-Gurion: 'We passed the Independence Day law and gave the Prime Minister the authority . . . and he, as in all things, has ruled out the Knesset.'[111] Sprinzak denied that the government had intervened in the matter and took the responsibility for it himself: 'There was no desire here to impair the sovereignty of the Knesset . . . the government has nothing to do with my suggestion that we decide not to hold the festive session. I am asking you to refrain from publicizing this whole argument in the press.'[112] Despite the position taken by the Speaker of the Knesset, who was much embarrassed by the situation into which the Prime Minister had pushed the Knesset, the committee decided to hold a festive session on the eve of Independence Day. Sprinzak was unable to carry out this decision in full. Instead he delivered a special address and read out the President's greetings. The Knesset members rose and sang the anthem. It was hardly a festivity, but only a brief affair, which was not even held on the day of the holiday itself.[113] Usually, the symbolic significance of a festive session is marked by the fact that no other meetings are held the same day. In this case, however, the ceremony took place at the end of a routine day of plenum sessions.

However, even this small event marked the only time in the history of the state that the plenum held a special session to mark Independence Day. In the coming years, there was not a single trace of the modest affair held in 1949. In order to avoid the mortifying scene that took place prior to the first Independence Day, the Knesset extended its Passover recess until after that day. The following year, in 1950, the Knesset was already in a recess that began a short time before Passover and ended several days after Independence Day. This arrangement was finally institutionalized in the Basic Law: The Knesset, passed in 1958. The law states that the summer sitting of the Knesset would begin 'within four weeks after Independence Day'. In this way, the Knesset avoided the awkward predicament it had found itself in owing to Ben-Gurion's objection to its symbolic participation in the Independence Day festivities. To make up for the fact that the Knesset does not hold a festive session on Independence

Day, the Speaker of the Knesset has been invited, since 1950, to take part in the torch-lighting ceremony on the eve of the holiday.

Ben-Gurion made extensive use of the powers granted him in the Independence Day law. Each year he issued special orders before the holiday. In 1951, for example, he decided that the state flag would be raised not only on every government or public building, but on every private building as well.[114] In 1956, he added that 'Deliveries of bread, milk and ice will be permitted on the holiday only until 9 a.m.'[115] In 1958, the Knesset added a clause to the law, authorizing the Prime Minister to establish, through regulations, the Independence Day symbols and their use.[116]

Ben-Gurion did nothing to emphasize the symbolic importance of the Knesset, for example, by inviting the Speaker of the Knesset to the reviewing stand during the military parades held on Independence Day. At the parade held in Jerusalem in 1950, the President of the State, the Prime Minister and the Chief of Staff reviewed the parade.[117] In 1954, when Ben-Gurion was no longer in the government, Prime Minister Sharett invited him to be present on the reviewing stand during the military parade.[118] Ben-Gurion refused to come, and in his reply to Sharett said: 'It would be presumptuous of me [to accept the invitation]. The only ones who ought to be on the stand are the President, the Prime Minister and the Chief of Staff.'[119] Following a remark made by one of his aides, a few days later, he added the Minister of Defence to the list, because Sharett, unlike Ben-Gurion, did not serve as Minister of Defence during his premiership.[120] In Ben-Gurion's view, there was no place on the reviewing stand for the Speaker of the Knesset, a view which illustrated well his negative attitude to the Knesset.

NOTES

1. Giora Goldberg, 'You Don't Need a Constitution to Plant Trees' pp. 29–48.
2. Yehudah Erez, 'The Prime Minister and the Candidate for the Presidency', *Yedioth Aharonoth*, Yamim veLeilot (Days and Nights) supplement, 7 April 1978.
3. Israel Labour Party Archives, meeting of Mapai's central committee, 26 November 1952.
4. *Davar*, 23 July 1948.
5. Ben-Gurion Research Center Archives, correspondence, Prime Minister's secretary to the Secretary of the Knesset, 30 August 1949.
6. *Knesset Record*, 7 November 1949, p. 12.
7. *Ma'ariv*, 8 November 1949.
8. *Knesset Record*, 8 November 1949, p. 13.
9. *Ha'Aretz*, 9 November 1949.

10. State Archives, meeting of House Committee, 22 November 1949.
11. Ibid., 28 November 1949.
12. Ben-Gurion Research Center Archives, correspondence, Ben-Gurion to unidentified addressee, 22 October 1950.
13. State Archives, meeting of House Committee, 26 June 1951.
14. Ibid.
15. Ibid.
16. Ibid.
17. Ibid., 3 July 1951.
18. Israel Labour Party Archives, Meeting of Mapai's political committee, 18 May 1952.
19. Ben-Gurion Research Center Archives, correspondence, Ben-Gurion to Navon, 23 February 1954.
20. Israel Labour Party Archives, meeting of political committee, 26 February 1953.
21. Ibid., meeting of Mapai faction in Knesset, 12 February 1958.
22. Ben-Gurion Research Center Archives, correspondence, Ben-Gurion to Bar-Yehuda, 17 December 1957.
23. Ibid.
24. Ibid.
25. Ibid., Bar-Yehuda to Ben-Gurion, 19 December 1957.
26. Ibid.
27. *Davar*, 27 January 1959.
28. *Davar* was the newspaper of the Histadrut, and in effect was controlled by Mapai.
29. *Davar HaShavuah*, 4 February 1959.
30. *HaPoel HaTzair*, issue no. 20, 3 February 1959, p. 10.
31. Giora Goldberg, 'On the Need to Increase the Number of Knesset Members' (Hebrew), *Netivei Irgun veMinhal* (Modes of Organization and Administration), year 23, issue no. 137–8 (Winter 1982), p. 20.
32. *Knesset Record*, 12 April 1951, pp. 1,067–8.
33. Israel Labour Party Archives, meeting of Mapai central committee, 16 September 1954.
34. Ben-Gurion Research Center Archives, correspondence, Ben-Gurion to Haim Zeidman, 30 September 1954.
35. Ibid., minutes of meetings, Ben-Gurion's meeting with leaders of Achdut Haavoda, 12 August 1955.
36. *Knesset Record*, 8 October 1956, p. 18.
37. David Ben-Gurion, *Yoman Hamilchamah* (War Diary), vol. 3, Tel Aviv: Ministry of Defence, 1982, p. 866.
38. Ben-Gurion Research Center Archives, correspondence, Shetner to Sherf, 6 November 1949.
39. *Knesset Record*, 13 December 1949, p. 281.
40. Ibid., p. 282.
41. Ibid., p. 287.
42. Bader, *The Knesset and I*, p. 30.
43. Israel Labour Party Archives, meeting of Mapai faction in the Knesset, 12 December 1949.
44. Yehiel P. Flexer, *Marot haKnesset* (Sights in the Knesset), Jerusalem: Daf Chen, 1980, p. 114.
45. State Archives, joint meeting of the foreign affairs and security committee and the constitution, law and justice committee, 18 January 1950.
46. *Knesset Record*, 23 January 1950, p. 611.
47. Israel Labour Party Archives, meeting of directorate of Mapai faction in the Knesset, 18 December 1949.
48. Ibid.
49. Ibid.
50. State Archives, minutes of meeting of House committee, 12 December 1949.
51. Ibid.

52. Ibid.
53. Ibid.
54. Ibid.
55. Ben-Gurion Research Center Archives, correspondence, Ben-Gurion to Harari, 26 December 1949.
56. Ibid.
57. Israel Labour Party Archives, meeting of directorate of Mapai faction in the Knesset, 2 January 1950.
58. Ibid.
59. Ibid., 9 January 1950.
60. Ibid.
61. Asher Tzidon, *Beit Hanivcharim* (The House of Representatives), Jerusalem: Achiassaf, 1964, p. 144.
62. Ibid., p. 89.
63. Flexer, *Marot haKnesset*, pp. 14–15.
64. Ben-Gurion Research Center Archives, correspondence, Sprinzak to Ben-Gurion, 2 June 1952.
65. Ibid., Ben-Gurion to Sprinzak, 4 June 1952.
66. *Knesset Record*, 22 July 1957, p. 2,475.
67. *Davar*, 5 September 1966, Ben-Gurion frequently utilized the weapon of boycott. For example, in February 1969, when he boycotted the funeral of Prime Minister Eshkol.
68. State Archives, meeting of constitution, law and justice committee, 3 May 1949.
69. Ibid.
70. Ibid., meeting of House Committee, 14 February 1950.
71. Ibid.
72. Ibid., 28 February 1950.
73. Ibid.
74. Ibid., 6 June 1950.
75. Ibid., 11 December 1950.
76. Ibid., meeting of constitution, law and justice committee, 24 January 1951.
77. One indication of how much influence the Prime Minister has in setting the time for government meetings is Benjamin Netanyahu's decision, taken immediately after his election to that office in 1996, to move the weekly meeting from Sunday to Friday.
78. David Ben-Gurion, *Yoman Hamilchamah*, vol. 2, Tel Aviv: Ministry of Defence, 1982, p. 592
79. Ibid., 14 June 1948, p. 517.
80. Ibid., 17 September 1948, p. 697; vol. 3, 23 December 1948, p. 897; 7 January 1949, p. 933; 13 January 1949, p. 949.
81. Ben-Gurion Research Center Archives, correspondence, Ben-Gurion to the Jubilee Convention of the Teachers Union, 12 August 1953.
82. Ibid., Ben-Gurion to Moshe Zmora, 18 May 1952.
83. Ibid., Ben-Gurion to Sherf, 28 October 1952.
84. *Knesset Record*, 29 February 1956, p. 1,238.
85. Ben-Gurion Research Center Archives, correspondence, Ben-Gurion to Sprinzak, 16 January 1957.
86. Ibid., Ben-Gurion to members of the Yad LeBanim center, 2 July 1950.
87. State Archives, meeting of House Committee, 2 August 1949.
88. Ibid.
89. *Knesset Record*, 16 August 1949, pp. 1,359–60.
90. Ben-Gurion Research Center Archives, correspondence, Ben-Gurion to Weisgal, 1957, no exact date.
91. *Knesset Record*, 22 April 1958, pp. 1,814–17.
92. Eliezer Don-Yehiya, 'Festivals and Political Culture: The Celebration of Independence Day in the Early Years of Statehood (Hebrew)', *Medina, Mimshal Vihasim Benleumiyim*, (State, Government and International Relations) 23 (Summer 1984), p. 12.

93. *Knesset Record*, 11 April 1949, p. 349.
94. Ibid.
95. Ibid., p. 350.
96. Ibid.
97. Ibid., p. 351.
98. Ibid., p. 352.
99. Ibid.
100. Ibid., p. 353.
101. Ibid., 12 April 1949, p. 355.
102. State Archives, meeting of House Committee, 12 April 1949.
103. Ibid.
104. *Knesset Record*, 12 April 1949, p. 356.
105. Ibid.
106. Ibid.
107. State Archives, meeting of House Committee, 27 April 1949.
108. Ibid.
109. Ibid., 3 May 1949.
110. Ibid.
111. Ibid.
112. Ibid.
113. *Knesset Record*, 3 May 1949, pp. 477–8.
114. *Yalkut HaPirsumim*, 1951, vol. 2, 19 April 1951, p. 910.
115. Ben-Gurion Research Center Archives, correspondence, 1 April 1956, instructions for the Independence Day Law.
116. *Knesset Record*, 25 February 1958, pp. 1,087–9; 12 March 1958, p. 1,276.
117. Yom-Tov Levinsky, *Sefer HaMoadim* (Book of Holidays), Tel Aviv: Dvir, 1957, p. 493.
118. Ben-Gurion Research Center Archives, correspondence, Sharett to Ben-Gurion, 30 March 1954.
119. Ibid., Ben-Gurion to Sharett, 10 April 1954.
120. Ibid., Ben-Gurion to Navon, 13 April 1954.

PART THREE

The Struggle Against the Knesset Members

6 The Immunity of Knesset Members

On the issue of parliamentary immunity, an unrelenting struggle was waged between the Knesset, which wanted legislation to ensure the elementary rights of its members, and Ben-Gurion, who strongly opposed such legislation. This struggle lasted for three years until it was resolved in 1951, to the Prime Minister's chagrin. The Law – Immunity of Members of Knesset – passed that year granted Knesset members very broad immunity, in comparison to other parliaments. One reason Knesset members wanted such broad immunity was apparently their profound distrust of the Prime Minister, who had been so vigorously opposed to the law. They evidently regarded the law as a form of protection against the Prime Minister's long arm and preferred to expand greatly the scope of their immunity. Over the years, this expanded immunity had an adverse implication for the Knesset. The negative attitude towards the Knesset among some segments of the Israeli public from the 1970s onwards resulted, among other reasons, from the sweeping immunity its members enjoyed. This right was interpreted as a cynical exploitation of legislative power to serve narrow personal interests.

As we will see later, the struggle over immunity was resolved in 1951 only when Mapai had lost its coalitional majority. In order to hold early elections to the Second Knesset, it was forced to reach a compromise with the other parties. The immunity law was so important to the Knesset members that the only demand made of Mapai, as part of that compromise, was its agreement to the passage of such a law.

THE NEED FOR PARLIAMENTARY IMMUNITY

Until the immunity law was passed, Knesset members were constantly under Ben-Gurion's watchful eye. The Prime Minister had control over the various security branches, and could restrict the rights of Knesset members by employing the secret services to learn every detail about them and their parties. As far back as the time of the Provisional State Council, Ben-Gurion was already being criticized in this regard. In October 1948, the interior committee of the Provisional State Council began to discuss political investigations.[1] Minister of Police Shitrit told the committee that during British rule there had been an organizational separation between criminal investigation and political investigation. The Israeli police had established a criminal investigation department, but not one for political investigation. In November, the committee once again discussed the subject, this time with the participation of the Minister of Police, the Police Commissioner and his deputy. The minister told the committee that the government had set up a committee of four ministers to look into the matter of a political investigation department. In wartime, he said, the army was responsible for this matter, but in normal times, he suggested, it would be better if the police were in charge of it. The Revisionist representative on the committee, Altman, demanded that a political investigation department be part of the police.[2]

At the time, a widespread network dealing in political investigation already existed and was under Ben-Gurion's control. In June 1949, the Prime Minister was not ashamed to write in his diary details of Herut's preparations for its convention. He gave the numbers of those registering in the various branches and in the army, and explicitly mentioned his source: 'According to a report by Shai'[3] which was the name used at the time for the General Security Service – the same political secret police that the members of the interior committee were taking an interest in. In this case, Ben-Gurion admitted that he was responsible for spying on a rival political party. The security service monitored the mail of ministers and Knesset members. As noted in Chapter 1, Bernstein and Kol complained that their correspondence was being opened and read. In October 1948, Minister Bernstein (General Zionists) claimed that letters arriving at his office were being surreptitiously opened and closed. Bernstein, a moderate, restrained politician, wrote to the Prime Minister about this matter, expressing his surprise that the responsible body would condone such an invasion of privacy.[4] He was even fearful that the very same letter, addressed to the Prime Minister, would be opened and read by 'spying hands' . . .[5] If this was Ben-Gurion's attitude towards ministers, it is not hard to imagine how much the Knesset members suffered at his hands. In January 1949, Ben-Gurion replied to a parliamentary question posed by Kol, who had complained that the censor was opening letters sent abroad by Knesset members. Ben-Gurion justified this by explaining that the country was in a state of war, adding that in Britain too, this kind of censorship had been practiced during the Second World War. He promised to instruct the censor to inform a Knesset member sending a cable if it was going to be delayed due to censorship.[6] In December 1949, he did not deny that letters arriving from abroad to Knesset members were examined by the military censor. In reply to a question by Yaacov Meridor of Herut, Ben-Gurion stated that in this regard, 'Knesset members are neither discriminated against nor shown any favouritism.'[7] In 1951, the House Committee discussed on several occasions the implications of there being no law of immunity. Bernstein, who was then no longer serving as a minister, remonstrated about the censor having opened a letter sent to him by the Israeli deputy consul in New York,[8] and on another occasion he showed the committee a letter from the same sender that had been opened, without the censor having attached a notification that he had examined it.[9] Joseph Serlin, also from the General Zionists, complained that many letters sent to him had been opened, and that once he had even received an envelope without a letter in it.[10] Knesset member Zakhariah Gluska (Yeminites) added his voice to these complaints.[11]

Ben-Gurion frequently made use of the military censor. He took the liberty of censoring the ministers and often banned their statements to the press. In December 1948, for example, he informed Minister Bentov (Mapam): 'I was given the wording of your statement to the press, and I forbade its publication.'[12] In the summer of 1948, the military censor, for whom Ben-Gurion, as Minister of Defence, was responsible, did not shrink from closing down Mapam's daily newspaper.[13] In August 1948, Ben-Gurion rebuked the military censor when something printed in the press constituted, in his view, 'clear damage to security', and instructed him 'to make sure that such items are not published'.[14]

In March 1949, the censor banned an announcement scheduled to appear in Mapam's newspaper, conveying greetings to Yigal

Allon from 'friends'. The reference was to the military successes of General Allon, who was then identified with the Achdut Haavoda wing of Mapam. The explanation given by the Prime Minister in the Knesset was that 'according to authorized instructions, names of soldiers and officers taking part in military operations were not to be published'.[15]

The long arm of the military censor extended as far as the Knesset plenum. Nathan Alterman, a well-known poet and declared supporter of Ben-Gurion, wanted to publish a poem praising the Palmach – a military organization affiliated with the Mapam leaders – after it was dismantled in May 1949. The censor prevented the publication of this poem in the Histadrut newspaper, *Davar*, but Ben-Aharon read it out in the Knesset plenum.[16] Bar-Yehuda, also of Mapam, complained that the censor 'instead of being a military censor had become the censor of a single party'.[17] Another Mapam Knesset member, Riftin, expressed his fear that articles written by members of his party would be rejected for publication.[18] Ben-Gurion professed his innocence in this regard, stating that the military censor was responsible for banning Alterman's poem and that he did not know whether there were really any grounds for doing so.[19] However, Ben-Gurion insisted on having his way, and after the poem had been read out in the Knesset, the military censor decided to delete it from the minutes. A week later, the affair was discussed at a joint meeting of the foreign affairs and security committee and the House Committee. The chairman of the foreign affairs and security committee, Aranne, was in favour of empowering the Speaker of the Knesset and his deputies (the Knesset presidium) to strike items from the minutes, but not the military censor. Bar-Yehuda was outspoken in his remarks:

> The impudence of the military censor in informing the presidium of the parliament that unless the Knesset Record was given to him, he would ban it, exceeds all bounds. I think the House Committee should react to this impudence so that the military censor will know in future who he is dealing with.[20]

It was common knowledge that the military censor had the Prime Minister's backing, and that the censor would never have gone so far as to threaten to ban Knesset documents unless he was sure the Prime Minister supported his action. The committee did not adopt the suggestion made by a Mapai member to authorize the Minister of Defence to delete items from the Knesset Record. Instead, the Speaker of the Knesset and his deputies were authorized to do so in the interest of state security. However, the opposition failed in its attempt to include in the resolution a clause that would allow such a deletion only in times of emergency. When the resolution was brought to the plenum for its approval, another clause was added, which did limit the authority of deletion to a time of emergency.[21] This did not satisfy Herut, however, and its representative, Katz, was very outspoken in his blunt criticism:

> The proposals before us do of course offer a partial solution to the problem, which is much broader and much more serious. The problem is one of infringement of the rights of the individual, infringement of the privacy of telephone conversations and correspondence. When anyone from our movement lifts the receiver, he usually alerts the party on the other end to the fact that someone in charge of 'the rights of the individual' is listening in. When I receive a letter from abroad, it has been opened before I see it.[22]

Against this background, it is easy to understand why in 1949 a subcommittee of the House Committee was set up to discuss immunity. But Ben-Gurion's opposition prevented it from reaching agreement on the issue.

Ben-Gurion imposed censorship on Ben-Aharon's words on other occasions as well. At the end of 1950, Ben-Aharon complained to the Prime Minister that the broadcast of his radio talk had been cancelled. Ben-Gurion replied: 'Your talk was not broadcast . . . and I take full responsibility for that . . . the "state officials", who you scorn for some reason, are not the ones who are responsible for prohibiting it, but rather the undersigned.' [23] In May 1951, Ben-Aharon submitted a parliamentary question to Ben-Gurion regarding the function of Freddy Harris, Chief Military Advisor to the Minister of Defence and the Chief of Staff. He asked whether it was true that Harris was privy to full information, including military secrets, while soldiers were forbidden to give information to civilians, including members of the foreign affairs and security committee. Ben-Gurion replied that Harris had been invited several times to attend meetings of the General Staff, and that he felt his services were very valuable.[24] The wording of the question and the reply did not appear in the *Knesset Record*.[25]

Since the Knesset members did not enjoy immunity, their freedom of movement was also restricted. Ben-Gurion felt so confident that he even allowed himself, in October 1948, to instruct the Ministry of Immigration to refuse to grant exit permits from the country, other than for reasons of health, national need or participation in a government delegation.[26] He did not exclude Knesset members from the need to obtain government approval to travel outside the country.

Occasionally, Knesset members were even prevented from travelling to certain places inside the country. On one occasion, for example, Mikunis of the Communist Party was scheduled to deliver a speech in the Arab quarter of Acre. When he arrived in that city, he was informed by the military governor, without being given any explanation, that the meeting had been cancelled and that he was forbidden to enter the Arab quarter: 'Such treatment of a member of the State Council is in contravention of the most elementary rights of Council members',[27] Mikunis protested. Ben-Gurion's response was that 'the rules of the state apply equally to all citizens, and members of the State Council enjoy no privileges in an area under military rule'.[28] In June 1949, a parliamentary question about the behaviour of the Communist Knesset members, Mikunis and Tufik Tubi, was posed to Ben-Gurion. The questioner asked whether they would be forbidden to enter Israel following the defamatory remarks they had made about the state while they were outside the country. Ben-Gurion stated that the House Committee ought to investigate whether it was true that the two had maligned the state, and if that was found to be the case, then the committee should submit its proposals to the Knesset.[29] It was most inappropriate for the Prime Minister to give instructions or advice to the House Committee. In October 1950, in his reply to another question on the same subject, Ben-Gurion said,

> It seems to me this is a matter in regard to which the House Committee should take measures against a Knesset member who has acted irresponsibly or improperly and has impugned the name of the State of Israel in fallacious propaganda.[30]

In December 1949, the Prime Minister tried to turn the House Committee against Tubi, following his criticism in the Knesset of searches by the army in Arab villages. In his letter to the committee, Ben-Gurion deplored the absence of a standing order setting limits between criticism and defamation. The reasons he gave for his initiative were: 'to uphold the honour of the Knesset and the state and to prevent anyone abusing the fact that no standing order exists in order to utter words of slander in the Knesset'.[31] The House Committee refrained from dealing with his complaint.[32]

In November 1949, Harari, the chairman of the House Committee, placed Katz's (Herut) complaint on the committee's agenda for discussion. Katz claimed that government employees were keeping tabs on Knesset members: 'They did not deny it, but they did not say who they were working for.'[33] Two weeks later, Katz gave the committee members details of the affair. He and two other Knesset members from Herut had travelled to an election rally in Haifa, and on their way back they realized a car was following them. They went to a police station. The men following them, who were wearing civilian clothes, did not flee but showed the policemen their papers and said they were on duty. The police informed the troubled Knesset members that they could not arrest the men following them or put them on trial. Katz added that it was clear that these men were agents of the government that was operating 'a black bureau. The Knesset has a right to know what bureaus exist in this state.'[34] The House Committee decided to summon the Minister of Police to the sub-committee on immunity. He appeared before the committee and said he was aware of this matter and that the police did not engage in political surveillance.[35] The House Committee decided to remove Katz's complaint from its agenda.

In February 1950, the interior committee of the Knesset held a discussion on political espionage in the presence of the Minister of Police and the Police Commissioner. MK Eliezer Peri of Mapam complained to the Minister that some of his party's branches had been broken into for political reasons. Nothing was stolen, but card files were examined and some material was photographed. Peri asked the minister whether the police had investigated these incidents and, if the police really had no political division, why it acquiesced to the operation of another government agency within its field of activity.[36] Tubi protested that policemen had searched his home on several occasions and had told him: 'We don't care if you are a Knesset member',[37] and that they wanted to search his home because of the very fact that he was a Knesset member. Tubi wrote to the commander of the Haifa police about it and the reply he received was: 'I do not know there is such a law called parliamentary immunity, and therefore we have the right to search your home once, and if that's not enough, twice, and if that's still not enough, then three or more times.'[38] Tubi asked the Police Commissioner to look into the matter, although the law of Knesset members' immunity had not yet been passed. The Police Comissioner admitted that the letter sent to Tubi by the Haifa police commander was 'written with a total lack of courtesy',[39] and added: 'I repeat once again – there is no political department in the police . . . there is no political espionage in Israel and we have no agents in any party. We do not send agents to political meetings, although such a thing does exist everywhere in the world.'[40] Sneh suggested that the police establish a department to supervise the government agency engaged in political espionage. In so far as the break-ins into the Mapam branches were concerned, the commissioner said that someone may have broken in, but the police had not received any information about it. He admitted that the Shai (the former name of the General Security Services) had a department of political espionage which did some fine work. Each morning, he affirmed, he received a full report of everything taking place in the country in the political realm: 'What was said here or there, who travelled and where.'[41] The important point here is that the Police Commissioner officially declared that a department of political espionage existed outside the police, under the aegis of the General Security Services, an organization directly subordinate to the Prime Minister.

Ben-Gurion's disparaging attitude towards the Knesset and Knesset members – in particular towards the Communists – led to a situation that permitted criticism of Knesset members even from the ranks of the army. In May 1950, for example, a junior officer wrote to Ben-Gurion about 'lies' by MK Vilner that had appeared in the Communist Party's newspaper, alleging that a sergeant-major had abused an Arab child: 'I am very surprised by the improper conduct of this Knesset member, interfering with the army in the fulfillment of its duties – while it is only thanks to this army that he has the honour to be a member of the parliament in the State of Israel.'[42] In June 1950, Tubi complained to the House Committee that during his visit to the Arab village of Teibe, he had learned that the military governor had opposed the visit: 'I told him he does not determine whether I have a right to visit the village.'[43] A similar matter was raised in the plenum in July 1950 by Vilner, another Communist Knesset member. He said he had desired to visit Teibe with other Communist leaders and had requested permission from the military governor, whose reply was:

> After the incident that occurred during your previous visit we are prepared to issue you entry permits to Teibe on the following conditions: (A) the visitors will be accompanied by a military unit to provide you with security throughout the visit; (B) the visit will be of a totally private nature without any large meetings or congregations. If you are prepared to accept these conditions, please notify me.[44]

Vilner asserted that these restrictions violated the rights of Knesset members: 'Knesset members are also prohibited from travelling freely. Even worse, one-time movement permits are not issued to them under normal conditions.'[45] The Prime Minister's response was evasive; he merely said that the immunity law was now under discussion in a committee.[46] In February 1951, the House Committee addressed Tubi's complaint that a few days earlier a police officer had come to his home, read him a charge sheet citing unlawful assembly on the same day and demanded that he sign it. Tubi refused on the grounds that it was improper to demand that of a Knesset member and the officer informed him that the police would take steps to put him on trial.[47] Tsizling of Mapam responded by stating that the police's conduct towards Tubi was disgraceful.[48]

In March 1951, MK Ben-Ami (Sephardim) complained in the constitution, law and justice committee that he had encountered difficulties in entering Jaffa, some of whose inhabitants were Arabs. He referred a parliamentary question to Ben-Gurion and was told in reply that these steps were taken to protect the personal safety of Knesset members. Ben-Ami protested that 'the entire state should be open to Knesset members, because they represent the whole state, not only those voters who elected them'.[49]

PASSAGE OF THE IMMUNITY LAW

As already mentioned, in 1949 a sub-committee of the House Committee was established to discuss immunity. The accumulation of incidents noted above increased pressure on Ben-Gurion in 1950 to agree to an immunity law. Even in Mapai, voices were heard in favour of such legislation. In February, Sprinzak expressed his frustration in a statement to members of the Mapai faction in the Knesset in favour of an immunity law: 'I will say but one thing in regard to the immunity law. This law must exist. Its implementation depends somewhat on our own people. The immunity law and the rules of procedure – these must be effective.'[50] The matter was raised again at a meeting of the faction directorate in May.[51] At the end of July, Sprinzak reiterated his support of the immunity law at a meeting of the faction directorate.[52] In October, he once again emphasized the urgent need to pass an immunity law.[53] According to Bader, 'Ben-Gurion has placed a veto on the proposed immunity law and Sprinzak has been co-operating with the government on this issue.'[54] Sprinzak refrained from presenting the proposed law to the plenum after it had been prepared by the House Committee. Bader contended that Ben-Gurion had said, 'I don't need immunity',[55] and added derisively that 'he was right'.[56]

In July 1950, after he realized he could no longer prevent the passage of an immunity law, Ben-Gurion finally revealed, at a meeting of the coalition directorate, his negative attitude to such a law:

> To this day, I have not read a single book on immunity. I would like to know why the Knesset members need immunity. They need it in order to fulfil their duties, namely: (A) to appear on the podium of the Knesset and express their views as representatives of their parties; (B) so that they can vote. Since they could be prevented from doing so, we have to ensure that no one can interfere with them. Immunity is not only a right, but a duty . . . According to the proposed immunity law, a Knesset member is not obliged to be present at the Knesset sessions. A Knesset member can obtain a passport and travel outside the country for several years. And this is impossible, a clause must be inserted into the immunity law obliging members to participate in the Knesset sessions and limiting the amount of time they can spend abroad. If there is a restriction on leaving the country for all citizens, why shouldn't it apply to Knesset members? In relation to this law, we have to take into account the situation the State of Israel is in now as well as its internal situation.[57]

He was opposed to the clause proposing a vote by two-thirds of the members to revoke any member's immunity, because that is liable to be helpful to the 'anti-democratic parties' existing in Israel. He demanded that Knesset members be legally obliged to fulfill their function. Anyone who does not appear at Knesset sessions, should be ousted from the Knesset. A Knesset member will be permitted to travel abroad with certain limitations:

> An exit permit for a Knesset member is justified in these three cases: (A) travel on behalf of the Knesset; (B) the need for medical treatment; (C) to conduct official business. There have recently been cases of Israelis besmirching the name of Israel in Europe, and the number of exit permits must be curtailed.[58]

Moreover, Ben-Gurion also demanded a significant reduction in the scope of immunity. According to the proposed law, the immunity would apply within and outside the Knesset. The Prime Minister insisted it should be limited to the Knesset. Since the House Committee intended to apply immunity not only to the votes, expression of opinions and acts of Knesset members in the fulfillment of their duties, but also 'as a consequence of the fulfillment of their duties', Ben-Gurion asked for an exact interpretation of this latter phrase. He was taken aback by the suggestion that Knesset members would have immunity from police searches, and raised the possibility that other people might reside in the homes of Knesset members. In regard to protection against searching the correspondence of Knesset members, he suggested that it would be limited to letters sent abroad, but not in the opposite direction.

Members of the coalition directorate raised several objections to the Prime Minister's comments. Argov protested that the Histadrut would be unable to send Knesset members abroad as its emissaries. Mazor of the United Religious Front was opposed to making attendance at Knesset sessions compulsory: 'I wouldn't mind, if, for example, Vilner spent all of his time outside the country.'[59] Bar-Rav-Hai, chairman of the sub-committee on immunity, was also opposed to Ben-Gurion's suggestion: 'I doubt whether anyone has the right to compel me to participate in the Knesset. I do not accept that.'[60] In view of the Prime Minister's reservations, the House Committee continued in early 1951 to discuss the details of the immunity law. Katz (Herut) and Bar-Yehuda (Mapam) demanded that excessive use should not be made of state security as a pretext for limiting the scope of immunity.[61] Argov expressed the Prime Minister's position in relation to the issuance of exit permits to Knesset members. They would have to obtain an exit permit to leave the country like all other citizens. The competent authority could refuse to issue an exit permit to a Knesset member for reasons of security, in which case the Knesset member could appeal to the House Committee.[62] Mapai representatives reported Ben-Gurion's demand that immunity be limited to the Knesset and not applied outside it, as had previously been agreed.[63] At a meeting of the constitution, law and justice committee in March 1951, Bader called for the passage of the immunity law.[64]

The opposition reacted to the delay in passing the immunity law by freezing the discussion on the election law, which was intended to bring about early elections to the Second Knesset. It did so, according to Bader, 'without a declaration, simply by the deed itself'.[65] Mapai was interested in early elections – since the government had lost its parliamentary majority. The other parties feared that Mapai might gain most of the votes of the masses of new immigrants, who were in large part from Arab countries, and hence had no interest in early elections. Mapai was in the minority in its demand for early elections, and hence the opposition, represented by Bader, linked earlier elections with the immunity law: 'We have no faith in the government's probity in relation to the opposition. Ben-Gurion utilizes the mechanism of the secret services to keep tabs on rival parties. And what more are he and his cronies likely to do during the elections?'[66]

In April 1951, a deal was in the making between the opposition and Mapai. Mapai would agree to the passage of the immunity law and in exchange, the opposition would agree to support legislation for holding early elections. According to Bader, the deal was made between him and Bar-Yehuda on behalf of the opposition and Argov from Mapai. Argov invited the two men to have a talk and asked them what they wanted. Their reply was an adamant demand for the passage of an immunity law and the three agreed that the Speaker of the Knesset would 'undertake to place the immunity law on the agenda and see to it that the debate reached its conclusion. Based on this agreement, on the same day, the Knesset plenum would pass the immunity law and the law for elections to the Second Knesset.'[67] Bader presented it at a meeting of the constitution, law and justice committee in April, and also demanded a clause be inserted into the elections law stating that if the immunity law was not passed, the law for earlier elections would not be applied.[68] The next day, Nir, the chairman of the constitution, law and justice committee, announced that the immunity law would be brought the following week for its first reading in the plenum.[69] According to a press report, Ben-Gurion was at first opposed to the deal,[70] however, he finally had no choice but to accept it.

A few days later, the Mapai secretariat convened to discuss the deal, and agreed that the Prime Minister would be informed about any progress made on the issue.[71] That same evening, the Mapai faction met, in the presence of Ben-Gurion. Argov, who had engineered the deal, explained its essence:

> All the other factions had demanded that an immunity law be passed together with the elections law. After the committee's negotiations, a compromise was reached that the first reading would take place tomorrow, and that the faction would give its commitment that immediately after the recess – in two weeks' time – there would be a second reading. The whole matter is peculiar and dubious, but we have no way out, because we're in the minority.[72]

Govrin was opposed to Mapai giving a commitment to the opposition. Argov told him: 'In order to avoid an argument, you have the choice. Either the elections law will not be passed, or we vote on the immunity law in a month's time at the second reading.'[73] Bar-Rav-Hai supported Argov and said that Mapai ought to proceed on the assumption that it had no majority, and 'any attempt to fight against the immunity law will not succeed'.[74] He appealed to Knesset members Lavie and Ada Maimon, who had openly supported Ben-Gurion in his opposition to the immunity law, to desist from their objection. MK Ephraim Tavory supported the passage of an immunity law, not only as part of the deal, but for substantive reasons:

> If we have introduced a democratic parliamentary system of government, then we have to draw all the conclusions. I think if England and countries in Western Europe have a parliamentary democracy, we can accept their basic elements.[75]

That same day, Bader declared in the plenum:

> We have demanded and continue to demand that together with the elections law, an immunity law for Knesset members be passed . . . and how will it be possible to get through the period of elections, if the members of parliament have no immunity? . . . and those opposed to the immunity law are the very ones who have no reason to demand immunity.[76]

The following day, Bar-Rav-Hai reported to the constitution, law and justice committee that the Speaker had confirmed, in the House

Committee, that two weeks after the Passover recess, the immunity law would be brought for its first reading in the plenum. Bar-Rav-Hai undertook, on behalf of Mapai, to carry out the agreement that had been reached.[77] On the same day, the two bills – on immunity and elections – were presented to the plenum. Still Lam of Mapai attacked Bader: 'But if MK Bader demands that we agree to a special, strange immunity law, one that is not customary in other countries, just to enable elections to be held – we cannot agree to that.'[78] Lavie, one of Ben-Gurion's most ardent supporters, went even further: 'What do we need immunity for? We have lived all this time without such a law.'[79] But that was the 'swan song' of the law's opponents, chief among them, the Prime Minister.

In June 1951, about a month before the elections, the immunity law had not yet been passed, and some suspicion arose that Mapai would not keep its part of the bargain. On 18 June, the plenum began its second reading of the law. Ben-Gurion suggested that the clause in the bill providing immunity against searches of the dwelling, body, possessions and papers of a Knesset member be deleted. In his speech, the Prime Minister admitted that he was still opposed to the bill as a whole and not only to that particular clause:

> If I were speaking as a member of Knesset, I would speak against the bill as a whole . . . as a member of Knesset I am ashamed of this bill, and will vote against it, even if I am the only one to do so. Immunity for Knesset members and their work inside the Knesset is necessary and justified, namely for their utterances and their votes in the Knesset – but there is no justification nor any moral and political grounds for granting excessive rights to Knesset members that are not connected with the fulfillment of their duties in the Knesset. And it is all the more odd and inexplicable that just before the Knesset dissolves, its members are rushing to grant themselves all sorts of privileges and inordinate rights that are not enjoyed by other citizens and which are unnecessary for the fulfillment of the duties of those elected by the people to serve in the Knesset. This bill does nothing to enhance the honour of the representatives of the people, on the contrary . . . one can assume that the members of Knesset are loyal to the state, but we cannot rely too much on this assumption; only the most naive person is unaware that in this country there are traitors to the State of Israel, in theory or in practice, who are ready to divulge infor-

> mation to real or potential enemies of Israel, not necessarily out of greed, and it is not impossible for such groups to be among those elected to the Knesset . . . I see in the existing conditions a grave danger to the security of the state.[80]

The formal objection to the clause on searches was submitted by Lavie of Mapai, but it was overruled by the majority.

After the plenum accepted the position of the House Committee and rejected the objections put forward by Ben-Gurion and other Mapai members in relation to the first two clauses of the bill, the government demanded that the debate on the second reading be discontinued. The opposition strongly protested the disruption of the normal parliamentary proceedings. Bader argued that it amounted to a violation of the agreement between the parties, since before the recess, the constitution, law and justice committee, the House Committee, the presidium (the Speaker and his deputies) and all the factions had decided that the immunity law would be accepted, that the House Committee would discuss the bill during the recess and that two weeks after the recess, the bill would be brought for final approval by the plenum:

> I am naive, and in this sense I am certainly more naive than the honourable Prime Minister, who claims he is also naive, and I believed those promises; I had no doubt that they would be kept . . . In this situation, I must protest about the fact that the debate on the immunity law is not going forward.[81]

Mapam joined in Herut's demand, and the opposition stirred up a parliamentary storm following the discontinuation of the debate on the immunity law. Nir, who was chairing the session, justified the discontinuation of the debate on the grounds that the government was entitled to determine the agenda, and refused to accede to the opposition's demand that a procedural vote be held on the discontinuation of the debate. Ben-Aharon said:

> We have reasons to assume that the Mapai members know – and the Prime Minister's words today have strengthened this impression and turned our suspicions into certainty – that there is a clear intent here to prevent the approval of the immunity law in this Knesset, a continuation of the sabotage they resorted to during the first two years of the Knesset's existence.[82]

Bader added, 'We listened with grave concern to the Prime Minister's opinion of the immunity law.'[83] The opposition's protest against the discontinuation of the debate on the law was of no avail.

At a meeting of the Mapai faction, the next day, Ben-Gurion was still entertaining the notion that the law could be rescinded: '[If] the immunity law is not completed, and the party gets a majority in the Second Knesset, it will rescind the law'.[84] However, six days later, on 25 June 1951, after Bader and Bar-Yehuda demanded that Argov and Sprinzak honour the deal, the debate on the second reading was reopened, and at its end the law was finally passed in the third reading. Just before the final vote, a member of Knesset made a facetious proposal: 'I suggest that we delay the final vote, to give the Prime Minister time to vote against the law.'[85]

The law granted the Knesset members extremely broad immunity in comparison to other countries. One reason for this, among others, was the members' apprehension about Ben-Gurion's possible actions. His opposition to the law may actually have intensified the Knesset members' desire to pass a law that would grant them very broad immunity. The immunity law was, in a sense, a 'revolt' by Knesset members, including those from Mapai, against the Prime Minister. After Ben-Gurion's time, the law was amended several times, reducing the scope of the immunity, but even after these changes it still provided very broad immunity. As previously mentioned, one of the reasons for the public's negative image of the Knesset is the sweeping immunity its members enjoy.

AFTER THE PASSAGE OF THE IMMUNITY LAW

Mapai did not succeed in obtaining an absolute majority in the 1951 elections. Nonetheless, after the elections there was some concern that Ben-Gurion would try to rescind the immunity law. The initial version of the basic guidelines of the new government stated that 'The immunity required for Knesset members in the fulfillment of their duties will be defined and their rights and obligations will be clarified.'[86] This statement could be interpreted as meaning the issue of immunity would be reopened and the immunity of Knesset members could be greatly curtailed, or perhaps annulled. In view of this concern about possible actions by Ben-Gurion, the wording was changed and the basic guidelines say: 'the powers of the Knesset will be defined', as well as 'the rights of and duties of Knesset members in accordance with the principles of parliamentary–democratic government'.[87] Ben-Gurion admitted that the change was made under pressure from the Progressives, 'because they said the separate paragraph might arouse the suspicion that we are going to rescind the law of immunity for Knesset members which was passed by the First Knesset'.[88] The immunity law was helpful to the Knesset on several occasions; for example, when, in November 1951, Riftin of Mapam read out in the plenum a poem whose publication had been banned by the censor.[89] In contrast to the earlier incident – when Ben-Aharon read Alterman's poem – Ben-Gurion was unable to demand, through the censor, that the poem be omitted from the minutes, and to threaten, again through the censor, the banning of the minutes.

Despite the fact that the immunity law was now in existence, Ben-Gurion continued on several occasions to instruct the censor to take a hard line in relation to Knesset members. In December 1951, Vilner complained in the plenum that the censor was making use of political considerations that had nothing to do with security. He said:

> I wrote a letter to someone abroad. First of all, I think it is forbidden to take scissors to letters by Knesset members and cut them up. My letter was received abroad cut into pieces. I won't speak now about the fact that letters written by Knesset members are being censored. But what was deleted from my letter? One sentence saying that the majority of residents in Israel are embittered and do not accept the government's foreign policy.[90]

The Prime Minister brushed aside Vilner's claims and asserted that he had abused his immunity:

> I am taking this opportunity to announce that we will enter an appeal to the House Committee about the procedure under which the Speaker of the Knesset – after a Knesset member has used his right of immunity to read in the Knesset excerpts of things banned by the Censor – allows these to be published in the press, and I will submit an appeal on this matter to the House Committee.[91]

There is no proof that Ben-Gurion actually carried out his intention to take action against the Speaker of the Knesset.

In January 1952, the Knesset was about to begin its debate on the reparations agreement between Israel and West Germany. Herut supporters demonstrated furiously in the streets of Jerusalem, throwing stones at the Knesset building and clashing with the police. Begin made threatening speeches outside and inside the Knesset. His address in the Knesset was stopped, and he threatened that if he were not allowed to continue, no one else would speak in the Knesset. There was also concern that violence would break out among the members.[92] Begin, very agitated, announced that day in the Knesset: 'As of 4 o'clock today, I, a member of Knesset, if the law of parliamentary immunity applies to me, regard this law as null and void.'[93] In fact, the law does not permit a Knesset member to waive his basic immunity nor can the Knesset lift that right, although his immunity on a specific point can be lifted by the Knesset.

Ben-Gurion decided, in the wake of the stormy incidents, to punish Begin and did so, blatantly violating the newly enacted immunity law. Even before the Knesset concluded its debate on means of penalizing Begin, the Prime Minister convened the secretariat of his party and succeeded in pushing through a decision in favour of establishing a party militia 'to protect the state and democracy in Israel'. Ben-Gurion then said:

> We cannot do this within the framework of the Histadrut because it will split and destroy the Histadrut . . . we must do this in the framework of the party . . . by organizing militant groups of workers . . . the core of this force to be established must be partisan . . . when it has to act, this force will not be subordinate to the police.[94]

The Prime Minister proposed that Iser Harel, head of the General Security Services, a man faithful to him, would look into the matter and engage in setting up the party militia.[95] In the meantime, the House Committee concluded its deliberations on Begin's punishment and decided to present a proposal to the plenum about preventing Begin's participation in Knesset sessions for several months (until the Passover recess) because he had threatened in his speech in the Knesset to resort to acts of violence.[96] The opposition was up in arms because the decision of the House Committee – adopted under the pressure brought by the Prime Minister – was a blatant violation of the immunity law, since Begin's immunity in relation to his utterances in the Knesset was absolute and could not be lifted.

Ezra Ichilov of the General Zionists attacked the House Committee, which in the absence of a constitution and parliamentary rules of procedure dealing with such situations, had attempted 'to set the first precedent, a grave and dangerous one, concerning the rights of the Hebrew elected representative'.[97] Bar-Yehuda of Mapam jeered at the decision:

> what you are proposing here now is one more emergency law on behalf of the majority of the Knesset against Knesset members . . . you are introducing some sort of law into the Knesset that makes a mockery of the basic right not only of MK Begin, but the right of every one here, and forbids him from openly expressing his thoughts as a representative of the people . . . I don't know why you suggest only until this Passover; in this way you could expel him until Passover of next year.[98]

Landau of Herut argued that the Knesset is not a court of law. Punishment was being levied on Begin without any legal basis, not even on a precedent or a custom: 'Your democracy is terror in nearly all spheres of our life.'[99]

Even the former Minister of Justice, Rosen of the Progressive Party, objected to the 'despicable proposal of the House Committee', and stated that it would be possible to try to lift Begin's immunity, but it was impossible to punish him without doing so.[100] He argued that there was no proof that Begin had in fact threatened the Knesset and facts to support this conclusion were lacking. 'This is a very dubious thing to do',[101] he added, and told of his experience as Minister of Justice in the previous Knesset in the debates on the immunity law, when 'representatives of the previous government waged an all-out war in the committee against the wording',[102] and the Prime Minister himself voted against the law.

Bader said:

> this is an example of a fascist regime . . . it is a fascist custom par excellence . . . this is a political trial . . . I have my own view about the trial on the Reichstag fire, but there at least there was the outward semblance of a trial, and Goering had threatened Ribbentrop that he would not get out of the trial alive. That is certainly a more persuasive reason than the one put forward by the Prime Minister.[103]

Nachum Chat of the General Zionists claimed that the decision was an 'out-and-out violation of the law' and Begin has the right to know what exactly he is being charged with.[104] Esther Vilenska of the Communist Party spoke about the 'destruction of parliamentary life in Israel'.[105] Ben-Gurion held to the opposite view:

> This does not contradict the immunity of the Knesset. On the contrary, the Knesset's immunity makes this imperative. People have to know they cannot threaten the Knesset or use acts of violence against it, and anyone who does so is punished first of all by the Knesset itself.[106]

Mapai's partners in the coalition were not happy about the steps taken against Begin. However, in the vote on the House Committee's proposal, Ben-Gurion won with a majority of 56 against 47 Knesset members.

On various occasions, Ben-Gurion expressed his aversion to the immunity law. In February 1952, in the Knesset, he attacked the President of the Supreme Court for having dared to criticize the statements made by the Minister of Justice in the Knesset about the overly lenient sentences meted out in the courts to attackers of policemen. The Prime Minister represented himself as the protector of the Knesset:

> I believe that in the immunity law passed in the First Knesset, members of the Knesset assumed for themselves excessive rights that are not justified and are not grounded in the notion of immunity. But fundamentally, the immunity law is correct and necessary. It is just and vital to ensure the elected representative of the people in the sovereign Knesset complete freedom in fulfilling his duties as a servant of the people, without the courts, the police and the army in the country being able to interfere in the performance of these duties. The courts and the judges are not in charge of the debates in the Knesset, and only the Knesset itself and its authorities, the Speaker, the House Committee, the plenum, are the sole judges.[107]

Ben-Gurion was of the opinion that the President of the Supreme Court had infringed upon the very idea of immunity. In fact, he was utilizing the law of immunity to defend his Minister of Justice since the Minister had expressed his criticism of the judges in the Knesset.

In July 1952, Ben-Gurion condemned what he regarded as the abuse of the immunity law by Tubi. Tubi had accused the army of conducting searches in an Arab village and demanded the establishment of a parliamentary inquiry committee. Ben-Gurion replied:

> We have immunity for Knesset members, so that they can fulfill their duties and express their thoughts, but I think there has never been such a disgraceful exploitation, as this, by MK Tufik Tubi, of the right of immunity, which in the final analysis also involves an obligation.[108]

The Prime Minister demanded that the House Committee examine 'to what extent the right of Knesset members can be abused'.[109]

In September 1952, the Prime Minister once again attacked the immunity law. During a meeting with leaders of the General Zionists, he said:

> If we pass an immunity law, knowing that there is a fifth column among us, I will not mention names, but we know that certain people will do exactly . . . what they are ordered to do by Soviet agents, . . . but it is impossible to search their homes, because they have immunity. Where else does such immunity exist?[110]

Three months later he wrote to Nahum Goldman about 'the strange immunity law that strengthens the position of spies and agents in the guise of representatives of the people'.[111]

Early in 1953, Ben-Gurion made a desperate attempt to enact new legislation that would curtail the immunity. He succeeded in passing a resolution in the government in favour of three amendments to the law: cancellation of the immunity from searches in the homes of Knesset members, cancellation of the freedom of Communist members of Knesset to leave the country, and cancellation of their right to enter every part of the country.[112] The chairman of the Mapai faction, Govrin, reported to the members of the faction on this plan of Ben-Gurion's, adding that in the debates held in the directorate of the faction and the directorate of the coalition, nearly everyone was opposed to the cancellation of the clause providing immunity from searches in the homes of Knesset members.[113] The government's resolution was never passed as legislation in the Knesset. The Prime Minister had no chance of amending the immunity law. The government's resolution was apparently connected with the 'doctors' trial' in the Soviet Union. After Ben-Gurion failed in this attempt to outlaw the Communist Party – the heads of Mapai were resolutely opposed to that[114] – he initiated a government resolution in favour of amending the immunity law, a move directly mainly against the Communists, hoping that the majority in the Knesset would support the government in this matter.

In October 1957, Tubi complained that his immunity had been violated when he was arrested by a military policeman at the entrance to an Arab village, but the Attorney General, to whom Tubi appealed, decided instead to demand that Tubi's immunity be lifted as a result of that same incident,[115] although in the end this did not happen. In August 1958, Ben-Aharon, whose party was then in the coalition, complained that the military censor or the General Security Services had confiscated an envelope sent to him by a representative of his kibbutz movement who had returned from Moscow. Ben-Aharon remonstrated that this amounted to a violation of the immunity law.[116] The head of the Defence Minister's bureau wrote that he was in possession of the material which he had received from the General Security Services.[117] The head of the General Security Services wrote to Ben-Gurion several weeks later, apologizing for the lack of judgement and the inefficiency of his people in this matter.[118] It is obvious from this incident that Ben-Gurion's office was involved in matters of this kind, although he failed in his attempts to deprive Knesset members of their parliamentary immunity.

NOTES

1. State Archives, minutes of meeting of interior committee of the Provisional State Council, 26 October 1948.
2. Ibid., 23 November 1948.
3. Ben-Gurion Research Center Archives, diaries, 13 June 1949.
4. Ibid, correspondence, Bernstein to Ben-Gurion, 16 October 1948.
5. Ibid.
6. Ibid., Ben-Gurion to Kol, 7 January 1949.
7. Ibid, Ben-Gurion to Yaacov Meridor, 22 December 1949.
8. State Archives, meeting of House Committee, 27 February 1951.
9. Ibid., 6 March 1951.
10. Ibid., 27 February 1951.
11. Ibid.
12. Ben-Gurion Research Center Archives, correspondence, Ben-Gurion to Bentov, 16 December 1948.
13. Ibid., Yigal Yadin to Ben-Gurion, 30 July 1948.

14. Ibid., Ben-Gurion to military censor, 16 August 1948.
15. *Knesset Record*, 11 April 1949, p. 333.
16. Ibid., 17 May 1949, p. 515.
17. Ibid., p. 516.
18. Ibid., 18 May 1949, p. 533.
19. Ibid., p. 534.
20. State Archives, joint meeting of the foreign affairs and security committee and the House Committee, 24 May 1949.
21. *Knesset Record*, 30 May 1949, pp. 592, 595.
22. Ibid., p. 593.
23. Ben-Gurion Research Center Archives, correspondence, Ben-Gurion to Ben-Aharon, 17 September 1950.
24. *Davar*, 10 May 1951.
25. Ibid., 7 May 1951.
26. Ben-Gurion Research Center Archives, correspondence, Ben-Gurion to Ministry of Immigration, 29 October 1948.
27. Provisional State Council, 6 January 1949, p. 4.
28. Ibid.
29. Ben-Gurion Research Center Archives, Ben-Gurion to Gluska, 29 June 1949.
30. Ibid., Ben-Gurion to Eliezer Levenstein (Livne), 10 October 1950.
31. State Archives, 20/25, Ben-Gurion to chairman of the House Committee, 4 December 1949.
32. Ibid., meeting of the House Committee, 6 December 1949.
33. Ibid., 15 November 1949.
34. Ibid., 28 November 1949.
35. Ibid., 13 December 1949.
36. Ibid., meeting of interior committee, 21 February 1950.
37. Ibid.
38. Ibid.
39. Ibid.
40. Ibid.
41. Ibid.
42. Ben-Gurion Research Center Archives, correspondence, Captain Gordon to Ben-Gurion, 29 May 1950.
43. State Archives, meeting of House Committee, 20 June 1950.
44. *Knesset Record*, 12 July 1950, p. 2,178.
45. Ibid.
46. Ibid. pp. 2,178–9.
47. State Archives, meeting of House Committee, 27 February 1951.
48. Ibid.
49. Ibid., meeting of constitution, law and justice committee, 27 March 1951.
50. Israel Labour Party Archives, meeting of Mapai faction in the Knesset, 5 February 1950.
51. Ibid., meeting of directorate of Mapai faction in the Knesset, 10 May 1950.
52. Ibid., 23 July 1950.
53. Ibid., meeting of Mapai faction in the Knesset, 12 October 1950.
54. Bader, *The Knesset and I*, p. 51.
55. Ibid.
56. Ibid.
57. Israel Labour Party Archives, meeting of directorate of the coalition, 18 July 1950.
58. Ibid.
59. Ibid.
60. Ibid.
61. State Archives, meeting of House Committee, 1 January 1951.
62. Ibid., 8 January 1951.
63. Ibid., 16 January 1951.

64. Ibid., meeting of constitution, law and justice committee, 12 March 1951.
65. Bader, *The Knesset and I*, p. 51.
66. Ibid.
67. Ibid.
68. State Archives, meeting of constitution, law and justice committee, 3 April 1951.
69. Ibid., 4 April 1951.
70. *HaTzofeh*, 6 April 1951.
71. Israel Labour Party Archives, meeting of Mapai secretariat, 9 April 1951.
72. Ibid., meeting of Mapai faction in the Knesset, 9 April 1951.
73. Ibid.
74. Ibid.
75. Ibid.
76. *Knesset Record*, 9 April 1951, p. 1,614.
77. State Archives, meeting of constitution, law and justice committee, 10 April 1951.
78. *Knesset Record*, 10 April 1951, pp. 1,623–4.
79. Ibid., p. 1,651.
80. Ibid., 18 June 1951, p. 1,998.
81. Ibid., p. 2,001.
82. Ibid., p. 2,002.
83. Ibid.
84. Israel Labour Party Archives, meeting of Mapai faction in the Knesset, 19 June 1951.
85. *Knesset Record*, 25 June 1951, p. 2,068.
86. Ben-Gurion Research Center Archives, minutes of meetings, meeting of designate ministers, 7 October 1951.
87. Ibid.
88. Ibid.
89. *Knesset Record*, 4 November 1951, p. 284.
90. Ibid., 12 December 1951, p. 637.
91. Ibid., p. 638.
92. Bader, *The Knesset and I*, pp. 62–3.
93. *Knesset Record*, 7 January 1952, p. 907.
94. Israel Labour Party Archives, meeting of Mapai secretariat, 10 January 1952.
95. Ibid.
96. *Knesset Record*, 21 January 1952, p. 1,030.
97. Ibid., p. 1,031.
98. Ibid., p. 1,032.
99. Ibid., p. 1,035.
100. Ibid., p. 1,037.
101. Ibid., p. 1,038.
102. Ibid., p. 1,048.
103. Ibid.
104. Ibid., p. 1,051.
105. Ibid., p. 1,053.
106. Ibid., p. 1,054.
107. Ibid., 27 February 1952, pp. 1,461–2.
108. Ibid., 2 July 1952, p. 2,522.
109. Ibid., p. 2,523.
110. Ben-Gurion Research Center Archives, minutes of meetings, meeting with leaders of the General Zionists, 11 September 1952.
111. Ibid., correspondence, Ben-Gurion to Goldman, 16 December 1952.
112. Israel Labour Party Archives, meeting of Mapai faction in the Knesset, 9 February 1953.
113. Ibid.
114. Giora Goldberg, 'The Jewish Factor in the Israeli Reaction to the Doctors' Plot in Moscow', in Eliezer Don-Yehiya (ed.) *Israel and Diaspora Jewry*, Ramat Gan: Bar-Ilan University, 1991, pp. 183–203.

115. Ben-Gurion Research Center Archives, correspondence, Baruch Azanya to Ben-Gurion, 29 October 1957.
116. Ibid., Ben-Aharon to Ben-Gurion, 21 August 1957.
117. Ibid., Chief of Defence Minister's bureau to an unknown addressee, 22 August 1957.
118. Ibid., the head of the General Security Service to the Prime Minister's bureau, 6 September 1957.

7 Collective Responsibility and Coalition Discipline

A parliament whose members are compelled to vote according to a party line can not properly fulfill its function. In a coalition system, of the type that has existed in Israel since its founding, the problem is even more complex, since the largest party in the coalition is likely to dictate to its coalition partners how they must vote in the parliament. When this occurs, the parliamentary majority is unable to criticize the government and its function is severely impaired. On the other hand, political parties are the major participants in parliamentary life, and if every member of the parliament is completely independent in deciding how to vote, this is damaging to the governance of the country. What is required, then, is a balance between the needs of government and the duties of the parliament. This balance is achieved by compromise, of the kind that exists, for example, in the British political system.

Ben-Gurion did not want a compromise between the opposing needs of the various branches of government. Instead he strongly favoured legislation that would totally quash the independence of the members of Knesset and the Knesset's ability, as an institution, to criticize and oversee the government. He did not get everything he wanted, but he did succeed in causing the Knesset a great deal of damage, which left its mark for decades after he had departed from the political scene. The provisional government, during its existence, had no collective responsibility towards the parliament.[1] Ben-Gurion's hopes that his party would obtain an absolute majority in the first elections in 1949, and would need no coalition partners, were dashed. The transition law, passed after the elections, stated, for the first time, that the government was collectively responsible to the Knesset for its actions. The principle of collective responsibility was also added to the basic guidelines of the government that were established following the 1949 elections.

STRUGGLES TO TIGHTEN COALITION DISCIPLINE

In February 1949, in a meeting with leaders of the General Zionists, Ben-Gurion revealed his position on coalition discipline. Rokach remonstrated with the Prime Minister about his past statement that 'it will not be easy for anyone in the minority in the government in so far as the forum of the parliament is concerned. He will have to keep silent in the parliament, and not appear there.'[2] Ben-Gurion replied that he was actually interested in hearing the members of his party criticize the government, but this would not be expressed in the Knesset or in votes taken there, nor as opposition.

> A government is a government. It is a unit . . . I am not saying, however, that parties in the government will not criticize one another. They will. I do not want to leave this task to Mr Peter Bergson; I want my associates to criticize the government.[3]

Peter Bergson was the former name of MK Hillel Kook of Herut, who was known for his persistent opposition to Ben-Gurion. The Prime Minister stressed that criticism could be voiced in the initial stage of internal debates, but once this stage was completed and a government decision had been reached, a party that chose to remain in the government had to take the responsibility for the implementation of that decision.[4] He was already suggesting that any party that chose to breach collective responsibility would either have to leave the government or be ousted from it. As the leader of the dominant party, which could easily choose its coalition partners, he was able to threaten this sanction since, during his tenure, Mapai did not depend on any particular party in order to set up a coalition. In the wake of the series of coalition crises that broke out in the 1950s, Ben-Gurion hardened his position and proposed legal solutions to deal with the problem. In February 1951, after the government was defeated, for the first time, in a confidence vote in the Knesset – on the issue of religious education – the Prime Minister wrote to Knesset members from the coalition factions: 'I will not serve in any government in which the members do not have collective responsibility and which does not have the backing of a majority in the Knesset.'[5] In October 1951, during a meeting of designate ministers for the new government, Ben-Gurion stressed the section in the basic guidelines that applied the principle of collective responsibility to the ministers and their parliamentary factions in relation to the government's decisions and its accepted programme.[6] In June 1952, Ben-Gurion called upon the members of the Mapai faction, and in fact the members of the other factions in the coalition, to tighten coalition discipline: 'Sometimes a member rises in the Knesset and says what he has to say without considering the consequences.'[7] The directorate of the coalition must decide that 'every member who wants to vote against a government decision, speak out against it, or abstain from voting',[8] will have to obtain the government's prior approval.

> No member can oppose a government decision without first receiving permission from the coalition directorate; if the coalition takes a decision opposed to that member's opinion, he has to give in. Although a member is permitted on occasion to differ with the government's view, he must do so within a general framework; no one of us was elected on a personal basis; we were elected as a collective body and we are responsible within this body.[9]

In fact, he was demanding of the Knesset members from Mapai and its coalition partners total obedience, not only preventing a Knesset member from voting according to his conscience, but also from speaking out in the Knesset and expressing criticism of the government's decisions. However, Ben-Gurion was not successful in getting a formal decision to this effect adopted in the coalition directorate.

There was opposition to Ben-Gurion's unyielding approach even in the ranks of Mapai. MK Shmuel Dayan, for example, spoke some harsh words at a meeting of the faction in November 1952 regarding the support demanded for a particular law, which the Prime Minister had not even taken the trouble to explain to the faction members:

> But in connection with these things that are brought to the Knesset on which we are required to vote, we must discuss them. I am not prepared to be an automaton, to raise my hand in favour of something that someone else has decided. I want to discuss it sometimes, to hear something about it. But when

> you bring a law here and say it was agreed upon somewhere else, I don't accept that.[10]

The chairman of the faction, Govrin, to whom Dayan's remarks were directed, replied that he supported Dayan's approach:

> I can do no more than that. I am not in charge around here, nor am I a member of the party secretariat. Today I asked Ben-Gurion to come to the faction in connection with this law. He told me it was physically impossible for him to come today, and he was very annoyed, justifiably so, asking: 'How many parties do we have?' On this matter, I think there is something wrong here. If Ben-Gurion had come today – this entire argument would not have taken place.[11]

In December 1952, when the Progressives were about to join the coalition, a dispute arose between them and Mapai about the scope of collective responsibility. Mapai demanded that collective responsibility be applied not only to topics connected with the accepted basic guidelines, but also to all government decisions. Rosen informed Ben-Gurion that his party was opposed to the automatic application of collective responsibility to all government decisions.[12] Even during his stay in Sede Boker, Ben-Gurion was still preoccupied with the subject of collective responsibility and coalition discipline. In August 1954, he wrote an indignant letter to Aranne:

> I am deeply concerned that the principle of collective responsibility will be undermined . . . The party must honour the signature of its representatives. But we all must honour the state, and if the principle of collective responsibility is undermined . . . [and ministers and Knesset members] . . . can vote as they wish and remain in government – then God have mercy on this state.[13]

In other words, Ben-Gurion was so extreme in his views on collective responsibility that he actually linked it with the very existence of Israel as a state. He was not prepared to accept any compromise on this matter, and his perception of it was both simplistic and dichotomic. In August 1955, he reported to the Mapai central committee on the coalition negotiations with the leader of Achdut Haavoda, Yigal Allon:

> They asked questions: 'Can't we write a letter to the newspaper? Can we not speak to the youth? Can we not lecture at a seminar?' I told him: 'Listen, Yigal, don't talk nonsense. It's impossible to be in the government and in the opposition. Either you accept this principle, or you don't.[14]

In June 1956, Justice Minister Rosen informed the Prime Minister that his party, the Progressives, had decided to abstain from a vote in the Knesset on Namir's joining the government.[15] Ben-Gurion was not prepared to accept that, and replied to Rosen the very same day: 'A member of the government is not entitled to abstain from voting on a government decision, unless he has received permission to do so . . . I would suggest to your members to vote in favour [of the decision] and make a statement.'[16]

An important point to make is that during Ben-Gurion's terms of office, discipline was rarely breached by the Mapai faction or the coalition partners. From the 1970s, a certain slackening of discipline was evident in both the faction and the coalition. Nonetheless, back in the 1950s, Ben-Gurion was already calling for changes to prevent any possibility of members voting or expressing opinions inconsistent with the government's position. In May 1957, at a meeting of the Mapai faction he attacked Mapam and Achdut Haavoda for having breached coalition discipline: 'There is a law of collective responsibility. It is in the basic guidelines, and this law has been breached.'[17]

In December 1957, the Prime Minister resigned in the wake of a crisis in the coalition, stirred up by a leak from a government meeting on Chief of Staff Moshe Dayan's visit to West Germany. Ben-Gurion took advantage of the crisis to further strengthen collective responsibility although the Knesset was not involved in the crisis. In a joint meeting of the faction and the party secretariat, he stressed that the principle of collective responsibility was not only laid down in the basic guidelines but 'is a basic law in this state'.[18] At the end of December, he held meetings with leaders of the coalition parties regarding his desire to tighten coalition discipline. To the leaders of the Progressives, he said: 'Collective responsibility is a law of the state, and we have violated the law.'[19] In a meeting with the leaders of Achdut Haavoda, he suggested the existing situation be changed, not by new legislation, but by a moral commitment, according to which if two-thirds of the ministers find that a minister has seriously undermined collective responsibility, he will have to resign.[20] In a meeting with leaders of Mapam he described his proposal in greater detail. The two-thirds rule would apply not only to an infringement of collective responsibility, but also to an act that undermined a security interest of the state or its international standing.[21] Mapam and Achdut Haavoda were opposed to the Prime Minister's proposal, since he could oust a minister from the government simply by obtaining the support of the Mapai ministers. Ben-Gurion recorded in his diary the details of his proposal which he had submitted to the coalition parties:

> A minister or his faction in the Knesset or on its committees may abstain in a vote on a position taken by the coalition only if he obtains the consent of the government. Anyone who cannot fulfill this commitment for any reason, must resign before the vote . . . every minister is obliged to resign if two-thirds of the government members have found, after an inquiry in the government, that a minister or his faction have seriously undermined the collective responsibility of the government or a security interest or the international standing of Israel. The press that is subordinate to the coalition factions is obliged to refrain from mutual incriminations and to meticulously maintain a civilized and collegial style in all debates. For this purpose, a committee will be established composed of all the newspapers subject to the will of the coalition factions.[22]

Ben-Gurion's intent was to expand collective responsibility to apply to party newspapers as well. But what is more important, he also aspired to apply collective responsibility not only to votes in the Knesset plenum but to all of its committees too. It is interesting that when he stated that 'Anyone who cannot fulfill this commitment for any reason, must resign before the vote',[23] he drew no distinction between ministers and Knesset members. This would mean that if a Knesset member from a faction in the coalition was going to abstain in a vote on a subject agreed upon by the government, he would have to resign from the Knesset to avoid violating collective responsibility. In fact, he was lumping together Knesset members and ministers from the same party that was a coalition partner. In March 1958, he stated explicitly in a meeting of the Mapai faction that the government would be dissolved if Knesset members from parties in the coalition did not vote with the government in the Knesset and in its committees.[24]

In the basic guidelines of the new government established in

January 1958, collective responsibility was applied to the ministers and their factions. These guidelines included a statement that all the ministers and the coalition factions were obliged to vote in the Knesset in favour of government decisions and laws proposed by it. They further stated that the government was entitled to permit a faction to abstain under certain circumstances, and that a faction may permit a member or several members to abstain, but a decision to this effect had to be taken in the government first. If a minister abstained in a vote without the government's consent, he was obliged to resign. A vote by a faction against a government decision is tantamount to a minister abstaining without the government's permission, which meant that ministers would have to resign owing to the vote of their faction in the Knesset.[25]

However, the inclusion of the principle of collective responsibility in an inter-party agreement did not satisfy Ben-Gurion, especially since neither its inclusion in the government's basic guidelines nor the statement in principle in the 1949 transition law had the effect of subjugating the majority in the Knesset to the will of the government. Ben-Gurion wanted an amendment to the 1949 transition law in order to achieve this aim.

LEGISLATION IMPOSING SANCTIONS FOR THE VIOLATION OF COALITION DISCIPLINE

After the 1959 elections, in which Mapai achieved the best electoral result ever under Ben-Gurion's leadership (47 mandates), he made the establishment of a coalition conditional on the enactment of strict legislation regarding coalition discipline. Any party that was not in favour of such legislation could not participate in the new government.[26] In December 1959 Ben-Gurion presented in the Knesset the new bill intended to endow the government and its head with vast power. According to the proposed amendment to the transition law,

> Collective responsibility is binding on members of the government and their factions. If a government member or his faction votes in the Knesset against the government or abstains in a vote in the Knesset, without the consent of the government, that act will be regarded as the minister's resignation from the government. This resignation will go into effect when the

> Prime Minister makes a statement on it in the Knesset. This statement does not require the approval of the Knesset.[27]

This wording was an expression of the maximum application of coalition discipline, since it applied to the Knesset plenum and its committees and referred to all subjects. Whereas in January 1958, the wording laid down in the basic guidelines was milder – referring only to decisions by the government and its proposed legislation – this time the wording was very strict, in that coalition discipline was applied to every vote 'against the government'.

The Prime Minister explained the reasoning underlying the proposed bill to the Knesset plenum as follows:

> In regard to collective responsibility, the transition law of the Knesset lacked any provision for sanctions, since the Knesset is not subordinate to the police and the courts of law . . . no one is required to remain in the government if his views on matters of principle and conscience differ from those of the government. Hence there is nothing in the bill we are proposing that infringes upon anyone's freedom of conscience.[28]

The leaders of the opposition vehemently attacked the proposed law. Begin argued that no parliamentary government anywhere has a provision in law stating that there is no possibility of introducing any changes in the parliament after a government decision has been taken: 'If the government has decided, there is no attempt at persuasion, there is no change, there is no possibility of voting otherwise; in effect, there is no point in a debate.'[29] Sneh held that the new law would endow Ben-Gurion with enormous power. The law 'changes the basic procedures of government and gives the Prime Minister the status of a sole ruler'.[30] Nir, whose party, Achdut Haavoda, was then in the coalition, announced on behalf of his party that the law was superfluous and apologized for the fact that its agreement to the law was a prior condition for its joining the coalition.[31]

Ben-Gurion rebuffed the opposition's attack on the proposed law: 'I am certain the unity of the Israeli people is far greater than is reflected in the Knesset with its numerous factions.'[32] He admitted that the purpose of the proposed law was to enable the Prime Minister to weigh whether or not to dismiss a minister, since the dismissal was not automatic, and his explanation was: 'There may be a case in which only one or two members will abstain; the faction may be absent, there may be some doubt about whether there was any ill will involved or not.'[33]

Not only did the proposed bill deprive the Knesset of the foundation upon which it rested, it also deliberately left the decision in the hands of the Prime Minister without the factions that were violating coalition discipline knowing in advance, with certainty, whether their ministers would be dismissed from the government or not. Although the bill did go through its first reading, Mapai's partners in the coalition hung back from pushing it through to the final stage. They succeeded, in co-operation with the opposition, in dragging out work on the bill until 1961, when early elections were held, and the primary version of the bill approved at the end of 1959 expired.

After the 1961 elections, Ben-Gurion renewed his efforts to amend the transition law. Since Mapai achieved poorer results in the elections (a decline from 47 mandates to 42) and Ben-Gurion's position in his party was weakened, the version presented to the Knesset in November 1961 was much more moderate than the one presented in December 1959. According to the new version, sanctions could only be imposed in relation to a number of issues: non-confidence, the state budget, proposed laws or provisions in the law that reduce the state's income or increase its expenditures, proposals relating to security or political matters or others in regard to which the government has decided that coalition discipline would apply. The Prime Minister's involvement in dismissing ministers did not appear in the new version. This time the authority of dismissal was granted to the government. Ministers could be dismissed even if they had voted in favour but their faction had voted otherwise. While in 1959, the bill also referred to votes in the Knesset committees, the 1961 version only spoke of votes in the plenum.[34]

At this stage, Mapai's coalition partners did not succeed in preventing the legislation. The opposition once again vigorously attacked the proposed law. Yosef Shofman of Herut said: 'We have learned that other than the present Prime Minister, no one else in this house, not even those who are going to vote for the law, is interested in its passage . . . again the Prime Minister has forced this proposed law on his colleagues in the coalition', and although the version proposed this time was more moderate, 'it is still a very harsh law'.[35] Begin contended that according to the new law, 'It is not the government that is responsible to the Knesset, rather the Knesset is responsible to the government.'[36] He criticized the freedom of manoeuvre that the government had left itself in regard to the dismissal of ministers. Since the sanction can be imposed, based on the will of the government, the latter determines what will be considered as a faction's vote against the government (the entire faction? the majority of the faction? one member of the faction?), 'the majority in the government will always be free to interpret what constitutes a faction',[37] Begin asserted.

Ben-Gurion replied to the opposition that, in the existing situation, it was possible at the same time to be in the coalition and to be in the opposition, and the purpose of the law was to prevent that.[38] He contended that the new law did not prevent members of Knesset from voting according to their conscience: 'This law . . . does not deal with the issue of what members of Knesset should do. Members of Knesset, according to this law are free to vote as they wish, no one intends to restrict this freedom.'[39] He meant that the law does not explicitly state that Knesset members are forbidden to vote against the government. However, this argument is somewhat demagogic, for it overlooks the heavy sanctions for doing so. He continued with this argument:

> The law does not restrict or diminish the freedom of voting of any faction, every faction is free to vote, according to this law, as it wishes . . . therefore it is sheer folly to claim that this law is intended to deprive Knesset members of their freedom to vote or that it in some way infringes on the sovereignty of the Knesset.[40]

Evidence of the Knesset's sovereignty was its authority to express non-confidence in the government. Ben-Gurion was opposed to the existing possibility that a parliamentary majority unable to unite in establishing a new government was entitled to overthrow the existing government.[41] The only means Ben-Gurion was prepared to leave in the hands of the Knesset was the harshest measure of all – a motion of non-confidence – and even that, in his view, called for a certain amendment. He added some words that indicated his unwillingness to differentiate between ministers and Knesset members from their parties:

> The members of government represent someone. When they do not represent anyone, they are not members of the government. Anyone joining the government does so by dint of the fact that he has the backing of a number of [Knesset] members.[42]

The new law came into effect in 1962. It states that a minister is responsible to the government for his vote in the Knesset plenum and the vote of his faction in the Knesset. If a minister votes against the government or abstains, without the prior consent of the government, and the latter wishes to enforce the principle of collective responsibility, the minister will be dismissed from the government when the government makes a statement to the Knesset to that effect. The maximum lapse of time between the vote and the presentation of the statement in the Knesset is two weeks. If the coalition faction has not voted with the government, or has abstained on votes of non-confidence, a proposed state budget, proposed bills and provisions of laws that either reduce state income or increase its expenditures, as well as bills, provisions of law and other proposals on security and political issues, and others on which the government has decided to apply collective responsibility – and if the government decides within a week of the vote that this amounts to a violation of discipline, the ministers of that same faction will be dismissed upon presentation of the government's statement to the Knesset to that effect. The statement can be given within two weeks from the date of the government's decision. The law authorized the government to, in advance, allow ministers and factions freedom to vote or abstain as they wish. It left the government broad freedom of action, since it is not obliged to dismiss a minister who has not voted in accordance with its decision; it has two weeks in which to resolve the crisis through negotiations. The dismissal of a minister due to the vote of his faction is even more complex; since the term 'faction' is not defined in the law (does it refer to the entire faction, a majority of its members, or some of them?), it is open to interpretation by the government; a formal stage of a government decision regarding the violation of discipline is required, a stage which is not mentioned in the law in relation to the dismissal of a minister because of his vote, and the government has three weeks between the vote and the dismissal. This lengthy period of time is meant to suffice to resolve the crisis that has arisen as a result of the vote. The 1962 amendment to the transition law has rather dangerous implications for parliamentary life. The compromise that Ben-Gurion was forced to accept after the 1961 elections in relation to the wording of the law prevented the passage of a much more extreme law which would have further weakened the Knesset and its members. If the process of legislation had dragged on for one more year, the law would probably never have been passed, since a year after its passage, Ben-Gurion resigned as Prime Minister. Most likely without him, Mapai would not have initiated such a law. Nonetheless, the law was not rescinded nor has it been altered since 1962. Parliaments do not hastily tend to change constitutional procedures, particularly since every government wishes to gain some benefits from a constitutional procedure introduced during another government's tenure. In general, it is more difficult to rescind an existing procedure than to establish a new one.

Chapter 8 deals with Ben-Gurion's influence on Israeli parliamentary life through intra-party politics and his control over the process of nominating Knesset members.

NOTES

1. Israel Labour Party Archives, Mapai Council, 12 January 1949, Ben-Gurion's speech.
2. Ben-Gurion Research Center Archives, coalition files, meeting between Ben-Gurion and General Zionist leaders, 24 February 1949.
3. Ibid.
4. Ibid.
5. Ibid., correspondence, Ben-Gurion to Knesset members in the coalition, 15 February 1951.
6. Ibid., minutes of meetings, meetings of designate ministers, 7 October 1951.
7. Israel Labour Party Archives, Mapai faction in the Knesset, 27 June 1952.
8. Ibid.
9. Ibid.
10. Ibid., Mapai faction in the Knesset, 8 November 1952.
11. Ibid.
12. Ben-Gurion Research Center Archives, correspondence, Rosen to Ben-Gurion, 22 December 1952.
13. Israel Labour Party Archives, Ben-Gurion to Aranne, document 9, 16 August 1954.
14. Ibid., Mapai Central Committee, 22 August 1954.
15. Ben-Gurion Research Center Archives, correspondence, Rosen to Ben-Gurion, 19 June 1956.
16. Ibid., Ben-Gurion to Rosen, 19 June 1956.
17. Israel Labour Party Archives, Mapai faction in the Knesset, 25 May 1957.
18. Ibid., Mapai secretariat and faction in the Knesset, 21 February 1957.
19. Ben-Gurion Research Center Archives, minutes of meetings, Ben-Gurion's meetings with leaders of the Progressives, 29 December 1957.
20. Ibid., minutes of meetings, Ben-Gurion's meeting with leaders of Achdut Haavoda, 29 December 1957.
21. Ibid., minutes of meetings, Ben-Gurion's meeting with leaders of Mapam, 29 December 1957.
22. Ibid., Ben-Gurion's diaries, 25 December 1957.
23. Ibid.
24. Israel Labour Party Archives, Mapai faction in the Knesset, 16 March 1958.
25. *Knesset Record*, 7 January 1958, p. 564.
26. Ibid., 28 December 1959, speech by MK Nir, p. 201.
27. Ibid., p. 181.
28. Ibid., p. 182.
29. Ibid., p. 184.
30. Ibid., p. 194.

31. Ibid., p. 201.
32. Ibid., 30 December 1959, p. 223.
33. Ibid., p. 224
34. Ibid., 27 November 1961, p. 451.
35. Ibid., 29 May 1962, p. 2,072.
36. Ibid., p. 2,076.
37. Ibid., p. 2,077.
38. Ibid., p. 2,084.
39. Ibid., p. 2,082.
40. Ibid., p. 2,083.
41. Ibid., p. 2,084.
42. Ibid.

8 Intra-Party Politics and Nominations

According to the law and the internal logic of a parliamentary system, the government is elected by the parliament. In fact, one of the major functions of a parliament is to elect the government. Since an elected body is supposed to be responsible to and dependent on the institution that elects it, the government ought to be responsible to and dependent on the parliament. In the Israeli case, Ben-Gurion created a virtually inverse situation. Formally, the Knesset does elect the government, but informally, the government, or to be more precise, the Prime Minister, has enormous influence on the election of a large percentage of Knesset members. For example, the members of Mapai had to seek Ben-Gurion's favour in order to get into the Knesset. His vast power in the party enabled him to choose members of Knesset from Mapai, while other Mapai leaders had very limited influence on the composition of the faction in the Knesset. Ben-Gurion did not make his choices randomly. They were directed mainly at weakening the Knesset vis-à-vis the government. Mapai Knesset members were all too aware that the fate of their personal careers was, to a great extent, in Ben-Gurion's hands. As a result, they did not really fulfill their tasks as Knesset members as they should have, by criticizing the government, supervising it and inquiring into its actions and policies. Even worse, they tried to prove their loyalty to Ben-Gurion, which led to disastrous results as far as the Knesset's functioning as an institution was concerned. It is natural for members of the opposition to fill the functions of criticizing and investigating, but the fate of a parliament is actually determined by the way in which members of the ruling party fulfill their roles. This chapter will first analyze Ben-Gurion's influence on the composition of the Mapai faction in the Knesset, and will then describe his attempts to weaken the Knesset by appointing Knesset members to government, or quasi-government positions. The next subject will be the appointment of Knesset members to positions of deputy ministers and, finally, the conflicts that erupted between the government and the Mapai faction will be analyzed.

MAKING UP THE LISTS OF CANDIDATES TO THE KNESSET

By the end of 1948, discussions about the composition of the Mapai list for the Constituent Assembly, to be elected in January 1949, had already begun. Abraham Brichta has found that Aranne had much impact on the makeup of the list of candidates.[1] It is not clear whether Ben-Gurion was a member of the nominations committee, but he certainly had a great deal of influence on it. At the end of December, he wrote in his diary about a meeting with Aranne, in which Aranne told him about the difficulties involved in making up the list.[2] Ben-Gurion and Aranne agreed that members of the Jewish Agency executive could not appear on the list of candidates and that Ben-Zvi would have a fairly high place on the list, that women (including Golda Meir) would be alloted seven places and six would be given to the kibbutzim and moshavim.[3] Additional proof of Ben-Gurion's influence on the composition of the list can be found in his correspondence on this matter with various figures in Mapai. At the end of December 1948, two representatives of the Tel Aviv cell of the Mapai lawyers organization contacted him, demanding that at least five or six places be promised to 'members whose life's calling and expertise are law and justice'.[4] A few days later, Ben-Gurion did reply to them, stating that he understood their reasoning, but regretted the fact that they had failed to take other factors and considerations into account.[5] The Prime Minister did not accept their demand. This is particularly important, since if he had assigned a greater role to experienced attorneys in the Mapai faction, that certainly would have strengthened the Knesset's legislative power, something Ben-Gurion was not interested in. Around the same time, two representatives of the Bulgarian immigrants also wrote to Ben-Gurion, asking that high places on the list be assigned to this sector of the population.[6] One of them wrote to Ben-Gurion again after the list had been made up, demanding that the two candidates of Bulgarian origin be moved up to higher places on the list, where they had a realistic chance of being elected.[7]

Early in January 1949, the decision of the nominations committee was brought to the party's central committee for approval. Aranne presented the list containing 61 names. Six of them were ranked, and the rest were supposed to be ranked after the central committee approved the list, 'because the committee did not have the time to arrange the order of the list'.[8] Lavon explained why he had refused to participate in the work of the nominations committee, his main argument being that the list was not composed in accordance with the needs of the parliament. He asserted that it did not contain enough 'people who could fill a vital role in their parliamentary work', and added, 'The committee, to my regret, did not accept this approach, and then I tried privately . . . I tried to make up two lists of candidates . . . it is abundantly clear to me that this composition does not meet the needs of an institution like the parliament.'[9] Beba Idelson also reported on her own absence from the meetings of the nominations committee, and demanded that only men and women who were not employed elsewhere should be elected to the parliament. Sprinzak was very frustrated by the composition of the list: 'Any talk on this subject is like rubbing salt into an open wound . . . in a delegation of 40 persons – we all know that the parliament works on laws, formulations – and one jurist is not enough for this . . . it will be funny if we all live under Nir's authority.'[10] Zeev Haring said: 'This list makes a very bad impression',[11] and Guri suggested that the work of making up the list be assigned to a different committee, particularly since he was doubtful whether 'the committee had taken into account that these members will have to devote their time mainly to the work of the Constituent Assembly'.[12] Joseph had some harsh things to say: 'It's clear to me that a number of these members, with all due respect, cannot and will not fulfill their duties as members of the Constituent Assembly, and that is not fair or just to the state . . . there are names of people here who will not be effective in parliamentary work.'[13] He suggested that ten of the candidates be replaced by others. Other members joined in the rebellion against the decision of the nominations committee, but when the vote was taken, the central committee approved the committee's proposal. Ben-Gurion was not present at this meeting, but he was obviously backing the committee's proposal. In fact, the composition of the list did not meet the needs of the Knesset; it had too few lawyers, too few young people and too many older members who were holding down full-time jobs in various institutions, for example, as managers in the various branches of the Histadrut or in extra-governmental Zionist institutions. This composition was in keeping with Ben-Gurion's approach that the Knesset was not a workplace, but a forum of notables that convened from time to time to receive reports from the government and to approve its proposals, including bills. The rebellion that several senior members of Mapai tried to carry out was in fact justified.

Two months after the elections, Ben-Gurion, speaking before a party forum, advocated an immediate change in the composition of the Mapai faction in the Knesset: 'In my opinion, it is essential to remove many people from the Knesset, or these people should leave their agricultural settlements or other matters they are preoccupied with, and engage only in their work in the Knesset.'[14] In May 1949, the party secretariat decided in favour of changes in the faction's composition, which were supposed to become effective during the First Knesset. The secretariat chose three ministers, including the Prime Minister, to serve on a committee authorized to replace several Knesset members.[15] However, the committee did not arrive at an agreement. The important point is that ministers, headed by Ben-Gurion, were the ones intended to determine the new composition of the Mapai faction in the Knesset.

In preparation for the elections to the Second Knesset, Ben-Gurion played a more active role than he had in the previous elections in determining the composition of the party's Knesset members. This time he chaired the nominations committee, which also included Sharett and Lavon. Aranne, who was actually the one who proposed the composition of the nominations committee to the party central committee,[16] reacted to the fact that he had been elbowed aside by resigning from his position as party secretary immediately after the elections.[17] Forty-two members of the central committee supported the proposed composition, six were opposed and 16 abstained. The fact that 22 were not in favour indicates that there was a certain amount of criticism of the proposed composition of the committee. Only one member, Zeev Shefer, dared to explain his opposition: 'I have nothing against the proposed members, but I'd like to say only one sentence – I have seen the Knesset choose a government, but I have never seen the government choose the Knesset.'[18]

Again, Ben-Gurion received requests for representation in the Knesset.[19] Within two weeks, the nominations committee, chaired by Ben-Gurion, had completed its work and its decision was brought to the central committee for approval. This time it was Sharett who presented the committee's proposal, as Aranne had done in 1949.

Sharett reported that the other committee members – Lavon and Ben-Gurion – had not accepted his view that a Knesset member ought not to serve in any other permanent capacity. In other words, Ben-Gurion did not want Knesset members who would invest all their time and energy in their parliamentary work. Sharett labelled this as 'contempt for the parliament', complained that the Knesset worked too little (two and a half days a week), and ascribed this to the fact that 'people are busy with other things'.[20] Ben-Gurion's influence on the composition of the list was greater this time than it had been two years earlier, also because he had chaired the nominations committee. The lack of any opposition to the committee's proposal – unlike the situation in 1949 – probably was because members of the central committee did not dare challenge the Prime Minister.

When the list was being prepared for the 1955 elections, the younger party members demanded that the nominations committee be cancelled. Instead, they proposed that primaries, in which all party members would participate, should be held in 60 regions. The party central committee would be authorized to rank those chosen in the primaries and could also disqualify a candidate chosen in the primaries.[21] Ben-Gurion led the struggle against this proposal: 'Regional elections in the party are absurd unless there are regional elections in the country . . . regional elections in the party are feasible only if there are regional elections in the country[22] . . . what you are proposing is not practical, it is not democratic.'[23] Ben-Gurion's proposal to stick to the oligarchic system of a nominations committee was approved by a majority of 33 members of the central committee, with 14 opposed and 15 abstaining.[24] There was greater opposition to Ben-Gurion's domination of the nominations committee than there had been in 1951. In the same discussion, a senior party member, Shmuel Rollbant, criticized Ben-Gurion's approach to the nominations. He objected to Ben-Gurion's perception of the Knesset as a 'house of notables' rather than a 'house of hard work . . . which requires specific qualifications and training'.[25] While other parties chose members who were suitable to the Knesset, Ben-Gurion preferred to allocate places to groups. 'I fear that Ben-Gurion will not be content until he has a majority of Yemenites in the Knesset . . . by doing so you are encouraging ethnicity as a profession.'[26] Rollbant enumerated three qualifications necessary for a legislator: 'the ability to learn, oratorical prowess and intelligence'.[27]

Prior to the 1955 elections, a five-member nominations committee was selected, only ten days before the final date for submitting the slate. This was done to minimize the various pressures that would be brought on members of the committee. The central committee did not accept the secretariat's recommendation to choose a broad nominations committee with 19 members. Instead it preferred a smaller committee chaired by Ben-Gurion, whose members included the ministers Sharett and Meir, as well as Namir and Kesse.[28] Representatives of various groups contacted Ben-Gurion, demanding to be given places on the slate that would offer them a good chance of being elected.[29] According to Brichta, the slate was made up 'without considering, in most cases, the recommendations of the branches or of other organized bodies affiliated with the party'.[30]

This time it was Ben-Gurion himself who presented the nominations committee's proposal to the central committee. He did this one day before the deadline for submission of the slate, leaving no time for any substantive changes. While prior to the 1949 and 1951 elections, the central committee had voted on the appointments committee's proposal, this time Ben-Gurion devised a new technique. He demanded that the central committee approve the proposed slate *before* it was read out, and authorize the committee to make changes in it. He asked if anyone opposed his suggestion, and no one dared open his mouth. Since the proposal was unanimously approved, Ben-Gurion agreed to read out the slate prepared by the nominations committee that he chaired.[31] Even before that, Ben-Gurion had expressed his dissatisfaction with the lack of democracy in the existing electoral system, stating that in some cases he had not agreed to the candidacy of members filling positions in institutions that were more important than the Knesset: 'There were some among the members of the committee who refused, in some cases I refused to have them run, because I know the work they are doing and must do, which is more important than sitting in the Knesset, and so I didn't agree.'[32] These words reflect his attitude towards the Knesset as an inferior institution. Although he had supported the formal decision that a Knesset member must devote all his time to the Knesset, he now equivocated: 'But now – no. Now there is some logic to having key figures in the central enterprises of the Histadrut and the party involved in the life of the Knesset.'[33] Ben-Gurion was in favour of setting aside places on the party slate for specific sectors of the population, but he was critical of the recommendations for filling these places that were put forward by several sectors. In relation to the kibbutz sector, he complained that among its five recommendees there was not a single soldier, 'and they have such men. If

I were the only one to decide, I would do that.'[34] He had a similar complaint with regard to the Tel Aviv branch, and when some of its members protested, he tried to explain, 'until today, there hasn't been a single member in the foreign affairs and security committee who is knowledgeable about military matters . . . but I want to have someone in the Knesset from our party who is familiar with military and security matters close up'.[35] If this was the case, why did he not do anything in this regard in the nominations committee for the 1951 elections? At the end of his speech, he expressed the hope that this would be the last time the Mapai slate would be made up in the nationwide system of a nominations committee.[36] Not only did Ben-Gurion manage to suppress the young generation's demand for democratization of the nominations procedure, but he almost completely controlled the composition of the slate. According to Brichta,[37] he decided he would have the final say as to who would represent Mapai in the next Knesset. He had so much influence over the composition of the slate that he even decided whose names would be the last on it, although they would only have symbolic importance. David Zakai wrote to Ben-Gurion that by not assigning one of the last places on the slate to the editor of *Davar*, Haim Shorer, he was revealing his attitude towards the paper as a whole.[38] Ben-Gurion replied that

> Shorer certainly was worthy of adorning the end of the slate, as one of the company of the 'princes of the tribe'. But, I believe you were wrong in protesting about the oversight when it was too late. Even committee members are human beings, not gods, and they are apt to forget one or another deserving person . . . Is it really morally necessary to lodge such complaints and reproaches?[39]

Representatives of the small towns reacted to the failure to include their representative in a promising spot on the slate by cancelling their membership in the party's central committee and secretariat. Ben-Gurion expressed his regret that he had been unable to dissuade them, and added: 'I do not know how it is possible to set up a slate of candidates based on the existing election system without assigning the job to a special committee.'[40] He referred to the cancellation of their membership in the party institutions as 'nullification of democracy in our party'.[41] On another occasion, in reply to the complaint of MK Neta Harpaz, who was not given a promising place on the slate, he stated his objection to the demands for representation made by the various sectors: 'I see a dangerous trend in the demands put forward by blocs in our movement for their own representation . . . a man from a moshav serving in the Knesset does not represent the moshavim, nor does an attorney in the Knesset represent the body of attorneys.'[42] He added that the task of composing the slate was an 'unpleasant' one, carried out by reaching compromises among the five committee members. He did not agree with the claim that the Jerusalem branch had been discriminated against, and added a few personal remarks: 'I am sure that your work outside the Knesset is more important than in the Knesset.'[43] In the nominations process, he stated,

> We only have to look into whether the candidate should be in the Knesset, or whether he can fill important assignments elsewhere. When Nahman Raz and Reuven Yafeh refused to be candidates for election to the Knesset and chose to continue working in the settlements of new immigrants, I was overjoyed.[44]

He wrote to Harpaz, demanding that he and his people abandon their threat to withdraw from the slate of candidates, that they desist from publishing their threat and ordered them: 'You must behave like loyal and disciplined soldiers.'[45] Activists of Libyan descent also complained to Ben-Gurion that they had been discriminated against, and added that HaPoel HaMizrachi had promised them places on their slate which gave them a good chance of being elected.[46]

Member of Knesset Ada Maimon remonstrated with Ben-Gurion about the insult she had suffered when she realized she had not been given a promising place on the slate when he read out the names at the central committee meeting.[47] Ben-Gurion replied that he had been told in the nomination committee's discussion that she had refused to be a candidate, and she had therefore been put at the end of the slate 'together with a number of authors and artists as "window dressing"'.[48]

At the convention of the Mapai younger generation in March 1956, the Prime Minister referred to the method of making up the slate for the Knesset. He was in favour of giving quotas to women, Israelis of Oriental descent and the younger generation. He asserted that if the internal elections were secret, it would be a 'catastrophe', because only Ashkenazi males would be elected: 'In this country, the

Ashkenazis control everything.'[49] In this discussion, a dialogue developed between the Prime Minister and Asher Yadlin, one of the heads of the younger generation's faction. When Yadlin stated that the party leadership had not been elected, Ben-Gurion asked, 'Who was not elected?'[50] and Yadlin's retort was: 'Beginning with David Ben-Gurion and all the way down to Asher Yadlin, your obedient servant. None of us was elected.'[51] Ben-Gurion denied this: 'We were both elected at the party convention.'[52] The principle underlying the argument between the two was the nature of the election process, was it really a democratic process, as Ben-Gurion argued, or was the election merely a sham, as Yadlin claimed. In July 1956, Zakai protested to the Prime Minister about the lack of democracy inside Mapai. He made a point of mentioning Ben-Gurion's derisive comment at the meeting of the party central committee when members of Mapai were being elected to the central committee of the Histadrut, saying that a vote would be taken, 'and we'll record the names of those abstaining in the golden book'.[53]

The nominations committee for the 1959 elections numbered 18 members, including the Prime Minister. Again, it was Ben-Gurion who brought the committee's proposal to the central committee for approval.[54] He had considerable influence on the composition of the slate, but less than in the past. For the first time, a certain degree of autonomy was granted to the party districts in choosing their representatives, but the change was not a dramatic one. Ben-Gurion noted that

> the work of the nominations committee took place in a pleasant atmosphere although 50 per cent of the representatives were chosen by the districts . . . since many members who could have demanded places high on the slate relinquished their right, it was possible to have a more diversified slate, from the standpoint of ethnic groups, as well as new members – of both sexes.[55]

For the 1961 elections, the last ones held while Ben-Gurion headed Mapai, a nominations committee was not appointed. Since the date of elections was moved backward, no changes were made except for the removal of Lavon's name from the slate, in keeping with Ben-Gurion's demand.

THE APPOINTMENT OF KNESSET MEMBERS TO GOVERNMENTAL OR QUASI-GOVERNMENTAL POSTS

One means that Ben-Gurion utilized to weaken the Knesset was to appoint Knesset members from his party to governmental or quasi-governmental posts. They would then become more closely identified with the executive arm and would no longer properly fulfill their parliamentary functions. In the chapter dealing with the Knesset's investigative function, a few instances were noted in which Ben-Gurion appointed Knesset members – from Mapai and other parties – to serve on government investigation commissions or government inquiry committees. However, he was not content with this ploy, and also appointed Knesset members as his assistants.

The Prime Minister had already begun using this tactic a short time after the 1949 elections. He appointed Knesset member Peretz Naftali from Mapai as his economic advisor: 'You are hereby appointed as the Prime Minister's economic advisor and it is within your authority to carry out any investigations or inquiries in state, private and public enterprises in the country.'[56] Bader submitted a parliamentary question to Ben-Gurion in this regard, and was told that Naftali had volunteered to advise the Prime Minister, was receiving no salary for doing so, 'and I know of no law that prohibits a Knesset member from assisting a minister or the Prime Minister during his tenure in the Knesset'.[57] Ben-Gurion did not bother to reply to another part of Bader's question, about the appointment of MK Rokach as a member of the government commission investigating the causes of the failure of the Independent Day parade.[58]

In July 1949, the Prime Minister appointed MK Hacohen of Mapai as his assistant for naval affairs:

> You are hereby appointed as assistant to the Minister of Defence on naval affairs. As a member of Knesset you will work in the Ministry of Defence gratis, and will be in charge in the Ministry of all the economic, organizational and other matters relating to the Navy, with the exception of the military command which is within the competence of the Commander of the Navy.[59]

This time it was not the appointment of a personal assistant outside of the administration, but a senior appointment to an existing, high-ranking position.

In June 1950, the Prime Minister apologized to the Mapai secretariat for not having notified the party that he had appointed MK Eliezer Livne as his emissary to US Jewry:

> I regret not having informed the party at the time of the mission I assigned to Mr Livne: to investigate the trends and directions in American Jewry after the establishment of the state, in connection with which he will be absent from the country for several months.[60]

In effect, the Prime Minister had sent a Knesset member from his party abroad for several months on a mission unconnected with his parliamentary work. It is no wonder, then, that in 1952 Ben-Gurion opposed the suggestion made in the political committee of Mapai to return to the proxy system that had existed in the Provisional State Council, and called it an 'absurd proposal'.[61] He was quite aware that the Knesset would benefit from the proxy method. Instead, he demanded that Knesset members should not leave the country:

> Knesset members do not need to travel to the UN. Knesset affairs are more important to us than the UN . . . a Knesset member receives a salary for his membership in the Knesset, and is it such a torture for him to sit in the Knesset for three days? Knesset members will not travel abroad.[62]

By that, he did not mean that Knesset members who were confined to the Knesset could oversee and criticize the government, but rather that they could support it. This statement was made during a coalition crisis that left Mapai with a small majority in the Knesset.

On other occasions, too, Ben-Gurion levelled criticism at Knesset members from his own party. In January 1953, he wrote to Aranne, complaining that Mapai's Knesset members were not active enough on behalf of the party, adding that 'Not all the members of the faction are so enterprising, but with some well-planned action, we can get most of the Knesset members to show more initiative',[63] including those from other parties that were in the coalition. After the 1955 elections, Knesset members from the moshavim sector of Mapai protested the fact that the Prime Minister had not appointed one of their people as Minister of Agriculture. For a while, they boycotted parliamentary activity. Ben-Gurion reacted vehemently, stating that they had been elected to the Knesset on behalf of the entire party and were not representing only the moshavim: 'It is unthinkable that they should absent themselves from the Knesset.'[64] At a meeting of Mapai's political committee, late in December 1955, he again criticized the Knesset members from the moshav sector: 'Shmuel Dayan cannot suddenly come and say he was elected by the moshavim and that they told him not to come to the Knesset. He was not chosen by the moshavim, but by the entire [labour] movement.'[65]

APPOINTMENT OF DEPUTY MINISTERS

According to Israeli law, government ministers, with the exception of the Prime Minister and his deputy, could, until 1996, come from outside of the Knesset. Deputy ministers, on the other hand, must be Knesset members. If a deputy minister resigns from the Knesset he is automatically discharged from his post as deputy minister. In the first years after the establishment of the state there was no legislation regulating the powers of a deputy minister and the way he was selected. At first, Ben-Gurion drew no distinction between an assistant to the minister and a deputy minister. In December 1949, he referred to his assistant in the Ministry of Defence, Shaul Avigor, as the deputy defence minister.[66] In October 1950, the Prime Minister informed the Knesset that ministers are authorized to appoint Knesset members as their deputies and that they will also transfer some of their powers to them.[67] It is very strange that the Prime Minister did not feel that such a basic constitutional matter was a fit subject for legislation. The opposition was not prepared to accept his notification as a substitute for legislation regulating the issue of deputy ministers. Ben-Gurion's notification had serious implications, not only from a constitutional viewpoint, but also for the Knesset. The appointment of Knesset members as deputy ministers meant that the Knesset would be weakened, since some of its members would be going over to the executive arm.

In October 1950, the Mapai faction in the Knesset discussed the subject of deputy ministers. Lam called upon the faction to discuss whether people who were not Knesset members could be appointed as deputy minister. Joseph said that the Prime Minister had already announced that the deputies would only come from the ranks of the Knesset.[68] In December 1950, at a meeting of the Mapai faction in the Knesset, Beba Idelson intimated that she did not accept Ben-Gurion's position that deputy ministers could only come from the ranks of the Knesset.[69] At another meeting of the faction that month, it reached no decision as to whether deputy ministers would come from the Knesset or outside the Knesset. Lavon commented that 'on the matter of deputy ministers who are not Knesset members, we have to wait for Ben-Gurion's arrival, for he made the announcement in the Knesset'.[70]

In November 1950, Minister of Justice Rosen explained to the House Committee the Prime Minister's statement about the appointment of deputy ministers. A deputy minister would come only from the ranks of the Knesset but, unlike a minister, he would not be responsible to the Knesset, but only to the minister. The deputy would be appointed by the minister without any need for approval by the Knesset or the government. Rosen doubted that the arrangement called for legislation.[71]

In January 1951, Ben-Gurion was summoned to the House Committee on the matter of MK Yosef Efrati's (Mapai) appointment as the Director General of the Ministry of Agriculture. The Prime Minister failed to draw a distinction between a deputy minister and a director general, which shows he intended to have deputy ministers fill distinctly administrative posts while continuing to serve in the Knesset. The chairman of the House Committee, Harari, pointed out that the Law of Elections to the Knesset states that a Knesset member cannot be a government official.[72] Ben-Gurion understood that the Knesset would not simply accept his notification in the plenum on this matter and issued instructions for the preparation of a government bill on deputy ministers. Bar-Yehuda insisted that until this legislation was passed, Efrati could not sign documents as director general and deputy minister. The Minister of Justice solved the problem for Ben-Gurion by agreeing that Efrati could have the status of an advisor for two weeks.[73]

A week later, the government hastened to propose to the Knesset an amendment to the Transition Law regarding deputy ministers. According to the proposed bill, the deputy would come only from the ranks of the Knesset, would be appointed by the minister with the government's approval, would act in the ministry and in the Knesset on behalf of the minister and would fulfill all the duties assigned to him by the minister. The Minister of Justice, who presented the bill on behalf of the government, admitted that it was being done urgently for the purpose of 'granting the deputy ministers a legal status'.[74] He also admitted that 'there is therefore some basis for the view that since the deputy minister is subordinate to the instructions of a member of government, he thereby is granted the status of an official'.[75]

The proposed bill aroused heavy criticism in the Knesset. Burg

(United Religious Front) also alluded to Ben-Gurion's inclination to appoint a deputy of his own in the Ministry of Defence: 'This rumour was denied, but nonetheless, it circulated for quite a few days in the public as well as in semi-official publications.'[76] Bar-Yehuda, expressing the fear that there might be an inflation of deputy ministers, asked: 'Where will the Knesset be?'[77] He went on to say: 'If you had only given the matter more serious thought, for the sake of the Knesset and your own sake, you wouldn't have brought the bill to us in this form.'[78] Bader expressed his concern that a situation might be created in which all the ministers (other than the Prime Minister) came from outside the Knesset and all the deputy ministers were Knesset members: 'I see this as a new form of the Knesset's dependence on a man who has a merely administrative position.'[79] Rubin of Mapam protested the fact that Efrati had already been serving for two months as a deputy minister 'in violation of the law'.[80] The opposition in the Knesset was of no avail, and the bill was transferred to the constitution, law and justice committee for handling.

Two days after the bill was approved in its first reading, the constitution, law and justice committee discussed the government's bill concerning deputy ministers. The Minister of Justice urged the committee to complete passage of the legislation, on the pretext that the ministers were overloaded with work. Rosen did admit that the bill was problematic, 'because he is placed in a position which can, in any event, be interpreted from a legal standpoint, although not from a political and administrative standpoint, as the position of an official, particularly when the bill states he will work "on behalf of the minister"'.[81] Bar-Yehuda, who represented parliamentary interests, made several demands. First, that the deputies should not come from the ranks of the Knesset, also that the Knesset be authorized to approve the appointments, that their number should not exceed the number of ministers, and that they could not appear in the Knesset in the name of the government.

Rubin explained why it was essential to limit the number of deputies:

> If 40 per cent of the coalition members are in the government, that rules out any possibility of a real debate in the Knesset, since most of the members would have no ability to express themselves and would be obliged to comply with the government's decisions. What then would be the point of the Knesset's existence? The Knesset would become an institution whose

task is to give a legal–formal stamp to government decisions, without any possibility of debate.

He added that the deputy should be prevented from acting within the ministry and his activity should be limited to the Knesset, since the director general is the man at the apex of the administrative pyramid. He objected to the proposed clause stating that the minister assigns tasks to his deputy, since 'a minister cannot assign tasks to a Knesset member'.[82] Rubin suggested that the law state explicitly that the deputy will not be regarded as a government official. Ari Jabotinsky of Herut argued that the government bill blurred the difference between the Knesset and the government, and suggested that the Knesset be authorized to appoint and dismiss deputy ministers.[83] A week later the Justice Minister replied to some of the opposition's demands. The government would inform the Knesset of the appointment of a deputy minister (although it would not require the Knesset's approval), and the number of deputies would be limited to one per ministry; the deputy would act in the name of the government, not on behalf of the government.[84] At the stage of the second reading, all the opposition's demands were rejected – the main ones being a limitation on the number of deputies, authorization of the Knesset to approve the appointment of the deputies and the stipulation that the deputies carry out their tasks in the Knesset only and not in the government ministries.[85]

Although Ben-Gurion had been compelled to agree to legislation in the matter of deputy ministers and was also forced to back down from his original proposal, which included, among other stipulations, an unlimited number of deputies from among the Knesset members, in the final analysis he did achieve his major goal. The lines between the Knesset and the government were blurred even further through the creation of the position of deputy minister, since these deputies had to come from the Knesset. The Knesset lost a bit of its independence and, most important of all, it lost some of its members to the executive arm.

THE RELATIONSHIP BETWEEN THE GOVERNMENT AND THE MAPAI FACTION IN THE KNESSET

The relations between Ben-Gurion and the Mapai faction had always been tense. To Ben-Gurion's mind, the major, perhaps even the sole, function of Knesset members from his party was to show their loyalty to the government's decisions and policies and to give them formal approval. The faction, naturally enough, strove for some degree of autonomy, and demanded that the government should at least consult it on certain matters.

Sometimes Ben-Gurion used the faction to contest decisions taken by party institutions that he disagreed with. As mentioned in Chapter 1, an interesting conflict between him and a party institution had already erupted in November 1948, during the tenure of the Provisional State Council, about whether voting rights for the elections to the Constituent Assembly should be granted to Jews still in Cyprus awaiting transfer to Israel. Ben-Gurion was opposed to allowing them to vote, and the government took a decision in line with his view. Following an initiative by Aranne, the party bureau took an opposite decision in November 1948, in favour of giving voting rights to the exiles in Cyprus. Its decision stated that a minister or a faction member opposed to the bureau's decision could abstain in the vote.[86] Ben-Gurion was not prepared to accept the bureau's decision. He appeared at a meeting of the Mapai faction and claimed that if the Cyprus exiles were permitted to vote, the existence of the state would be endangered and other countries might express doubt about its legality. Aranne related to this view with derision at the bureau's meeting: 'When anyone of us tries to put this forward as a reason, it doesn't seem important, but when Ben-Gurion says it, then it is important.'[87] Following Ben-Gurion's speech at the faction meeting, all the members voted in favour of his position, and in fact, reversed the decision of the bureau taken the week before. The party found itself in an embarrassing position, because following the bureau's decision its leaders had sent a cable to the Cyprus exiles, informing them that the party had decided to grant them the right to vote. Ben-Gurion won this struggle, this time using the faction to rebuff the decision of the bureau – a party institution. After the 1949 elections, the forum of the Mapai faction became institutionalized in the Knesset, while the party's institutions lost their influence on parliamentary matters. The party's secretary, Aranne, wanted the members of the Mapai secretariat to take part in the faction's meetings, and demanded that parliamentary matters be discussed by the secretariat: 'This is an absolute necessity, if we want to avoid a very unpleasant development.'[88] Sprinzak complained before the party secretariat that the government was neglecting the Knesset's affairs and that there was no minister in charge of parliamentary matters:

> I have already held back Livne on several occasions, he has a hobby-horse on this subject and wants to make a big speech about the absence of ministers at the Knesset sessions. He is waiting for me to give him the floor so he can do so . . . It's an impossible situation for the government to send proposed bills or amendments to the Knesset 24 hours before it meets. I am surprised there is not a general uprising about this situation.[89]

The Speaker of the Knesset expressed his disappointment at the way the Mapai faction was functioning:

> I am not prepared to conceal it, because I sit up here and see the opposition in a good situation . . . the opposition of Etzel[90] is a top-notch opposition in the parliamentary sense. On every occasion, they know what they are talking about . . . it is no wonder that theirs is a good faction, these are young, fresh, intelligent people, they have no other interest now, they no longer are living in the underground . . . I do not feel that the members of our faction all have the feeling that they now belong to the Knesset. The faction is composed of various people who have never in their lives had anything to do with parliaments. They have filled some important public positions, but not in this area . . . I can see that the Mapai faction in this Knesset is very weak.[91]

Minister Joseph said a ministerial committee had convened four times in order to prepare rules of procedure for the Knesset, and even 'Ben-Gurion had spoken about that several times'.[92] The very fact that ministers, including the Prime Minister, had been engaged in preparing rules of procedure for the Knesset is very peculiar, since in democratic governments the rule is that the executive arm does not interfere in the internal procedures of the parliament. Shazar, Minister of Education and Culture, said that the Knesset ought to constitute a compromise between the British model of an active parliament and the model of the Zionist Vaad HaPoel – a formal, passive institution of mainly symbolic significance: 'It is neither the Zionist Vaad HaPoel nor the English parliament; it is something else.'[93] He was critical of Ben-Gurion for devoting most of his time to the Ministry of Defence and not being active enough as Prime Minister. The faction co-ordinator, Yehudith Simchoni, admitted that 'the situation of our faction is very poor'.[94]

On 14 July 1949, a joint meeting of the faction and the secretariat was held, to discuss with Ben-Gurion whether he would appear the following day before the Constitution, Law and Justice Committee on the issue of a constitution. At the time, it was already a well-known fact that the Prime Minister opposed the framing of a constitution.[95] The decision taken was to recommend to Ben-Gurion that he postpone his appearance before the committee.[96] This time, the Prime Minister accepted the faction's recommendation.

In November 1949, the faction discussed the organization of its activity. Lavie reported that the economics committee was not holding meetings because the ministers absented themselves from its meetings.[97] He asked the faction directorate for permission to speak in the plenum on Ben-Gurion's forestation plan, which he opposed, but he was not granted permission:

> I spoke to Ben-Gurion about this matter, and he said that first we have to talk about it in the faction. Okay, we'll talk about it in the faction, but when? . . . There has to be an opportunity to talk about it in the faction when Ben-Gurion is present, and there is no chance of doing so . . . This has got to stop . . . if the state of affairs is such that a member feels as if he were a *nuchschlepper* [Yiddish slang for one who follows others], then he ought not to be a member.[98]

During Lavie's speech, when he mentioned Ben-Gurion's refusal to allow him to speak in the plenum, Lavon cynically remarked about the Prime Minister: 'He's a great democrat.'[99]

Duvdevani spoke about his impressions of the Knesset: 'I'm in a very low mood in the Knesset, because I have to say amen to everything the government says. That's unacceptable. In such a situation, the Knesset member has no desire to work.'[100] Shraga Goren reported on what was going on in the economics committee: 'I am a member of the economics committee. But what can we do if the government is virtually killing this committee? They are not letting it work. I'd like to suggest that we cancel this committee.'[101] Ada Maimon remarked: 'If Ben-Gurion had read his last speech in the Knesset to us, we could have deleted several things.'[102] The atmosphere among the faction members at this meeting was tense. In the wake of the sharp criticism voiced at the meeting, the faction's activity was reorganized. The party secretary was authorized to handle negotiations with the ministers on legislation. Three co-ordinators of

Knesset meetings, three members of the inter-coalition committee, a co-ordinator of faction meetings, and ten members of the faction directorate were appointed.[103]

In December 1949, the Speaker of the Knesset, at a meeting of the faction's directorate, protested to the Prime Minister that the government was presenting too few bills to the Knesset and was keeping it occupied only with 'administrative laws'.[104] Ben-Gurion admitted that this situation was causing some damage, but ascribed it to disagreements in the government and to the slow pace of the Ministry of Justice's work, due to a shortage of jurists.[105] In February 1950, a year after the Knesset was founded, the faction held a meeting from which all the Mapai ministers were absent. Aranne expressed his dissatisfaction with the government's attitude towards the Knesset: 'The government is part of the faction, they are delegates of the party faction.'[106] Aranne stated that the government surprised the faction members by initiating things in the Knesset without advising them, and that there should be a special minister to co-ordinate between the ministers, the faction and the party.

Sprinzak said that 'one of problems of the parliament is that the government existed before the parliament . . . there is also the attitude of government members to the Knesset – they treat the Knesset as a burden, a necessary burden, but a burden nonetheless. It is not so easy to remedy this situation.'[107] He added a few more very harsh words:

> What is going on here? It's chaos . . . This is ruining our work, and sometimes we arrive at absurd situations. At times I want to ask the government during a session what to do. But very often they are too loaded with work, and they do not have any grounding in parliamentary affairs, they are not mentally prepared for the meetings . . . not all the government ministers present matters properly from the podium of the Knesset.[108]

He blamed the non-productivity of the faction on the absence of ministers at the Knesset sessions, and continued:

> The faction has to tell itself that the parliament is important. It would have been better if they had never created it. But since it has been created, it must be important. Criticism of the conduct of government members should not be levelled out of dissatisfaction, but out of a desire to make the necessary reforms.[109]

In July 1950, at a meeting of the faction, Duvdevani remonstrated about the absence of ministers from the Knesset.[110] In August 1950, the faction held a discussion with the secretariat and senior members of Mapai in the Histadrut, in Ben-Gurion's presence. Lavie protested about the fact that certain subjects were not being discussed at the meeting, in particular the issue of Knesset members' salaries: 'Why am I not allowed to put that on the agenda?'[111] he asked, and Aranne replied that in future, the faction would hold a discussion with ministers from the party on that subject.

In October 1950, when changes were being made in the composition of the government, a joint forum of the faction and the secretariat discussed the faction's working procedures. This subject was not supposed to have been on the agenda, but as soon as the meeting opened, several members demanded that it be discussed immediately. Lam said: 'There is nothing more urgent than the faction's working procedures. For two years we have been living without any set procedures.'[112] Bahir suggested that a discussion be held immediately on the subject, and his suggestion was accepted. Sprinzak criticized the government: 'The members of government are always checking each other. It's too bad they don't check themselves. The atmosphere in the government is not one of talking and discussing, but one of axioms.'[113]

Bahir demanded that the faction chairman, Argov, inform Ben-Gurion in the name of the faction that he should not decide on the composition of the government before the faction had discussed it. Argov replied that he was unable to do that. At the very most, he could tell the Prime Minister that the faction requested that he and his ministers come to a meeting of the faction to report to its members on the changes in the government's composition. He added that when he had asked Ben-Gurion to attend meetings of the coalition management, his request had not been met. Eliahu Hakarmeli criticized the government for its attitude to Knesset members from Mapai: 'We are not kept informed of either major or minor things. A member who knows what is going on only because he reads about it in the newspaper might as well not be a member.'[114] He demanded that he and others be given the right to speak in the plenum: 'What is there to be afraid of? Every Knesset member should be given the opportunity to express himself and get answers to his parliamentary questions. A member ought not to stand like a beggar at the door.'[115] Bahir added that he accepted the principle that the Prime Minister was entitled to form the government,

> But he has to come to the faction and hear our opinions. That's how it should be, but the faction meeting was never even held. If the meeting had been held, there would be minutes and the ministers would read them. I know that Ben-Gurion reads the minutes of the meetings that he does not attend.[116]

The meeting was recessed and there was an immediate demand by the faction for a ministerial report on the government's composition. Minister of Finance Kaplan was sent to the faction meeting and only then was it renewed. This time, the Knesset members voiced their protests to the Minister of Finance. Lam asserted that 'Frequently the government surprises us by proposing bills we are opposed to. After these have already been passed by the government, they are brought to us all of a sudden and we are supposed to defend them.'[117] Goren was sceptical:

> It would be a good idea for us to talk about the work of the faction, but I despair of ever finding a solution to this issue. I am one of the members who has hardly ever missed a meeting in the Knesset, and I regularly attend every committee I belong to. Nonetheless, I am not in the know. I don't know what is going on in the faction directorate and I don't know what is going on in the faction itself. Our faction does not live the life of a faction. Its members do not know what is happening, they are constantly being confronted by surprises. Quite often, the government confronts us with a surprise and we have to raise our hands . . . Until when will this go on? We are sometimes forced to drink a beverage that is neither tasty nor pleasant to swallow . . . in the second year of the Knesset's existence we have taken huge strides backwards.[118]

Guri deplored the fact that Yaacov Gerry, the first non-partisan minister, was appointed as Minister of Trade and Industry without any discussion in the faction: 'On all major matters, we hold a discussion after the fact. And this means that the matter has already been decided.'[119] In his view, the faction ought to be informed in advance on major matters: 'The government has to tell us what it is going to do in this sitting.'[120] Deborah Netzer said

> This is the first time I have worked in an institution without knowing what is going on. I don't know what is awaiting me.

> It's a good thing that I sometimes read a newspaper too. Before the vote, I believe I have the right to hear and be heard too. We are disciplined, we raise our hands, but is this the right way? Even when you vote, you must know what it is all about.[121]

Govrin said he had called for a special meeting of the Knesset because of the government crisis, 'but our members in the government did not agree'.[122]

The Mapai backbenchers continued their revolt. They were not satisfied by the appearance of the Finance Minister before them, and demanded that the Prime Minister should appear as well. Five days after the long day on which two meetings were held, one of them with the Finance Minister, Ben-Gurion was supposed to attend a meeting of the faction, but at the last minute he cancelled his appearance. The chairman of the faction, Argov, stated that the day before, Ben-Gurion had promised to attend the meeting.[123] The Speaker of the Knesset was furious:

> I think it is not normal for the faction to meet in Ben-Gurion's absence. He either has to accept the view of the faction, or to state his own view to the faction. It is Ben-Gurion's duty to be in this faction at this moment. I believe that the faction directorate should demand that Ben-Gurion be here.[124]

Argov was in favour of taking a decision as to whether to continue the meeting without the Prime Minister or to cancel it. He suggested that the meeting be recessed for half an hour, 'and some of our members will go to him and demand that he come here'.[125] The meeting was in fact recessed and a delegation sent to the Prime Minister, who refused to come to the faction meeting, but did agree to talk to its delegates. After lunch the meeting was renewed, although the obstinate Prime Minister did not condescend to attend.

In November 1950, at a meeting of the faction, the Speaker of the Knesset once again criticized the ministers for their failure to attend: 'When it is necessary to approve a law, the government comes, otherwise they are not in the Knesset.'[126] A week later, the faction held a debate on its working procedures. Aranne reproved the ministers for their poor attendance at the Knesset and suggested that they set up a rotation system of attending Knesset meetings. In addition, a minister would be obligated to be present in the Knesset when matters concerning his ministry were under discussion.[127] Aranne said:

> The government ought to be interested in the faction, because without the faction it won't exist. They fail to recognize this fact. If the Knesset has recently been divested of all its content and attendance at its meetings has declined, then you, members of the government, have had a hand in that, because your attitude determines the attitude Knesset members have toward you.[128]

Netzer argued that 'the government, to my regret, does not ask for our help'.[129] Govrin was particularly critical of the government: 'When we relate to a proposal on the agenda, we do not know exactly what the government wants . . . either or, either the government will rely somewhat on the faction or it will not rely on it at all.'[130] He stated that he would not accept the government's view regarding the removal of certain subjects from the agenda in every instance, 'because there are some subjects which the atmosphere does not allow us to remove from the agenda', and he added that he had told the ministers that they had to bring up the issue of the black market in the Knesset, and if they did not, 'they must allow us to do so, but they didn't allow me to do that'.[131] He demanded that the ministers attend Knesset meetings and that a twice-weekly meeting be held between the ministers and the faction members: 'They must be induced to come, even by going so far as to write a severe letter reprimanding a member of government who is obliged to appear.'[132] At that meeting, Argov admitted that the Knesset was not functioning properly – the debates were boring, important issues were removed from the agenda, and overly detailed laws were brought for discussion. He blamed the government: 'If we gave the Knesset some more substance, its members would not spend all their time in the cafeteria . . . we are faced with faits accomplis when it comes to legislation.'[133] Minister of Finance Kaplan tried to place the responsibility for the faction's humiliating position on Ben-Gurion: 'He is not just another member of government . . . all the work of the government is largely determined by its head.'[134] Sprinzak estimated that Ben-Gurion would probably not agree to Kaplan's suggestion to set up regular contacts with the Knesset, and added that 'If such an arrangement were introduced, it would solve many problems.'[135]

Members of Mapai were so frustrated that the faction held yet another discussion, a few days later, about the attitude of the government, particularly of Ben-Gurion, towards it. Shmuel Dayan praised Kaplan for being the only minister who sometimes attended faction meetings, and added: 'There was a time when Ben-Gurion participated in our meetings, but even then, for a short time.'[136] He protested the fact that the government did not consult the faction and refused to inquire into certain issues. Beba Idelson was more incisive and directed her criticism at the Prime Minister:

> I am sorry that I have to say this in Ben-Gurion's absence, because I am referring to him. The faction is confronted by facts that it has never heard about before . . . I had to make excuses for something I had been opposed to from the start . . . none of us knew. We read about it in the newspaper . . . There must be criticism, especially of Ben-Gurion. I want there to be an institution, either the faction or the party central committee, that will supervise what is going on in the government . . . I want to know what institution oversees the government.[137]

Sprinzak poured out his heart to all those present: 'I just cannot manage with the government . . . every agenda is a product of unending improvisation. This morning it was clear that I had to adjourn the session, because the government was not sticking to the agenda.'[138]

At a faction meeting in January 1952, following the serious parliamentary incident in the debate on German reparations, Beba Idelson remarked, 'We have reached some sort of labyrinth in our parliamentary life.'[139] Minister of Labour Meir admitted that the Knesset in its third year was in a poor state: 'There is a sense that no one is really concerned about the Knesset and its work. We all should be very anxious about what is going to happen.'[140]

On 13 February 1952, in the meeting of the faction, Aranne was extremely pessimistic: 'The Knesset is dying – from a parliamentary point of view – these may be its last moments. I hope that it is still possible to save it.'[141] Yaacov Shapira said: 'We get no guidance from the government . . . the government does not participate in the work of the Knesset.'[142] Izhar Smilansky was also pessimistic: 'What is demanded of a Knesset member is not to hear or to understand, but just to vote. That is sometimes said cynically.'[143]

On 9 March 1952, Ben-Gurion finally made an appearance at a faction meeting. Not only was no criticism of him voiced, but he was the one who was critical. He urged the faction members to finish passing the budget law:

> It depends only on the coalition. There is something called a majority and we have to use it. It is possible to sit one day for seven hours and complete it . . . An amendment needs to be made: if three members of the opposition have the same objection, only one of them will speak.[144]

In May 1952, Govrin complained at a meeting of the faction about the absence of ministers at Knesset meetings, and remarked, 'The situation in the Knesset as far as legislation is concerned is very bad. The members do not attend committee meetings . . . the government does not assist in the work of the Knesset.'[145] When Ben-Gurion attended a meeting of the faction at the end of May 1952, Idelson confronted him: 'I have a question for the Prime Minister. Are members of the faction to learn about changes in the government from the newspaper?'[146] She was referring to Kaplan's anticipated resignation from the government. Ben-Gurion replied that he knew nothing about any changes in the government.

In August 1952, at a joint meeting of the faction and the political committee, an argument developed between Ben-Gurion and Govrin. Ben-Gurion was angry about having been forced to come to explain why Lavon had been made a member of the government. He questioned the authority of the faction:

> I thought that the political committee was the supreme authority of the party. Now Govrin tells me that he has to go back and bring the matter to the faction . . . it is unthinkable to have two party institutions deciding on the same matter . . . we cannot turn democracy into a caricature of democracy.[147]

Govrin did not relent and replied that he did not accept the Prime Minister's view and insisted that members of the faction have a right of inquiry. The party cannot deny the faction this right by means of another party institution. Govrin stated that he would demand an inquiry into the issue of authority in the party. On this occasion, Ben-Gurion used the political committee as a means of ignoring the Mapai faction in the Knesset.

In November 1952, at a meeting of the faction, Livne remonstrated about the fact that Ben-Gurion had offered the position of President to Albert Einstein without consulting the faction.[148] In May 1953, Govrin resigned from his position as co-ordinator of the Mapai faction and chairman of the coalition management, and Ami

Assaf was elected in his place. In October 1953, Assaf stated at a meeting of the faction that it was necessary to hold a meeting of the faction directorate and the Mapai ministers: 'We cannot continue in this manner, with you acting alone and we acting alone, and being surprised by all kinds of proposed laws.'[149]

About two weeks after the 1955 elections, the faction held a long meeting in Ben-Gurion's office about organizing the Knesset after the elections. Ben-Gurion proposed that the election of the Knesset presidium be postponed since a coalition had not yet been formed, and it would preferable for the coalition to have a majority in the presidium. The date when the elected Knesset would convene was also discussed. Sprinzak wanted to convene the Knesset as early as possible, but Ben-Gurion proposed 'leaving that up to the government'.[150] The faction took no decision on this matter. Four weeks later, it held another meeting, this time without Ben-Gurion. In the coalition negotiations, one of Hapoel Hamizrachi's demands was chairmanship of the constitution, law and justice committee. The faction tended to agree to this demand, but Minister Joseph blocked its acceptance, arguing that in Ben-Gurion's absence it was impossible to take any decision on the matter.[151]

In October 1955, at the faction meeting, MK Avraham Harzfeld wanted to speak about the composition of the coalition. Another member, Kesse, remarked that in Ben-Gurion's absence there was no point in doing so. Assaf suggested to the disappointed Harzfeld that he 'request a meeting with Ben-Gurion'.[152] At the faction meeting on 19 December 1955, the Speaker of the Knesset was particularly irate about the conduct of the ministers in the Knesset:

> All of a sudden there's no minister, not a single minister . . . then we have to close down the Knesset. I understand that 14 ministers do not have to sit there, basking in the divine light, but not a single one – that's a disgrace . . . that's bankruptcy for Mapai – the conduct of the faction in the Knesset – ugly bankruptcy, unwarranted, devoid of any public integrity.[153]

Aranne concurred with Sprinzak's criticism: 'In so far as the ministers are concerned, it's a very serious matter', and commented that the Mapai faction 'had crumbled even before it had arisen.'[154]

In May 1956, Govrin, who in the meantime was leading the faction again, called a joint meeting with Ben-Gurion about relations between the faction and the government. At that meeting, he bemoaned the fact that there was no communication between the faction and the Mapai ministers. Ben-Gurion complained that the meeting was lasting too long and that some of the participants were not speaking to the point. Govrin explained that the meeting was lengthy because Ben-Gurion had not come to the faction's meetings for a long time.[155] He also protested about the inferior status of the faction, whose members were content only to raise their hands, and knew nothing about the laws before they were brought to the plenum: 'If we don't want to play with words, then it [the faction] is not responsible for anything nor does it decide anything.'[156] Ben-Gurion insisted that he give an example. Govrin gave him several, and demanded that resolutions be presented to the faction before they are brought to the Knesset.[157] In April 1957, the chairman of the finance committee, Guri, sent a letter of protest to the Prime Minister about the absence of the ministers at the second reading of the budget law: 'It is incumbent upon the government to make an effort to resolve this problem; it is not beyond its power to do so.'[158]

In May 1957, the Prime Minister attended a meeting of the faction and turned to the Speaker to demand that the presidium decide, before the following day's meeting, that it would not recognize the urgency of motions to the agenda on a certain matter.[159] Sprinzak stated that it was impossible to do that unless one of the ministers were to announce, in the name of the government, that it would make a statement to that effect to the Knesset the following week. Ben-Gurion was not willing to do that, and stated that Minister of Justice Rosen would inform the presidium the following day that the government had not yet completed its discussion or reached a decision. Sprinzak defended his position by asserting that it would be hard for the coalition to obtain a majority on the presidium since one of the deputies, Beba Idelson of Mapai, was abroad. Ben-Gurion was furious: 'Members cannot take on authoritative positions. If she is a member of the presidium, she cannot be busy travelling when the Knesset is re-opening its session.'[160] The Speaker was not prepared to accept the Prime Minister's demand in full, and stated that the presidium would take a decision based on the announcement by the Minister of Justice.

In June 1957, Govrin wrote to Ben-Gurion in the name of the faction directorate, on the matter of passing the Basic Law: The Knesset. He asked the Prime Minister for guidelines: 'If you should decide to present the entire bill to the government, it is necessary to ensure, by sending a government delegate, that the constitution, law and justice committee, which is dealing with this law, will stop discussing it in the meantime.'[161] Moreover, Govrin asked the Prime Minister to meet with him regarding the Knesset rules of procedure. This letter shows how much influence Ben-Gurion had on the Knesset's internal affairs. In September 1957, at a faction meeting, Govrin protested about the changes the government was making in the Knesset's agenda.[162] Guri claimed at that meeting that the Knesset was in a decline and that the faction was 'more in the nature of a mouthpiece explaining the actions and activities of the government than a body that exerts some influence before decisions are finally taken'.[163] If the faction were made a more active participant, it could contribute to the Knesset's status and to Israeli democracy, Guri remarked.

This tendency to relegate the faction to the sidelines was also reflected in the Mapai constitution (1957) and the coalition by-laws (1956). The constitution states that the faction is responsible to the party central committee, and that decisions taken by the party institutions are binding on all members of the faction voting in the Knesset. The constitution drew a distinction between foreign affairs and security issues, which Ben-Gurion dealt with more than any other matters, and other issues. On matters of foreign affairs and security, the faction could hold a debate, but it was not entitled to take any decisions. On other matters, the faction could hold discussions and take decisions too. The coalition by-laws made it very difficult for Knesset members from the coalition factions to initiate any parliamentary activity. A Knesset member wishing to submit a motion to the agenda had to submit it to the chairman of the coalition management, who would find out what position the minister involved had taken on the matter and would inform the coalition factions of its content. If the chairman of the coalition management did not agree to raise the proposal, the matter would be brought to the coalition management. Knesset members would vote in the plenum in accordance with the decision of the coalition management, and if they had not had the time to discuss the matter, they would vote according to the minister's position on it.

In March 1958, Ben-Gurion reported to the faction on foreign policy and on the need to encourage competent young men to remain in the regular army, but immediately stated that the faction was not authorized to discuss the matter.[164] Bahir disagreed with the Prime Minister, pointing out that although the faction was not authorized to take any decisions on the matter, it was entitled to discuss it, and according to the party constitution, he was in fact right. Bahir also complained to Ben-Gurion that members of the faction did not have enough information to appear before the public and asked that he meet with them each month to provide them with information. This time Bahir spoke to Ben-Gurion in a more temperate tone: 'We do not want to take up too much of your time at faction meetings.'[165] But Beba Idelson did not hesitate to remonstrate with Ben-Gurion about the faction's inferior status, even in comparison to the opposition factions:

> They are allowed to talk about everything, while we, the largest faction, the one that has to fight and explain, are in the idiotic situation of being the last to know anything . . . and to go on for a long time as we are now, that is not very dignified. There ought to be a minister who meets with the faction and explains things to it. Otherwise, we cannot exist.[166]

The Prime Minister was not opposed to the suggestion that the faction would receive information from the government every month.

In July 1958, the faction met with the secretariat to discuss the crisis that had erupted following Minister of the Interior Bar-Yehuda's issuance of guidelines regarding the registration of nationality. The Prime Minister ruled that neither the government nor the Knesset was authorized to discuss matters of religion.[167] The Speaker of the Knesset argued that the government ought to leave the matter to a parliamentary committee that would discuss it and arrive at a conclusion, but his proposal was not even brought to a vote. Ben-Gurion reacted to it with derision and said that a few months earlier, the Minister of Religion had, without the government's knowledge, issued regulations about burial, and that this subject would now come to a government meeting: 'On this too, it is possible to select a Knesset committee', he remarked cynically to the Speaker of the Knesset. The problem of the minister's attendance at the Knesset remained on the agenda. In October 1958, the Minister of Commerce and Industry, Pinhas Sapir, said, at a meeting of the faction, that the ministers 'were obliged to come to the Knesset'.[168]

In June 1960, MK Gideon Ben-Yisrael wanted the faction to discuss the shortage of manpower in the development areas, particularly in the Negev.[169] The Prime Minister stated that this 'is not the affair of the faction, but rather of a party or Histadrut institution'.[170] In August 1960, at a faction meeting, Ben-Yisrael complained that the faction was not taking any decisions, but just listening to information, and pointed out that parliamentary questions and motions to the agenda were controlled by the opposition.[171] Harzfeld again mentioned that the ministers were obliged to attend the plenum.[172] That same month, at a faction meeting, MK Yisrael Kargman inveighed against the government's publication of tax orders during the Knesset's recess, although it had promised not to use this executive tool during the recess.[173]

In August 1962, harsh criticism was voiced at a faction meeting against the government. The faction chairman, Govrin, protested that the government had not yet submitted to the Knesset several basic laws that it had undertaken to enact in its basic programme.[174] Avraham Harzfeld inveighed against the separation between the faction and the Mapai ministers:

> The faction is on its own and the ministers are on their own. They have apparently decided that everything they say, wisely or unwisely, rightly or wrongly – is an example to be followed . . . such a situation has never existed since the establishment of the Knesset . . . they are not even interested in hearing what the members have to say . . . I understand that they take the position that they bear greater responsibility, but to go so far as to completely ignore us? . . . We have to disabuse them of the notion that we are dummies who do nothing but vote . . . I will not raise objections in the Knesset, I will not cause any provocation, nor will I defeat a proposal in a committee of which I am a member, but they have to at least explain why they are proposing it and why I must accept it. Perhaps I also am capable of understanding something?[175]

Hacohen criticized the lack of communication with the ministers. Kargman concurred with him and expressed his regret that the Prime Minister was not present at the meeting, 'because it is his duty to see to it that a minister or two sits in the Knesset'.[176] Beba Idelson said she felt ashamed when not a single minister was present during the vote on the budget in the plenum. Assaf directed the barbs of his criticism not only at the coalition and Mapai, but at the Prime Minister himself. Moshe Baram protested the fact that 'the opposition asks questions and we sit there like mummies . . . we do not want to sabotage anything . . . the ministers come to us when there is a state of emergency'.[177]

Three months after this stormy meeting, Govrin resigned his position as chairman of the faction, giving as his reason the contempt the ministers revealed towards the faction and the fact that the secretariat had encroached upon the faction's powers.[178] He read out those clauses in the party constitution that give the faction the right to discuss and decide on issues that are not connected with foreign policy or security. Ben-Gurion interrupted at this point and found fault with the wording of the constitution, stating that it was 'a bit too far-reaching' and created a situation in which 'the faction discusses and decides, which means that the party does not exist and that no other institution exists, but that the Knesset members are the only ones who determine the party's policy'.[179] It was Ben-Gurion's suggestion not to accept Govrin's resignation. Kargman supported Govrin:

> Knesset members do not want to be automatons even in the era of automation, in particular an elected representative will not wish to be an automaton, will not want to come to the Knesset to vote, for the Knesset, in the final analysis, is a matter of voting.[180]

Bar-Rav-Hai said: 'I should not have to travel to the Knesset on Monday and read in the paper what our ministers are going to present, and at the end, just vote. That situation creates indifference ... If you don't feel you can have some influence, then it is no longer interesting.'[181]

This fierce criticism was voiced against the background of Ben-Gurion's shaky standing in Mapai following the quarrel pivoting on the Lavon affair. At the end of the meeting the members passed a resolution not to accept Govrin's resignation, and several weeks later an arrangement was found that enabled him to resume his post as chairman of the faction. The years during which Ben-Gurion headed the government were marked by a series of endless complaints lodged by Mapai Knesset members about his tendency to ignore them and treat them with contempt.

NOTES

1. Abraham Brichta, *Democracy and Elections* (Hebrew), Tel Aviv: Am Oved, 1977, p. 107.
2. David Ben-Gurion, *Yoman Hamilchamah*, vol. 3, p. 907.
3. Ibid.
4. Ben-Gurion Research Center Archives, correspondence, A. Ankorion and Z. Bar-Shira to Ben-Gurion, 26 December 1948.
5. Ibid., Ben-Gurion to Ankorion, 5 January 1949.

6. Ibid., A. Kinori and L. Konorti to Ben-Gurion, no specific date.
7. Ibid., A. Kinori to Ben-Gurion, 19 January 1949.
8. Israel Labour Party Archives, meeting of Mapai central committee, 4 January 1949.
9. Ibid.
10. Ibid.
11. Ibid.
12. Ibid.
13. Ibid.
14. Ben-Gurion Research Center Archives, minutes of meetings, talk with party members, 6 April 1949.
15. Israel Labour Party Archives, meeting of Mapai secretariat, 17 May 1951.
16. Brichta, *Democracy and Elections*, p. 107.
17. Israel Labour Party Archives, meeting of party central committee, 7 June 1951.
18. Ibid.
19. Ben-Gurion Research Center Archives, correspondence, J. Lam to Ben-Gurion, 12 June 1951; A. Ankorion to Ben-Gurion, 21 June 1951.
20. Israel Labour Party Archives, meeting of Mapai central committee, 22 June 1951.
21. Ibid., 22 May 1955.
22. Ibid., 19 May 1955.
23. Ibid., 22 May 1955.
24. Ibid.
25. Ibid.
26. Ibid.
27. Ibid.
28. Ibid., 29 May 1955.
29. Ben-Gurion Research Center Archives, correspondence, headquarters of Mapai young generation to Ben-Gurion, 2 June 1955; A. Ankorion to Ben-Gurion, 15 May 1955; Y. Simchoni to Ben-Gurion, no specific date.
30. Brichta, *Democracy and Elections*, p. 110.
31. Israel Labour Party Archives, meeting of Mapai central committee, 9 June 1955.
32. Ibid.
33. Ibid.
34. Ibid.
35. Ibid.
36. Ibid.
37. Brichta, *Democracy and Elections*.
38. Ben-Gurion Research Center Archives, correspondence, Zakai to Ben-Gurion, 20 June 1955.
39. Ibid., Ben-Gurion to Zakai, 1 July 1955.
40. Ibid., Ben-Gurion to Feinberg and Shapira, 30 June 1955.
41. Ibid.
42. Ibid., Ben-Gurion to Neta Harpaz, 15 June 1955.
43. Ibid.
44. Ibid.
45. Ibid.
46. Ibid., activists of Libyan origin to Ben-Gurion, 1955, no specific date.
47. Ibid., A. Maimon to Ben-Gurion, 26 August 1955.
48. Ibid., Ben-Gurion to Maimon, 2 October 1955.
49. Israel Labour Party Archives, national convention of the young generation, 3 March 1956.
50. Ibid.
51. Ibid.
52. Ibid.
53. Ben-Gurion Research Center Archives, correspondence, D. Zakai to Ben-Gurion, 4 July 1956.
54. Israel Labour Party Archives, meeting of Mapai central committee, 6 September 1955.

55. Brichta, *Democracy and Elections*, p. 122, based on *Davar*, 7 September 1959, p. 1.
56. Ben-Gurion Research Center Archives, correspondence, Ben-Gurion to Naftali, 22 April 1949.
57. Ibid., Ben-Gurion to Bader, 5 June 1949.
58. Ibid., *Knesset Record*, 5 June 1949, p. 641.
59. Ben-Gurion Research Center Archives, correspondence, Ben-Gurion to Hacohen, 6 July 1949.
60. Ibid., Ben-Gurion to Mapai secretariat, 4 June 1950.
61. Israel Labour Party Archives, meeting of Mapai political committee, 24 September 1952.
62. Ibid.
63. Ben-Gurion Research Center Archives, correspondence, Ben-Gurion to Aranne, 28 January 1953.
64. Ibid., Ben-Gurion to Yitzhak Koren, 12 December 1955.
65. Israel Labour Party Archives, meeting of Mapai political committee, 28 December 1955.
66. Ben-Gurion Research Center Archives, correspondence, Ben-Gurion to Avigor, 4 December 1949.
67. *Knesset Record*, 30 October 1950, p. 102.
68. Israel Labour Party Archives, meeting of Mapai faction in the Knesset, 12 October 1950.
69. Ibid., 13 December 1950.
70. Ibid., 19 December 1950.
71. State Archives, minutes of meeting of House Committee, 25 October 1950.
72. Ibid., 16 January 1951.
73. Ibid.
74. *Knesset Record*, 22 January 1951, p. 829.
75. Ibid., p. 830.
76. Ibid.
77. Ibid., p. 831.
78. Ibid.
79. Ibid., p. 832.
80. Ibid., p. 836.
81. State Archives, minutes of meeting of constitution, law and justice committee, 24 January 1951.
82. Ibid.
83. Ibid.
84. Ibid., 31 January 1951.
85. *Knesset Record*, 7 February 1951, pp. 1,016–21.
86. Israel Labour Party Archives, meeting of party bureau, 16 November 1948.
87. Ibid.
88. Ibid., meeting of Mapai secretariat, 9 June 1949.
89. Ibid.
90. The reference was to the Herut faction. This party was based on the Etzel, which was active in the underground prior to the establishment of the state.
91. Israel Labour Party Archives, meeting of Mapai secretariat, 9 June 1949.
92. Ibid.
93. Ibid.
94. Ibid.
95. Giora Goldberg, 'You Don't Need a Constitution to Plant Trees' p. 36.
96. Israel Labour Party Archives, meeting of Mapai faction in the Knesset with the secretariat, 14 June 1949.
97. Ibid., meeting of Mapai Knesset faction, 13 November 1949.
98. Ibid.
99. Ibid.
100. Ibid.

101. Ibid.
102. Ibid.
103. Ibid., meeting of Mapai Knesset faction and Mapai secretariat, 22 November 1949.
104. Ibid., meeting of management of Mapai Knesset faction, 7 December 1949.
105. Ibid.
106. Ibid., meeting of Mapai Knesset faction, 5 February 1950.
107. Ibid.
108. Ibid.
109. Ibid.
110. Ibid., 30 July 1950.
111. Ibid., meeting of faction with secretariat and Mapai members on the Histardrut Executive, 6 August 1950.
112. Ibid., meeting of faction with secretariat, 12 October 1950.
113. Ibid.
114. Ibid.
115. Ibid.
116. Ibid.
117. Ibid., afternoon meeting.
118. Ibid.
119. Ibid.
120. Ibid.
121. Ibid.
122. Ibid.
123. Ibid., meeting of Mapai Knesset faction, 17 October 1950.
124. Ibid.
125. Ibid.
126. Ibid., 28 November 1950.
127. Ibid., 4 December 1950.
128. Ibid.
129. Ibid.
130. Ibid.
131. Ibid.
132. Ibid.
133. Ibid.
134. Ibid.
135. Ibid.
136. Ibid., 13 December 1950.
137. Ibid.
138. Ibid.
139. Ibid., 15 January 1952.
140. Ibid.
141. Ibid., 13 February 1952.
142. Ibid.
143. Ibid.
144. Ibid., 9 March 1952.
145. Ibid., 6 May 1952.
146. Ibid., 26 May 1952.
147. Ibid., joint meeting of faction and the political committee, 13 August 1952.
148. Ibid., 18. November 1952.
149. Ibid., 28 October 1953.
150. Ibid., 11 August 1955.
151. Ibid., 15 August 1955.
152. Ibid., 25 October 1955.
153. Ibid., 19 December 1955.
154. Ibid.
155. Ibid., 7 May 1956.

156. Ibid.
157. Ibid.
158. Ben-Gurion Research Center Archives, correspondence, Guri to Ben-Gurion, 5 April 1957.
159. Evidently the subject was the strike that had broken out in the Ata factory.
160. Israel Labour Party Archives, meeting of Mapai Knesset faction, 19 May 1957.
161. Ben-Gurion Research Center Archives, correspondence, Govrin to Ben-Gurion, 12 June 1957.
162. Israel Labour Party Archives, meeting of Mapai Knesset faction, 19 September 1957.
163. Ibid.
164. Ibid., 16 March 1958.
165. Ibid.
166. Ibid.
167. Ibid., joint meeting of Mapai Knesset faction and Mapai secretariat, 13 July 1958.
168. Ibid., meeting of Mapai Knesset faction, 21 October 1958.
169. Ibid., 6 June 1950.
170. Ibid.
171. Ibid., 9 August 1960.
172. Ibid.
173. Ibid., 23 August 1960.
174. Ibid., 6 August 1962.
175. Ibid.
176. Ibid.
177. Ibid.
178. Ibid., 5 November 1962.
179. Ibid.
180. Ibid.
181. Ibid.

PART FOUR

Parliamentary Style and Conflicts with Political Rivals

9 Attacks on the Knesset and Knesset Members

In the opening chapter, we learned that one means extra-parliamentary elites employ against the parliament is vehement verbal attacks on it and its members. The purpose of these attacks is to diminish the parliament's legitimacy in the eyes of the public, which expects the parliament to be a respected institution, whose members speak and behave in a manner fundamentally different from that of people in the street, the market or the sports stadium. It expects their demeanour and speech to be restrained, their parliamentary manners to be proper, based on mutual respect and integrity. Members of parliament are supposed to use a moderate style of speech, avoiding exaggerations, lies and incitement. They are also supposed to act according to the parliamentary rules of the game. So they must abstain from maligning and besmirching their rivals. In part, their parliamentary skill lies in their ability to level incisive criticism without becoming offensive, or using a style characterized by invective, derision, coarseness and getting sidetracked from the subject at hand. They are expected to be present at parliament sessions during which they are criticized, to listen to their political rivals and to show some degree of readiness to be influenced by what their rivals have to say, particularly if they have presented them with new facts.

Since one of the major roles of the parliament is to constitute a supreme national arena for public debate, the style that takes shape in it is of paramount importance. A large part of the public cannot really evaluate how the parliament fulfills its other traditional functions – investigation, supervision and control – but it is easy for citizens to form an opinion about how the parliament fulfills its function of discussing and debating. The quality of parliamentary style constitutes a major criterion for evaluating this aspect of the parliament's work as well as its functioning in general.

One of the causes of the Knesset's negative image is the cheap and common style, often termed 'verbal violence', that has become a permanent feature of parliamentary life in Israel. The public has a far more favourable opinion of the judicial system than it has of the parliamentary system. When a sample was asked in July 1991 to what extent various political and social institutions contribute or do damage, substantive differences were revealed between the Knesset and the High Court of Justice: 39.6 per cent believed that the High Court contributed greatly, versus only 13.9 per cent who thought the same regarding the Knesset; 48 per cent were convinced that the High Court made some contribution versus 43.8 per cent in relation to the Knesset; 32.8 per cent believed the Knesset both contributed and caused damage while 10.2 per cent held this view in relation to the High Court of Justice; 7.7 per cent believed the Knesset caused damage and 1.9 per cent that the Knesset caused a great deal of damage, while only 0.8 per cent believed the High Court caused damage and 1.3 per cent that it caused a great deal of damage.[1] One of the reasons for the differences found may be the dignified and restrained style that characterizes the judges in contrast to the legislators' boisterous style of speech.

Ben-Gurion is also largely responsible for the non-parliamentary style that developed in the Knesset. In blatant contrast to his vision of statehood that would surmount all divisions and differences, Ben-Gurion endowed the Knesset with all the features of a boxing ring in which no rules of fair play apply. His own unruly style prepared the ground for virulent expressions by other Knesset members. One would naturally expect the Prime Minister to have a restrained style, for he is not supposed to engage in levelling criticism. The opposition – the most critical factor in any parliament – might be expected, on the other hand, to tend much more towards a non-parliamentary style. The Israeli reality is the reverse. Ben-Gurion, as Prime Minister, tended to adopt a non-parliamentary style, replete with often unbridled outbursts directed at Knesset members, in particular those from the opposition. Ben-Gurion's fractious style, including goads and taunts, was not the result of an irrepressible emotional approach. On the contrary, he deliberately adopted this manner to achieve certain objectives. One was to degrade the Knesset in public opinion. Another was to 'induce' the opposition to adopt an uncompromising, caustic non-parliamentary style, that would reduce its chances of ever attaining power.

Ben-Gurion's desire to disparage the Knesset in the public eye did not derive only from the almost natural rivalry between the legislative arm and the executive arm; rather, it reflected his belief that the Knesset was adversely affecting state interests, as well as his fundamental hostility towards the Knesset and parliamentary life. This is how he described the Knesset in April 1951, speaking before the Mapai faction and its political committee:

> Anyone can see what is taking place in the Knesset nowadays in relation to the elections law and the immunity law, this bizarre combination, the close alliance between Mikunis, Sneh, Rokach, Shag, Bader and Rosen, what a strange thing it is. Everyone knows there are traitors in the Knesset. The Communists are unquestionably agents of a foreign country. Mapam is not an agency, the Shomer Hatzair states explicitly that it would under no circumstances fight against Russia. And the Zionists, although they are general Zionists and feel no sympathy for Russia, are strongly allied with them. This is liable to be revived in other situations as well, particularly in the Second Knesset, in which there are apt to be ten Arabs, who can play a decisive role, and others will dance around them . . . we can see how the General Zionists, the Mizrachi and the Agudah are abandoning state interests, and if they need an alliance with Mikunis, they will become partners, and we can see how the state's interests are being forfeited.[2]

Ben-Gurion's words to members of the Mapai secretariat in May 1952, show how rational his choice of parliamentary style was:

> The party must be a militant party. The major shortcoming of the faction is that it is not a fighting faction. We should never have to defend our position. We need to explain . . . but not to defend, only to attack the opposition, to reveal its malevolence, its daily acts of sabotage, to give them no respite.[3]

The price the opposition was meant to pay for non-parliamentary conduct was far higher than the price Ben-Gurion was prepared to pay for it.

In the first two Knessets, a commonality of interests was created between Ben-Gurion and the chief opposition party – Herut. The former underground members were having a hard time adjusting to the new situation brought about by the establishment of the state. Its leaders were glad of every opportunity for a parliamentary confrontation with the government, particularly with the man at its head. Beginning with the Third Knesset, in particular after the party convention in 1956, new, different winds began to blow in Herut.[4] Its leaders understood that the only way they could bring the party closer to power was to move closer to the centre, which meant giving up every possibility of extra-parliamentary oppositional activity, creating ties with other parties and gaining entry to public institutions which, until then, had banned Herut. In the Knesset, this turnabout was markedly expressed by the fact that Herut no longer constituted an opposition that in principle automatically opposed every act and proposal by the government, and whose leaders tried to adopt a proper parliamentary style, which entailed observing all the rules of the parliamentary game and refraining from clashes and quarrels with the government, in particular with its head. Ben-Gurion did not make this easy for Herut and did nothing to help it in its transition from an underground to a political party. He understood that from his standpoint, it was better to leave Herut as an extremist, loud, militant opposition, which was out of the running as a coalition partner. As long as large segments of the population perceived it as such, Herut would have a very hard time constituting an alternative to the party in power. Ben-Gurion initiated a series of parliamentary conflicts, which at times developed into scandals, in order to 'drag' the Herut leaders by their tongues and induce them to behave in an unparliamentary manner, which they were trying to avoid doing. He did this in particular by emotional references to historical events, still fresh in everyone's memory, connected with the bitter quarrel between his movement and the Revisionists. These attempts were successful. From this viewpoint Ben-Gurion differed from other members of his party and his movement. During the period (January 1954–November 1955) when Sharett was Prime Minister, the kind of dramatic parliamentary conflicts that typifyied Ben-Gurion's tenure as Prime Minister did not occur. After Ben-Gurion resigned from the prime ministership in 1963 and was succeeded by Eshkol, the acrimonious clashes between Herut and Mapai, centring on grievous historical memories, stopped almost completely too.

PARLIAMENTARY CONFLICTS BETWEEN BEN-GURION AND THE OPPOSITION PARTIES

Ben-Gurion's first parliamentary attack against Herut and Begin took place several weeks after the first elections. On 8 March 1949, after he had succeeded in forming a government, Ben-Gurion informed the Knesset of its composition and its programme. That same day an extensive debate began, with the participation of representatives of all the factions, and lasted for three days. Begin made his first programmatic speech in the Knesset. It was a very restrained address, in which he made no mention of past events that had divided his party and Mapai, and promised a pragmatic approach to the new government:

> We will be in opposition to this government and will judge it by its actions. We shall praise its good deeds, and denounce its bad deeds, fearlessly and undaunted . . . We shall participate in every constructive endeavour . . . we shall participate in settling the pioneering village and in defending the freedom of the people and the state . . . no one will disqualify us or keep us from playing a role in carrying out great deeds . . . no one here is competent to judge who among the Jewish people is constructive and who is not constructive.[5]

He called on Ben-Gurion, without specifically mentioning his name, to adopt a statesmanlike approach:

> By virtue of the change that has take place in reality – and it is in the blood of all Jews, with all their parties and classes, and no one will dare to discriminate against Hebrew blood, which was shed for the sake of Jerusalem's sanctity and for its victory.[6]

Ben-Gurion's reply to Begin, two days later, was particularly rancorous. He accused Begin and his associates of spouting speeches and declarations but doing very little, and said they had not been partners in the supreme national effort of the War of Independence:

> I must say that there is a fundamental difference between us and you, and not only on the question of Jerusalem, but on all issues. We do not put much faith in declarations and declamations . . . I know a little about your actions in Jerusalem, before

> the Israel Defence Forces liquidated your armed dissidence. And at this point, I don't want to rake up the past either. But it is my duty to tell you that your actions then did not help in the independence of Jerusalem . . . Something, I believe, was done when you were outside, for Jerusalem . . . I know who was there, I didn't see you there. I know about battles near Latrun after the invasion . . . and a lot of blood was spilled there, a lot of blood . . . I know who was there. I also know who was not there . . . And I saw the fighters who spilled their blood on that road . . . on that descent called 'Burma' . . . I know who was there, I also know who was not there.[7]

Later on in his speech, Ben-Gurion took on the leaders of Mapam, and spoke with pride about his battles with the Revisionists:

> I fought against Revisionism no less than those from Mapam, and the Revisionists justifiably cannot forgive me, although I do not use the term 'fascist' very much – even though they took that name for themselves . . . for me the name Revisionism was something that had to be fought against, and I fought . . . when there was a danger to the State of Israel in connection with the *Altalena*, I took a certain responsibility upon myself, a responsibility that I am proud of! . . . I also have some share in liquidating the armed dissident forces in Jerusalem . . . when the Agency Executive decided to fight against the Etzel . . . I did not shrink from Sneh's opposition either, and I carried out the fight.[8]

The Herut Knesset members did not reply to these accusations at the same meeting, but only several weeks later. In a debate on the Discharged Soldiers Law, Yaacov Meridor claimed that the Etzel forces were prepared for the battles at Latrun but were not called upon to take part in them: 'I don't know why we were not asked to, maybe they were waiting for an opportunity to count who was there and was not there.'[9] In addition, Meridor said: 'We were not the ones who opened this subject; it was the Prime Minister who began.'[10]

In the same debate, Arye Ben-Eliezer also referred to the clash that Ben-Gurion had initiated several weeks earlier:

> But in this Knesset . . . someone was interested in making a reckoning with the past. We hardly reacted at all, and thought we wouldn't react in the future either. But I ask: please don't

> exaggerate, if you want a reckoning, remember there are two sides to it . . . I want to believe the Prime Minister and Minister of Defence will also take that into account. Because how long will he live with the past? How long will he live with hatred? . . . Let's end this question.[11]

From the time Ben-Gurion hurled these accusations at Herut, until November 1949; for eight months, he boycotted Begin's speeches in the plenum. Every time Begin was called to the speaker's podium, the Prime Minister would leave the hall, making a grand exit. The Prime Minister's boycott of the head of the opposition's speeches showed how non-parliamentary his style was. The next instance of a systematic boycott was in the Eleventh Knesset (1984–88), when nearly all the members left the plenum hall whenever Meir Kahane spoke. However, a boycott by one man, all the more so when he is Prime Minister, was regarded as an exceptional phenomenon in Israeli parliamentary life. On 9 November 1949, Begin was surprised when he was about to speak and Ben-Gurion remained in the hall: 'I have to open with the blessing "*Hechiyanu*" [that we have lived to see this day]. Here I have risen to the podium, and the Prime Minister is still seated in the hall.'[12] A few days later, Ben-Gurion replied with a series of derisive remarks, castigating Herut, and implying that they had fascist leanings:

> MK Begin recited the *Hechiyanu* prayer about the fact that the Prime Minister was sitting in the Knesset listening to his speech. I very much regret that I cannot reciprocate and say the same about his speech that I heard. Although it was the first time I heard Mr Begin, the speech was not new to me. I have heard such speeches – not in Hebrew and not in this country – several years ago, before the Second World War, and to tell you the truth, I was really sorry that here in our midst such speeches are delivered. I had hoped – and perhaps I was too naive – that the members of Herut, that grew out of the Etzel, had learned something in the State of Israel, when they sat together with representatives of the public, and I refer to representatives from the coalition and from the opposition – that built the country, established the state, fought its wars and won. I regret that this speech proved that the leader of Herut has learned nothing and has forgotten nothing, since the time the members of Etzel appeared beyond the camp of the Zionist movement and of the organized

> Yishuv. This speech was very instructive for me in one sense: it didn't leave in my heart even an iota of doubt about the essence of the movement that the speaker heads. This essence has no Hebrew name, and you know I don't like to use foreign terms.[13]

A few months earlier, in April 1949, during his speech on the Armistice agreements, Ben-Gurion attacked the opposition factions, Herut in particular:

> it is strange, that those factions who are not interested in democracy, but rather in the rule of a single party, in the oppression of every freedom of opposition, are the very ones who speak about the sovereignty of the Knesset. I only wish they would maintain the sovereignty of the Knesset.[14]

He had some very harsh words for Herut: 'But our task and our desire in the Arab world was not Dir Yassin. Our task was not to annihilate the Arab people.'[15] He continued to taunt the Herut members: 'You didn't bring a single Jew here with your declamations.'[16]

After Begin demanded, in January 1950, an investigation into the fall of the Old City of Jerusalem, he was the object of a veritable flood of criticism by the Prime Minister in the plenum:

> Mr Begin ought to have known that he was speaking not at a Purim festival but in the Knesset, and when you speak in the Knesset you need to know a little about the subject, some words of truth and some responsibility . . . there are individuals who I believe have the moral right to ask me questions about wartime matters, and I answer them. I recognize their moral right, whether it's the son of a soldier, the father of a solider, the mother of a soldier, or a soldier himself. I do not recognize Mr Begin's right. He is not the son of a soldier, he cannot yet be the father of a soldier. Nor is he, to the best of my knowledge, a soldier. He was not a soldier in the Israel Defence Forces . . . he was not with those who fought for the freedom of Israel, for our independence and our success, he did not join in the battle. At the moment, I have no complaints to him. Before the elections to the Knesset, an amnesty law was passed and it also applies to Mr Begin. But I do not recognize his right to inquire and to ask, and because of the amnesty law, I will not ask him any personal questions.[17]

In effect, the Prime Minister was treating the head of the opposition as if he were a criminal who, due to special circumstances, was not being punished for shirking his military service.

Ben-Gurion's caustic style in the Knesset was not limited to attacks on Herut and the Communists. He usually did not shrink from waging battles with other factions in the opposition. For example, in November 1952, several weeks before he saw fit to add the General Zionists to his government, he criticized them in the plenum for not having contributed enough to the national effort:

> I am interested in doers, not in talkers. The state is built by those who do work and not by those who give forth words. Two weeks ago, I was in the Negev; I looked for you there and to my regret I found no sign of a General Zionist. Who prevented you three years ago from going down to the southern plain? Who kept you from establishing a plant in Elath? I didn't find any trace of you there. And I sometimes walk in the hills of Jerusalem and the Galilee looking for your footsteps there, and I do not find them.[18]

In February 1956, during his speech on the budget law, Ben-Gurion spoke about the possibility of a war between Israel and its neighbours, and fiercely attacked the members of the Communist party:

> We will win despite everything. We will suffer, perhaps our settlements will be destroyed, our streets and cities will be damaged, many of us will be killed, but we will win, because those who the Israeli Communist faction regards today as allies – King Hussein of Jordan and the Egyptian tyrant rule a people who do not know why they are being sent into battle, just as they didn't know eight years ago.[19]

Sneh, astonished, reacted by saying: 'You don't know what your lips are saying. Mr Prime Minister, you are talking nonsense.'[20] The Prime Minister's words caused a parliamentary ruckus.

In March 1956, the Knesset was in an uproar again when Ben-Gurion hurled accusations at Begin. The fracas broke out after Begin's speech explaining the reason for the no confidence proposal – what Herut viewed as the restrained policy that the government was adopting in relation to the growing Egyptian threat. Begin said:

'When the order is given, there will be no difference – we will all fight until victory', and concluded his speech by emotionally calling on the government: 'You must resign!'[21] Ben-Gurion opened his reply very aggressively: 'There is one thing in his speech I agree with. That our fighters will fight. But he is exaggerating somewhat in relation to himself. He said, we have fought and we will fight. The speaker did not fight in the War of Independence and he will not fight.'[22] At this point, a noisy commotion broke out in the plenum. Begin reacted sharply:

> Here we have a hero! When I was fighting for the sake of my people, you were informing against fellow Jews . . . I will teach all of you to speak with respect in this house . . . Did I say even one word to offend him personally? What sort of invective is he uttering here?[23]

The following day MK Assaf of Mapai sent a reproachful letter to the Prime Minister:

> In our system of government, the obligation to exercise restraint, and to control oneself falls first of all on those in power, and not on the opposition. The former has the authority to make decisions, the power to implement them, to demand obedience and assign tasks. The opposition can do nothing but criticize and caution. Accordingly, it is the ruler's obligation to placate and to conciliate . . . what took place yesterday was the very opposite.[24]

Further on in his letter, Assaf referred to Begin:

> We cannot dismiss the self-sacrifice and commitment that his people have exhibited . . . Neither we, nor especially the Prime Minister in our name, have any need, and even more so any purpose, to anger him, to show him disrespect. The result is disparagement of the Knesset's standing at a time when the responsibility rests upon us . . . I sincerely hope that you will accept my words with all the feelings of respect I have for you, but also with all the severity of the claim I permit myself to make of you.[25]

Ben-Gurion was not prepared to accept Assaf's criticism. In his reply to Assaf, he depicted what had occurred in the Knesset as 'the hooliganism and unrestrained behaviour of Begin and his people',[26] and defended his own conduct in the plenum:

> In the Knesset no one implements or rules; they just argue and make inquiries. When a demagogue tries to deride the government (maybe that is his right) and tries to instigate a war, which may lead to the loss of the state, and boasts that he fought in the War of Independence – things have to be set straight and I have to point out that he did not take part in the war, and he has no right to include himself among the fighters. In your eyes, it may be unimportant, to me it is important . . . and a shirker cannot boast that 'we fought and we will fight' . . . in your opinion, I ought not to comment on that – but it is hard to argue about opinions . . . but if some fellow who shirked his duty (and maybe he had good reasons for that) to participate in the War of Independence, and boasts that 'we fought and we will fight' – I will deny his lies to his face. Even if Gruner sacrificed his life in acts of terror against the British, Begin is not entitled to brag that he participated in the War of Independence, when that is a lie.[27]

Evidently Assaf did not agree with Ben-Gurion's reply, for, at a meeting of the Mapai faction in August 1962, he voiced some implicit criticism of Ben-Gurion's style in dealing with the opposition.[28]

In June 1956, during the debate on Sharett's resignation as Minister of Foreign Affairs, Ben-Gurion attacked Begin without explicitly mentioning his name: 'I would like to say that in Mapai, and I believe I can say in all the other parties in the government, there is not a single maniac or clown who would say to himself or to his associates that God had chosen him to rule.'[29] He was distinguishing between a demagogue and a statesman. This is how he described the demagogue:

> The path of a demagogue is an easy one. There is nothing he cannot do; there is no country he cannot conquer; there is no enemy he cannot destroy; there are no desires of the public that he cannot satisfy; there are no interests of the masses that he cannot gratify – because all his power lies in the words he utters. He is a talker – and there is no impediment to his tongue . . . he is a political parasite. The demagogue always praises and glorifies the army, because he knows how much the people love

> the army, to what extent the people's security depends on the army, but he himself never has raised a finger for the sake of the army . . . when the people is attacked, the demagogue makes a pretence of being so essential to the people, that it is more important for him to remain working in the party than to join in the war as one of the soldiers. And as a party activist he obtains an exemption from the army and from the war, and when the battles are over, when the army has won, he does not stop boasting: 'We have fought and we have won' . . . and it is no wonder that one never finds the demagogue on the borders, in the Negev, and usually one only meets him in Zion Plaza or Mugrabi Square.[30]

In October 1956, less than two weeks before the outbreak of the Sinai War, the Prime Minister once again initiated a clash with Herut in the plenum. The Knesset was holding a debate on foreign affairs and security, in which Begin harshly criticized the government for not launching a military offensive against Egypt after it had blockaded the Strait of Elath: 'Why, then, did you promise in the elections to send ground, air and sea forces to break through the blockade?'[31] Before Ben-Gurion began his reply to Herut, he first attacked the Communists for 'having taken the Egyptian tyrant under its wings, maybe because most of the weapons he received and all the weapons he is now getting, come from the Soviet Union'.[32] This sentence led to a sharp exchange between him and Sneh:

BEN-GURION: Perhaps you will allow me to talk; there is freedom of speech here, Mr Sneh.

SNEH: Of course, there is freedom of speech, for me too.

BEN-GURION: No. You have no freedom of speech now. You have to shut up.

SNEH: The Speaker is the one to say, I will listen to him, not to you.[33]

Ben-Gurion's attack on Herut was particularly vociferous. He claimed that Begin was lowering 'the level of moral argumentation in the Knesset and making a laughing-stock of himself'.[34] This is how he related to Herut's support of a military initiative:

> I am unable to define the true nature of this advice because I don't want to dishonour the Knesset nor do I want to use the word that is appropriate to this advice here, in the Knesset. And the people who give such advice, unlike MK Hazan, I do not

> believe in the crocodile tears they shed over the fallen soldiers of the IDF.[35]

This statement aroused irate reactions from the Herut benches. Begin demanded that Sprinzak rebuke the Prime Minister and yelled: 'Shameless . . . This is a disgrace to the honour of Israel . . . You have no scruples . . . he may speak, but he cannot give free rein to his tongue.'[36] Esther Raziel-Naor cried out: 'Don't we have any sons who were killed? . . . Don't we have widows and orphans?'[37] Ben-Gurion did not back down, but carried on with his attack:

> And I am expressing my complete certainty, that the people of Israel will never place the glorious Israel Defence Forces in the hands of such irresponsible people, who would lead us to the slaughter, whenever they think it is a fitting time for what they call Independence, nor will they ever give them power in the State of Israel . . . a distinction must be drawn between those in the state who are responsible and those who are irresponsible, and we have to tell the people that, and no one will stop me from telling that to the people.[38]

At the start of the next session of the Knesset, about a week before the Sinai War, Sprinzak made two announcements, on behalf of the Prime Minister and on behalf of Herut, both of which related to the serious incident. Ben-Gurion wrote: 'If during the argument, a word slipped from my mouth that I should not have said in the Knesset, I regret that and take it back wholeheartedly and without any reservations.'[39] Herut's announcement was worded as follows:

> We do not want, and never have wanted, any insults to be voiced in the Knesset. Between us and our rivals there are very deep controversies. As free men, with sincerity and without fear, we will clarify them in the Knesset, in the ears of the people who have elected us and judge us. We are all bound to hold our debates with mutual respect, as befits delegates chosen by an ancient people of culture. In this way we will elevate the status of the Hebrew legislature in the eyes of the nation and the world.[40]

It is not improbable that the Prime Minister took the step, unusual for him, of employing a conciliatory tone because he knew that the war about to break out would call for national unity and solidarity. However, even in this state of emergency, Ben-Gurion was not entirely committed to the reconciliation that had been achieved. When he learned about the agreement reached between Mapai and Herut about defusing the parliamentary incident, he was furious at Minister of Finance Eshkol, who was supposed to give the announcement in the plenum in the Prime Minister's name. The Mapai leaders used Ben-Gurion's letter in order to reach a compromise with Herut, based on which Herut would also write a letter of reconciliation of its own, and both letters would be read out by the Speaker. Ben-Gurion protested to Eshkol about the fact that his letter had been shown to members of Herut before it had been read out in the plenum, and added: 'In my announcement, I was only replying to the Speaker's remark, and no one had any permission to use it in a negotiation with any faction whatsoever, in particular not with the Herut faction.'[41]

In November 1957, during a debate on foreign policy and security, Ben-Gurion attacked Bader and the other members of Herut: 'Mr Bader belongs to that happy group, which according to the leader of Herut, was chosen to rule by God himself . . . A man who by divine decree was chosen for such an important state position.'[42] Another conflict between the Prime Minister and the head of the opposition arose in June 1958. The verbal clash broke out following a motion to the agenda raised by Begin about officers in the regular army attending party assemblies. Begin's speech was fairly moderate and contained no attacks on Ben-Gurion. But the latter replied with sound and fury, accusing Begin of shirking military service and describing his speech as 'slander of people who took part in the War of Independence by a man who did not take part in it'.[43] In reply to Raziel-Naor's question: 'Who did not take part in the War of Independence?' Ben-Gurion said: 'Mr Begin did not take part in the War of Independence. Anyone who did take part in the war does have a little more right than a man who refused to take part in it.'[44]

Following this deliberate provocation by Ben-Gurion, a week later Herut proposed a motion of no confidence in the government. Begin, who explained the reasons for the motion on behalf of his faction, accused the Prime Minister of 'hatred, animosity, libel, war between brothers, shedding innocent blood – up to the point of vengefulness that has no expression in human language, vengefulness beyond death'.[45] Begin appealed to the Knesset members of Mapai to restrain their leader:

> Overcome your fear and tell your leader that he must know how to hold his tongue. The Knesset is not a party council of Mapai, here there will be no monologues . . . Here he will get as good as he gives or more. And if you don't tell him that, then the opposition will see to it that he does not let his tongue run away with him in the Hebrew house of representatives.[46]

After Ben-Gurion called Begin the 'talker', Begin retaliated by calling him the 'rowdy little tyrant',[47] a good illustration of how successful Ben-Gurion was in inducing Begin and his associates to resort to a non-parliamentary style of speech.

In December 1958, the Prime Minister accused Herut of being incapable of establishing pioneering endeavours.[48] In January 1959, he lashed out at Herut again: 'I did not make up this whole business about fascists in Israel', and recalled the incident when stones were thrown at the Knesset building in January 1952.[49] The members of Herut tried not to raise a parliamentary storm, although Ben-Gurion was attacking them furiously, classing them with the Communists: 'I make an exception of two groups: the Communists and Herut.'[50] Ben-Gurion did not let go, and began running through the details of the events linked to the *Altalena* affair, which he called a 'revolt against the government'.[51] At last, the members of Herut fell into the trap he had laid for them. Ben-Eliezer shouted: 'This matter is not yet finished. You will end it. You will stand trial . . . You murdered.'[52] Begin reminded Ben-Gurion of his request that he refrain from raising painful past events in the Knesset:

> First, I will appeal personally to the Prime Minister: Although you have never spoken to me and never will speak to me, we are sitting here in the house of representatives of the State of Israel, and I turn to you as one man to another, as a Jew to a Jew: how many times have you, Mr Ben-Gurion, turned to me and to members of the Herut faction, in writing or orally, asking us not to bring up from this podium affairs of the past. Do you deny that? How many notes have you sent to me and to MK Ben-Eliezer?[53]

Ben-Gurion did not confirm Begin's claim about his requests and demanded that he present proof.

Five days later, Herut reacted to the Prime Minister's accusations by proposing a no confidence motion. This time the Knesset was in an uproar after Ben-Gurion had adamantly refused to accede to Begin's demand that a thorough investigation be made into the *Altalena* affair: 'I will not go anywhere with you outside of the Knesset . . . except for this place, I do not intend to be in the same room with you.'[54] The Prime Minister's response to some interjections by Yosef Shofman was acerbic: 'Have you also gone up to the gallows with MK Begin?'[55]

However, Ben-Gurion was not always successful in baiting the members of Herut and stirring up a parliamentary storm. In December 1959, for example, he began to settle an account with Herut and Begin in the course of the debate on the amendment to the Transition Law, which was supposed to set up sanctions for violations of coalition discipline. At first he taunted Begin: 'The important speaker on behalf of Herut', and later began to quote from the *Herut* newspaper about the fact that Begin had joined a group of motorcyclists on a jaunt outside Tel Aviv on the eve of the 1959 elections. His conclusion was that 'Any normal person viewing this comical journey could only feel pity for those poor people who had lost their senses, thinking that by arranging such ludicrous displays, and publicizing them in the paper a day before the elections, they could win the voter's hearts.'[56] The members of Herut reacted by interjecting remarks, but they were careful to avoid creating parliamentary mayhem.

In February 1960, however, Ben-Gurion did succeed in drawing the members of Herut into a parliamentary commotion. He opened with a caustic attack on Herut, in which he even related to the incident, eight years earlier, when its members had thrown stones at the Knesset: 'I said that I understood the mood of the mob that gathered here and threw stones at the Knesset, but I called out the army to stop them. Why did I understand their mood? Because a demagogue had incited them.'[57] The Prime Minister had particularly harsh words for Begin: 'I don't think your speech was motivated by patriotism.'[58] In July 1961, on the other hand, Ben-Gurion failed to provoke Herut into a parliamentary conflict. During a speech on the Lavon Affair, he launched a vigorous attack on Begin, referring to various stormy events, such as the stone-throwing at the Knesset building in 1952 and Begin's expulsion from the Knesset. All the Herut members remained silent, without interjecting a single remark.[59] In May 1962, Ben-Gurion clashed with Begin during a debate on four no confidence motions. Begin was infuriated by the Prime Minister's words:

> I was in a government that demanded real sacrifices and the people responded favourably, and were also proud of the achievements these sacrifices brought about. When I say the people are proud of these achievements, I must make one exception: Mr Bader and his cohorts who argued that these sacrifices did not bring us achievements, but a third Ninth Day of Av [a day of national mourning] . . . But you are the only ones who say this, you and the people are two different things.[60]

When he referred to Begin as 'the man now sitting to the right of Mr Bader', Begin reacted angrily, asking, 'Even when I do not talk, do you have to rebuke me?'[61]

That same month, the Prime Minister attacked Herut during his speech in the plenum on the legislation connected with sanctions for violations of coalition discipline:

> Afterwards we heard some odd things that only can be said if the speaker doesn't understand what is going on. I understand that it's possible to go to a gathering of youth or children, where there are no grownups, to take a room there and hang up a sign saying: 'God has chosen us to rule'.[62]

Again, the members of Herut were content to merely shout a few interjections and refrained from creating a parliamentary uproar.

'WHEN THEY PRAISED HITLER AND GLORIFIED HIS NAME'

The last parliamentary clash between Ben-Gurion and Begin and Herut took place in May 1963, about a month before Ben-Gurion left the prime ministership. It was the worst as far as its language was concerned. While replying to those attending a debate on the political and security situation, Ben-Gurion began casting serious aspersions on the Herut members: 'However, I once again must admit that I do not share, nor did I ever share, the view taken by Mr Landau and his friends in relation to Germany. I did not join them when they glorified and praised Hitler and took him as a model.'[63] This sentence was expunged from the Knesset Record. The Prime Minister's outburst was followed by vehement reactions from the Herut benches: 'How do you permit yourself to say such things? You made an agreement with them',[64] Landau shouted. Begin called

Ben-Gurion 'black', an 'informer', a 'collaborator', and demanded that the Knesset Speaker, Kadish Luz, reprimand the Prime Minister for his remarks.[65] Ben-Gurion continued speaking despite loud disturbances by Herut members. Landau called out: 'He will not speak!'[66] but Ben-Gurion obstinately continued: 'and they placed Hitler among the grandest names of our time'.[67] Three times, Luz asked Ben-Gurion to repeat the words that had so stirred up the Knesset, so he could be sure he had in fact said them. The Prime Minister refused to submit to the Knesset Speaker. The Herut members continued their deliberate interference until Luz was forced to adjourn the session. In this conflict, Ben-Gurion got no help from the other members of his party. A newspaper report said: 'Even the members of the Mapai faction were silent, in keeping with the instructions of their whips.'[68] As soon as the session was adjourned, the Knesset presidium was convened for an urgent meeting. Luz asserted that Ben-Gurion ought to be asked to repeat what he had said and if Luz found that his words were inappropriate, he would insist that he retract them. If Ben-Gurion were to refuse, his words would be expunged from the minutes. At the meeting of the presidium, Herut demanded that Ben-Gurion declare that he was taking his words back, and then the session could be renewed. The presidium finally adopted a compromise resolution – that Ben-Gurion would retract his words and the House Committee would decide on sanctions against the Knesset members who had disrupted the session. Nonetheless, the plenum session was not reopened, because Ben-Gurion refused to accept the presidium's decision and to retract his words. The presidium was reconvened to try to find a way out of the impasse. Joseph Serlin (Liberals) suggested that Luz invite Ben-Gurion and Begin to separate talks in order to reach a compromise. The Knesset Speaker agreed and said: 'I take upon myself the risk of a meeting with Ben-Gurion.'[69] In the meantime, Foreign Minister Meir succeeded in persuading the Prime Minister to take back what he had said. During that whole time, Ben-Gurion remained in the plenum hall, which had emptied out. Once Meir's inducements had the desired result, Ben-Gurion met with Luz and a meeting was later held between Begin and Luz. After a recess of nearly three hours, the plenum session was renewed.

When the session was reopened, Ben-Gurion did not express any regret for his remarks, but simply stated that he was prepared to expunge three and a half lines from his speech,

> in accordance with the Speaker's instructions, since I believe that the Speaker's instructions are binding on every person in the Knesset, no matter who the Speaker is, in particular since we are fortunate enough to have a speaker who is one of the finest men of our nation.[70]

The meaning of his statement was that he did not accept the decision of the Knesset presidium, but was complying with the Speaker's instruction. After Ben-Gurion's statement, the session continued without any further disturbance. According to a press report, the Prime Minister had intended to utter the harsh comments against Herut at the closing state ceremony on the Remembrance Day of the Holocaust and Heroism that had taken place in Jerusalem a few weeks earlier, but at the last minute this invective was deleted from his speech.[71]

On the day after this incident, an editorial was printed in *Ma'ariv*, openly criticizing Ben-Gurion: 'In the Knesset session yesterday, the Prime Minister achieved what he had set out to do – to enrage the Herut faction and to cause a commotion.'[72] The next editorial in *Ma'ariv* was even more blatant, calling on the Knesset not to give in to the pressures brought by Mapai to impose sanctions on Herut members. The article placed full responsibility on Ben-Gurion:

> The Prime Minister misused the Knesset podium in order to disparage an entire faction and to portray it as 'glorifiers of Hitler' . . . if he had complied with the Speaker's instructions to repeat his words or to retract them, the commotion might have been avoided . . . the fact that the Knesset was of the opinion, along with all the members – including the members of Mapai who were stunned and silent during the hubbub and refrained from coming to the Prime Minister's aid . . . [that] the comments made by Ben-Gurion are a gross provocation and should not only be retracted but also expunged from the minutes . . . Mapai is demanding the punishment of Herut members more out of fear of their leader than out of any respect for the Knesset,

and if the Herut members are penalized in the final analysis . . . 'that will amount to a disservice to Israeli parliamentary life'.[73]

Mapai had a hard time enlisting a majority in the House Committee to denounce the conduct of the Herut members and to invoke the clause in the rules of procedure that would exclude Herut from five sessions of the plenum. The opposition, including Mapam, supported Herut in this instance. Two of Mapai's coalition partners, the National Religious Party and Poalei Agudat Israel, also refused to join in the condemnation. The Minister of the Interior, Moshe Shapira of the National Religious Party, informed the chairman of the coalition management, Govrin, that his party was opposed to the condemnation because 'the Prime Minister's action was improper'.[74] Other than Mapai, only Achdut Haavoda was a party to the condemnation initiative.

Moreover, even among the two parties that called for condemnation, some criticism of the Prime Minister was voiced. Two days after the incident, the author Haim Guri wrote an extremely virulent article about Ben-Gurion in *LaMerchav*, the Achdut Haavoda newspaper. In it, he wrote:

> If he did it in cold blood, then that's horrible . . . to utter such a sentence today . . . in the Knesset in Jerusalem . . . No, that is unforgivable. In the three and a half lines that were expunged, Ben-Gurion caused a grievous injury . . . he has no right to spill the blood of Knesset members, the representatives of the people . . . more than the shouts of Herut members, this time the dignity of the Knesset was debased by the sentences uttered by the man who is in charge of the army.[75]

The most interesting aspect was the criticism levelled against Ben-Gurion from Mapai circles. Some of it can be understood against the background of the internal crisis in which the ruling party found itself as a result of the residue of the Lavon Affair. Abraham Wolfensohn, one of the Prime Minister's most loyal supporters, referred to the incident when speaking to the young members of Mapai: 'How is it possible that the leadership of the party and its faction in the Knesset were stunned into silence, and the *Davar* newspaper actually attacked Ben-Gurion on a matter of principle.'[76] The Prime Minister 'in fact has remained isolated, without a party and without a press'.[77] This suggests that the desire of the Mapai representatives on the House Committee to punish the Herut members who disrupted the stormy session did not reflect a cohesive stand by all members of Mapai behind the Prime Minister.

Wolfensohn's criticism of *Davar* related to the editorial printed by the paper two days after the incident, which found some fault with the Prime Minister:

> One cannot help being somewhat taken aback by the Prime Minister's comments, which provoked the members of Herut to such an unprecedented tumultuous outburst, and which were so out of keeping with the need for as united a political reaction as possible on the part of the Knesset in these dire times. Unquestionably, the entire populace of Israel expect their leaders and elected representatives to discuss all issues, even the most delicate and complex, while maintaining a maximum degree of unity as the nation faces its enemies.[78]

Never before had such an editorial so critical of the Prime Minister been published in the ruling party's newspaper. As a consequence, Shorer, the editor of *Davar*, was summoned to an inquiry by the party secretary, Reuven Barkat, and the party bureau.[79] They were all so furious at *Davar*, that Ben-Gurion's old, forgotten idea about publishing a new daily under Mapai's aegis was taken out of mothballs.[80]

The press reported that 'Ben-Gurion's outburst aroused much dissatisfaction among members of Mapai, several of whom did not conceal their disapproval of the Prime Minister's behaviour'.[81] The 'Min HaYesod' group, which disagreed with Ben-Gurion on the Lavon Affair, attacked the Mapai leadership for lacking the courage to condemn the Prime Minister's behaviour in the Knesset and for the fact that Shorer had been summoned to an inquiry in the party bureau.[82] In Mapai's Yiddish-language newspaper, *Letzte Neis*, the editor described Ben-Gurion's action in the Knesset as a 'blood libel against Jews' and 'desecration of the Knesset's podium'.[83]

The National Religious Party's refusal to co-operate with Ben-Gurion in this matter nearly led to a coalition crisis. According to a press report, threats were made against the National Religious Party that if it failed to support Mapai's condemnation motion in the House Committee, a government would be established without its participation.[84] But its leaders apparently understood that since not all members of Mapai automatically supported Ben-Gurion, the threat was not a serious one. The House Committee spent several meetings deliberating the incident. The committee's chairman, Haim Zadok of Mapai, suggested that Begin and Landau be punished by expelling them from two sessions. However, since the National Religious Party was opposed to the suggestion, the support of the Mapai representatives, the Arab factions that were attached to Mapai and Achdut Haavoda did not suffice to carry the motion.[85] The House Committee adopted a resolution expressing regret over the Herut faction's grievous violation.[86] Ben-Gurion failed in his attempt to expel members of Herut from the sessions of the Knesset. It is possible that this failure of his, in particular his inability to bring the coalition to a united stand and the absence of backing by some of the leaders of his party, hastened his decision to resign from the government. He publicly announced his decision to resign 11 days after the House Committee failed to adopt the decision he wanted.

BEN-GURION ASSOCIATES HERUT WITH THE COMMUNISTS

The attacks on Herut and the defamation of its leaders were not, as already noted, the result of an emotional outburst. In fact, they had been well planned in advance. Ben-Gurion lumped Herut and the Communists together although he was well aware of the fundamental differences between them. In public, he would never have anything good to say about Herut, but in private he made a clear distinction between these two parties. In a meeting of Mapai's political committee in November 1952, he compared Begin and Mikunis and hinted that the former was preferable because the Communists were dependent on an outside power. A tone of contempt for Begin was obvious in his comments: 'Anyway, why bring the question of Begin into this, Begins do not rule in he world, the Communists do rule a large part of the world.'[87] Nonetheless, he did not shrink from saying, referring to the *Altalena* affair, that 'I am not saying which one of them is better, I haven't yet had the privilege of shooting at Mikunis, but I did have the privilege of giving an order to shoot at Begin.'[88] In a letter he wrote in August 1955 to a citizen, Ben-Gurion stated that

> The issue of security is an exception, and to that the members of Herut are no less loyal than any others, but we need security for a particular purpose, and that purpose is lacking in Herut – it is the pioneering effort to build the country, to integrate Jews from all the diasporas, and to mould a free people with equal rights.[89]

When he was asked by Govrin in October 1957 whether he ought to agree to add Herut and the Communists to the list of factions proposing Ben-Zvi for a second term as President, Ben-Gurion replied that if Herut wished it could be added to the list, but not the Communists, because 'they are traitors and agents of a foreign power'.[90] In May 1962, again he drew a distinction between Herut and the Communists. This occurred at a convention of the secretariats of the Mapai branches:

> If I exclude one party – the Communists – then I do not cast any doubt on the fundamental loyalty of any party to the needs of the state . . . if I come to the Knesset, to the finance committee or the foreign affairs and security committee to demand an increase in the budget, and explain why, I know in advance that I will get it from all the parties except the Communist Party.[91]

Not only did Ben-Gurion draw a clear distinction between Herut and the Communists, but he was also aware of the importance of a restrained parliamentary style. In October 1960, he related to that in the plenum: 'Our Knesset discusses all issues with complete freedom, and if anyone complains of boredom due to the absence of any scandals, we have but to pray that we will have an abundance of such "boredom".'[92]

BEN-GURION'S CRITICISM OF THE STYLE OF DEBATES IN THE KNESSET

Despite Ben-Gurion's own impetuous style of speech, he did not refrain from expressing his disapproval of the general conduct of the Knesset. From time to time, he would comment about it and demand that some steps be taken to improve it. For example, in December 1949, he wrote to Harari, the chairman of the House Committee, that there was a need to do something about the parliamentary style in light of the conduct of Tufik Tubi of the Communist Party. The cause of his complaint was Tubi's speech in the plenum in November 1949, in which he made some very acrimonious comments about the government and the IDF following searches carried out by the army in Arab villages, and said: 'The government is conducting a chauvinistic and undemocratic policy against the Arab inhabitants . . . these actions are not campaigns to get rid of infiltrators, but rather pogroms. No more and no less.'[93] The Prime Minister reacted immediately to these accusations, expressing his astonishment:

> this bizarre custom, that has been taking place here, of taking the floor, under the pretext of the agenda, to defame the State

> of Israel . . . I do not know if this Knesset member is authorized to assign grades as to whether this is a democratic state or not . . . a distinction must be made between freedom and unbridled behaviour . . . I suggest . . . to instruct the House Committee to adopt measures to defend the honour of the Knesset from this unconstrained behaviour and to enact regulations to prevent the repetition of such incidents.[94]

In his letter to Harari, the Prime Minister wrote:

> I have looked into a number of questions put by this Knesset member and have found that his accusations are always unfounded . . . To our regret, until today there is no rule of procedure in the Knesset that determines the boundary between criticism and defamation and deliberate incitement.[95]

Some step in this direction should be taken urgently 'in view of the systematic defamatory statements made in the Knesset', and the House Committee has the responsibility to 'bring before the Knesset a proposal to prevent shameful conduct of this kind'.[96] The Prime Minister attached to his letter one written to him by the officer serving as commander of the military government, in which he denied all the allegations made by Tubi in the plenum.[97] Although the House Committee discussed Ben-Gurion's complaint, it was unable to agree upon a resolution regarding Tubi.[98]

Ben-Gurion did not even spare Harari the rough edge of his tongue. This is what he said about him at a meeting of Mapai's political committee in July 1951: 'Harari is an honest man, but he is an idiot. He has ruined the Knesset. He has a concept of liberalism like Krensky's.'[99] In November 1950, he went so far as to criticize the parliamentary style of Knesset members to the Chief of Staff, Yigal Yadin, to whom he wrote: 'The army's actions and the progress it has made this past year have disproved the aspersions certain persons inside and outside the Knesset have, for various reasons, cast against the IDF.'[100] Further on in the letter, the Prime Minister made it clear to the Chief of Staff that he was referring to Knesset members from Mapam, like Galili and Ben-Aharon.

The extent of Ben-Gurion's hostility to the First Knesset is obvious from his February 1951 letter to Aranne:

> This Knesset was a display of disintegration, impotence and shameful, dangerous irresponsibility. From the bottom of my

> heart I sincerely believe that it is not a true reflection of the people – this clique that is trying to run the show and is motivated only by hatred and ambition, devoid of any inner anxiety or faithful concern for the dangers threatening our existence and the awesome tasks facing our generation, is not the people. But I am certain there is a people – and we have to find paths to reach it, to educate and mobilize it.[101]

That same month he wrote to Justice Minister Rosen, that he had no 'illusions about the sense of responsibility of most of the Knesset factions'.[102] A month later, in March 1951, he made similar comments to the members of his party's political committee: 'We have an unruly Knesset, and this situation is liable to bring about the dissolution of the state.'[103]

In the summer of 1951, the Prime Minister accused the opposition of not having restrained itself even while bloody battles were being fought with the Syrians. He was referring to military clashes over the land near the Huleh which broke out in May 1951 and culminated in the Tel-el-Mutillah battle. In a meeting with members of the agricultural settlements, he spoke of the large number of casualties – 40 – in this battle, 'and instead of the nation being united at such a time, there are only minorities in the Knesset . . . it is impossible for the army to fight alone, we have to stand by it'.[104] In an election rally with professionals active in the party, Ben-Gurion referred to the Tel-el-Mutillah incident as 'the most serious after the war' and added that:

> At the same time, the Knesset was carrying on in a shameful manner, at that very moment, for the people's representatives to behave in such a way . . . when I see this Knesset I am filled with dread. If we are condemned to have a Knesset of this sort for the next four or six years, we will have to pray to God to protect this state . . . this disorderly behaviour, instead of dealing with the matter at hand in a time of danger, only creating ruses and intrigue.[105]

After lashing out at the Knesset, he began criticizing the judges: 'I wanted to say that I would have liked to take the judges and put them in prison – but that is forbidden.'[106]

At another party convention, Ben-Gurion cautioned against any co-operation between Herut, the General Zionists, Mapam and the Communists in Knesset votes, depicting it as a 'danger to the governance of the state and to the existence of the state'.[107] As a result, he said, 'We have concluded that the correct way is to turn to the people and to dissolve this Knesset.'[108] He expressed his fear that the Knesset that would be elected would also not function properly.

> If we have a Knesset that for a year or two will demonstrate its inability . . . if it turns into an arena of battles between factions and sub-factions and devious intrigues that no one could possibly approve of . . . a helpless democracy is the primary cause of the emergence of fascism, whether rightist or leftist fascism . . . An ineffective Knesset and devious machinations will undermine the faith large segments of the people have in the efficacy of democracy, and without democracy this state will not endure.[109]

In September 1951, after the elections, Ben-Gurion stated before his party's political committee that 'If it's up to us, there will not be the kind of disorderly behaviour that we saw in the previous Knesset.'[110] In November 1951, the Prime Minister delivered an aggressive speech to the political committee of Mapai during a discussion of the merchant seamen's strike:

> The sabotage begins in the Knesset . . . it is unthinkable that these hooligans will not allow us to talk. If there is already a law that prevents such acts in the Knesset – we need to use it. If there is no law, we can pass one . . . first of all, we have to stop the terror in the Knesset. I do not understand why a member of ours cannot speak in the Knesset. Quite often, I feel like leaving the Knesset and not speaking, but I don't want to cause any scandals in the Knesset . . . When Vilner imprecates and slanders, he shouldn't be allowed to speak . . . but no one interferes with him . . . we must first of all stop the terror in the Knesset. Terror is stopped by force . . . These hooligans only know how to use force and chutzpah . . . a law in itself is not enough, we need to have a special police force of the Knesset.[111]

The stormy events in the Knesset and outside it, following the decision to accept reparations from West Germany, reached their peak on 7 January 1952 when mobs of demonstrators hurled stones at the Knesset and the session was recessed after Begin's inflammatory speech and his refusal to accept the decision of the session's chairman. As mentioned in Chapter 6, it was clear that the law for the immunity of Knesset members, enacted several months earlier, protected Begin, and the Rules of Procedure did not allow any punishment to be meted out to him. Nonetheless, Ben-Gurion decided to punish him severely. He proposed that the House Committee adopt a resolution expelling Begin from the Knesset for several months – until the Passover recess – alleging that he had threatened acts of violence in his speech.[112]

A few weeks after the stormy incident, the decision of the House Committee was approved by the plenum with a majority of 56 against 47 Knesset members. The spokesmen for the factions that were Mapai's coalition partners did not take part in the debate that preceded the vote. The only one of them who spoke, Nurok of the Mizrachi Party, expressed his disagreement with the House Committee's decision.[113] Their silence attested to their dissatisfaction with the Prime Minister's eagerness to punish Begin. Even Rosen, who had served as Justice Minister in previous governments, expressed his firm opposition to the 'worthless proposal of the House Committee'.[114] The opposition spokesmen stated the most adamant objection to the House Committee's decision, and stressed the fact that there was no basis either in the law or in the Rules of Procedure for meting out punishment. Ben-Gurion, however, was adamant. In contrast to his usual anti-parliamentary strategy, this time he asserted that the Knesset had full authority to take such a decision, since 'everyone should know that one cannot threaten the Knesset or use acts of violence against it, and anyone doing so is punished first of all by the Knesset itself'.[115]

The same month, January 1952, in a letter to his daughter Renana, who was in the United States, he was critical of the manner in which Knesset debates were conducted, referring specifically to the parliamentary storm that raged around the issue of reparations:

> The arguments in the Knesset have also not changed much in their nature or their content, although after the honourable Mr Begin was expelled, things have become calmer in the Knesset. And Begin's colleagues have come back 'in keeping with the leader's request' and have been very charitable to the State of Israel.[116]

He also took the opportunity to disparage the press: 'The yellow press continues to appear incessantly, although in recent days in a somewhat abbreviated form, due to a shortage of paper, but the shortage, to my regret, is not sufficient.'[117]

In May 1952, the Prime Minister complained to the Speaker of the Knesset about Ben-Aharon who had called out, 'This is vileness' during Ben-Gurion's speech in the Knesset. In his letter to Sprinzak, Ben-Gurion stated that

> I personally don't care what MK Ben-Aharon says, but I doubt whether it is respectful to the Knesset when such words are uttered in the Knesset and recorded in the *Knesset Record* – as if this were the accepted and approved procedure in the Knesset. I consider it my duty to draw your attention to this.[118]

In July 1952, the Speaker of the Knesset ordered Tubi to leave the podium and adjourned the session in the wake of the storm aroused by Ben-Gurion in response to Tubi's speech. Tubi had suggested that a parliamentary inquiry commission be set up regarding the action by the army in the village of Arab a-Shibli near Nazareth and had continued: 'Every week Ben-Gurion's government opens a new page of racist provocation and national oppression.'[119] The Prime Minister interrupted him:

> That is not a motion to the agenda, you are defaming the government and the state . . . never before has the right of immunity, which also involves some obligations, been so shamefully exploited as is being done by MK Tubi . . . I suggest that the House Committee discuss these false charges which are totally groundless . . . and MK Tubi ought to know the boundaries of what is permissible; and if he does not, the House Committee should inform him of them. It is imperative that the House Committee examine this conduct which is not new and discuss to what extent members of Knesset can take undue advantage of their right and hurl accusations at the army which have no basis in truth.[120]

The House Committee did in fact discuss the affair and decided to expel Tubi from two sessions of the plenum.[121] The reason for the expulsion was not the content of Tubi's words, since the law for immunity of Knesset members passed in 1951 protected him, rather it was his digression from the framework of the debate. Tubi entered an appeal to the plenum:

> Since when has there been censorship on the words of Knesset members? . . . In actual fact, the Speaker did not intervene while I was speaking, but only after the intervention of the Prime Minister, Mr Ben-Gurion, who interrupted my speech with a virulent attack, and only then did the Speaker come to his aid . . . this trial conducted at the request of the Prime Minister and representatives of the government is a violation of the freedoms of Knesset members inside this house. It is an attempt to intimidate Knesset members, to prevent them from disclosing the government's disgraceful actions . . . Prime Minister Ben-Gurion was the first to stir up the atmosphere in the Knesset . . . and instead of the Speaker coming to the aid of the speaker by calling the Prime Minister to order, he took the reverse course . . . the Prime Minister has tried to blur the facts by a wave of imprecations and condemnations . . . the Prime Minister has several times used expressions such as 'hooligan', 'base'. By using such expressions, the Prime Minister has permitted himself to stoop to this level . . . the Prime Minister should be put on trial.[122]

The plenum denied Tubi's appeal by a majority of 39 against 17 Knesset members.

In December 1952, Ben-Gurion attacked the Knesset and the opposition, in particular the Communists, at a meeting of Mapai's political committee:

> What is happening around us worries me a great deal; what is going on inside is disgracing this Knesset, the unruly behaviour of the Communists after the ignominious trial in Prague, the Knesset's habit of allowing them to do what they want . . . the minority parties who have no responsibility, are not looking after the interests of the state, but their own interests, and these require that there ought not to be a strong government, that there ought not to be rule of law, that everyone can do in the Knesset what he wishes.[123]

That same month, the Prime Minister levelled some extremely serious accusations against two of the opposition parties. In a letter to Nahum Goldman, the chairman of the World Jewish Congress, he wrote, following the Prague trial: 'It turns out that we have two blocs that serve as a fifth column, one in its entirety, openly and unhesitatingly; the second, undercover and with some hesitation.'[124] He was evidently referring to the Communists who were acting openly and to Mapam that was acting undercover. Further on in his letter, he attacked the small parties and their behaviour in the Knesset:

> Small factions that have no chance of bearing responsibility for the state on their own, are not concerned about the state; rather their considerations are based solely on the faction's interests – the determining factor is not what is good for the state, but what is good for the faction. And that's the cause of the unbridled behaviour in the Knesset.[125]

In February 1953, the Prime Minister complained to the Knesset presidium and the House Committee about the behaviour of the Communist Knesset members:

> The existing arrangements in the Knesset render it nearly impossible to speak there. If the speaker is not to the liking of the Communists, then the unruly behaviour of MKs Vilner, Vilenska and Mikunis knows no bounds . . . either the Knesset Rules of Procedure are not effective or they are not being applied . . . this amounts to a continual insult to the chosen representatives of the state and to the honour of the Knesset. This situation, in particular when this is being done in a systematic manner, and by persons clearly and openly enemies of the State of Israel, is intolerable. And it is unthinkable that the presidium and the House Committee are unable to find a way to put a stop to this shameful situation.[126]

In November 1953, he spoke at a Mapai council about 'the civil war that we have in the Knesset, these disputes'.[127]

In March 1956, the Prime Minister wrote to the Speaker, complaining about Sneh (Communists) who had heckled him during his speech in the Knesset:

> Is the Knesset defenceless against such unruly behaviour, can we not enact regulations and take effective steps against such disorder? I do not ask this because I was offended, because I don't get offended by anything said by members of the Communist faction. However, I am asking whether there is no obligation seriously to see to it that the Knesset is respected.[128]

Sprinzak replied that he had summoned Sneh and informed him and his faction that their behaviour in the Knesset would no longer be tolerated, 'and we will find the legal means for that purpose'.[129] In July 1956, Ben-Gurion expressed his surprise at the words of MK Shofman (Herut) praising the police, 'because we are not accustomed to hearing in the Knesset any appreciative comments about the work of the police. Usually in the Knesset what we hear are words of scorn and abuse, which this service does not deserve.'[130] As far back as November 1951, Ben-Gurion had already made adverse comments in the Knesset about 'the unfair attitude shown by important segments of the public, journalists and some Knesset members as well, towards policemen, in the fulfillment of their difficult tasks'.[131]

In August 1956, during his speech at the eighth convention of Mapai, the Prime Minister was critical of the level of parliamentary debate. He deplored the vast gap 'between the greatness of the actions and the baseness of the speech', and carried on with a venomous attack on the press and Herut. Referring to the press he said: 'Scores of years after the pages of the worthless newspapers are covered with dust and eaten by moths, and all the derogatory, vile words of the pen-pushers who befoul everything sacred are long forgotten, the creative endeavours and the heroic deeds will endure in all their glory.'[132] And about Herut he stated:

> A fascist movement has emerged in Israel . . . We are witnessing the growing fascistization of the right wing. In the Second Knesset, the fascist wing had only about a quarter of the representatives of the Right, today it has more than half of them, and this movement draws upon the poor neighbourhoods, the immigrant transit camps and from the immigrants who have not yet been integrated, and it utilizes pseudo-patriotic demagoguery.[133]

In December 1956, the Prime Minister demanded that the Knesset presidium punish Tubi for having called out in the Knesset 'You are murderers' following the massacre in Kfar Kassem. Ben-Gurion said:

> For the sake of the honour of the Knesset and of the State of Israel, I consider it my duty to draw your attention to Tubi's interjection in the Knesset, immediately after the Speaker

> announced the adjournment of the session, when he shouted 'You are murderers!' Is it possible that this, by a Knesset member who is nothing but an enemy of Israel and a traitor to the state as a member of the Communist faction, will be permitted and go unpunished?[134]

The Speaker reported to Ben-Gurion on the discussion held by the Knesset presidium on this matter. It had not seen fit to punish Tubi, because his cry had not been recorded in the minutes, since it was not at all clear whether he had indeed uttered these words.[135] Tubi himself denied it in a letter to the Knesset secretary and added: 'It is clear that there was nothing unparliamentary in my words.'[136] Ben-Gurion's complaints about the style of speech used in the Knesset attest to the fact that he clearly understood how much damage can be caused to the status and power of the Knesset by a reprehensible style of speech.

In December 1957, Ben-Gurion replied to a no confidence motion by the Communists regarding foreign policy. The basis for the motion was explained by Mikunis, who in his speech did not deviate from the opposition's usual norms in regard to style. However, the Prime Minister refused to relate to the substance of Mikunis' complaints, and limited himself to a brief reply: 'Mr Chairman, the style employed by the last speaker may be in accordance with the Rules of Procedure and proper manners, but I think it is beneath the Knesset's honour to argue with this speaker.'[137] This reply reflected blatant contempt for the Knesset and the government's obligation to deal with the substance of the opposition's claims. Ben-Gurion did not feel he was obliged to reply to every question he was asked in the Knesset as the Prime Minister. In 1952, he had already stated that 'not everyone's comments are deserving of a reply'.[138] Which member of Knesset was in fact worthy of a reply by the Prime Minister? Anyone who merited Ben-Gurion's 'confidence in the sincerity of his words and his loyalty to democracy'.[139] At a meeting of the Mapai central committee in December 1958, Ben-Gurion severely criticized what was being done in the Knesset: 'What is being done in regard to our political affairs is a disgrace that sullies our honour. I will not speak now about the Knesset and the "honour" that it bestows upon us.'[140]

CRITICISM IN THE KNESSET OF BEN-GURION'S STYLE

Occasionally, criticism of the Prime Minister's style of speech was voiced in the House Committee and in the plenum. In a debate held in February 1950 on the amount of time to be allocated in the plenum on the subject of a constitution, Meir Yaari of Mapam turned to Sprinzak and said in an ironic tone: 'I should like to ask the Speaker of the Knesset whether when the Prime Minister assigns epithets to the factions, that [time] is also taken into account. This is an important cause of scandals in the Knesset.'[141] In June 1950, the Prime Minister's style of speech was very harshly criticized in the House Committee. Bar-Yehuda announced on behalf of Mapam that:

> If there is a recurrence of these systematic comments by the Prime Minister which contain provocations questioning the Zionism and Jewishness of an entire faction, we hereby announce that we will feel free to react to all these provocations, as we see fit without considering what form of speech would facilitate the management of affairs in the plenum.[142]

The chairman of the House Committee, Harari, concurred with this criticism: 'As soon as the Prime Minister digresses from the agenda, the Speaker ought to stop him. The chairman of the session did not stick to the agenda.'[143] At this stage, Nir, the deputy speaker, who was running that stormy plenum session, intervened:

> In my own view as well, I ought to have stopped the Prime Minister, but I did not want to stir up a quarrel between the chairman and the Prime Minister. That would bring no honour either to the Prime Minister or to the Knesset. Someone has to speak in private to the Prime Minister so that such things will not occur again.[144]

In June 1951, Sapir (General Zionists) sharply criticized Ben-Gurion's style in the plenum:

> Permit me to say in all brutality, that if the Prime Minister can say from the podium of this Knesset to the Knesset members, the elected representatives of the people: 'Goodbye, but not *au revoir*', then is it any wonder that these words reach the very ends of the state, and are interpreted as they are? This is proof that your arrogance has reached its peak.[145]

In June 1950, Ben-Gurion reacted virulently to Feige Ilanit's (Mapam) speech in the plenum on the inquiry into education in the immigrant camps. Ilanit protested the government's decision to inquire into the matter by means of an 'engagé committee', despite the fact that the education and culture committee had previously assigned the task of inquiry to a sub-committee composed of some of its members.[146] The Prime Minister objected to the use of the term 'engagé committee' and added some extremely blatant comments:

> Only someone living with the feeling of being a foreign people in a foreign state could deliberately use this term . . . only someone who has no Jewish feelings and is not a party to Jewish independence and lives in a foreign world . . . and regards Israel's independence, the State of Israel and the government of Israel as something 'engagé' – only he would use this expression, knowing its true meaning.[147]

In July 1950, the House Committee once again debated the issue of style. The Speaker of the Knesset asked that the interjections be toned down: 'The ethic of interjections in the Knesset is ruining the Knesset's image in the public . . . one speaks of the Knesset as if it were the Temple',[148] but the style employed in the Knesset was causing heavy damage: 'And these words are used by children who argue that they are entitled to use them since Knesset members do so as well.'[149] Bar-Yehuda placed the blame on the Prime Minister, since his expressions were so reprehensible that one could not avoid reacting to them. He added: 'I am prepared to provide you with a list of expressions recorded in the minutes and some not – those that were expunged – by the Prime Minister.'[150] Raziel-Naor of Herut and Mazor of the United Religious Front were also critical of the Prime Minister's style. The latter remarked: 'After all, he is the Prime Minister and it is not fitting that he use such expressions.'[151]

A few weeks later, the Speaker of the Knesset informed the House Committee that he had asked the government to discuss 'the question of the House's honour'.[152] Tsizling of Mapam, Minister of Agriculture in the Provisional Government, stated during the committee's discussion that Ben-Gurion was the one who planned and orchestrated the parliamentary scandals:

> I should like to state that it is the Prime Minister who sets the tone . . . As soon as the Prime Minister rises, tension sets in. I

> know that anything in writing is not an interjection. It is not an outburst, but rather something prepared in advance . . . In my view, the whole issue begins from the top, from the Prime Minister. We ought to know that, because that sets the tone.[153]

Ilanit was particularly enraged at Ben-Gurion in the wake of her clash with him in the plenum several weeks earlier:

> I will not call Ben-Gurion Prime Minister until he calls me by the name given me by those who voted for me, and no factional discipline will apply to me. One member may be opposed to another's opinion, and can try to persuade him, but I cannot agree to be called 'this woman' . . . I will adopt the measures of a cold war . . . he did not say that incidentally but deliberately . . . Ben-Gurion cannot determine what my attitude to Zionism is – I have no intention of learning Zionism from him.[154]

Klebanov of the General Zionists suggested that the Speaker or members of the Mapai faction ought to deal with the problem:

> Unquestionably, the Prime Minister very often speaks with such aspersion that is befitting neither to the place nor the time, and is also totally unjustified . . . If the Speaker of the Knesset or other members of his party wish to point out to him the error of his ways or his weakness in this regard, it would really be worthwhile for them to do so.[155]

Yosef Baratz of Mapai spoke about the negative effect of the parliamentary style: 'What interests me is the adverse influence of what takes place in the Knesset inside the country . . . Both children and adults speak about the way Knesset members behave . . . the situation has become intolerably worse.' He also referred to Ben-Gurion's role in this regard: 'I will speak candidly, I do not always agree with comments made by the Prime Minister and the manner of his speech, but I cannot accept the approach that his words are the source.'[156] Sprinzak said that when the Prime Minister referred to MK Ilanit as 'this woman', it 'was not in good taste'.[157] He stated that he had discussed the matter of style in the Knesset with the Minister of Justice ('one of the members of government with whom one can talk about manners') and had called upon the government to hold a discussion on the subject. The Speaker did not withhold his criticism of the Prime Minister:

> When Ben-Gurion gets into an argument with his most intimate friends – with those who were his most intimate friends – there is no hope that he'll stop. He won't listen to me, I don't exist for him at that moment . . . Ben-Gurion sometimes makes me angry, but not with words, rather vis-à-vis his temperament.[158]

At a meeting of the Mapai faction in December 1950, Sprinzak once again was pessimistic about the possibility of getting the Prime Minister to moderate his style, this time after Minister of Finance Kaplan had suggested that relations between the Knesset and the government might be improved by holding talks with the Prime Minister.[159]

Sprinzak's comments at meetings of the House Committee and the Mapai faction show that he did not hold out much hope of being able to deal with the problem created by the Prime Minister's acerbic expressions. His pessimism may have resulted from his long-time acquaintance with Ben-Gurion. He probably remembered that in February 1923, at the Histadrut's second convention, Ben-Gurion had made it difficult for him to chair the meetings. He had spoken out blatantly against Yizhak Yizhaki's faction and Sprinzak had had to call him to order for that. At the time, Ben-Gurion was the leader of Achdut Haavoda while Sprinzak was one of the leaders of HaPoel HaTzair. Already then, Sprinzak had been critical of Ben-Gurion's style of speech: 'When Ben-Gurion spoke, it was a speech inciting everyone against all those who were not members of Achdut Haavoda. Ben-Gurion should not have spoken to inflame everyone's emotions.'[160] Ben-Gurion did not sit idly by, he countered with his own words of criticism about the restrained management of the Histadrut's first convention, held in 1920 in Haifa in his absence:

> I do not agree with the way the Haifa convention was run, where we related to them with the Christian patience of our comrade Sprinzak. We have to fight against them . . . If I used the wrong expressions, I'll retract them. If my words are not the truth, I am prepared to accept any penalty levied on me.[161]

Bader reported on a meeting that Sprinzak had initiated during the Second Knesset with representatives of the factions to discuss the parliamentary style: 'the stormy sessions in the Knesset grew more frequent. Sprinzak invited the representatives of the factions and demanded of all of us: "The scandals must be stopped", and Ben-

Aharon said: "Tell Ben-Gurion not to cause any scandals, then there won't be any."'[162] The meeting Bader was referring to may have been held in June 1953. At a meeting of the Mapai faction on 29 June 1953, Assaf reported on a meeting of the Knesset Speaker with heads of the factions to discuss the parliamentary style. According to Assaf, the Communists 'found one cause for all the feelings of discrimination and insult that led to an outburst, and that was the Prime Minister'.[163]

CRITICISM IN MAPAI OF BEN-GURION'S STYLE OF SPEECH

Ben-Gurion's unparliamentary style and the severe clashes between him and the opposition aroused the disapproval of Mapai Knesset members. This discontent had emerged several years before the rift created in the party by the Lavon Affair. The subject had been raised a number of times on the agenda of faction meetings and meetings of the faction's management. In July 1950, for example, the Speaker referred to the subject indirectly at a meeting of the faction management: 'At the House Committee I submitted a formulation for manners in the Knesset. There is a demand that this should also include the government itself, and it should be presented to the government.'[164] In October 1950, the subject came up again at a meeting of the management. Several Knesset members complained about Sprinzak's soft approach to Herut members. Argov told the Speaker: 'You have to bang the gavel sooner', but Sprinzak placed the blame on the Prime Minister: 'When Ben-Gurion is yelling from the podium, my gavel will not silence him.'[165]

In February 1952, the Mapai faction discussed Ben-Gurion's parliamentary style. Harzfeld asserted that the Prime Minister's speech in the plenum several days earlier had done nothing to calm spirits in the house: 'There are already results from this speech, it does not enhance the prestige of the Knesset.'[166] Aranne fired barbs at Ben-Gurion, who was not present at the meeting: 'His conduct towards the opposition is, in my view, a catastrophe. My opinion of Ben-Gurion and my attitude to him are favourable, but we must talk to him; if we speak to him as friends, that may do some good.'[167] When Harzfeld and Aranne voiced some criticism of Ben-Gurion's style, Deborah Netzer and David Hacohen came to his defence. The latter was of the view that 'we have to forgive Ben-Gurion, out of our admiration for him. But we have to bear in mind that other circles do not feel this admiration, to the same extent as we do.'[168] In May 1952,

Ben-Gurion's style came up for discussion, in his absence, at a meeting of the Mapai faction. Aranne made some implicit remarks, stating that 'Important members of the government forget that what is permissible for a Knesset member is not permissible for a minister.'[169] Livne criticized the Prime Minister's style of speech and conduct towards the Knesset factions. Beba Idelson expressed her regret that Ben-Gurion 'voices trenchant remarks in the Knesset against factions like the General Zionists, and immediately afterwards makes peace with them in the Knesset corridors'.[170] Lavie tried to defend the Prime Minister: 'We all respect him, his impulsiveness and his life – we cannot judge him according to our concepts.'[171] Govrin said that the rules of collegiality required remarks about Ben-Gurion's style to be made in his presence.[172] At a meeting of the Mapai central committee in September 1957 Guri asserted that since the establishment of the state there had been a decline in the Knesset's prestige, and ascribed it to the sharp attacks on the electoral system to the Knesset: 'I do not know if we are doing a good service to the state and to the Knesset by day in, day out, speaking out against the existing election system without doing something to fundamentally correct it.'[173] However, the most persistent and venomous attacks on the election system came from Ben-Gurion, in the Knesset and outside it.

NOTES

1. Gad Barzilai, Ephraim Yaar-Yuchtman and Zeev Segal, *The Supreme Court in the Eyes of Israeli Society* (Hebrew), Tel Aviv: Papyrus, 1994, p. 217.
2. Israel Labour Party Archives, meeting of faction in the Knesset with the political committee, 11 April 1951.
3. Ibid., meeting of Mapai secretariat, 28 May 1952.
4. Giora Goldberg, 'The Struggle for Legitimacy: Herut's Road from Opposition to Power', in Stuart Cohen and Eliezer Don-Yehiya (eds) *Comparative Jewish Politics – Conflict and Consensus in Jewish Political Life*, Ramat Gan: Bar-Ilan University, 1986, pp. 146–69.
5. *Knesset Record*, 8 March 1949, pp. 67–8.
6. Ibid., p. 65.
7. Ibid., 10 March 1949, p. 135.
8. Ibid., pp. 138–9.
9. Ibid., 29 March 1949, p. 253.
10. Ibid., p. 254.
11. Ibid., p. 256.
12. Ibid., 9 November 1949, p. 20.
13. Ibid., 21 November 1949, pp. 125–6.
14. Ibid., 4 April 1949, p. 305.
15. Ibid., p. 306.
16. Ibid., p. 307.

17. Ibid., 4 January 1950, pp. 435–6.
18. Ibid., 3 November 1952, p. 15.
19. Ibid., 29 February 1956, p. 1,239.
20. Ibid.
21. Ibid., 6 March 1956, p. 1,308.
22. Ibid.
23. Ibid., p. 1,309.
24. Ben-Gurion Research Center Archives, correspondence, Ami Assaf to Ben-Gurion, 7 March 1956.
25. Ibid.
26. Ibid., Ben-Gurion to Ami Assaf, 11 March 1956.
27. Ibid.
28. Israel Labour Party Archives, meeting of Mapai faction in the Knesset, 6 August 1962.
29. *Knesset Record*, 19 June 1956, p. 2,066.
30. Ibid., pp. 2,067–8.
31. Ibid., 15 October 1956, p. 70.
32. Ibid., 17 October 1956, p. 111.
33. Ibid., p. 112.
34. Ibid., p. 113.
35. Ibid.
36. Ibid.
37. Ibid.
38. Ibid.
39. Ibid., 22 October 1956, p. 117.
40. Ibid.
41. Ben-Gurion Research Center Archives, correspondence, Ben-Gurion to Eshkol, 25 October 1956. A copy of the letter was sent to the Speaker of the Knesset, Yosef Sprinzak. Ben-Gurion's first letter to Eshkol was sent on 19 October 1956.
42. *Knesset Record*, 18 November 1957, p. 178.
43. Ibid., 18 June 1958, p. 2,114.
44. Ibid.
45. Ibid., 24 June 1958, p. 2,135.
46. Ibid.
47. Ibid.
48. Ibid., 9 December 1958, p. 491.
49. Ibid., 7 January 1959, p. 799.
50. Ibid., p. 800.
51. Ibid., p. 801.
52. Ibid., p. 802.
53. Ibid., p. 804.
54. Ibid., 12 January 1959, p. 831.
55. Ibid., p. 832.
56. Ibid., 30 December 1959, p. 224.
57. Ibid., 24 February 1960, p. 720.
58. Ibid., p. 722.
59. Ibid., 3 July 1961, p. 2,132.
60. Ibid., 15 May 1962, p. 1,939.
61. Ibid., p. 1,938.
62. Ibid., 29 May 1962, p. 2,082.
63. *Ma'ariv*, 14 May 1963, p. 2.
64. Ibid.
65. Ibid.
66. Ibid.
67. Ibid.
68. Ibid.
69. Ibid., p. 15.

70. *Knesset Record*, 13 May 1963, p. 1,822.
71. *Ma'ariv*, 14 May 1963, p. 2.
72. Ibid., p. 16.
73. Ibid., 15 May 1963, p. 12.
74. Ibid., p. 2.
75. *LaMerchav*, 15 May 1963, p. 2.
76. *Ma'ariv*, 27 May 1963, p. 4.
77. Ibid.
78. *Davar*, 15 May 1963, p. 1.
79. *Ma'ariv*, 17 May 1963, p. 1, and *Ma'ariv*, 18 May 1963, p. 1.
80. Ibid., 26 May 1963, p. 1.
81. Ibid., 15 May 1963, p. 1, based on *HaBoker*.
82. Ibid., 23 May 1963, p. 15.
83. Ibid., 19 May 1963, p. 4, based on *Letzta Nayes*, dated 17 May 1963.
84. Ibid., 16 May 1963, p. 1.
85. Tzidon, *The House of Representatives*, p. 113; *Davar*, 6 June 1963, p. 2; *LaMerchav*, 6 June 1963, pp. 1–2.
86. Tzidon, *The House of Representatives*, p. 113; *Davar*, 6 June 1963, p. 2; *LaMerchav*, 6 June 1963, pp. 1–2.
87. Israel Labour Party Archives, meeting of Mapai's central committee, 23 November 1952.
88. Ibid.
89. Ben-Gurion Research Center Archives, correspondence, Ben-Gurion to Israel Galiner, 14 August 1955.
90. Ben-Gurion Research Center Archives, correspondence, Govrin to Ben-Gurion, 7 October 1957; Ben-Gurion to Govrin, 8 October 1957.
91. Israel Labour Party Archives, conferences, conference of secretariats of Mapai branches, 17 May 1962.
92. *Knesset Record*, 31 October 1960, p. 78.
93. Ibid., 16 November 1949, pp. 71–2.
94. Ibid., p. 72.
95. State Archives, 20/25, Ben-Gurion to Harari, 4 December 1949. A similar letter with a later date, 26 December 1949, was found in the Ben-Gurion Research Center Archives, correspondence, Ben-Gurion to Harari, 26 December 1949. Since the House Committee discussed the letter on 6 December, it is likely that the actual date is 4 December.
96. State Archives, ibid.
97. Ibid., Colonel A. Mor to Ben-Gurion.
98. Ibid., minutes of meeting of House Committee, 6 December 1949.
99. Israel Labour Party Archives, meeting of political committee, 22 July 1951.
100. Ben-Gurion Research Center Archives, Ben-Gurion to Yadin, 27 November 1950.
101. Israel Labour Party Archives, file 6/3, Ben-Gurion to Aranne, 22 February 1951.
102. Ben-Gurion Research Center Archives, correspondence, Ben-Gurion to Rosen, 19 February 1951.
103. Israel Labour Party Archives, meeting of Mapai political committee, 29 March 1951.
104. Ibid., conferences, conference of members of agricultural settlements, 21 June 1951.
105. Ibid., election convention with activists from the academic professions, 1 July 1951.
106. Ibid.
107. Ibid., elections conference of Mapai members on committees of workers and clerks in cities and towns, 6 July 1951.
108. Ibid.
109. Ibid.
110. Ibid., meeting of Mapai political committee, 10 September 1951.
111. Ibid., 28 November 1951.
112. *Knesset Record*, 21 January 1952, p. 1,030; Bader, *The Knesset and I*, pp. 62–4.
113. *Knesset Record*, 21 January 1952, p. 1,039.

114. Ibid., p. 1,037.
115. Ibid., p. 1,054.
116. Ben-Gurion Research Center Archives, correspondence, David Ben-Gurion to Renana Ben-Gurion, 31 January 1952.
117. Ibid.
118. Ibid., Ben-Gurion to Sprinzak, 7 May 1952.
119. *Knesset Record*, 2 July 1952, p. 2,522.
120. Ibid., pp. 2,522–3.
121. Ibid., 27 August 1952, p. 3,184.
122. Ibid., pp. 3,185–6.
123. Israel Labour Party Archives, meeting of Mapai political committee, 10 December 1952.
124. Ben-Gurion Research Center Archives, correspondence, Ben-Gurion to Goldman, 16 December 1952.
125. Ibid.
126. Ben-Gurion Research Center Archives, correspondence, Ben-Gurion to the presidium and to the House Committee, 17 February 1953.
127. Israel Labour Party Archives, meeting of Mapai Council, 27 November 1953.
128. Ben-Gurion Research Center Archives, Ben-Gurion to Sprinzak, 1 March 1956.
129. Ibid., Sprinzak to Ben-Gurion, 5 March 1956.
130. *Knesset Record*, 11 July 1956, p. 2,265.
131. Ibid., 20 November 1951, p. 410.
132. Israel Labour Party Archives, Mapai's eighth convention, 26 August 1956.
133. Ibid.
134. Ben-Gurion Research Center Archives, Ben-Gurion to Knesset presidium, 12 December 1956.
135. Ibid., Sprinzak to Ben-Gurion, 24 December 1956.
136. Ibid., Tubi to Moshe Rozetti, 24 December 1956.
137. *Knesset Record*, 23 December 1957, p. 469.
138. Ibid., 6 February 1952, p. 1,231.
139. Ibid.
140. Israel Labour Party Archives, meeting of Mapai central committee, 25 December 1958.
141. State Archives, minutes of meeting of House Committee, 14 December 1950.
142. Ibid., 20 June 1950.
143. Ibid.
144. Ibid.
145. *Knesset Record*, 26 June 1951, p. 2,081.
146. Ibid., 19 June 1950, p. 1,758.
147. Ibid., p. 1,761.
148. State Archives, minutes of meeting of House Committee, 18 July 1950.
149. Ibid.
150. Ibid.
151. Ibid.
152. Ibid., 6 August 1950.
153. Ibid.
154. Ibid.
155. Ibid.
156. Ibid.
157. Ibid.
158. Ibid.
159. Israel Labour Party Archives, meeting of Mapai faction in the Knesset, 4 December 1950.
160. Mordechai Sever (ed.), *The Second Convention of the General Federation of Hebrew Workers in Eretz-Israel, 1923* (Hebrew), Tel Aviv: The General Federation of Labour, 1968, p. 59.

161. Ibid., p. 60.
162. Bader, *The Knesset and I*, p. 61.
163. Israel Labour Party Archives, meeting of Mapai faction in the Knesset, 29 June 1953.
164. Ibid., meeting of management of Mapai faction in the Knesset, 23 July 1950.
165. Ibid., 22 October 1950.
166. Ibid., meeting of Mapai faction in the Knesset, 13 February 1952.
167. Ibid.
168. Ibid.
169. Ibid., meeting of Mapai faction in the Knesset, 6 May 1952.
170. Ibid.
171. Ibid.
172. Ibid.
173. Ibid., meeting of Mapai central committee, 19 September 1957.

10 Attacks on the Political Opposition and the Parties

In addition to the verbal skirmishes that Ben-Gurion instigated in the Knesset, he also regularly vilified all political parties, those in the opposition, some of those in the coalition, as well as parliamentary opposition in general. This had the indirect effect of lowering the Knesset's prestige, since an opposition and parties are essential elements of parliamentary life, in particular in a parliamentary form of government. Contrary to what is generally thought, Ben-Gurion did not limit himself to attacks against Herut and the Communists; he also directed his barbs at other parties, including some that belonged to the labour movement, which he headed.

ATTACKS ON PARTIES AND ON THE OPPOSITION UNTIL HIS RETIREMENT TO SEDE BOKER IN 1953

In a meeting with Mapam leaders in February 1949, Ben-Gurion called Herut 'a gang without a conscience', and stated that when he served as chairman of the Provisional Council of State, he had treated the Communists with respect even though he loathed them: 'I have to treat them with respect, even though they are not deserving of this respect, these Commies don't deserve any respect!'[1] While speaking to Mapam leaders, he would accuse Herut and the Communists of various wrongdoings, but this did not stop him from criticizing Mapam itself. In July 1949, speaking to the Mapai leadership, he asserted that the parties of the extreme right and the extreme left (including Mapam) advocated seizing power by force, but were not doing that 'since they do not have enough power'.[2] A month later, he repeated this allegation to members of the Mapai central committee:

> We have in the Knesset and outside the Knesset, Communists, Herut and Mapam, namely three parties, whose programme, ideals and practical theory calls for the seizure of power by force. They say this is now only a formal democracy. Do you think this is just idle talk? As far as Herut is concerned, we have already seen them try to do this and fail. However, in Mapam too this is more than just theory. If we don't take some measures, we will not have an army to ensure the state's security.[3]

Mapam was convinced that Ben-Gurion was trying to liquidate it. Aranne, who, after the elections, held talks with Mapam, reported to the Mapai secretariat in October 1949, that 'They see us in the image of Ben-Gurion, who is determined to destroy them (of course, not in the physical sense).'[4]

Ben-Gurion was well aware that one favourable way to change the parliamentary style was by enlarging the coalition. At a meeting of the Mapai secretariat in August 1949, he said that if Mapai were to add Mapam and the General Zionists to the coalition, that would raise 'the prestige of the Knesset, because many of the offensive things being done there would not be done'.[5] However, he did not make a serious effort, either in the First or at the beginning of the Second Knesset, to add them to the coalition. The General Zionists joined the coalition only in 1952 and Mapam after the 1955 elections.

The fact that he did not want to add these parties to the coalition did not keep Ben-Gurion from treating their non-participation as a real crime. This is what he said at a meeting of the Mapai council in March 1951:

> We ought to seat many of them in the dock of the accused of Jewish history; there can be no forgiveness or atonement for the acts of sabotage some of them have caused to the State of Israel . . . serious, constant injury . . . criminal sabotage to the endeavours of this generation . . . and the two parties guilty of criminal activity will be seated in the dock to face trial by the people in Zion . . . they will not be judged by their words, not for the things they say, but for what they failed to do, for not extending a loyal hand, wholeheartedly, without any conditions, without asking for any privileges.[6]

In January 1954, he wrote to the journalist, Levi Yizthak HaYerushalmy, that Mapam's refusal to join the government after the 1949 elections was 'the most serious undermining of the state's stability, much greater than all the injuries that our enemies from without have attempted to cause us'.[7] The leader of the General Zionists, Bernstein, wrote to Ben-Gurion in September 1955, stating his objection to the idea that every 'opposition in the State of Israel is damaging, and that the only criterion for responsibility is participation in the government... a responsible opposition has a positive role to play in the development of the state, and our party proved that when it was in the opposition'.[8]

In April 1951, Ben-Gurion attacked the General Zionists at a meeting of the Mapai council, for having 'sabotaged the work of the state and making the government's work more difficult . . . these attempts at sabotage have not ceased throughout these two years... two years ago, they threw off the yoke of the state and took up a position as the enemy of the elected government'.[9] In September 1951, at a meeting of Mapai's political committee, Ben-Gurion actually spoke out against the addition of the General Zionists to the coalition owing to the danger that they might grow stronger and take over the government, since in the elections held a few weeks earlier, they had moved up from seven to 20 mandates. 'They will be strengthened if they participate in the government', [10] he cautioned. In the same speech, he harshly disparaged them: 'I do not regard the General Zionists as a party. It has no ideology. It is just a group with vested interests at the expense of the population at large and the state . . . They are not Zionists.'[11] He took the same opportunity to lash out at Hapoel HaMizrachi: 'Hapoel HaMizrachi is in my view, a bunch of clerics. They are not religious people, but simply clerics, who cannot stomach the notion of freedom of religion and conscience, who do not understand what this freedom is or what it means.'[12]

At a meeting of the Mapai faction in the Knesset, in January 1951, the Prime Minister vilified the religious parties, the General Zionists, Herut and the Communists: 'I know the religious bloc, with a few exceptions, they are all rapists... There are several parties that advocate rape. One we call the fascists, and there is a second one we call Communists.'[13] In February 1951, the Prime Minister complained to President Weizmann about the opposition parties: '[They consider] every injury caused to the government as legitimate, even if it was damaging to the interests of the state.'[14] A few days earlier, after the government resigned following its defeat in the Knesset on the issue of education in the new immigrant camps, Ben-Gurion wrote to Minister of Justice Rosen in a critical vein about the Knesset factions, and to a lesser degree about the President:

> The matter is now in the hands of the President and the Knesset. I have no illusions about the sense of responsibility of most of the Knesset factions, and I know that the President's good will and integrity far exceeds his ability, and he cannot compel the various factions to show responsibility.[15]

At a meeting of the foreign affairs and security committee in March 1951, Ben-Gurion remonstrated about the leaks from the committee's discussions about drafting women into the army, and censured the religious newspaper *HaTzofeh,* which he claimed had published this information:

> I don't know what religion is. According to the religion that I know, the newspaper *HaTzofeh* is not a religious newspaper, because in the Jewish religion there is a commitment to truth, and a newspaper that does not adhere to the truth, is not religious.[16]

At an election rally with teachers held early in July 1951, Ben-Gurion accused the small parties of pettiness and indifference to the needs of the state. A small party's acts are solely based on electoral considerations,

> and its members will do anything for this purpose. This end justifies any means. It [the party] will slander, will fabricate libel, will unite with the Communists, will unite with Herut, will do anything that is forbidden, just as long as it can obtain two or three more mandates.[17]

This time he called the General Zionists 'bloodsuckers' and characterized the system of elections as 'corrupting the best of men'.[18] A few days later, at a convention of Israelis of Bulgarian origin, he attacked the parties:

> A conspiracy is a collusion between factions that have nothing in common except hatred and opposition . . . The General

> Zionists and the Communists have nothing in common except hatred, and on the basis of this hatred, it is impossible to run a state.[19]

The following day, addressing a women's conference, Ben-Gurion continued in the same vein, impugning the opposition parties. First, he attacked the General Zionists for not having participated enough in the war effort and later accused the 'factions in the Knesset' as well as the press, of defending the 'black market'. The quarrels between the parties and their unrestrained polemics are unnecessary, he stated.[20]

In a memorandum that he wrote for the Mapai central committee prior to the elections, he demonstrated an extremely hostile attitude towards the General Zionists:

> We must incessantly denounce the rightist and reactionary nature, so replete with animosity towards the workers, of those who call themselves 'General Zionists', and their inability to gain power without entering into an alliance with Begin and the blacks . . . let the right-wing (the General Zionists) prove that they are not part of the semi-fascist black bloc (alliance with Begin) . . . The enemy is the right – not the religion.[21]

This memorandum shows just how far Ben-Gurion was willing to go in order to win at the ballot box. He suggested that the party be active even among army reservists:

> A large part of the population is now organized in the reserve army. Although it does include mostly men . . . this public is not an army, it is made up of civilians, but organized in the framework of reserves in units – companies, battalions, brigades, and all that on a territorial basis. The organization of loyal members in every unit, and in particular the enlistment of those of our members who served in the Haganah and the army to maintain personal contact and to provide information to this civilian public that is attached to the reserve army, would be of decisive importance in the comprehensive educational programme that I propose as a basis for the election war . . . We have to get to every citizen from all sides – at his workplace, in his professional organization, his ethnic group, his community – and the place where he lives.[22]

In July 1951, about two weeks before the elections, the Prime Minister expressed doubts about whether they would take place:

> There are some who say they are going to blow up the elections by force. I am not responsible for that. Some members who deal with the matter came and told me that. As far as I know those involved, I know that according to their views it would be permissible . . . I am not sure they will let us set up a new Knesset . . . I don't believe in the elections and I don't believe in the Second Knesset.[23]

These doubts turned out to be totally unfounded.

In August 1951, after the elections, speaking to Mapai's political committee, Ben-Gurion revealed his attitude to Herut and the Communists:

> I am not taking the Communists into account, as if they simply didn't exist, because I do not consider them to be an Israeli party, but rather an agent of a foreign party . . . In my view, there are two disqualified parties: the Communists and Herut.[24]

That same month, at a meeting of Mapai's central committee, he attacked the parties and the press: 'The bad thing in this country is the parties and the press, which is lacking all sense of responsibility . . . we won't get rid of this press and these parties in the near future . . . but we ought not to be frightened by the press or by the parties.'[25] In December 1951, he wrote to Chief of Staff Yadin about his visit to Haifa following the seamen's strike: 'The civil war manoeuvres of Mapam and the Communists are a more serious matter.'[26]

Three days after stones were thrown at the Knesset by Herut supporters, the Prime Minister suggested, as mentioned above, that the Mapai secretariat establish a party militia to act in co-ordination with Iser Harel, the head of one of the state security arms:

> The establishment of a force to protect the state and democracy is a political matter. We cannot do this in the framework of the Histadrut because that would destroy and split the Histadrut . . . We must do it within the framework of the party . . . by organizing armed groups of workers . . . the core of the force to be set up must be partisan . . . when there is a need to act, this force will not be subordinate to the police, but if necessary it can be

> attached to the police. I suggest we select one man, Iser Harel, to check out the people, to give us one of his men, and together with another man, they will command this force.[27]

The secretariat approved his proposal and decided that 'the party will establish a guard to defend the state and the democracy in Israel. A national headquarters for this guard will be established.'[28] Ben-Gurion avoided involving the Histadrut in this proposal because of the rift with Mapam, which at the time opposed the government.

In September 1952, Ben-Gurion, speaking to leaders of the General Zionists, asserted that the opposition has only 'hatred and opposition to the state', and continued his reproof,

> The Knesset ought to be an example . . . we ought to know that we are all sitting in a school. We are all children, and a few are teachers, and what the teacher does is very important. The whole nation learns from teachers, and the members of Knesset ought to be the teachers of the people, but these teachers are not educating for democracy, but the very opposite.[29]

He also had some serious complaints about the General Zionists:

> I have a lot of faults to find with you. Knowingly or unknowingly, you are giving a hand to those who are trying to subvert democracy . . . you and everyone else are prepared to do anything, just to undermine the government.[30]

At a meeting that same month with Bernstein, a leader of the General Zionists, he again complained about the parliamentary opposition: 'There are oppositions in all countries throughout the world, but this hatred, God in heaven, what will become of us?' and stated, 'Begin is not a normal man.'[31] Against the background of his criticism of the opposition, he erupted into a diatribe about the Jewish people:

> This is a nation of swindlers . . . the Jews have always been swindlers . . . Zionism changed my opinion about anti-Semitism, where I was, there was no small measure of anti-Semitism. As a Zionist, I saw that the anti-Semites were right, this is a contemptible people that does not become a part of the

> people in whose midst it lives, it is not loyal to the authorities, even if it takes an oath to be loyal.[32]

In October 1952, Ben-Gurion got hold of a handbill of the Shomer Hatzair, the youth movement that gave birth to Mapam. Infuriated by it, he demanded that the Minister of Justice, Haim Cohen, investigate to see what could be done against those who had composed it and against the organization itself, even going so far as to raise the possibility of dismantling the Shomer Hatzair, asking: 'Is it possible to dismantle this organization?'[33]

In December 1952, Ben-Gurion attacked Mapam and the Communists at a meeting of the Mapai central committee and its faction in the Knesset:

> In Israel there are two parties that are prepared to stick a knife into the heart of the state for the sake of a foreign country . . . I cannot imagine that in any other state there could be anyone like Mikunis – such complete identification with enmity against the people of Israel, against the State of Israel, openly, with pride and arrogance.[34]

Early in 1953, after having announced his resignation from the government, Ben-Gurion was particularly enraged. In January Mapai's political committee had rejected his demand to propose legislation to outlaw the Communist party, and thereby liquidate it. His pretext for this demand was the Communists' support of the Soviet line concerning the 'doctors' trial'.[35] The things he said about the Communists before the political committee were particularly acrimonious:

> It is unthinkable that we should have in our midst a Nazi party . . . Can the laws of Israel permit the appearance of their newspapers, their attendance at the Knesset? I am told that this would mean setting up concentration camps. If it is necessary to make concentration camps, we'll do that; if it is necessary to shoot, we'll shoot. On more than one occasion it was necessary to shoot people even closer to us . . . Will I come into such a Knesset? Is this how we are going to educate our youth?[36]

The failure of his proposal to outlaw the Communist party reflected his isolation in the Mapai leadership on the issue of the party's attitude towards the Communists. In February 1950, Sprinzak, during a meeting of the Mapai faction of the Knesset, had already expressed his aversion to Ben-Gurion's attitude towards the Communists. He demanded that any action against the Communists be taken within the existing law, and added: 'Ben-Gurion said "let's throw out this dog". It's not good to say that in a meeting. But when there is a law – we should act according to the law.'[37]

At the end of January 1953, Ben-Gurion wrote a letter of protest to the ministers regarding the Minister of the Interior's decision to close down the newspaper of the Communist party, *Kol Ha'am,* for only ten days.

> I do not believe this step is either sufficient or purposeful enough . . . either you really do something . . . or you do nothing, and at least you won't be turning the government into a ridiculous, helpless organ. Closing down a newspaper – if it is justified and mandatory – it should be closed down for good and not allow the Communists to publish newspapers.[38]

In February, Ben-Gurion delivered an impassioned speech to the political committee about the refusal of members of the Kibbutz HaMeuchad movement (the movement affiliated with the Achdut Haavoda faction of Mapam) to accept the decision taken by the Histadrut following the split in Ein Harod:

> There is a greater force than that of the Kibbutz HaMeuchad, just as there was a greater force than that of the Etzel . . . they will have to accept the ruling of the Histadrut or will have to leave; if not, we will use force against them, we will use firearms against them. That is the only reasoning that will persuade people like them.[39]

In June, he wrote to the Minister of Trade and Industry, Bernstein, denouncing the parliamentary form of government: 'The present parliamentary system, to my understanding, is nothing but a distortion of the image of the people and its will. The people is not as divided and shattered as is reflected in its official form.'[40]

THE STRUGGLE FROM SEDE BOKER AGAINST THE OPPOSITION AND THE PARTIES

Even after he resigned from the government in December 1953 and retired into political exile in Sede Boker, Ben-Gurion did not stop pressuring the parliamentary opposition. In July 1954, he wrote to Moshe Goldstein, secretary of the Progressive Party that

> We have several parties, on the right and on the left, who, either covertly or overtly, favour a totalitarian regime . . . in our Balkanized method of elections . . . the electees are not in fact elected by the voters, but rather by those who make up the lists . . . this electoral system is nothing other than a caricature and falsification of democracy.[41]

In December 1954, at a party convention, he referred to the electoral system as a 'disaster for the state and for the people . . . a disaster that is apt to lead to total destruction'.[42] The method made it impossible to close the wide gaps between the various ethnic groups. These gaps worried him a great deal because of his attitude towards the Oriental Jews. If war should break out before the gaps were closed, he said,

> We are lost. These people will not fight, they will run away . . . because they have no awareness, they did not come here out of Zionism. They do have anti-Arab sentiments, but that is not enough. They have no awareness of a homeland, they have no bonds to this country.[43]

About the Jews of Iraq he said:

> For them, work is shameful, they are a bunch of petty merchants, and the distance between us and them is vast, the moral, spiritual distance. Over time, we can overcome that, but we have devised an electoral system that makes that impossible.[44]

In February 1955, at a meeting of friends, he spoke out against the opposition and the electoral system. 'The unity of the nation is irreconcilable with this idiotic system that artificially divides the people.'[45] He complained about the fact that the opposition did not give the Prime Minister backing during his visits abroad, and demanded that it show responsibility 'instead of defaming and vilifying him and sending Begins to incite against him'.[46]

In May 1955, at a meeting of his party's central committee, Ben-Gurion attacked 'the subversive opposition of the two parts of Mapam, Herut and the Communists throughout these seven years', and linked this to the nature of the new immigrants:

> The catastrophe of this state, the catastrophe of this people, is that we do not have a responsible opposition . . . we have an opposition devoid of any responsibility, such an opposition would be dangerous even in the most well advanced of states, but it is several fold more dangerous in a country of immigration, in which the immigrants come from backward communities and are incapable of making proper judgments.[47]

Later in his speech, he maligned the form of government in Israel, going so far as to cast doubt on the state's ability to exist under the conditions created by this system:

> This form of government is likely to bring a disaster upon the state . . . We will not meld the Jews into one people under such a system. And in a state of emergency, I am not certain that we can face up to the enemy if the government is not based on the will of one people, and not as it is today, based on intrigues.[48]

In June 1955, he wrote to Ophira Erez that Achdut Haavoda is 'a sterile and harmful opposition' and that its members are 'dissenters from the labour movement'.[49] On the eve of the 1955 elections, he virulently criticized the electoral system: 'How worthless, pointless and devoid of all democracy the existing system is.'[50]

A RETURN TO ATTACKS ON THE PARTIES AND THE OPPOSITION FROM THE POSITION OF PRIME MINISTER

After the elections, in which Mapai lost five mandates, Ben-Gurion lashed out furiously at the parties and the opposition in a meeting with two Mapam leaders, Meir Yaari and Yaacov Hazan, held in August 1955. He asserted that 'the parties in Israel are doing their utmost to hasten the destruction of the state'.[51] At a meeting of Mapai's central committee held a day later, he began to criticize the parties for their lack of concern for the interests of the state:

> There has never been anything so shameful here as the way the parties conducted the elections . . . these elections have dealt a fatal blow to any chances of merging the Jews into one people; they have widened the gaps even more. These elections have not completely destroyed every chance, but they have dangerously harmed the state's ability to act, have undermined the security of the state and have increased the possibilities of corruption. More and more, they are forcing the state to become a federation of political parties.[52]

His impression of the parties with which he had opened coalition negotiations was a very poor one:

> It has become clear to me for the hundredth time that these are not parties but rather pressure groups. And the difference, in my view, between a party and a pressure group is that a party regards itself as responsible for the affairs of the state . . . a pressure group has its own special, private interest – irrespective of what happens to the affairs of the country at large.[53]

At the next meeting of the Mapai central committee, he spoke out harshly against the opposition:

> There is no opposition in this country, there are only saboteurs. Whoever does not bear the burden of government is a saboteur, because those parties that call themselves parties, but are not parties, have no notion of what an opposition is . . . and even if they should want to engage in constructive opposition, they would still engage in sabotage, because in this country the major goal of the opposition is to see the government fail . . . in England they want to take the government's place, but they do not want to see the government fail . . . We have to deal with Jews who call themselves parties, but they're really something different.[54]

In September 1955, during the negotiations for setting up a coalition, he wrote to the leader of the Progressive Party, Rosen, that his party has no right not to participate in the government, because 'bearing the burden of government is a duty, not a kind deed . . . if you do not give us a hand in establishing a government, I will regard that as a serious injury to the state'.[55] In other words, in his view, the right to serve in the opposition was not reserved for any party, and if it insisted on doing so, that was a deliberate injury to the state.

At a convention of Mapai's younger generation in March 1956, Ben-Gurion expressed his very low opinion of Israeli parties: 'I doubt if we have one party worthy of the name. Most of the existing parties are only sects . . . Mapai too is not yet a party in the true sense of the word, although it is the only one that comes anywhere near this concept.'[56] Later, he referred to the other parties with derision: 'If it is a party that has no chance of being in the government, then it is not a party; and for this reason all the others are not parties either, because they certainly know what their prospects are.'[57] At a party convention in December 1954, he gave an example of the sectarian nature of Mapam and Achdut Haavoda: 'They are very interested in being in the Knesset, not for the good of the state . . . they have two interests that concern them greatly: they want to expand their agricultural settlements, they want to gain a foothold in the army.'[58]

In a plenary debate in June 1957 about the functions of the security services, the Prime Minister justified granting these services broad powers because there were serious internal dangers:

> To our regret, we have in this country circles that are an actual fifth column or are capable of becoming one in certain circumstances . . . therefore, we need to keep our eyes open to watch these people or circles that are a fifth column or may become one.[59]

At a meeting of Mapai's central committee in July 1957, he cautioned against Begin's 'demonic nature and lack of judgment': 'I haven't the slightest doubt that if he came into power and carried out his programme, he would destroy the state within ten days.'[60] In October 1957, speaking to leaders of Achdut Haavoda, he expressed his fears of Herut, which was benefitting from the lack of co-operation between the labour parties: 'Herut represents a threat, a serious threat, particularly since there is "a primitive population" in the country . . . there are a great many primitive people here.'[61] He had already revealed a similar attitude towards Jews of Oriental origin in January 1950 at a meeting of leaders of his party when he stated:

> The question is whether we want to push these immigrants – which will be the major immigration in the coming years – into the arms of Herut and the Mizrachi, on the one hand, or on the

> other, into the arms of the Communists. Because those elements, in particular the Moroccans, will join Herut as easily as they joined the Communists. They have no roots in political understanding. We cannot demand of them that they make the same sort of judgements as we do. We are not just one of the parties, we are the state.[62]

Although the leaders of Achdut Haavoda were often at the receiving end of Ben-Gurion's invective, once that party had joined the coalition, he had no compunctions about making derogatory remarks about the other parties to them. At a meeting with Bar-Yehuda and Ben-Aharon in December 1957 he had some very acrimonious things to say about the leaders of the Communist party: 'If they receive an order, no matter what it is, they will carry it out.'[63] Later he referred in a somewhat more conciliatory tone to Begin, saying that 'Even Begin, that scoundrel, who if he does what he says he will, will bring about the destruction of the state, still I do not suspect him of deliberately wanting to undermine the security of the state.'[64]

In January 1958, he spoke out vituperatively again the plethora of parties and the electoral system, which, added to the custom carried over from the diaspora, of idle bickering about anything and everything, exacerbated the partisan divisiveness: 'there are ten Jewish factions, and these have to justify their separate existence'.[65] During his speech in the plenum about the Basic Law: The Knesset, in February 1958, the Prime Minister expressed his blatant contempt for the parties and the Knesset. The main topic on the agenda was the system of elections to the Knesset. He said that although he knew very well that his party was in the minority in this regard and that he did not delude himself that he could persuade the leaders of the small parties, 'I nonetheless regard it as my civic duty to say what I think, that other than the factions in the Knesset there is the public at large which is not subject to or connected with any faction . . . and it is to this public that I want to briefly explain from this podium.'[66] By speaking directly to the people, above the head of the Knesset, he was seriously slighting the parliament's status. Begin immediately hastened to defend the Knesset's honour and fiercely disputed the claim that the existing electoral system was nothing other than a 'deceit and a fraud', and said: 'If you say that you absolutely condemn this system of elections, even if only from a moral standpoint, knowing that the Fourth Knesset will be elected by this method, will that have the effect of strengthening the unity of the state, or of destroying it?'[67] It is perhaps then logical to assume that one of the aims of Ben-Gurion's repeated attacks on the electoral system was to undermine the moral basis of parliamentary life. If the very election of the parliament is basically flawed and immoral, then the parliament is clearly not a legitimate and honourable institution. But Ben-Gurion's desire to change the electoral system did not stem primarily from his desire to dwarf the Knesset, but rather from his belief that with the personal–district-majority system based on the British model, Mapai would gain an absolute majority of the Knesset seats, and would have no need of a coalition. This explains the firm, consistent and united opposition of all the parties to Ben-Gurion's and his party's desire to change the system. Of course, Ben-Gurion could not publicly reveal his motives, but he did try to present an altruistic position, suggesting that the existing system would actually ensure Mapai's stay in power, while under a new system, his party might lose its position. Mapai, he said, was prepared to make this sacrifice, 'because of the state's need, which takes priority over the interests of any party'.[68]

In his speech on the budget law, in March 1958, Ben-Gurion attacked the opposition:

> A fragmented opposition cannot be a responsible, national opposition . . . and in this situation, it is abundantly clear that an opposition so fragmented and divided has a hard time imagining that anything can be done in the state without turning to the parties.[69]

In November 1958, during his speech at a meeting of the Mapai faction in the Knesset, he maligned the opposition: 'The opposition is not an opposition, but the intrigues of small cliques.'[70] He continued this tirade a week later at a meeting of the Mapai central committee: 'What kind of opposition is this? Is this an opposition at all?'[71] He attributed the grotesque state of the opposition and the grievous ills of Israeli politics to the faulty system of elections:

> A democracy made up of ten parties is a caricature of democracy . . . If we want sovereignty for the Knesset, that sovereignty must be drawn from the people . . . the existing system is a disaster, it undermines democracy, destroys all faith in democracy, destroys all respect for the government, holds the opposition up to ridicule, makes the entire Knesset a laughing stock . . .

> there is no other regime like this anywhere in the world . . . it is a Jewish invention, an invention of the Jewish people which never had a state and does not know what parliamentary life is . . . we will not last much longer unless we have a responsible government and a responsible opposition, and that situation will surely lead to the defeat of democracy and to a coup, and there is no avoiding that, because a stable democracy can only exist where there is a system of regional elections.[72]

He did not even refrain from questioning the manner in which the electoral system had been introduced: 'Who made the existing system of elections? There were 36 people who were not elected by anyone, nor could they have been.'[73] He was referring to the Provisional State Council that had determined the method of elections for the Constituent Assembly. He mentioned the number 36, because he did not include himself among those who had established the system.

Prior to the elections to the Fourth Knesset, Ben-Gurion renewed his attacks on the parties, the opposition and the electoral system. In January 1959, he said to Sneh in the Knesset: 'We have no common ideological or moral grounds.'[74] In the same speech, he said that Herut 'does not deserve to join a national coalition based on mutual faith, on loyalty to the state and only to the state'.[75] At a meeting of immigrants from North Africa, held in Netanya in May 1959, he accused the parties of obstructing the ingathering of Jews from all parts of the world:

> There is one thing that obstructs the ingathering of all Jews, and that is the separatism, divisiveness and factionalism we have in our midst. For example, the parties . . . this unnecessary, ridiculous multiplicity of parties, which is a result of life in the diaspora, of our people's dispersion and schism, that is what makes it hard to gather and integrate them.[76]

To prove how much the State of Israel needed to take in Jews from all over the world, he described to those present – immigrants from North Africa – the nature of North African immigration: 'I don't know of any advanced people among the Jews of North Africa, any people who are not backward, who have the intellectual or mental capability or the education to be among the more advanced in this country.'[77]

THE PARTIES AND THE OPPOSITION AS A DANGER TO DEMOCRACY AND THE EXISTENCE OF THE STATE

In June 1959, speaking at a seminar of Mapai activists, Ben-Gurion asserted that Mapam and Achdut Haavoda were not political parties, but are rather kibbutz movements, and that the abominable state of the parties was threatening the democratic character of the country:

> I am not sure that democracy in Israel will last another ten years, if this regime remains in place . . . if the nation finds itself in such situations of inefficiency and beset by dangers, they will say the hell with democracy! We are sick and tired of all these parties, and there are people for whom the existence of the state, the security of the state are serious matters. And they think that in such a state as this it is impossible to ensure their security, and I am one of those who think that.[78]

While France can endure under any form of government, Israel cannot. There is the danger of a coup in Israel: 'A fascist party will be at its head. If only ten commanders in the army are replaced, then it will be a different army . . . they'll forcibly grab power and disperse the Knesset.'[79] He said it was a fact that Herut had already tried to do that in 1952:

> We have seen that they wanted to do that already, when the Knesset was compelled to do something that the fascist party objected to, and they did not obey the police, the police fell and they trampled policemen, and when I succeeded in calling in the army, the army came and saved the day and this mob of hooligans did not break into the Knesset and carry out a massacre, as might have happened.[80]

In September 1959, the Prime Minister spoke to attendees of a national non-partisan convention. Before speaking about the parties, he launched into a horrendous description of the state:

> This is Sodom and Gomorrah. There is no state as despicable, ridiculous, corrupt, lacking in power and capability as the State of Israel . . . I will not speak of the parties for which I have no

> respect. There are two parties which I do not respect and I did not sit with them in the government, nor will I ever. They will never come into power . . . I would not leave the country even if they attained power, I would do everything I could to remove them.[81]

Later, he attacked Mapam and Achdut Haavoda, who had joined his government after the 1955 elections: 'In actual fact, these are not two parties. There is no such party as Achdut Haavoda, it's a bluff. There is no party such as Mapam; that too is a bluff.'[82] 'We have no opposition', the Prime Minister stated, describing the opposition as 'corrupt, debased'.[83] The electoral system, in his view, was 'so worthless and damaging that it has no parallel in the world . . . the form of elections is a question of life and death for this state'.[84] The very survival of the state under the existing regime was

> a miracle, a miracle that is not assured. It was only thanks to the fact that this party was the major force . . . I am certain that in another ten years the state will not endure under this corrupt regime, which is the result of these proportional elections.[85]

At another convention of non-partisans, in October 1959, he asserted that the large number of parties creates 'a caricature of elections . . . we are turning the whole issue of elections into a farce . . . the system of proportional elections is liable to split the Jews . . . it is a cancer that is eating into the body of the nation, and we must uproot this disease'.[86]

In March 1961, the Prime Minister declared to his party's central committee that other than Mapai, 'There are no other parties in the state. There are sects, there are factions, Mapam and Achdut Haavoda are not parties, they never were, and if they stay as they are, they never will be parties.'[87] In April 1961, he delivered a belligerent speech at a meeting of Mapai's election headquarters. He prepared his party's activists for the elections by saying:

> As usual, we will face the united animosity of the nine small factions in the Knesset . . . these are not political parties in the true sense of the word, but fragments of parties . . . we cannot ignore the impure source of the common attack launched by all of these bodies that are so disparate and opposed to one another.[88]

Again, he attacked the electoral system, which he described as 'the fruit of the legacy of our diaspora past and of backward, underdeveloped countries'.[89] A month later, he once again resorted to such strident language at an internal meeting of his party: 'All the great troubles of the state come not from Nasser, but from the divisiveness that poisons our political life and prevents us from ingathering the Jews from all the diasporas.'[90]

After the elections, he complained about the stormy manner in which they were conducted, for which he blamed the small parties: 'This time the animosity was worse than ever before, descending to an unthinkable moral and ideological low.'[91] He found it difficult to reconcile himself to Mapai's poor showing in the elections and said: 'I regard the results as a disaster for the state.' He jeered at the opposition for its inability to create order and co-operation within its ranks: 'Three members of "Haagudah" and three members of the Communists are not six, instead they cancel each other out, because as far as each is concerned, the other is a minus, in other words, the complete opposite.'[92]

When he presented his new government in the Knesset after the 1961 elections, Ben-Gurion once again attacked the parties, except for Mapai:

> We just have small sects, because all the small factions, even those with 17 members, are nothing but sects, and they each have some special programmatic 'hobbyhorse' that is not accepted by the whole populace and is not at the centre of life, but has some 'appeal' for a small number of voters. In this way, they are splitting the people . . . stressing some marginal detail that is of importance mainly to members of the sect, and concentrating around them an unimportant minority of the nation and thus fragmenting the Knesset.[93]

At a meeting of Mapai's younger generation, on the eve of his retirement from the party, Ben-Gurion once again reviled the parties, that are 'debasing themselves in the eyes of the youth' and spoke about the

> distrust of the parties among a large segment of the population – of all the parties. This contempt for the party entails a great danger, it is likely to lead to a dictatorship – which is what they now have in France. They felt contempt for the parties and

> were glad when a great man appeared, and said to him: all the power is in your hands. They are fortunate that he is not a dictator like Stalin was, but it is a dictatorship.[94]

His reference to France's Fifth Republic as a dictatorship and to De Gaulle as a dictator is rather puzzling. On the one hand, Ben-Gurion depicted himself as the protector of democracy, but on the other, he did not always express total loyalty to the democratic system of government. For example, he was rather ambiguous in speaking about democracy in April 1949 at a meeting with members of Mapai:

> It is possible to form a party that rules by force of terror and is the only one in the state. I am not saying whether that is good or bad, but that won't happen here. It is possible to form a second party that rules by force of persuasion . . . that is the party that we must have.[95]

The fact that he refrained from expressing firm opposition to a one-party regime was apparently linked to the belief he still adhered to at the end of the 1940s, that it was necessary to create a socialist regime, a version of social democracy closer to the East European model than to the West European.

Ben-Gurion's fears that Herut might be recognized as a legitimate party also led him to object to bringing Zeev Jabotinsky's remains to Israel for internment there. The attempts at persuasion of some Mapai leaders were to no avail. He even rebuffed President Ben-Zvi's request, replying in an unequivocal tone: 'I see no point in bringing the bones of dead people who have always lived in the diaspora. I make only two exceptions: Herzl and Rothschild. Those it was proper to bury in Israel . . . Are we in need of dead Jews? Are we going to turn our country into a land of graves?'[96] In the same vein he wrote to Yosef Schectman: 'This country needs live Jews, not dead bones . . . and we should not turn the country into a graveyard.'[97] One of Eshkol's first decisions as Prime Minister was to bring Jabotinsky's bones to Israel. When he first presented his new government, in June 1963, he showed a totally different attitude from that of his predecessor:

> We should like to hope that arguments and disagreements between us will relate to common and general goals, and that

> these will be conducted with good will and in a decent and relevant manner. And that criticism will be levelled for the sake of the matter at hand, and not for its own sake.[98]

The head of the opposition, Begin, agreed with him immediately: 'I propose that we build the relations between the government and the opposition on the basis that our new Prime Minister was speaking of.'[99] And as a matter of fact, from the time that Eshkol replaced Ben-Gurion, relations between the government and the opposition improved immensely, and the tone of parliamentary clashes between Mapai and Herut became far more moderate.

We cannot overlook the fact that Ben-Gurion's reasoning in favour of 'a defensive democracy', one that defends itself against internal enemies of the democratic regime who try to exploit its advantages in order to destroy it, was far more relevant in his time than in later years. There was a real danger to the existence of democracy then. The fact that, contrary to his bleak forecasts, a democracy remained in force, and even was strengthened after his retirement, does not refute the logic that underpinned his claims. Ben-Gurion felt he had an enormous responsibility to ensure the existence of the state and its democratic character, and against the background of events inside and outside Israel in his time, one can, to some extent, understand his approach. Nonetheless, it is impossible to accept his harsh language and his excessive tendency to condemn almost completely the opposition and the political parties which, as noted, form the cornerstone of a democratic regime. In some of his more scathing diatribes, described in this and the previous chapter, he may have been the victim of his own volatile and aggressive personality. However, the psychological dimension is outside the scope of this book, which deals only with the historical dimension.

NOTES

1. Ben-Gurion Research Center Archives, minutes of meetings, coalition files, meeting with Mapam leaders, 24 February 1949.
2. Israel Labour Party Archives, meeting of Mapai central committee with members of the Knesset faction, 23 July 1949.
3. Ibid., meeting of Mapai secretariat, 7 August 1949.
4. Ibid., meeting of Mapai secretariat, 20 October 1949.
5. Ibid., meeting of Mapai secretariat, 28 August 1949.
6. Ibid., meeting of Mapai secretariat, 16 March 1951.

7. Ben-Gurion Research Center Archives, correspondence, Ben-Gurion to Levi Yitzhak HaYerushalmy, 11 January 1954.
8. Ibid., Bernstein to Ben-Gurion, 1 September 1955.
9. Israel Labour Party Archives, Mapai council, 29 April 1951.
10. Ibid., meeting of Mapai political committee, 13 September 1951.
11. Ibid.
12. Ibid.
13. Ibid., meeting of Mapai faction in the Knesset, 9 January 1951.
14. Ben-Gurion Research Center Archives, correspondence, Ben-Gurion to Weizmann, 27 February 1951.
15. Ibid., Ben-Gurion to Rosen, 19 February 1951.
16. Israel Labour Party Archives, personal file of Meir Argov, minutes of meeting of foreign affairs and security committee, 26 March 1951.
17. Ibid., conventions, elections meeting with teachers, 5 July 1951.
18. Ibid.
19. Ibid., meeting of Jews of Bulgarian origin, 10 July 1951.
20. Ibid., women's rally, 11 July 1951.
21. Ibid., file 6/3, proposal to party central committee, 20 February 1951.
22. Ibid.
23. Ibid., meeting of Mapai faction in the Knesset, 17 July 1951.
24. Ibid., meeting of Mapai's political committee, 5 August 1951.
25. Ibid., meeting of Mapai central committee, 13 August 1951.
26. Ben-Gurion Research Center Archives, correspondence, Ben-Gurion to Yadin, 19 December 1951.
27. Israel Labour Party Archives, meeting of Mapai secretariat, 10 January 1952.
28. Ibid.
29. Ben-Gurion Research Center Archives, minutes of meetings, meeting with leaders of the General Zionists, 11 September 1952.
30. Ibid.
31. Ibid., minutes of meetings, meeting with Peretz Bernstein, 26 September 1952.
32. Ibid.
33. Ibid., correspondence, Ben-Gurion to Haim Cohen (Minister of Justice), 31 October 1952.
34. Israel Labour Party Archives, meeting of Mapai central committee and the faction in the Knesset, 15 December 1952.
35. Giora Goldberg, 'The Jewish Factor in the Israeli Reaction to the Doctors' Plot in Moscow', pp. 183–203.
36. Israel Labour Party Archives, meeting of Mapai political committee, 16 January 1953.
37. Ibid., meeting of Mapai faction in the Knesset, 5 February 1950.
38. Ben-Gurion Research Center Archives, correspondence, Ben-Gurion to members of government, 29 January 1953.
39. Israel Labour Party Archives, meeting of Mapai's political committee, 26 February 1953.
40. Ben-Gurion Research Center Archives, correspondence, Ben-Gurion to Bernstein, 17 June 1954.
41. Ibid., correspondence, Ben-Gurion to Moshe Goldstein, 14 July 1954.
42. Ibid., minutes of meetings, convention in Ohalo, 16 December 1954.
43. Ibid.
44. Ibid.
45. Ibid. minutes of meetings, meeting of members with Ben-Gurion, 19 February 1955.
46. Ibid.
47. Israel Labour Party Archives, meeting of Mapai central committee with representatives of the branches, 19 May 1955.
48. Ibid.
49. Ben-Gurion Research Center Archives, correspondence, Ben-Gurion to Ophira Erez, 15 June 1955.

50. Israel Labour Party Archives, meeting of Mapai central committee, 9 June 1955.
51. Ben-Gurion Research Center Archives, minutes of meetings, meeting with leaders of Mapam, 7 August 1955.
52. Israel Labour Party Archives, meeting of Mapai central committee, 8 August 1955.
53. Ibid.
54. Ibid., meeting of Mapai central committee, 22 August 1955.
55. Ben-Gurion Research Center Archives, correspondence, Ben-Gurion to Rosen, 6 September 1955.
56. Israel Labour Party Archives, conventions, national convention of the younger generation, Kfar Vitkin, 3 March 1956.
57. Ibid.
58. Ben-Gurion Research Center Archives, minutes of meetings, convention in Ohalo, 16 December 1954.
59. *Knesset Record,* 19 June 1957, p. 2,194.
60. Israel Labour Party Archives, meeting of Mapai central committee, 21 July 1957.
61. Ben-Gurion Research Center Archives, minutes of meetings, meeting with leaders of Achdut Haavoda, 7 October 1957.
62. Israel Labour Party Archives, meeting of Mapai faction in the Knesset with the secretariat, with members of Mapai on the executive of the Histadrut and with Mapai members on the plenum of the education center, 26 January 1950.
63. Ben-Gurion Research Center Archives, minutes of meetings, meeting with leaders of Achdut Haavoda, 29 December 1957.
64. Ibid.
65. *Knesset Record,* 7 January 1958, p. 587.
66. Ibid., 11 February 1958, p. 878.
67. Ibid., p. 882.
68. Ibid., p. 879.
69. Ibid., 27 March 1958, p. 1,722.
70. Israel Labour Party Archives, meeting of Mapai faction in the Knesset, 20 November 1958.
71. Ibid., meeting of Mapai central committee, 27 November 1958.
72. Ibid.
73. Ibid.
74. *Knesset Record,* 7 January 1959, p. 799.
75. Ibid., p. 803.
76. Israel Labour Party Archives, conventions, convention of North African immigrants, Netanya, 6 May 1959.
77. Ibid.
78. Ibid., seminar of Mapai activists, 20 June 1959.
79. Ibid.
80. Ibid.
81. Ibid., national convention of non-partisans, HaKfar HaYarok, 30 September 1959.
82. Ibid.
83. Ibid.
84. Ibid.
85. Ibid.
86. Ibid., national convention of non-partisans, Tel Aviv, 20 October 1959.
87. Ibid., meeting of Mapai central committee, 19 March 1961.
88. Ibid., conventions, convention of election headquarters, Tel Aviv, 5 April 1961.
89. Ibid.
90. Ibid., convention of election headquarters in the branches, 4 May 1961.
91. Ibid., convention of election headquarters, 20 August 1961.
92. Ibid.
93. *Knesset Record,* 2 November 1961, p. 243.
94. Israel Labour Party Archives, conventions, convention of secretariats of young generation circles, 15 February 1964.

95. Ibid., meeting with members of Mapai in Prime Minister's office, 8 April 1949.
96. Ben-Gurion Research Center Archives, correspondence, Ben-Gurion to Ben-Zvi, 3 June 1956.
97. Ibid., Ben-Gurion to Schectman, 3 October 1956.
98. *Knesset Record*, 24 June 1963, p. 2,161.
99. Ibid., p. 2,166.

Conclusion

Conflicting interests and rivalry between heads of state and parliaments are natural occurrences; Ben-Gurion's relations with the Knesset were not unusual in their essence, but only in their vehemence. All the prime ministers who took office after Ben-Gurion – Sharett (1954–55), Eshkol (1963–69), Meir (1969–74), Rabin (1974–77 and 1992–95), Begin (1977–83), Shamir (1983–84 and 1986–92), Peres (1984–86 and 1995–96), Netanyahu (1996–99), Barak (1999–2001) and Sharon (2001–) – clashed to some extent or another with the Knesset, albeit far less frequently and intensely than did Ben-Gurion. Ben-Gurion influenced the shape of parliamentary life a great deal more than the ten prime ministers who came after him, in part because he served in that office much longer than they did, but particularly because he was Prime Minister during the formative period of the state, in which political patterns, which last for a long time, were shaped and institutionalized. Moreover, he wielded enormous power and influence within his governments and in his party – more than any other Israeli Prime Minister has done. Also, during the entire period of his terms as Prime Minister, his party was the dominant one.[1] A dominant party possesses a great deal more influence than is reflected by its proportionate share in the parliament, because it has a veto power, without which no government can be established. A prime minister who is the head of a dominant party can base his standing on that party's strength and gain enormous influence.

Unlike certain clashes between heads of state (kings, presidents or prime ministers) and parliaments, which are based mainly on power struggles, the conflict between Ben-Gurion and the Knesset was not over who held the power, and the sources of the discord were not deeply rooted. Therefore, the intensity of the conflict was disproportionate to the slight potential of the forces that fed it. Not only was Ben-Gurion totally identified with the state he had established, he felt he owned it, and passionately loved it. He perceived the Knesset as an institution that was challenging him and questioning – even trying to undermine – the feelings of identification, ownership and love that he felt for the state. He found it very difficult to draw a distinction between the Knesset and the other government institutions, and thought it ought to serve as a means of achieving national aims. Routine parliamentary life did not fit the revolutionary and messianic atmosphere that prevailed during Ben-Gurion's terms as Prime Minister.

In his view, the Knesset did not play a sufficient or proper role in building the state. It was not fully aware of the momentous nature of the time and instead was preoccupied with petty issues, while constantly interfering with the great national endeavour. In contrast, other organizations, like the Israel Defence Forces, the state apparatus and the kibbutz and moshav movements were, in his view, filling a vital role in the process of nation-building. The work of the parliament was appropriate for mundane life and everyday routine, but not for the making of history.

Ben-Gurion's struggle against the Knesset was not a matter of principle. If the Knesset had fulfilled his expectations, probably he would have supported it. If it had assisted the government and placed the good of the state as its highest priority, it would have gained Ben-Gurion's support. However, the parliament's role in a democracy is not to assist the government, but rather to criticize, investigate and supervise it. As a representative institution, it has to protect the particular interests of all the citizens vis-à-vis the executive arm, which is concerned with furthering the collective interests. This was the point of contention underlying Ben-Gurion's volatile relations with the Knesset.

By its very nature, parliamentary work has many formalistic aspects, which were not consistent with Ben-Gurion's revolutionary approach. The verbal and declarative element of parliamentary life is a basic and important one, but Ben-Gurion viewed it as fruitless verbosity, perhaps even as indolence, in the face of the great tasks that had to be carried out. To him, the Knesset's desire to play a significant role in the system of government that was taking shape was a disservice to the vision of statism. According to Don-Yehiya and Liebman, this vision, which also emerged in several Third-World countries after they achieved their independence, was not suited to a democratic regime of the kind that existed in Israel.[2] This contradiction between statism and democracy – which never arose in the Third-World undemocratic states that fostered statism – was one of the factors that led to the decline of statism in Israeli society. And, in fact, as it declined, the democratic basis of the state was strengthened and the power of the Knesset began to increase.

There were two impetuses for Ben-Gurion's attitude towards the Knesset. In the sphere of practical politics, he regarded the Knesset as a rival and an impediment that ought to be weakened. In the broader philosophical sphere, he believed that the needs of a nascent state taking its first steps are not compatible with a strong parliament possessed of many powers. His attitude towards the Knesset did not merely reflect despotism; rather it was based on a crystallized world view. While this world view may seem odd today, more than 50 years after the establishment of the state, it had a certain justification during the time Ben-Gurion was at its head, particularly in the early years after independence. Moreover, just as Ben-Gurion fought the Knesset from his position as Prime Minister, the obstreperous demands by the opposition parties that the Knesset be strengthened and aggrandized stemmed from their position as an opposition. In other words, it is natural for the head of the executive branch to refrain from defending the rights of the parliament, while the members of that parliament will rise to its defence.

Criticism, supervision, investigation and comprehensive public debate – all these intrinsic functions seemed superfluous to Ben-Gurion in that momentous time. He competed with the Knesset over the function of representation. Although he was not directly elected by the voters, he regarded himself as their direct representative, and did not even leave the Knesset its most natural function – representation of the public. He perceived the Knesset as a divisive element, while, in his view, the good of the state called for cohesion and unity. Moreover, by impairing the prestige of the Knesset, Ben-Gurion was able to undermine oppositional elements, for whom the Knesset was the major sphere of activity and with which they strongly identified. Ben-Gurion's negative attitude towards the Knesset was only part of a broader approach – his resentment of other vital elements of democracy, like the parties, the press and the courts of law.

In functional terms, as well as in a long-range view, there is some justification for Ben-Gurion's negative attitude towards the Knesset. In a nascent state, engaged in a war for its existence from its very establishment, a strong executive arm was able to help it survive and withstand the threat of its external enemies. However, this justification was acceptable only, if at all, in the first years after the state's establishment. As time went by, there was no longer any justification for strengthening the executive arm at the expense of the legislative arm. Nonetheless, over the years no substantive change occurred in Ben-Gurion's attitude towards the Knesset. In his struggle against the Knesset, he achieved some striking successes early on. But when he returned to head the government, after the elections to the Third Knesset (1955), his achievements were fewer and his attempts to weaken the Knesset were blocked to some extent. As the years went by, Knesset members, even those of Mapai, became less willing to accept his dictates. This change took place against the background of the state's emergence from the initial stage of its independence. The Sinai campaign (1956) returned Israel to a critical state of emergency that to a certain extent arrested the process of normalization, and this enabled Ben-Gurion to persist in his negative attitude towards the Knesset. While in the short term, there were reasons, although not truly compelling ones, for Ben-Gurion's antagonism towards the Knesset, from a long-term view, this attitude was damaging and destructive, not only from the standpoint of the Knesset, but also from the standpoint of the national interest.

Israel was not the only state in which independence resulted in a weakened legislative branch. Le Vine found that in African states that had been under French control until the end of the 1950s and the early 1960s, after they achieved independence, there was a marked decline in the status of parliamentary institutions, attended by an increase in the power of governmental institutions, particularly of the presidents.[3] There was a similar phenomenon from the mid-1990s among the Palestinians, even before they achieved independence. The head of the Palestinian Authority, Yasser Arafat, adopted a basically negative attitude towards the legislative institutions.

Fierce battles between heads of states and parliaments are apt to break out in a number of situations. In a presidential regime, when the president and the parliamentary majority are from rival parties, there is a potential for a severe conflict. Situations of this kind existed for many years in the United States. The 1996 elections gave the Democratic president, Bill Clinton, an overwhelming majority, and a clear majority to the Republican party in both houses of Congress. In Fifth-Republic France, a situation like this lasted for several years and has been in existence again since 1997. In a parliamentary system, clashes between the head of state and the parliament are very likely if minority governments exist over a long period of time, and somewhat less likely if the parliament has several times forced the government to resign. Even if the government has not been forced to resign and the parliamentary majority has been preserved, a conflict is apt to break out if the parliamentary majority is very narrow and impairs the government's functioning and stability. None of these scenarios fits the situation that existed in Ben-Gurion's time. He usually set up very broad coalitions and was always able to enlarge them in return for a relatively low payment, because his potential coalition partners were never in a good bargaining position. The Knesset in no way posed a threat to Ben-Gurion's rule, which was never in question. Although Mapai did not succeed in gaining more than 40–47 mandates in Ben-Gurion's time (46 in 1949; 45 in 1951; 40 in 1955; 47 in 1959; and 42 in 1961), the labour parties (including the Arab lists attached to Mapai) had an absolute majority in all of the Knessets elected during that period.

The damage that Ben-Gurion caused the Knesset was twofold. He weakened the legislative arm in relation to the executive arm and, at the same time, caused partisanship to grow in strength. At first, he saw no need for a clear separation between the legislative and the executive branches. He was not satisfied to stand at the head of the executive branch; he regarded himself as a national leader above any other institution or organization. As a result of the refusal of the legislative branch, in the early years, to accept its subordination to the government and to Ben-Gurion, as well as the absence of any separation, Ben-Gurion created too great a separation between the two branches, removing the Knesset from the national cycle and relegating it to the sidelines. In other words, once the Knesset did not totally accept Ben-Gurion's authority and objected to the lack of any separation between the branches, he began to view it as a rival and embarked on a struggle against it. As he saw it, if the Knesset wanted separation, it would get a full separation and would pay a heavy price for it. He rejected the normal midway situation, in which there is a certain separation between the parliament and the government attended by a system of checks and balances and the notion of a functional separation between the two branches. Because of his monistic concept of the political process, he did not believe in a multiplicity of functions and the need to separate between them by establishing special institutions to fulfill specific functions. A similar phenomenon, underpinned by a lack of separation between the two branches, was noted in Third-World countries. In Kenya, for example, a large part of the public holds to the notion of 'government as a single unit, rather than one composed of distinct and possibly competing branches',[4] which made it easier for President Kenyatta to relate to 'his' government 'as embracing all of its divisions and all spheres of action'.[5]

This monistic approach was not accepted in Israel as it was in Third-World countries like Kenya. The Knesset also refused to accept this simplistic and non-democratic concept. Consequently, Ben-Gurion reached the conclusion, an inevitable one as far as he was concerned, that the Knesset was a serious threat to the government and indirectly, to the state as well, and that the government and the Knesset were permanently competing for rule of the country. This power-play between the two was a kind of zero-sum game, in which every gain made by one side was always at the expense of the other and vice versa. The conclusion was that the recalcitrant Knesset had to be distanced – perhaps even expelled – from his administration and substantively weakened by a series of various measures.

One consequence of Ben-Gurion's struggles against the Knesset was that it was constantly on the defensive. Ben-Gurion was always the initiator, while the Knesset became the reactor. This passive position had an adverse effect on the Knesset. One result was that Knesset members initiated hardly any legislation, leaving the major portion of such initiatives to the government. The proportion of private members' bills proposed during Ben-Gurion's time was low: in the First Knesset not a single private bill was proposed. In the Second Knesset, finally two bills were enacted that originated in private legislation; however, the share of such bills in the overall legislation passed was not even 1 per cent. In the Third Knesset there was an increase to 6.5 per cent and in the Fourth to 8.9 per cent. In the Fifth Knesset, in the middle of which Ben-Gurion ended his term as Prime Minister, there was a rise to 11 per cent. After Ben-Gurion's resignation, this growth trend continued and in the Eighth Knesset (1974–77) reached 17.3 per cent.[6] This trend grew much stronger in the 1980s and 1990s, although it did not stem only from Ben-Gurion's resignation, but from other factors as well, such as the rise of competitiveness and the loss of party dominance.

Another study has described in detail the improvement in the Knesset's functioning, with a stress on the role of the opposition, since one-party dominance ended in 1973.[7] This improvement did not occur only in the number of private members' bills, but in several other spheres as well. Parliamentary tools, such as questions, motions of no confidence and motions to the agenda, which were atrophied in Ben-Gurion's time, became more effective after he left the political scene. A marked change for the better occurred in the Knesset committees. The progress, albeit slow, of the Knesset over time was so pronounced, that even during the tenure of the national unity government in the 1980s, its functioning was not impaired, and, compared to earlier periods in which a national unity government was in power, actually improved.[8]

In the opening chapter, the claim was put forward that a high degree of inter-party competitiveness enhances a parliament's functioning. This is only true up to a certain level of competitiveness; when it exceeds this level, this trend is likely to be reversed, so that the status of the parliament may actually be worsened. Neither a high level nor a low level of competitiveness have a favourable effect on the parliament's status. The establishment of a national unity government following the 1984 elections to the Knesset led to a certain decline in competitiveness (from a situation of very high competitiveness) attended by an improvement in the Knesset's functioning. When the threat to a state's existence is attenuated by the establishment of a very broad coalition, the potential for the fulfillment of the classic parliamentary functions of criticism, supervision, investigation and incisive public debate increases. This rule ought to have led to very effective parliamentary functioning during Ben-Gurion's terms in office, since the threat to the government was almost nil. However, his negative attitude to the Knesset precluded this natural development. The reform introduced in 1996, when the new system came into force based on the direct election of the Prime Minister, may result in a slight reduction in inter-party rivalry (particularly in the periods between elections) and in a further improvement in the Knesset's status.

Ben-Gurion's attitude to the Knesset reflected not only his attitude to other democratic institutions, such as the press, the courts and the parties, but also the fact that during this period, Israel was a mobilized democracy. This partial form of democracy was also linked to other factors. It is impossible to overlook several facts: first, that during those years, the state's Arab citizens were under a military government; second, that some of the parliamentary parties – on the right, the left and in the religious camp – did not openly accept fundamental democratic principles; and third, that several extra-parliamentary undergrounds and movements posed a direct threat to the democratic form of government.

In light of these constraints, and the fact that Israel was a young state devoid of any parliamentary tradition, one could not expect to find in it then a form of parliament like the lustrous British version, or an authority that legislates, investigates, supervises and criticizes, like the two US Houses of Congress. The British Parliament and the American Congress of the second half of the twentieth century do not have the same status they had in their initial stages. It would have been absurd to entertain such unrealistic expectations of the Knesset during the years that Ben-Gurion served as Prime Minister. For example, in Israel during the period 1948–63, it would have been impossible to have militant Knesset committees engaging in intensive investigation of the executive branch, the way the American Congress does. Similarly, one could not expect to find the extreme British version, where the Prime Minister appears twice weekly in parliament to reply to questions, anxiously anticipating additional questions from the opposition benches after giving his replies, and after having thoroughly prepared for the occasion.[9] However, even if the discrepancy between young Israel and the well-established Western democracies was vast during Ben-Gurion's terms of office, one could have expected far more of the formative Israeli democracy than of the new states of the Third World. The immense parliamentary experience accumulated in the institutions of the Zionist movement and of Knesset Yisrael, along with the participation of Jews in other parliaments, the positive influence of the mandatory period on the parliamentary system and the high proportion of political institutions existing at the time of the state's founding – all these ought to have contributed to the emergence of a legislative branch, which, while not similar in status to those of Britain and the United States, was a far cry from the parliaments of Third World states. Ben-Gurion was one of the main factors that prevented this development.

Some of Ben-Gurion's methods described throughout this book were also utilized by heads of state in the Third World. Attempts like Ben-Gurion's to introduce constitutional reforms, such as his failed attempt to dissolve the Knesset or his successful one in relation to coalition discipline were also pronounced among leaders of Third-World countries. In Chile, for example, in 1969, President Peri initiated a series of constitutional reforms, including one relating to the dissolution of the parliament by the President, intended to strengthen the executive arm – the President in particular – and to weaken the parliament.[10] These changes came into effect with the socialist Allende's victory in the elections and ended up by so worsening the rift between the executive and the legislative branches that the democratic regime collapsed.[11]

The co-optation that Ben-Gurion tried to effect by appointing Knesset members as deputy ministers was also common in African states like Kenya. Hopkins, who studied relations between the parliament and the President in Kenya, found that Kenyatta was in the habit of rewarding several dozen parliament members by appointing them as assistants to ministers:

> Such positions provide useful patronage posts for the president. They can reward the 'faithful' from peripheral areas, bolster the appearance of an equitable balance in government, and co-opt about one-third of the Assembly to an obligation to support, or at least not oppose, government policy.[12]

The Tanzanian president, Nyerere, was also in the habit of personally attacking members of parliament, just as Ben-Gurion had frequently done in the Knesset. He deplored the failure of members of the Tanzanian parliament effectively to fulfill their function.[13] A series of studies on the functioning of parliaments vis-à-vis heads of states in the Third World has shown that members of parliament were active primarily in their constituencies. They were engaged mainly in mediating between citizens and the central government and in enlisting support for the central government. The heads of states were pleased with this situation, since the legislators were busy with local politics and hardly interfered in the affairs of the central government.[14] One can assume that one of Ben-Gurion's motives for supporting a regional system of elections – in addition to his desire to enlarge Mapai's share in the Knesset and to make it the majority party – probably was his interest in distancing Knesset members from the national scene by creating a commitment on their part to their respective constituencies. There is no basis for this assumption in Ben-Gurion's writings, but neither is there any for his putative motive to change the electoral system in order to increase Mapai's strength. While a political leader is not likely to reveal his true motives in relation to such a cardinal issue, Ben-Gurion's centralistic approach and his disdain for the local arena suggest that these two assumptions are not entirely detached from reality.

Ben-Gurion's hostile attitude to the Knesset did have at least three positive implications:

1. As a result of his pressures on the Knesset, the axis of the struggle between the Knesset and the government was no less important than the other axis of the struggle between the coalition and the opposition.
2. As a result of the threat posed by Ben-Gurion, situations sometimes arose in which the opposition parties co-operated with parties in the coalition.
3. Opposition parties on both ends of the political spectrum co-operated in an attempt to thwart Ben-Gurion's schemes.

Clashes and quarrels between heads of states and parliaments also occur in properly run democracies, and at certain times there have been prime ministers who have struggled against the parliament. However, in sound, well-administered democracies one would not find such deep-set hostility and so constant a battle against a parliament, as existed in the case of Ben-Gurion. Several Canadian prime ministers were not as tolerant of the parliament as they should have been. Pearson, for example, speaking about the importance of a prime minister emerging from the ranks of the parliament, said:

> As for Parliament, you can't really establish leadership there as Prime Minister unless – I don't want to be too dogmatic about this – you have a deep and genuine feeling for parliamentary institutions. For this, it is a great help to have had a parliamentary experience; to have risen from the ranks in Parliament where you can acquire, if you have not had it instinctively, a feeling for Parliament, of its importance and its traditions. I always had a feeling of deep respect for Parliament (after all, I had been a constitutional historian!), but I entered at the top, on the front benches. I had been in civil service for many years before being elected and I had never done any Parliament apprenticeship. And I confess I never had any great love for parliamentary battle and rows. I could get worried up about issues as much as anybody else, as a competitive human being, but I always thought debates which were repetitive and prolonged and too violent wasted too much time. I used to get impatient because you couldn't get things done quickly enough because of those struggles in Parliament that other people may have loved.[15]

Indeed, it is impossible to blame Ben-Gurion for his lack of parliamentary experience. As the first Prime Minister, he could not have brought any parliamentary experience with him, nor was he involved in the pre-state representative institutions, but rather in executive institutions. This problem of a lack of parliamentary experience was also the lot of the other prime ministers from Mapai/Labour (with the exception of Peres) and was particularly marked during the first term in office of Rabin, the first Prime Minister from the young generation. All four Prime Ministers from the Likud did have parliamentary experience, although Begin had more than Shamir, and Netanyahu had less than Shamir.

Another Canadian Prime Minister, Trudeau, was less restrained than Pearson. Both men were interested in making the parliamentary debates less drawn out and more effective, but Trudeau was far more caustic in his speech than Pearson. This is how he referred to members of parliament from the opposition who used a filibuster to block his attempt to change the parliamentary rules about the allotment of time in the parliament: 'When they get home, when they are out of Parliament, they are fifty yards from Parliament Hill, they are no longer honourable members – they are just nobodies.'[16] On another occasion, Trudeau attacked the parliamentary style of the members, as Ben-Gurion used to do from time to time: 'When I say I don't like the Commons, it's because it's a place where men are shouting, where people yell at each other – yell as one wouldn't dare in a classroom. I find that vulgar. It offends me.'[17]

Although Trudeau was certainly more blunt than Pearson, compared to Ben-Gurion he was polite and mild-mannered. Medding asserts that Ben-Gurion's leadership was neither charismatic nor revolutionary in character, but rather that it was transformative.[18] Transformative leadership is evolutionary and incremental; a transformative leader sets goals for the society and justifies them in terms of ideological values adhered to by his supporters. Medding tends to regard transformative leadership as a special type of democratic leadership, particularly because it depends on institutional, rather than personal, sources of support. Medding went to great lengths to refute the claim that Ben-Gurion's leadership was not democratic. He refused to accept Anita Shapira's conclusions that Ben-Gurion tended to retain unlimited power while suppressing and humiliating his adversaries and that he was a leader along the lines of a Leninist military commander.[19] This book cannot settle the argument between Medding and Shapira, since it is limited to the narrow aspect of Ben-Gurion's relations with the Knesset. Nonetheless, the findings that have been presented on its pages tend firmly to reinforce Shapira's claims and to weaken Medding's line of defence.

Duverger and Derfler, who studied the relationship between the executive and the legislative branches during De Gaulle's term as president of France, called it a 'republican monarchy'.[20] In the context of the relations between the Knesset and Ben-Gurion during the time he served as Prime Minister, this term is also appropriate for the State of Israel.

NOTES

1. For an explanation of the term a 'dominant party', see Giora Goldberg, *The Parties in Israel – From Mass Parties to Electoral Parties* (Hebrew), Tel Aviv: Ramot, Tel Aviv University, 1992, pp. 23–51.
2. Eliezer Don-Yehiya and Yeshayahu Liebman, 'The Dilemma of a Traditional Culture in a Modern State: Changes and Developments in the "Civil Religion" of Israel' (Hebrew), *Megamot*, vol. 28, no. 4 (August 1984), pp. 461–85.
3. Victor T. Le Vine, 'Parliaments in Francophone Africa: Some Lessons from the Decolonization Process', in Joel Smith and Lloyd D. Musolf (eds) *Legislatures in Development: Dynamics of Change in New and Old States*, Durham, NC, Duke University Press, 1979, pp. 125–54.
4. Raymond F. Hopkins, 'The Kenyan Legislature: Political Functions and Citizen Perceptions', in G. R. Boynton and Chong Lim Kim (eds), *Legislative Systems in Developing Countries*, Durham, NC: Duke University, 1975, p. 221.
5. Ibid.
6. Giora Goldberg, 'The Parliamentary Opposition in Israel (1965–1977)', p. 162.
7. Ibid.
8. Giora Goldberg, 'The Knesset: Development, Stability, or Decay?' in Daniel J. Elazar and Shmuel Sandler (eds) *Israel's Odd Couple*, Detroit: Wayne State University, 1990, pp. 193–220.
9. Patrick Weller, *First Among Equals*, Sydney, London and Boston: George Allen & Unwin, 1985, pp. 170–1.
10. Arturo Valenzuela and Alexander Wilde, 'Presidential Politics and the Decline of the Chilean Congress', in Joel Smith and Lloyd D. Musolf (eds) *Legislatures in Development: Dynamics of Change in New and Old States*, Durham, NC: Duke University Press, 1979, pp. 209–10.
11. Ibid., pp. 211–13.
12. Raymond F. Hopkins, 'The Influence of the Legislature on Development Strategy: The Case of Kenya and Tanzania', in Joel Smith and Lloyd D. Musolf (eds) *Legislatures in Development: Dynamics of Change in New and Old States*, Durham, NC: Duke University Press, 1979, p. 173.
13. Ibid., p. 176.
14. See various articles dealing with this subject in Joel Smith and Lloyd D. Musolf (eds) *Legislatures in Development: Dynamics of Change in New and Old States*, Durham, NC: Duke University, 1979. See in particular Lloyd D. Musolf and J. Fred Springer, 'The Parliament of Malaysia and Economic Development: Policy Making and the MP', pp. 289–310.
15. Cited from Weller, *First Among Equals*, pp. 168–9.
16. Ibid., p. 169.

17. Ibid.
18. Peter Y. Medding, *The Founding of Israeli Democracy, 1948–1967*, New York and Oxford: Oxford University Press, 1990, pp. 217–18.
19. Ibid., pp. 212–13. Anita Shapira, *From the Dismissal of the Chief of the Haganah to the Disbandment of the Palmach* (Hebrew), Tel Aviv: Hakibbutz HaMeuchad, 1985, pp. 9, 64.
20. Leslie Derfler, *President and Parliament: A Short History of the French Presidency*, Boca Raton FL: University of Florida, 1983, p. 202.

Bibliography

ARCHIVES

Ben-Gurion Research Center Archives, Sede Boker
Israel Labour Party Archives, Beit Berl
State Archives, Jerusalem
Central Zionist Archives (CZA), Jerusalem

OFFICIAL PUBLICATIONS

Government Yearbooks
Knesset Record
Provisional State Council (minutes)
The People's Council (minutes)
Yalkut HaPirsumim

DAILY PRESS

Al HaMishmar
Chadashot
Davar
Ha'Aretz
HaBoker
HaTzofeh
Herut
Kol Ha'Am

LaMerchav
Letzte Neis
Ma'ariv
Yedioth Aharonoth

BOOKS AND ARTICLES

Bader, Y. *The Knesset and I* (Hebrew), Jerusalem: Idanim, 1979.

Barzilai, G., Yaar-Yuchtman, E. and Segal, Z. *The Supreme Court in the Eyes of Israeli Society* (Hebrew), Tel Aviv: Papyrus, 1994.

Ben-Gurion, D. *The War of Independence: Ben-Gurion's War Diary* (Hebrew) 4 vols, Tel Aviv: Ministry of Defence, 1982.

Blondel, J. *Comparative Legislatures*, Englewood Cliffs, NJ: Prentice-Hall, 1973.

Bondi, R. *Felix* (Hebrew), Tel Aviv: Zmora-Bitan, 1990.

Boynton, G. R. and Chong Lim Kim (eds) *Legislative Systems in Developing Countries*, Durham, NC: Duke University, 1975.

Brichta, A. *Democracy and Elections* (Hebrew), Tel Aviv: Am Oved, 1977.

Daskal, A. 'The Activities of the Extra-Parliamentary Opposition during the First Years of the State: Brit Kanna'im and Malkhut Yisrael', MA thesis (Hebrew), Ramat Gan: Bar-Ilan University, Department of Political Studies, 1990.

Derfler, L. *President and Parliament: A Short History of the French Presidency*, Boca Raton FL: University of Florida, 1983.

Don-Yehiya, E. 'Festivals and Political Culture: The Celebration of Independence Day in the Early Years of Statehood' (Hebrew), *Medina, Vihasim Mimshal Benleumiyim*, (State, Government and International Relations) 23 (Summer 1984).

Don-Yehiya, E. and Liebman, Y. 'The Dilemma of a Traditional Culture in a Modern State: Changes and Developments in the "Civil Religion" of Israel' (Hebrew), *Megamot*, 28, 4 (August 1984), pp. 461–85.

Flexer, Y. P. *Sights in the Knesset* (Hebrew), Jerusalem: Daf Chen, 1980.

Goguel, F. 'Parliament under the Fifth French Republic: Difficulties of Adapting to a New Role', in Loewenberg, G. (ed.) *Modern Parliaments: Change or Decline?*, Chicago and New York: Aldine-Atherton, 1971.

Goldberg, G. *The Parliamentary Opposition in Israel (1965–1977)*

(Hebrew), Jerusalem: The Hebrew University, Ph.D. dissertation, 1980.

——'On the Need to Increase the Number of Knesset Members' (Hebrew), *Netivei Irgun veMinhal* (Modes of Organization and Administration), 23, 137–8 (Winter 1982).

——'The Struggle for Legitimacy: Herut's Road from Opposition to Power', in Cohen, S. and Don-Yehiya, E. (eds) *Comparative Jewish Politics – Conflict and Consensus in Jewish Political Life*, Ramat Gan: Bar-Ilan University, 1986, pp. 146–69.

——'The Knesset: Development, Stability or Decay?' in Elazar, D. J. and Sandler, S. (eds) *Israel's Odd Couple*, Detroit MI: Wayne State University, 1990, pp. 193–220.

——'The Jewish Factor in the Israeli Reaction to the Doctors' Plot in Moscow', in Don-Yehiya, E. (ed.), *Israel and Diaspora Jewry*, Ramat Gan: Bar-Ilan University, 1991, pp. 183–203.

——'Ben-Gurion and the "People's Front"' (Hebrew), *Medina, Mimshal Vihasim Benleumiyim* (State, Government and International Relations), 35, (Autumn–Winter 1991), pp. 51–66.

——*The Parties in Israel – From Mass Parties to Electoral Parties* (Hebrew), Tel-Aviv: Ramot, 1992.

——'You Don't Need a Constitution to Plant Trees – On State-Building and Framing a Constitution' (Hebrew), *Medina, Mimshal Veyahasim Beinleumiyim* (State, Government and International Relations), 38, Spring–Summer 1993.

Hopkins, R. F. 'The Kenyan Legislature: Political Functions and Citizen Perceptions', in Boynton, G. R. and Chong Lim Kim (eds) *Legislative Systems in Developing Countries*, Durham, NC: Duke University, 1975, pp. 207–31.

——'The Influence of the Legislature on Development Strategy: The Case of Kenya and Tanzania', *Legislatures in Development: Dynamics of Change in New and Old States*, Durham, NC: Duke University, 1979, pp. 155–86.

King, A. (ed.) *The British Prime Minister*, London: MacMillan, 1969.

Le Vine, V. T. 'Parliaments in Francophone Africa: Some Lessons from the Decolonization Process', in Smith, J. and Musolf, L. D. (eds) *Legislatures in Development: Dynamics of Change in New and Old States*, Durham, NC: Duke University, 1979, pp. 125–54.

Levinsky, Y. *Book of Holidays* (Hebrew) Tel Aviv: Dvir, 1957.

Likhovski, E. S. *Israel's Parliament: The Law of the Knesset*, Oxford: Clarendon, 1971.

Loewenberg, G. (ed.) *Modern Parliaments: Change or Decline?*,

Chicago and New York: Aldine-Atherton, 1971.

Markesinis, B. S. *The Theory and Practice of Dissolution of Parliament*, Cambridge: Cambridge University Press, 1971.

Medding, P. Y. *The Founding of Israeli Democracy, 1948–1967*, New York and Oxford: Oxford University Press, 1990.

Mezey, M. L. *Comparative Legislatures*, Durham, NC: Duke University, 1979.

Musolf, L. D. and Springer, J. F. 'The Parliament of Malaysia and Economic Development: Policy Making and the MP', in Smith, J. and Musolf, L. D. (eds) *Legislatures in Development: Dynamics of Change in New and Old States*, Durham, NC: Duke University, 1979, pp. 289–310.

Naor, M. *Laskov* (Hebrew), Tel Aviv: Ministry of Defence and Keter, 1988.

Olshan, Y. *Controversy and Contention* (Hebrew), Jerusalem and Tel Aviv: Schocken, 1978.

Sager, S. 'On the Sources of the Parliamentary System in the State of Israel' (Hebrew), *Molad*, 4, 22 (December 1971), pp. 327–39.

——'A Reform during Question Time in the Knesset' (Hebrew), *Quarterly on Social Research*, 9–11 (August 1975), pp. 105–10.

——*The Parliamentary System of Israel*, Syracuse, NY: Syracuse University, 1985.

Segal, Z. *Israeli Democracy* (Hebrew), Tel Aviv: The Ministry of Defence, 1988.

Sever, M. (ed.) *The Second Convention of the General Federation of Hebrew Workers in Eretz-Israel, 1923* (Hebrew), Tel Aviv: The General Federation of Labour, 1968.

Shapira, A. *From the Dismissal of the Chief of the Haganah to the Disbandment of the Palmach* (Hebrew), Tel Aviv: Hakibbutz HaMeuchad, 1985.

Sherf, Z. *Three Days* (Hebrew), Tel Aviv: Am Oved, 1965.

Smith, J. and Musolf, L. D. (eds) *Legislatures in Development: Dynamics of Change in New and Old States*, Durham, NC: Duke University, 1979.

Sprinzak, Y. *Letters* (Hebrew), vol. 3, Tel Aviv, Ayanoth, 1969.

Tzidon, A. *Beit HaNivcharim* (Hebrew) (The House of Representatives), Jerusalem: Achiassaf, 1964.

Valenzuela, A. and Wilde, A. 'Presidential Politics and the Decline of the Chilean Congress', in Smith, J. and Musolf, L. D. (eds) *Legislatures in Development: Dynamics of Change in New and Old States*, Durham NC: Duke University, 1979, pp. 189–215.

Weiss, S. *The Knesset: Its Functioning and Output* (Hebrew), Tel Aviv: Achiasaf, 1977.

Weller, P. *First Among Equals*, Sydney, London and Boston: George Allen & Unwin, 1985.

Williams, P. 'Parliament under the Fifth French Republic: Patterns of Executive Domination', in Loewenberg, G. (ed.) *Modern Parliaments: Change or Decline?*, Chicago and New York: Aldine-Atherton, 1971, pp. 97–109.

Wright, V., *The Government and Politics of France*, New York: Holmes and Meier, 1978.

Index

www.ingramcontent.com/pod-product-compliance
Ingram Content Group UK Ltd.
Pitfield, Milton Keynes, MK11 3LW, UK
UKHW020401010325
455677UK00021B/562

9 781138 870123